Reporting from the Field:

SAS® Software Experts Present Real-World Report-Writing Applications

Donglei Chen

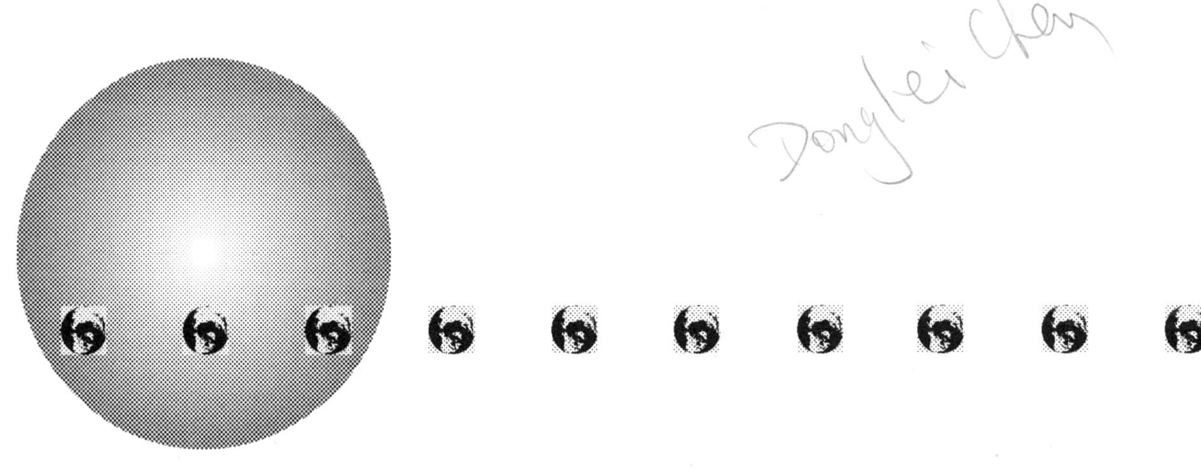

The correct bibliographic citation for this manual is as follows: SAS Institute Inc., *Reporting from the Field: SAS® Software Experts Present Real-World Report-Writing Applications*, Cary, NC: SAS Institute Inc., 1994. 329 pp.

Reporting from the Field: SAS® Software Experts Present Real-World Report-Writing Applications

ISBN 1-55544-644-2

SAS Institute Inc., SAS Campus Drive, Cary, North Carolina 27513.

1st printing, September 1994

CONTENTS

FOREWORD

by Frank C. DiIorio

The SAS System's range of applications is vast, and in no area are the diversity and the potential for frustration greater than in presentation of results. Tools for the report-writing process range from the simple (PROC PRINT) to the mysterious (PROC TABULATE) to the numbingly complex (the DATA _NULL_ step). All, however, have a common thread: they are routinely and effectively implemented by seasoned SAS professionals, some of whom have shared their knowledge in this volume.

The prospectus of my first book, *SAS Applications Programming: A Gentle Introduction*, proposed a comprehensive treatment of report-writing topics. Reality and page limits conspired to tone down my expectations. I considered making these topics a separate volume, code-named "Saying It with SAS."

No need to do this now, and I'm delighted to be part of the reason. *Reporting From the Field* is a collection of report-writing strategies whose greatest strength is the diversity of its authors. No one author can do the subject justice. The range of industrial settings and formatting requirements represented here exceeds the experience of any single user. What this book brings to all SAS programmers is a great variety of input on tool selection, techniques for report implementation, and just plain creativity.

Beginning and intermediate programmers will benefit from the chapters' tips on report program design and tool selection. Those involved with specific applications such as survey research and quality control will be the beneficiaries of chapters devoted specifically to these topics. Even the most accomplished and jaded SAS professional will regard this collection as a useful addition to his or her "toolbox."

Regardless of application area or level of treatment, it is interesting simply to observe how those in the field go about the problem solving and reporting process. This book may not cure your PUT statement blues (that's what the other four feet of manuals is for), but it may open your eyes to new ways of approaching the report-writing process.

CHAPTER 1

Tips and Tricks

by Sheree H. Andersen

Abstract

The SAS System, like the venerable magician's bag of tricks, has a number of capabilities that can be incorporated to facilitate report writing programs. This chapter highlights some features of SAS software including data set options, functions, macro variables, and procedures that have proven invaluable. Being aware of SAS software capability is primary to successful programming. Knowing the intricacies of the SAS System avoids the dilemma of "you can't get there from here!"

Specifications

The code in this chapter was developed and tested with Release 6.08 of the SAS System under the Windows environment. Use of the code with other releases of the SAS System or other environments may require user modification. Modified code is not supported by the author.

About the Author

Sheree H. Andersen is an independent SAS consultant with 14 years of experience using SAS software. Sheree has a BS degree in Statistics from Brigham Young University and an MS degree in Biostatistics from the University of Utah. Her areas of expertise include base SAS software, report writing, and the SAS macro facility.

Questions and Comments Should be Directed to:

Sheree H. Andersen
1530 E. Deer Haven Drive
North Logan, UT 84321
Telephone: 801-750-0908

Examples from this book are available online, see inside back cover for details.

Tips And Tricks

Sheree H. Andersen

Introduction

This chapter is intended for beginning- to intermediate-level SAS users. It is a collection of techniques that have proven useful over the years for report-writing. The chapter covers topics relating to the flexibility and power of the SAS System as a data processing package, but it focuses on less common applications. Topics include:

. DATA step processing
. Data set options (to subset data, to process observations or variables, to specify data sources or the final observation)
. The SAS function library
. Other helpful SAS features
. Some powerful procedures

DATA Step Processing

When one considers the wealth of possibility available in the DATA step, the expression "panaceSAS!" doesn't seem too optimistic. SAS software may not cure all ills, but a good understanding of the SAS System reveals almost unlimited potential for satisfying reporting requests. The capability of available tools is limited only by a user's knowledge and skill in implementing them.

This section will not attempt to cover ordinary DATA step processing. Rather, it features a relatively little-known capability of the DATA step.

One distinct advantage of the DATA step is that it assumes control over traditional programming processes like value initialization and record output. Occasionally the need arises for these automatic processing features to be suppressed. The automatic value initialization feature is suppressed with a RETAIN statement. The automatic output feature is managed with the OUTPUT statement. These two statements and their use are described below.

The RETAIN Statement

The normal processing of an observation through a DATA step includes the automatic initialization of all variables. The RETAIN statement prevents variables in the program data vector (PDV) from being initialized at each new execution of the DATA step. RETAIN may appear on a statement by itself or it may be followed by one or more variable names. If RETAIN appears by itself, it retains all the variables in the PDV. If RETAIN is followed by a list of one or more variables, only those variables will be retained.

RETAIN can be useful when dealing with the hierarchal summary output of PROC MEANS. The higher levels of summary, designated by the values of the _TYPE_ variable (discussion follows), can have values retained and used as the denominator for calculating percent of total. A simple example which calculates the state percent of national sales is shown below. Output 1 is a partial listing of the STATES data set. It shows the retained denominator value of NATSALES.

```
proc means noprint data=national;
   class state;
   var sales;
   output out=states sum(sales)=;
data states;
   set states;
   retain natsales;
   if (_type_=0) then do;
      natsales=sales; delete;
      end;
```

```
   pctsales=(100 * sales) / natsales;
proc print;
title 'State Percentages of National Total';
```

Output 1: State Percentages of National Total

```
                 State Percentages of National Total

OBS        STATE      _TYPE_     _FREQ_     SALES     NATSALES  PCTSALES

 1         ALABAMA      1          1         215        2520      8.5317
 2         ALASKA       1          1         103        2520      4.0873
 3         ARIZONA      1          1         318        2520     12.6190
 4         ARKANSAS     1          1         284        2520     11.2698
```

PROC FREQ also calculates percent-of-total information and can produce output data sets. If, however, the report request requires statistics that are available in PROC MEANS but not in PROC FREQ, like MIN, MAX, MEAN, or STD, it is more efficient to program the percentages as shown, rather than to add another procedure step involving an output data set that would have to be merged later.

The OUTPUT Statement

The OUTPUT statement is an efficient way to create one or more data sets. If no OUTPUT statement is used, each observation or input record that satisfies subsetting criteria is automatically placed in the output data set. The OUTPUT statement effectively overrides the automatic output facility of the DATA step. If an OUTPUT statement is used conditionally, only the observations overtly output will be kept.

The OUTPUT statement can be used to accomplish several data processing tasks:

- Create simultaneous data sets
- Duplicate observations for modification
- Generate data for testing
- Transpose variables into observations

These processes are discussed next, with examples.

Creating Simultaneous Data Sets

It is possible to create simultaneous data sets using the OUTPUT statement. Assume 5 years' data has been stored in a permanent SAS data set that needs to be partitioned into annual data sets based on the value of the variable YEAR. These statements would perform the task:

```
data db.year90 db.year91 db.year92 db.year93 db.year94;
   set db.all;
   if (year=90) then output db.year90;
    else if (year=91) then output db.year91;
    else if (year=92) then output db.year92;
    else if (year=93) then output db.year93;
    else if (year=94) then output db.year94;
```

Duplicate Observations for Modification

The OUTPUT statement can also create additional observations in an application that requires multiple, modified records. The OUTPUT statement is executed immediately upon encounter in the DATA step. This permits an observation to be output, as is, then modified by additional programming statements and output again. The modification/output process can be repeated as many times as needed to satisfy reporting requirements.

An example illustrates how to output an observation and then modify it for additional output.

Consider a customer satisfaction report format that requires the number of product defects to be shown by the opinion categories shown in Table 1.

Table 1: Opinion Category Descriptions

Original Value of OPINION	Modified Value of OPINION	Value Description
1,2	0	completely or very satisfied
1	1	completely satisfied
2	2	very satisfied
3	3	somewhat satisfied
4	4	somewhat dissatisfied
5	5	very dissatisfied

The first category is actually the sum of the following 2 categories. The program below uses the OUTPUT statement to output each observation as it is, then conditionally modifies the observations that fall into the combined category and outputs them again. PROC MEANS summarizes the number of product defects. In this example, specifying NWAY is important to prevent double-counting of the duplicate records. A numeric format, OPINFMT, defined by relating the data values and descriptions in Table 1, enhances the printed output shown in Output 2.

```
data satisfy;
    set satisfy(keep=opinion defects);
    output;

/**** Assign a lower sort order value to print this category first. ****/
    if (opinion in (1,2)) then do;
       opinion=0;
       output;
       end;
proc means noprint nway;
   class opinion;
   var defects;
   output out=report sum=;
proc print data=report;
   format opinion opinfmt.;
title 'Number of Defects per 1000 by Satisfaction';
```

Output 2: Number of Defects per 1000 by Satisfaction

```
            Number of Defects per 1000 by Satisfaction

OBS  OPINION                          _TYPE_    _FREQ_    DEFECTS

 1   completely/very satisfied           1         92        25
 2   completely satisfied                1         45        10
 3   very satisfied                      1         47        15
 4   somewhat satisfied                  1         15        33
 5   somewhat dissatisfied               1         36        39
 6   very dissatisfied                   1         11        46
```

Generating Data

The OUTPUT statement may occur inside an iterative DO/END block, which causes an observation to be output for each execution of the DO/END. When developing and testing a report-writing program, it is sometimes easier to generate a "dummy" data set rather than to work with real data. This situation is excellent for using an OUTPUT statement within an iterative DO/END block. For example, while testing a program module or benchmarking one process against another, a data set with ample observations can quickly be generated.

Perhaps testing the true uniformly distributed randomness, over the integers 1 to 10, of the RANUNI function (discussed later in the chapter) seems indicated. The following statements could be submitted:

```
data uniform;
   do i=1 to 1000;
      point=round(ranuni(0) * 10 +.5),1);
      output;
      end;
proc freq;
   tables point;
title 'Distribution of Uniform Random Variable';
```

POINT, a uniformly distributed random variable, is multiplied by 10 to change its values to the interval 1 to 10. A correction factor of .5 is added and the result is rounded to the nearest integer to ensure that only 10 values are generated. The UNIFORM data set has one thousand observations, each one produced by the OUTPUT statement contained within the DO/END block. The value of the RANUNI seed is 0, however, other seeds could similarly be tested and compared. Output 3 shows the results of this program:

Output 3: Distribution of Uniform Random Variable

POINT	Frequency	Percent	Cumulative Frequency	Percent
1	105	10.5	105	10.5
2	111	11.1	216	21.6
3	96	9.6	312	31.2
4	97	9.7	409	40.9
5	114	11.4	523	52.3
6	103	10.3	626	62.6
7	94	9.4	720	72.0
8	88	8.8	808	80.8
9	101	10.1	909	90.9
10	91	9.1	1000	100.0

Transposing Data

The OUTPUT statement can transpose data, that is, turn variables into observations. A good illustration of this technique comes from surgery data which has been stored with HOSPITAL as the observation key. The layout of the final report requires 3 columns, corresponding to the nested levels of summary: hospital, group, and state. The rows correspond to the type of surgery performed. A separate page is required for each hospital. The report template is shown in Table 2.

Table 2: Surgery Report Template

Hospital Name ______________

Type of Surgery	Hospital	Hospital Group	All Hospitals within State
Abdominal			
Head & Neck			
Extremities			
OB/Gyn			
Thoracic			

The raw data is organized with observations containing several hospital-identifying variables, as well as 5 variables corresponding to frequency counts of the type of surgery rendered for each of the specified levels of summary, namely HOSP1-HOSP5, GROUP1-GROUP5, and STATE1-STATE5. A program to transpose the data into the format needed for the report follows:

```
proc format;
value typefmt
1='Abdominal'
2='Head & Neck'
3='Extremities'
4='OB/Gyn'
5='Thoracic';

data report;
   set hospital;
   keep type hospital group state;
   array hosp hosp1-hosp5;
   array grp  group1-group5;
   array st   state1-state5;
   do _i_ = 1 to 5;
     type=put(_i_,typefmt.);
     hospital=hosp;
     group=grp;
     state=st;
     output;
     end;
```

Each group of related variables is placed in an array. The DO/END block executes 5 times and iteratively equates the variables in the arrays to the variables HOSPITAL, GROUP, and STATE, respectively, which are then output. This format can easily be extended to include more columns for reporting percentages or other data.

Data Set Options

Data set options control access to a SAS data set. Several types of control are possible:

. Subsetting control with WHERE=
. Observation control with POINT=
. Variable control with DROP= or KEEP=
. Data source control with IN=
. Terminal processing control with END=

These data set options can be used alone or in conjunction with each other.

Subsetting Control with WHERE=

You can select a subset of the data with the data set option WHERE= by using any logical selection criteria. All observations in the data set are processed against the selection criteria. Only observations which satisfy the expression are available for further processing in the DATA step.

The WHERE= data set option has a corresponding statement that performs the same subsetting task. There is an advantage in using the WHERE= data set option instead of the WHERE statement when 2 or more data sets are being combined. In this circumstance, the subsetting criteria can be customized to the data set. For example, if regional data sets are being combined, but only observations from a single state from each region are needed, the following statements would perform the subsetting:

```
data states;
   set midwest(where=(state='MI'))
       noeast(where=(state='NY'));
```

As long as there is no overlap of the values used to subset the data, the foregoing example could also be coded using the WHERE statement:

```
data states;
   set midwest
        noeast;
   where state in ('MI', 'NY');
```

A benchmark run shows the first example to have a slightly more efficient processing time. This efficiency advantage would increase if the selection criteria had greater complexity.

Observation Control with POINT=

The POINT= data set option on the SET statement allows direct access to the observations in a data set. Observation control of this kind is most efficient when fewer than 25% of the observations are to be processed. The variable named after the equals sign must contain the values of the observation numbers to be selected. This variable is temporary and is not added to the output data set. It is important to include a STOP statement whenever you are using the POINT= data set option to prevent execution of a continuous loop.

An easy method for selecting a systematic sample is by use of the POINT= and NOBS= data set options. The variable named after NOBS= has a value corresponding to the number of observations in the data set. In this example, every tenth observation is written to the output data set:

```
data sample;
   do pick= 1 to obs by 10;
      set all point=pick nobs=obs;
       output;
       end;
   stop;
```

Variable Control with DROP= or KEEP=

Processing is more efficient when only those variables essential to the process are available to the programming environment. A limited number of variables may be processed by means of the DROP= or KEEP= data set options.

Both these data set options have analogous statements, although the statement form has a slightly different processing effect. When used as options on the SET statement, DROP= and KEEP= restrict access to variables not referenced. In the statement form, they allow access to all variables in the data set but prevent variables not referenced directly on the KEEP or DROP statement from being written to the output data set.

The choice of which option to use, DROP= or KEEP=, depends upon the application. Assess how many variables are to be dropped compared to how many are to be kept. The shorter list is easier to code. If there is no apparent advantage in using one option over the other, KEEP= is preferred because it provides some self-documentation. You may not use DROP= and KEEP= for the same data set.

Data Source Control with IN=

The source of data may be specified with the IN= data set option. The IN= option sets up a binary variable that is temporary and therefore omitted from the output data set. The variable name is specified after the equals sign; it determines which data set the observation currently being processed originates from. This variable has the value of 1 if the observation is from the corresponding data source, otherwise it has the value 0.

When IN= is used in conjunction with a MERGE statement, you can determine if the observation has matching BY variables in the data sets being combined. A simple example illustrates how non-matches are identified. Consider 2 data sets, the first containing data on parts ordered, the second containing data on parts in inventory. To procure the number of parts not in stock, you need to create a data set that identifies them:

```
data notstock;
   merge orders(in=orders) stock(in=stock);
   by part;
   if (orders & ^ stock);
```

Terminal Processing Control with END=

Terminal or last observation processing may be specified with the END= data set option. This option assigns a variable name that determines when the last observation is processed.

An example shows how the value of a counter variable can be output to the log when the last observation is processed. The counter variable is incremented whenever the variable MILES exceeds 10,000:

```
data service;
   set fleet(end=last);
   if (miles>10000) then count+1;
   if (last) then put 'Number over 10,000 ' count=;
```

The SAS Function Library

The SAS function library incorporates an impressive array of data processing tools. The SAS compiler recognizes many functions that process data in a proscribed way within the DATA step. Complete documentation of the available functions and their usage is contained in Chapter 11 of *SAS Language: Reference, Version 6, First Edition.*

When reading about these functions, remember the metaphor of a SAS data set as a rectangular table composed of rows and columns which correspond to observations and variables, respectively. DATA step functions work horizontally on an observation, or across a row. They should not be confused with SAS procedures, which summarize and process data vertically and include all observations.

Function Arguments

Each executed reference to a function invokes a subroutine which processes the arguments specified. For example, when you specify the MEAN function and give a number of valid numeric arguments, the SAS System computes their arithmetic mean.

Most functions have one or more required arguments and they often have optional ones also. Usually SAS functions permit flexibility in what may constitute an argument. In the following list, each component qualifies as an argument:

. constants
. variables
. expressions (which may contain embedded functions)

Table 3 shows a simple example of the MEAN function and demonstrates the difference between each type of argument.

Table 3: MEAN Function and Different Argument Types

Type of Argument	Function Specification	Result
constant	mt=mean(10,15,20);	The variable mt would have a value of 15 for each observation in the data set.
variable	mt=mean(t1,t2,t3);	The variable mt would have the computed average of the 3 variables: t1, t2 and t3. The result may be different for each observation depending on the degree of similarity between observations.
expression involving an embedded function	mt=mean(t1,lag(t1));	The variable mt would have the computed average of the values of t1 on the current and prior observation.

Function Categories

There are several categories of related functions in the SAS System, as listed below. Some of these categories and a few of their corresponding functions are introduced in the following sections.

- Arithmetic
- Array
- Character
- Date and Time
- Financial
- Mathematical
- Probability
- Quantile
- Random Number
- Sample Statistic
- Special Functions
- State and Zip Code
- Trigonometric and Hyperbolic
- Truncation

Character Functions

Character functions operate on text strings which contain alpha-numeric data. This type of function performs data manipulations like justification, substring, string searches, character translations, and verification, just to name a few. Some particularly useful character functions are described below.

The SUBSTR Function

Substring operations can be performed using the SUBSTR function. Portions of text strings can be extracted into new variables. It is also valid to express the SUBSTR function on the left of an equation, allowing for transitional value testing.

The first argument of the SUBSTR function identifies the constant, variable, or expression that is to be substringed. The second argument indicates the relative position to begin the substring operation. The last argument specifies the substring length and is optional. If it is specified, the substring result is the text beginning in the position indicated in the second argument and ending with the relative displacement of the third argument.

The values created from the SUBSTR function are padded with blanks so the new variable has the same length as the variable or constant in the first argument. It is possible to conserve space by limiting the length of the result variable with a LENGTH statement prior to the SUBSTR function reference.

The INDEX Function

The INDEX function can search a string to find the first occurrence of a specified substring. The flexibility in how the arguments may be specified allows the INDEX function to perform many useful tasks.

You can easily select an observation with the INDEX function when the value of the selection variable is of length 1. Consider the situation in which record type, REC_TYPE, is a character variable with 8 possible values such as the letters A through H. If similar processing is required for record types A, B, and C, a simultaneous data check can be done by setting up the INDEX function in this way:

```
if (index('ABC',rec_type)) then do;
```

This statement has the effect of comparing the value of the variable REC_TYPE for any of the values juxtaposed in the first argument and returning a "true" condition if there is a match. Alternate ways of performing the same task are given below:

```
if (rec_type='A' | rec_type='B' | rec_type='C') then do;
if (rec_type in ('A','B','C')) then do;
```

A simple benchmark, run under Windows using SAS version 6.8, selects a subset of the A, B, and C record types and demonstrates the relative efficiency of the three methods. Interestingly, the first method is most efficient in a smaller data set, as noted in Table 4.

Table 4: Benchmark Results on Subset Example

Method	Subset of 10,000 obs.	Subset of 40,000 obs.
INDEX	1.14 sec.	5.0 sec.
REC_TYPE=	1.2 sec.	4.07 sec.
REC_TYPE IN	1.26 sec.	5.21 sec.

Another helpful task that INDEX can perform deals with data that has been transposed by PROC TRANSPOSE. A transpose results in the exchange of observations and variables. An automatic variable, _NAME_, is created; it contains the original variable names. The INDEX function can assist in the logical processing of related variables from the original data set that have been given common root names such as AGE1-AGE10. If, for example, the age variables were encoded and require an algorithm to restore their original values, the INDEX function can readily identify the transposed observations to process. The following statement illustrates how this is done:

```
if (index(_name_,'AGE')) then do;
```

This statement selects all the observations that correspond to the original variables with the common root name AGE for similar processing.

The VERIFY Function

The VERIFY function provides a quick validation check of the values of a character variable. Quite often variables are defined as character even though they contain numeric values. This is done for efficiency in storage, as well as because these variables have a nominal value scale. A nominal value scale means that the variables do not have intrinsic numeric properties such as order, natural zero points, or relative values. Consequently mathematical computations performed on them are meaningless. You can validate that only numbers make up the values of a such a variable by using the VERIFY function. Zip code is an example of a variable that can be defined as character yet contains only numeric data. The following statement omits an observation from the output data set if the Zip code contains other than numeric data:

```
if (verify('ZIP','0123456789'));
```

Variations of this example would enable data validation for only alpha characters or for some specific alpha-numeric mix.

The SCAN Function

SCAN breaks a character string into "words" which are designated by one or more delimiters. SCAN returns the "word" in the nth position as specified in the function. One use of the SCAN function is to restructure date data. For example, if date values have been stored following the value template of YYYY.JULIAN, where YYYY represents a year value which may have a length of 2 or 4 and JULIAN represents the Julian day count, SCAN could isolate the date components into new variables:

```
year=scan(jdate,1,'.');
julian=scan(jdate,2,'.');
```

This code scans the variable JDATE and places the first "word" that is delimited by a period (.) into the variable YEAR. Similarly, the second "word" is placed into the variable JULIAN.

Date and Time Functions

The date and datetime functions permit quick translation of the many representations of date and time data. Many of the functions convert conventional date and time data into values known as SAS date, SAS time, or SAS datetime values. Reciprocal functions that restore conventional date and time values are also available.

The SAS date and time values are numerically standardized to facilitate time sequencing and time manipulation processes. A common programming error occurs when the date and datetime functions are invoked without regard to whether the data has SAS date, SAS time, or SAS datetime values. It is important to use functions compatible with the data or inaccurate results will be produced.

SAS date values are the number of days either before or after the pivotal date of January 1, 1960 (12:00 a.m.). Leap years have been accounted for. SAS time values, independent of date values, are the number of elapsed seconds since midnight of the current day. Finally, SAS datetime values represent the number of elapsed seconds between midnight, January 1, 1960, and the specified datetime.

One function of interest in this category is INTNX which moves a SAS date or time forward or backward by the number of elapsed time intervals specified. An example demonstrates the use of the INTNX function in scheduling a force of volunteer firemen. Three of four firemen share call for 9-week shifts while the 4th is on a rotating 3-week relief. Firemen A, B, and C begin their shift January 2, 1994. Three weeks later Fireman D replaces Fireman C. The relief period rotates until Firemen B and A have been relieved, then the process begins again. The following statements produce the schedule for the first 4 shifts, shown in Output 4:

```
data schedule;
   i=0;
   do fireman='A','B','C','D';
      begin='02jan94'd;

/**** Prevent D from a pre-schedule start. ****/
      if (fireman='D') then do;
         begin=intnx('WEEK',begin,3);
         i=0;
         end;
      do shift=1 to 4;
         on=begin;
         off=intnx('WEEK',on,9);
```

```
/**** Initiate staggered reliefs. ****/
        if (shift=1) then off=intnx('WEEK',on,9 - (3 * i));
        begin=intnx('WEEK',off,3);
        output;
        end;
    i+1;
    end;
proc print;
   by fireman;
   id shift;
   var on off;
   format on off date9.;
title 'Volunteer Fireman Schedule';
```

Output 4: Volunteer Fireman Schedule

```
              Volunteer Fireman Schedule

FIREMAN=A

SHIFT                 ON                OFF
  1               02JAN1994          06MAR1994
  2               27MAR1994          29MAY1994
  3               19JUN1994          21AUG1994
  4               11SEP1994          13NOV1994

FIREMAN=B

SHIFT                 ON                OFF
  1               02JAN1994          13FEB1994
  2               06MAR1994          08MAY1994
  3               29MAY1994          31JUL1994
  4               21AUG1994          23OCT1994

FIREMAN=C

SHIFT                 ON                OFF
  1               02JAN1994          23JAN1994
  2               13FEB1994          17APR1994
  3               08MAY1994          10JUL1994
  4               31JUL1994          02OCT1994

FIREMAN=D

SHIFT                 ON                OFF
  1               23JAN1994          27MAR1994
  2               17APR1994          19JUN1994
  3               10JUL1994          11SEP1994
  4               02OCT1994          04DEC1994
```

Random Number Functions

A variety of random number functions is available in the SAS System. These related functions enable the value of a random variate to be returned from many of the common statistical distributions. They allow Monte Carlo simulation techniques to be applied for the purpose of testing assumptions and behaviors about data of unknown distribution.

The RANUNI or RANDOM Function

The RANUNI or RANDOM function is particularly helpful when you are drawing a random sample of size n from a finite population of size N. Assume the population of interest has been numbered from 1 to N. The following algorithm compares a uniformly distributed variate with the ratio of the currently selected sample size to the remaining sample points in the population and prints the number of the selected sample points. In this example, a sample of 10 is selected from a population of 100. Output 5 lists the numbers of the selected sample in the variable PICK.

```
data pick;
   retain sample 10 pop 100;
   do pick = 1 to 100;
      random=ranuni(0);
      if (random < sample / pop) then do;
      sample=sample -1;
      output;
      end;
   pop=pop - 1;
   end;
proc print data=pick;
title 'Randomly Selected Sample';
```

Output 5: Randomly Selected Sample

Randomly Selected Sample

OBS	SAMPLE	POP	PICK	RANDOM
1	9	90	11	0.09551
2	8	89	12	0.09765
3	7	87	14	0.07574
4	6	83	18	0.05304
5	5	80	21	0.02948
6	4	74	27	0.04552
7	3	71	30	0.03985
8	2	49	52	0.03018
9	1	37	64	0.01768
10	0	23	78	0.03450

Special Functions

These functions operate on both character and numeric variables. They provide assorted data processing capabilities like recoding values through informats or formats and allowing access to values or variables on previous observations.

The LAG Function

The LAG function returns the value of a variable on the prior observation. More complicated data structures can be handled with the LAGn function, where n can range from 1 to 100. In other words, one is not limited only to values on the prior observation. The lagged values are available in memory and can be used in logical constructs that depend on more than one observation at a time. This function is especially useful when calculating differences that exist between 2 observations. For example, data structured to contain paired observations, related to each other in some logical way, can be processed.

One or many variables may be lagged. If many variables are to be lagged it is easier to set up an array and iteratively process them rather than to lag them individually.

You should not use the LAG function conditionally. When the LAG function is used with an IF-THEN statement, unexpected results may occur. If lag processing is needed, it should be executed for each observation, even if the logic involving the lagged variable is processed for a subset of the data. Keep in mind that the first observation processed will have missing values for the lagged variables.

Other Helpful SAS Features

The SAS System has many other features which help you process data. A few of them are presented in this section.

Using Concatenation to Build a Value

A concatenation feature indicated by the double vertical bar symbol (||) enables constants, symbols, and variables to be spliced together to form the value of another variable. The following example develops a confidence interval and shows concatenation being used. The mean, standard deviation, and frequency of a sample are in the data set STATS. The upper and lower boundary of the confidence interval are calculated using the statistical formula. The constant 2.48 used is taken from a Student's t distribution and corresponds to an alpha level of .01 and a sample size of 26. The results are shown in Output 6.

```
data limits;
   set stats;
   lower=round(mean - (2.48 * std / sqrt(_freq_)),.1);
   upper=round(mean + (2.48 * std / sqrt(_freq_)),.1);
   ci='(' || trim(lower) || ' , ' || trim(upper) ||')';
proc print;
title 'Confidence Interval Value From Concatenation';
```

Output 6: Confidence Interval Value From Concatenation

```
          Confidence Interval Value From Concatenation

OBS     MEAN        STD      _FREQ_    LOWER    UPPER     CI

 1       105         15        26       97.7    112.3     (97.7 ,112.3)
```

%INCLUDE Files

Executing the %INCLUDE statement includes contents of an external file, which may contain any valid SAS text, at the point of encounter. The external file name must be specified on the %INCLUDE statement, or the FILEREF of a corresponding FILENAME statement must appear in the program that references it. Storing repetitious code makes the processing portion of the program uncluttered and less complicated. One particular use of the %INCLUDE statement is when a program has many label definitions. Storing the labels in a file, separate from the program, simplifies the code.

Another possible use of the %INCLUDE statement is when a report has been defined at both a detail and summary level. If all other aspects of the report are identical, the portions that vary could be compiled conditionally by use of the Macro language facility, coupled with the %INCLUDE statement. %INCLUDE needs to have a symbolic parameter governing the level of report, that is, D for detail or S for summary. Simplified pseudo code illustrates how this is done:

```
%macro report(level);
data report;
   set info;
   %include &level.report;

/**** remainder of report processing ****/
%mend;
%report(D)
```

Macro Variables

Macro variables are extremely useful in providing flexibility within a report. Macro variables defined at the beginning of a report program can be modified or updated quickly. Values of the macro variables are then substituted anytime the macro variable is referenced. If the same report is required for multiple years, the easiest way to change all occurrences of the year value is through macro variable substitution.

Macro variables are an efficient means of parameter substitution. They are flexible because they can be defined to be any valid SAS code from a length of 0 up to the current available memory. This permits you to use them creatively to fit any situation. In general, they are handled more efficiently by the SAS compiler than by a Macro definition contained within the %MACRO and %MEND statements. Exceptions to this general rule are macro variables that are defined as a recursive or nested reference, or one that utilizes quoting functions.

A simple example illustrates the flexibility of macro variables. Only the value of the macro variable YEAR needs to be changed in the %LET statement for the identical report to be processed for another year.

```
%let year=94;
data new;
   set survey&year;

/**** additional program statements ****/

proc print;
title "Report for &year";
```

Macro Variables and Data Set Incompatibility

Macro variables also can serve as a "patch" for incompatibilities among data sets you need to combine. Some types of data that are organized by chronological sequence, particularly survey data, tend to become incompatible over time because of changes in the way the data is gathered or in the questions that are asked. The incompatibilities may be variable name changes, added or deleted variables, or even value scale recoding. Since macro variables can be defined to DROP or RENAME inconsistent variables, these types of problems can be effectively addressed.

Consider an actual situation in which four otherwise compatible data sets differed in the variable name used for the observation weight. The algorithm to calculate the weight variable changed between 2 consecutive years. Originally a non-integer weight had been used, then it was determined that integer weights, based on a different time frame, suited the analytical circumstances best. However, to match published reports, it was necessary to retain the non-integer weight for the earlier data sets instead of retroactively recalculating the newly-defined integer weight. The new weighting scheme differed enough to justify assigning another variable name. A problem arose when several years' data had to be combined for a report. Macro variables provided the solution (extraneous code omitted):

```
%let keepers=keep=model year class target;
%let refit=blue_wt rename=(blue_wt=obs_wt);
data size;
set db.cars90(&keepers obs_wt)
    db.cars91(&keepers obs_wt)
    db.cars92(&keepers &refit)
    db.cars93(&keepers &refit);
```

In this situation, it would have been possible to code data set options separately for each data set, making them compatible, but this method makes the code less cluttered and easier to maintain.

Variations of macro variables providing a "patch" are limitless. Another circumstance involved combining monetary data from 5 European countries for 4 years. Macro variables readily enabled the conversion, to the extent that the final report showed currency in equivalent U.S. dollars.

Automatic Macro Variables

The SAS System provides automatic macro variables that can be used anywhere in a program. Only a partial list is given here; refer to Chapter 20 of *SAS Language: Reference* for the complete list.

- SYSDATE - contains date job began execution
- SYSDAY - contains day of week job execution began
- SYSDSN - contains most recently created data set name
- SYSERR - contains return code from PROC or DATA step
- SYSJOBID - contains current job, session or userid

Some Powerful Procedures

The SAS System offers many statistical and data processing procedures. They have considerable flexibility in the number of observations and variables that can be processed and in the appearance and content of output reports. The sophistication of data management, accuracy, ease of use, and optional features are impressive. A few of the most valuable procedures and their applications are introduced and described here.

PROC PRINT

PROC PRINT is the easiest way to generate a report, and it is also the least flexible. Its function is to print variables in a data set. By specifying the optional statements that can be used in conjunction with PROC PRINT, you can customize the output.

The VAR statement controls the order and selection of variables to be printed. If no VAR statement is issued, all variables in the data set will print, in the order they were defined. By default, observation numbers print on the left. These may be suppressed by using the procedure option NOOBS. An ID statement causes the variable or variables listed in it to be moved to the left of the observation, as an identifier, instead of the observation number. BY variable processing breaks output into groups within the report and the level of totaling if a SUM statement is also specified. The procedure option LABEL requests that labels, instead of variable names, print as the column headings.

PROC MEANS

PROC MEANS with the noprint option is identical to PROC SUMMARY. It efficiently computes a full range of multi-level summary statistics. The CLASS statement enables rapid computation of subgroup statistics on data that has not been previously sorted. The CLASS statement controls the number and type of summary observations to be produced. An automatic variable named _TYPE_ identifies the hierarchal level of summary. The values of _TYPE_ depend upon how many variables are specified in the CLASS statement. The distinct values of _TYPE_ can be derived from the formula 2^n, where n is the number of variables on the CLASS statement. If the NWAY option is specified, the output is restricted to include observations only of the highest _TYPE_ value.

PROC MEANS Output

To identify the level of summary, consider the CLASS statement variables. Each one-way to n-way variable value crossing is automatically computed. The _TYPE_=0 observation is the overall summary level. All observations in the data set are used to compute the statistics at this level. The _TYPE_=1 observations contain subgroup statistics where subgroups are defined by unique values of the variable listed last on the CLASS statement.

An example shows the effect of using the CLASS statement. A manufacturing company with 4 divisions seeks summarized expenditure information at the company and division level for the last quarter. This request is easily handled using PROC MEANS with a CLASS statement. A partial listing of the first few observations in the detail data set is shown in Output 7. It is followed by the PROC MEANS statements used to summarize it, with final results shown in Output 8. Notice the values of the variable _TYPE_, the first observation, where _TYPE_=0, corresponds to the company total.

Output 7: Partial Listing Detail Data

Partial Listing MFR Data

OBS	DIV	MONTH	EXPENSE
1	A	JAN	2432
2	B	JAN	3615
3	D	FEB	220
4	A	JAN	1277

```
proc means data=mfr;
   class div;
   var expense;
   output out=mfrsum sum=;
title 'Summarized MFR Data by Div';
```

Output 8: Summarized MFR Data by Div

Summarized MFR Data by Div

OBS	DIV	_TYPE_	_FREQ_	EXPENSE
1		0	40	38281
2	A	1	15	18362
3	B	1	10	10875
4	C	1	6	1755
5	D	1	9	7289

Additional levels of summary are computed by adding variables to the CLASS statement. In the example above, the variable MONTH is added to the class list of variables. Table 5 illustrates the effect of this change.

Table 5: CLASS Statement with 2 Variables

TYPE	Maximum # of Obs of same _TYPE_	Level of Summary Description
0	1	All expenditures for all months and all div
1	3	All expenditures by month
2	4	All expenditures by div
3	12	Expenditures for each div by month

When the variables DIV and MONTH are listed on the CLASS statement, the _TYPE_=1 observations correspond to the subgroups defined by unique values of MONTH. _TYPE_=2 observations correspond to the subgroups defined by unique values of DIV. Finally, the _TYPE_=3 observations correspond to the lowest level of summary, that is, unique combinations of the values of the variables DIV and MONTH. The maximum number of _TYPE=3 observations is the product of unique levels of DIV and MONTH, or 4 * 3. Fewer _TYPE_=3 observations will be produced if there is no data for some combination of DIV and MONTH.

Additional variables on the CLASS statement continue this crossing pattern of subgroup identification with the highest _TYPE_ value corresponding to the n-way classification.

Percent-of-Total in Combination with Other PROC MEANS Output

Report writing requests often include percent-of-total information for categorical or attribute data. Although PROC FREQ does compute percents, it does not compute means, standard deviations, or most of the other statistics available in PROC MEANS. Furthermore, PROC FREQ cannot output to the same data set results from more than one table request. The most efficient method of computing percent-of-total information when other report statistics are needed (or more than one table specification) is PROC MEANS. While PROC MEANS does not actually calculate the percents, it does provide the values, that is, numerator and denominator, to do so. This can be accomplished through additional programming statements in a DATA step following PROC MEANS.

A simple example demonstrates how to create a report that includes 2 attribute variables for which percent of total is needed and a mean. This technique can be extended to simultaneously process many different attribute variables. Consider a data set with the demographic data shown in Table 6.

Table 6: Demographic Data

Variable	Category	Data Value
age	under 20	10
	20 - 34	27
	35 - 49	42
	50 - 64	57
	65 & over	72
gender	female	F
	male	M

The age data is represented by the midpoint of the categories indicated and is assumed to be uniformly distributed over the intervals, allowing an estimate of the mean to be computed from the midpoint. The oldest category midpoint is arbitrarily selected to be 72, although another reasonable value could be substituted. The initial DATA step inputs the data and creates AGE1-AGE5, GEN1, and GEN2, variables used to indicate category frequencies, which are needed for calculating the percent-of-total in the second DATA step. A simple PROC PRINT displays the mean age and percents for the attribute variables, AGE and GENDER, in Output 9. Since a CLASS statement is not specified, the data is summarized into a single observation. However, the same technique also works when a CLASS statement is used and subgroup statistics are desired.

```
data setup;
   infile in;
   input age gender $;
   if (age=10) then age1=1;
    else if (age=27) then age2=1;
    else if (age=42) then age3=1;
    else if (age=57) then age4=1;
    else if (age=72) then age5=1;
   if (gender='F') then gen1=1;
    else if (gender='M') then gen2=1;
proc means noprint;
   var age age1-age5 gen1-gen2;
   output out=stats mean(age)= sum(age1-gen2)=;
data report;
   set stats;
   array pct age1-age5 gen1-gen2;
   do over pct;
      pct=round((100 * pct) / _freq_),.1);
      end;
proc print;
title 'Mean Age Plus Age & Gender Percents';
```

Output 9: Mean Age Combined with Age and Gender Percents

Mean Age Plus Age & Gender Percents										
OBS	_TYPE_	_FREQ_	AGE	AGE1	AGE2	AGE3	AGE4	AGE5	GEN1	GEN2
1	0	26	43.46	7.7	19.2	22.1	33.1	17.9	38.7	61.3

One consideration when using this technique is the effect of missing data. The automatic variable_FREQ_ contains the number of observations for a given level of summary. If there were missing data for the variables AGE or GENDER, a frequency count of the non-missing data would have to be established, or the observations with missing data deleted, for the percents to add to 100%.

PROC TABULATE

This flexible table procedure allows customization of the appearance and content of tabular reports. PROC TABULATE does not produce an output data set and therefore customization is limited to the options defined for the procedure. Data can be raw or summarized at the point when PROC TABULATE is invoked. If data is raw, the requested statistics are tabulated and displayed according to specification. Summarized data may need to be weighted using the WEIGHT statement.

The table dimension expressions, specified on the TABLE statement, are virtually unlimited if the table format can be logically structured. Rules to remember when defining a table are:

- Commas separate the table dimensions, i.e. rows, columns, and pages.
- An asterisk indicates a variable crossing.
- A blank space indicates a variable concatenation.
- Angle brackets <> specify the denominator definitions needed for percent calculations.
- Analysis variables, those which are to have statistics computed, may be specified in only one dimension.

Variables can be crossed or concatenated in any table dimension. This example shows the difference between these possibilities. Consider the categorical data corresponding to TEMP and BLEACH in Table 7:

Table 7: Categorical Data

Variable	Category	Data Value
temp	10-40 C 41-60 C 60-90 C	COLD MED HOT
bleach	no bleach bleach	NO YES

Many choices are available to define a table consisting of these classifications. A 2-way table is specified by the dimension expression: TEMP, BLEACH. This table request has the effect of placing the values of TEMP in the row dimension and BLEACH in the column dimension as shown in Table 8.

Table 8: 2-way Table

		BLEACH	
		YES	NO
TEMP	HOT		
	MED		
	COLD		

The crossed dimension expression: TEMP * BLEACH, produces a table heading like that shown in Table 9:

Table 9: Crossed Table

BLEACH					
YES			NO		
TEMP			TEMP		
COLD	MED	HOT	COLD	MED	HOT

The concatenated dimension expression: TEMP BLEACH, produces a table heading with each level of the concatenated variables represented side by side, not contained within the value of another variable, as shown in Table 10:

Table 10: Concatenated Table

TEMP			BLEACH	
COLD	MED	HOT	YES	NO

PROC TRANSPOSE

Often the best way to report data is not the most logical way to store or retrieve it. The natural orientation for reports frequently has summarized values for rows and the columns correspond to values of specific attribute variables. This is contrary to how data is stored. For this reason PROC TRANSPOSE is a useful procedure to invoke after all the data summarization has been performed. It can change the data structure by making observations into variables.

For example, consider automotive data which contains customer satisfaction information. Each observation corresponds to an individual response to a survey. One attribute variable in the data set is MODEL, which indicates the type of model being evaluated. There are many observations for each model type. For ease of comparison, the different model types are reported, side by side, in columns after the data has been summarized. The report rows correspond to the average satisfaction, based on a scale of 1 to 10 (with 10 representing the highest level of satisfaction), and the sample size. PROC TRANSPOSE is used to rotate the data into the desired format. Output 10 shows the result.

```
proc means noprint nway;
   class model;
   var opinion;
   output out=average mean=;
proc transpose data=average out=report;
   id model;
   var opinion _freq_;
```

```
proc print data=report;
   var _name_ basic small sport luxury;
   format _numeric_ 6.1;
title 'Average Opinion by Model';
```

Output 10: Average Opinion by Model

```
                  Average Opinion by Model

OBS         _NAME_    BASIC       SMALL    SPORT     LUXURY

 1          OPINION      7.9         8.2      8.5        8.8
 2          _FREQ_    1056.0      1121.0    406.0      191.0
```

PROC DATASETS

PROC DATASETS is a utility for data base maintenance. It has the capability of renaming or deleting data sets, modifying variable names within a data set, or creating indexes for variables. It cannot delete observations or drop variables because it works only on the data set descriptor information, not the data set itself.

Chapter Summary

Being familiar with the capabilities of the SAS System contributes greatly to programming success. Together, the DATA step and various reporting procedures can handle almost any request. You have a choice of methods to generate any given report. Knowledge and experience help you select the best method, where best is defined as the easiest to code, the most accurate, the most appropriate to the task, and the most processing-efficient.

CHAPTER 2

Getting the Bugs Out

by Sheree H. Andersen

Abstract

Finding no errors in the log of an executed SAS report writing program comes close to maximizing a programmer's exhilaration. It can happen fairly consistently if careful planning and disciplined program development are followed. As code is assembled there are elemental steps that can ensure a high rate of first-time success. Let the SAS System assist in the testing of logic and syntax, as well as printing intermediate steps to reduce programmer stress.

Specifications

The code in this chapter was developed and tested with Release 6.08 of the SAS System under the Windows environment. Use of the code with other releases of the SAS System or other environments may require user modification. Modified code is not supported by the author.

About the Author

Sheree H. Andersen is an independent SAS consultant with 14 years of experience using SAS software. Sheree has a BS degree in Statistics from Brigham Young University and an MS degree in Biostatistics from the University of Utah. Her areas of expertise include base SAS software, report writing, and the SAS macro facility.

Questions and Comments Should be Directed to:

Sheree H. Andersen
1530 E. Deer Haven Drive
North Logan, UT 84321
Telephone: 801-750-0908

Examples from this book are available online, see inside back cover for details.

Getting the Bugs Out

Sheree H. Andersen

Introduction

This chapter is intended for beginning- to intermediate-level SAS users. It discusses errors typically found in report writing applications and makes suggestions on how to handle them. Several examples illustrate the subject matter. The topics covered are:

. Minimizing errors
. Efficiency
. Avoiding logical errors (flowcharting, program planning, multiple data sources, summarizing and subsetting data, testing program modules)
. Managing syntactical errors

Minimizing Errors

A worthwhile objective of any report developer is to minimize the number of errors in a SAS program. This is true particularly because an exponential relationship seems to exist between the number of errors and the programmer stress level. A development plan should include:

. efficiency considerations
. flowcharting
. testing
. space requirement calculations

Following this plan will generally reduce the number and type of errors that the programmer must deal with. Errors are usually thought to be logical and syntactical in nature because they prevent a program from successful completion. However, a well-trained user community also recognizes inefficient processing as a type of error even though inefficient programs can execute successfully and lead to accurate results. For this reason, efficiency is discussed before suggestions to identify and resolve logical and syntactical errors.

Efficiency

For most applications, it is possible to develop more than one method of programming a task. Obviously some methods utilize more resources than others. Being aware of the relative efficiency of alternate methods is the first step toward quality SAS programming. If there is a question about which method is most efficient, it is worthwhile to do an application-specific benchmark run, particularly if the application will process large amounts of data or will be run on a frequent basis. A benchmark run is done by developing in SAS code simple representations of the proposed process using various methods, then submitting them to the SAS System for execution. A large enough data sample should be used to discern true variability between the methods. The benchmark run is complete once a comparison of CPU utilization for the various methods is made. It is important to document the version of SAS software and the platform used when performing a benchmark run, since dramatically different results may occur under different circumstances. A benchmark example is given later in this chapter.

You can maximize DATA step efficiency by being aware of these conditions:

. Formatted input using the pointer control and format specification is more efficient than either list or column input.

. Reading a particular field to test record selection criteria while holding the record with a trailing @ is more efficient than reading a complete record which does not satisfy processing criteria.

- Direct access, that is, SET with the POINT= option is more efficient when the sampling is less than 25% of the data set.

- The efficiency of formats compared with IF and IF/ELSE constructs used for data translations depends upon the size of the format and the number of observations processed.

- PROC APPEND is more efficient than a SET which vertically concatenates two similar data sets.

- Data stored in SAS data sets is accessed more efficiently than data stored in flat files.

In general, it is more efficient to handle as much as possible of the data preparation needed within a DATA or PROC step. It has been estimated that as much as 90% of the CPU required is consumed in I/O. With that in mind, a method that limits the number of transitions between DATA and PROC steps is best because each transition requires that data be read from or written to some computer device.

Avoiding Logical Errors

Careful thought in a program's planning phase usually avoids logical errors. These errors typically occur when assumptions do not reflect reality. For this reason, users need to become thoroughly familiar with the processing methods of SAS software. A logical error might be something as simple as not considering the effect of missing data values in a process. A report program that contains logical errors may generate the desired report, but the information reported could be spurious if not all possible situations have been managed. Logical errors may occur when expected output from a DATA or PROC step differs from actual output. An example is a MERGE performed on two data sets, each with duplicate BY-variable values. The situations where logical errors can occur are limitless, so the best defense is a strategic one:

- Ask questions.
- Understand the process.
- Know the procedures and what they can do.
- Start with a flowchart.
- Walk through the process, logically.
- Test program modules.
- Continue to develop SAS programming skills.

Each step listed above is important. A discussion on flowcharting and testing program modules follows.

Flowcharting

It is always a good idea to plan out a program's flow. A flowchart sequences the process logically, by indicating the necessary PROC and DATA steps and defining the required elements and their sources. These elements may include text strings, sums to be used in calculations, or mathematical computations. The flowchart also provides means of communication with others about the program process and documentation for subsequent maintenance or support. A flowchart helps the program organization stay "on task" without the clutter of detail. Time spent in developing good flowcharting skills will more than pay for itself in quality output.

Flowcharting doesn't have to be elaborate unless you are developing a complex reporting system of integrated components, in which very explicit documentation is required for subsequent maintenance and support. For ad-hoc or one-time analysis, the flowchart can be very simple.

The most useful flowchart symbols are shown in Table 1.

Table 1: Flowchart Symbols

Symbol	Name	Function
	terminal	indicates beginning or end of a process
	decision	specifies logical point
	process step	describes process
	arrows	connects the symbols and indicates sequence relationship
	on-page connector	same page reference
	off-page connector	different page reference

It is helpful to keep the flow of the diagram moving from top left to bottom right for readability. In general the decision symbol should have the normal process or the most common outcome flowing from the bottom with the exceptions or special processing flowing to the side. When special processing for certain observations or subgroups of the data is flowed to the side, the normal flow can continue vertically on the page. To accomplish this, you may need to rephrase the decision in a way counter to conventional thought. For example, if special processing is required for a subgroup of observations, like students, the decision symbol can reflect the normal process by stating "Non-student" as opposed to "Student," as shown in Table 2.

Table 2: Decision Symbols

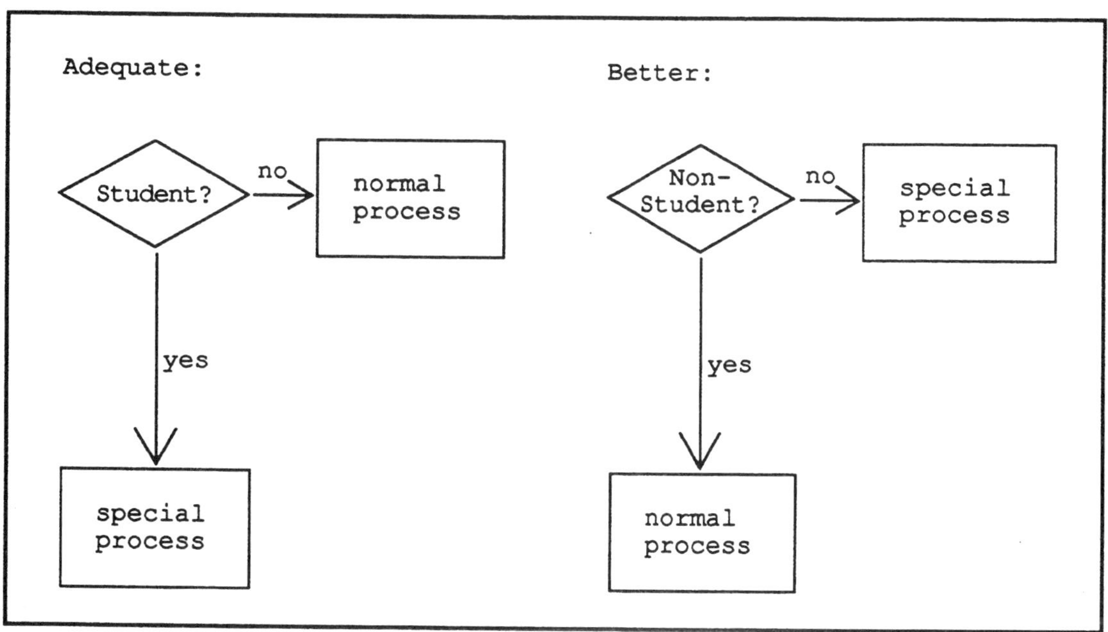

Data Sources

You can indicate sources of data in the flowchart. Some relevant questions you may ask are:

- Does the data come from different sources?
- How is the data to be combined?
- What variables do the data have in common?
- Is the data summarized or "raw"?
- Are all observations to be included or only selected ones?
- What combination of DATA and PROC steps is needed to obtain the desired report output?

Some of these questions and their ramifications are considered below.

Combining Data: MERGE, SET or UPDATE?

Data from multiple sources will need to be combined. How the data is to be combined is important because common logical errors arise in mismanaging data combination. If the data sources are similar, that is, contain many of the same variables but perhaps for different years or different locations, a vertical concatenation is probably needed. On the other hand, if the data sources are dissimilar and contain relatively few variables in common, a horizontal merge is probably needed. Before data from two or more sources can be combined, all data must be in SAS data sets. Data combinations are then executed by using a SET statement for vertical concatenation or a MERGE statement for a horizontal merge.

Understanding the effect of a MERGE statement is important in obtaining the desired results. Usually a merge is performed where there is either a one-to-one or one-to-many match. Unexpected results may occur when there are duplicate BY-variable values in both data sets.

When a one-to-many merge is executed, the data set listed last on the MERGE statement overwrites or replaces the values of any variables that are common to both data sets but not used on the BY statement. Also, with a one-to-many merge, the values of variables contained in the smaller data set are repeated until a new observation is processed from that data set. This feature is extremely useful when calculating percentages but could lead to problems if not anticipated.

Value repetition is useful, for example, when the smaller data set is the summary of the data set to which it is being merged. In this case, the smaller data set could contain the denominator on which percentages are to be calculated. The denominator value is effectively "carried down" or is available to each observation in the larger data set so the computation can be done. In the following example, the data set STATE contains observations for each state. A variable named SALES contains the total sales of a product for each state. If the percentage of sales by state is needed, the data set STATE is summarized using PROC MEANS, and a national total sales is calculated. Then, using the MERGE statement to combine the summarized data set and the STATE data set, calculate the state percentages based on the national sales total, as shown in the following code:

```
proc means data=state noprint;
   var sales;
   output out=national sum(sales)=totsales;
data percent;
   merge state national;
   pctsales = (sales * 100) / totsales;
```

Users should be aware of the other combining options, like UPDATE, because some of them offer unique processing features that may manage the required processing more easily. For example, UPDATE allows observations in a master file to be replaced with observations from a transaction file. If variables are on the master file but not on the transaction file, the values on the master file are preserved.

Data Set Compatibility

When data combination is required you need to carefully evaluate the variables in their respective data sets. Length and data type incompatibility are frequently overlooked pitfalls. Length incompatibility causes value truncation if the length in the first or primary data set is shorter than that of the merged or secondary data set. Data type incompatibility occurs when a variable has been declared numeric in one source and character in another. These problems can be averted by running PROC CONTENTS on all the data sets involved in a merge or concatenation and cross-checking their compatibility.

A LENGTH statement can be issued prior to the SET or MERGE statement to handle length incompatibility. This extends the length of the variable for the primary data set and prevents subsequent truncation of the variable from the secondary data set.

Data type incompatibility requires a rename of the variable with the data set option RENAME= at the time of the SET or MERGE. For example, suppose two data sets are to be combined vertically and the variable MONTH exists on both data sets. Assume that MONTH in the first data set has been declared numeric, with a length of 2, and has values 1 through 12, corresponding to the months. Further assume that the variable MONTH has been declared character in the second data set with similar values '1' to '12'. A data combination is still possible but the data type incompatibility must be addressed. The following SAS code, which uses the RENAME= and IN= data set options, would permit the concatenation to occur without error:

```
data all;
   set first
       second(rename=(month=mon) in=in2);
   if (in2) then month=input(mon,2.);
   drop mon;
```

Summarizing Data

It is important to recognize the level of detail required for each step in the process. The final output typically includes summarized data because data at its lowest level of detail, however voluminous, doesn't say much. Only when data is summarized and condensed can meaningful comparisons and objective analysis be made. SAS software has several summary procedures available, each capable of BY-group processing. To produce meaningful output, you need to know the distinctions and capabilities of these summary procedures:

- PROC MEANS (alias PROC SUMMARY)
- PROC FREQ
- PROC UNIVARIATE
- PROC TABULATE

PROC MEANS is a powerful procedure capable of computing statistics for all possible subgroup combinations, named on a CLASS statement, in one pass of the data. It is a quick and efficient way to compute sums, means, the number of non-missing values, standard deviations, and variances, as well as other statistics. Please refer to the *SAS Procedures Guide, Version 6, Third Edition*, for a complete list of the additional statistics. This procedure can produce many elements frequently needed in report writing. It can also produce one or more output data sets that can be further processed in DATA or PROC steps.

PROC FREQ summarizes categorical data by producing frequency counts and percentages. It can compute numerous contingency table statistics used for analyzing the association between variables. It can also produce output data sets, which may be processed further for report writing applications.

PROC UNIVARIATE produces descriptive and order statistics for continuous variables. The PLOT option produces stem-leaf distributions and boxplots. Tests for normality of the data are also available. PROC UNIVARIATE also produces output data sets containing the requested statistics.

PROC TABULATE is a very flexible procedure that can formulate simple to complex statistical tables. The variables in the row, column, and page dimensions can be crossed or concatenated, according to specification. Unlike the other procedures mentioned, PROC TABULATE does not produce output data sets.

Subsetting the Data

Reports are frequently needed for subsets of the data. When a logical statement identifies observations of interest, the SAS System processes only those observations. The software has several methods for subsetting:

- Subsetting IF statement
- WHERE statement or data set option
- DELETE statement
- OUTPUT statement

In general, these subsetting methods can be used interchangeably. You do need to understand the minor distinctions among them; otherwise errors in data processing may occur. You can choose the method that is most suitable and efficient for your task.

Subsetting IF Statement

The subsetting IF is perhaps the easiest form of subset to code in the SAS System. Only observations satisfying the criteria are available for further processing in the DATA step. The syntax is simple:

```
if (logical expression);
```

The logical expression can be as simple or complex as necessary to accurately define the observations of interest. For example:

```
/**** simple subsetting IF ****/
if (state='CA');

/**** complex subsetting IF ****/
 (state='CA' & 1000 < altitude < 3000 & ((status='Y'  & area>1000) |
   (status='N' & area<=1000) & rainfall^<12));
```

WHERE Statement or Data Set Option

The WHERE statement or data set option, new with version 6, allows subsetting of SAS data sets to occur before observations are brought into the program data vector (PDV). The advantage is that you can now subset the data in PROC steps without first creating a subset with a DATA step.

DELETE Statement

The DELETE statement is another way to subset data. If certain observations do not meet a logical condition, the DELETE statement excludes them from the output data set. DELETE can be used alone or as part of an IF-THEN statement. If you can specify which observations are to be excluded more easily than those to be kept, then a DELETE statement is preferred. It is important to realize that DELETE acts upon a complete observation; it should not be confused with the DROP statement, which acts upon variables.

OUTPUT Statement

The OUTPUT statement has the opposite effect of a DELETE statement. OUTPUT can be used alone or as part of an IF-THEN statement. When part of a conditional statement, OUTPUT selects only the observations which meet the specified condition. If the logical expression for including observations is easier to write than the one for deleting, use the OUTPUT statement.

One advantage of the OUTPUT statement is that you can create several output data sets simultaneously by directing observations to specific data sets. That is, OUTPUT can create multiple subsets of the data at one time. For example, if a data set has national data which must be split into regions, the following SAS code creates four output data sets:

```
data north south east west;
   set national;
   if (region='N') then output north;
    else if (region='S') then output south;
    else if (region='E') then output east;
    else if (region='W') then output west;
```

Observations are omitted from the regional data sets if they have either missing values or values for REGION other than those specified. To avoid the logical error of inadvertent omission, you can create another data set to which all remaining observations are directed.

Relative Efficiency of Subsetting Methods

A benchmark run was performed to assess the relative efficiency of the various subsetting methods. The process being evaluated selects only specific zip codes in a geographic region. This benchmark preceded development of an application to process over 2 million records.

```
/**** A format designating selected zipcodes is created. ****/
proc format;
   value $zip
   '84001' = 'Y'
   '84005' = 'Y'
   '84010' = 'Y'
   '84013' = 'Y'
   '84050' = 'Y'
   '84070' = 'Y'
   '84088' = 'Y'
   '84100' = 'Y';

/**** A 10000 observation data set with incremental zipcode values is
generated. ****/
data zips;
   do j=1 to 100;
      do I=1 to 100;
         zip=put(84000 + I,5.);
         output;
      end;
   end;
```

```
/**** A subset is selected using the subsetting IF statement. ****/
data sub_if;
   set zips;
   if (put(zip,$zip.)='Y');

/**** A subset is selected using the WHERE data set option. ****/
data wheredso;
   set zips(where=(put(zip,$zip.)='Y'));

/**** A subset is selected using the DELETE statement. ****/
data deletes;
   set zips;
   if (put(zip,$zip.)^='Y') then delete;

/**** A subset is selected using the OUTPUT statement. ****/
data outputs;
   set zips;
   if (put(zip,$zip.)='Y') then output;
```

The results obtained are shown in Table 3.

Table 3: Seconds of CPU Time for Various Subsetting Methods

Operating System..... Version of SAS.......	Windows 6.08	MVS 6.08	UNIX 6.09
Subsetting IF	2.08	.21	.43
WHERE data set option	57.95	.63	.60
DELETE statement	2.08	.21	.39
OUTPUT statement	1.37	.21	.36

Table 3 shows that very different results occur according to different platforms and versions of SAS software, underscoring the importance of making the benchmark specific to the site and circumstances under which the application will be run. In general, the WHERE data set option is less efficient than the other methods. These results should not dissuade use of WHERE in either its statement or data set option form. Used appropriately, it can also provide efficiency. If a procedure is to be executed for only a subset of data, it is more efficient to execute it in conjunction with WHERE than to first subset the data in a DATA step.

Testing Program Modules

It is good programming strategy to keep operations within the program modular, that is, in independent sections. Modularity facilitates testing and debugging because these sections can be isolated. Focusing on one module is easier than attempting to debug an entire program.

Once the flowchart has been defined, it needs to be translated into SAS code. Some modules may be logically difficult to code. These portions of the program should be thoroughly tested in a pseudo environment. Setting up the environment in an interactive SAS session is a good approach; immediate feedback is available and the code can easily be modified and resubmitted using the RECALL and SUB commands (or their respective function keys).

If the outcome of a given set of instructions is not predictable, try reducing the instruction set to the simplest form for expressing the essence of the process. Submit the reduced instruction set and print out intermediate results as well as final results. Intermediate results follow the evolution of data values *within* a DATA step. They require the PUT statement after each modification to the variables, and they are written to the log. Final results track the modifications *between* DATA or PROC steps that do not produce output. To view them, use PROC PRINT.

Modifications Within a DATA Step

Follow the evolution of a variable that is modified in several calculations by printing the values before and after each modification. The PUT statement may specifically name variables to be written to the log, or it may be followed the keyword _ALL_. Specifying _ALL_ writes to the log all the variables defined in the DATA step, as well as some automatic variables like _N_, along with their current values. The result is a snapshot of each variable's value at the moment the PUT is executed.

This feature of SAS software is useful because named output is produced with very little programming effort. The drawback of using PUT _ALL_ is that all the variables appear in the log and only a limited number may be of interest. In that case, the variables of interest should be named on the PUT statement, each one followed by an equal sign to produce named output. Without the equal sign, the values will be written to the log in the order specified on the PUT statement without a variable name identifier. An example of the PUT statement with named and unnamed output follows:

```
put age= educ= surname;
```

The log would include named output for the variables AGE and EDUC, where a missing numeric value is represented as a "." and a missing character value is represented as a blank. Unnamed output is produced for the variable SURNAME as shown in Output 1.

Output 1: PUT Statement Output

```
AGE=35          EDUC=HIGH          BOWEN
AGE=24          SCH                HICKES
AGE=.           EDUC=COLLEGE       FELLOWS
AGE=29          EDUC=POSTGRA
```

Another consideration with a PUT statement is the number of observations in the data set being processed. If a pseudo environment has been set up and there are a limited number of observations, this is not a problem. However, if many observations are being processed, a corresponding number of entries will be written to the log. Generally, you need to print only a few observations to the log to ascertain the effect of an instruction set. Set up a counter, or use the automatic variable _N_ to limit the number of observations printed to the log. If the observations that are of interest are not sequential, or if they are modified conditionally, it is better to set up a counter variable inside the DO/END block to identify them for printing to the log. Use an accumulator variable to create a counter as shown in the following statement:

```
x + 1;
```

This statement creates a numeric variable X and increments it by 1 with each execution of the DATA step. Unlike other SAS variables in the PDV, it is not initialized as a new observation is processed. Use the counter variable in a conditional statement to logically limit the number of PUT statements executed.

The next example uses the automatic variable _N_ and a counter variable X to demonstrate the evolution of variable values within a DATA step. Assume that a transformation of a variable is needed to first subtract a constant and then divide the result by another variable:

```
data transform;
   set random;
   if (_n_<4) then put 'ORIGINAL VALUE ' z=;
   z = z - 100;
   if (z < 0) then do;
      x+1;
      if (x < 4) then put 'Z NEGATIVE ' z=;
      end;
   z = z / std;
   if (_n_<4) then put 'VALUE DIVIDED BY STD ' z= std=;
   drop x;
```

Regardless of how many observations are in the data set, only 3 lines will be written to the log for each PUT statement executed. Depending upon whether the conditional statement is ever executed, as few as 6 lines could be written to the log or as many as 9. Each PUT statement shows the value of Z when it is executed. Output from this code is shown in Output 2.

Output 2: Evolution of Variables Within a DATA Step

```
ORIGINAL VALUE Z=230.0
VALUE DIVIDED BY STD Z=8.1 STD=16.0
ORIGINAL VALUE Z=612.0
VALUE DIVIDED BY STD Z=11.4 STD=45.0
ORIGINAL VALUE Z=90.0
Z NEGATIVE Z=-10.0
VALUE DIVIDED BY STD Z=-4.0 STD=2.5
```

It is easy to extend this technique to create several counters if different modules are being tested simultaneously. Dropping the counter variables prevents them from being needlessly carried along on the output data sets.

Printing Results Between Steps

PROC PRINT is the quickest way to view the final result of a DATA or PROC step that does not produce output. You can use PROC PRINT between steps in the program to follow the process. Limiting the number of observations to be printed (with an OBS=n data set option) reduces the paper burden but still provides enough information to determine if the program is functioning as expected. The use of titles helps associate the print output with the corresponding code.

Using the Right Combination of DATA and PROC Steps

For most reporting applications, some processing of the raw data is needed. Processing includes data manipulations, new variable definitions, setting up the data structure, and/or subsetting the data. All these operations can be performed in a DATA step. As noted previously, summarized data is usually needed for reports, so follow the initial DATA step with one or more of the SAS summary procedures discussed earlier.

If the printed output is inadequate because of aesthetics, content, or some other reason, the output data sets created by the summary procedures can become the source for reporting elements. The output data sets that are generated from the reporting procedures are organized by observations and variables which can be processed in a subsequent DATA step using FILE and PUT statements to meet very exacting requirements.

Managing Syntactical Errors

After you have tested each module thoroughly, you can assemble the complete program. Although the SAS compiler is very liberal concerning position and placement of statements on a line, a consistent coding structure makes subsequent program maintenance much easier. For example, DATA and PROC statements, as well as OPTIONS, FILENAME, and LIBNAME statements, should dominate all others by being placed at the left-most margin. Subordinate statements should be indented by 3 or more spaces. Additional indenting should follow the same spacing pattern. It is helpful for statements within a DO/END block to be indented for clarity.

After the code exists in machine readable format, submit it to the SAS System with OPTIONS OBS=0 as the first line of code. This permits a quick, efficient check of the syntax without your wasting resources by preventing initial steps from processing actual data when syntax errors are in subsequent code. Note that if a permanent data set is named in the DATA statement and OBS=0 is specified, the permanent data set will be overwritten. You can prevent this from happening by substituting a temporary name and proceeding with the syntax check. The syntax check highlights spelling problems, missing infix operators, and unmatched DO/END statements in the log. Notes, which are as important as warnings, are also written to the log. They should be evaluated and managed appropriately.

If a WHERE statement or data set option has been used, the OPTIONS OBS=0 will not work. Checking syntax is still possible by commenting out any WHERE reference. For example, the following code would allow a syntax check to be performed:

```
options obs=0;
data new;
   set old   /*   (where=(target='Y'))   */   ;
proc print data=new  /*   (where=(state='MI'))   */   ;
```

The Most Common Syntactical Errors

The most common syntactical errors are shown in Table 4, which appears at the end of this chapter. If the offending statement is not apparent, and the recommended action fails to resolve the problem, try commenting out increasingly smaller sections of the program code until the problem reoccurs. First, try executing just the DATA statement in conjunction with either its corresponding SET, MERGE, or INFILE statement. If that processes without error, restrict the commented section further so that additional statements are processed. This approach can be repeated until the offending statement is isolated. Then you can review its syntax to determine what is causing the program to abort.

Planning for Adequate Space

Another problem frequently overlooked in report writing is space, which you should not leave to chance, especially when large volumes of data are being processed. Calculate required space for observations in both temporary and permanent data sets. Each computer environment is different, so it is not possible to give specific instructions for managing space requirements. However, you can make a rough estimate by multiplying the number of bytes per observation by the number of observations. Both of these pieces of information can be obtained from PROC CONTENTS. Note that the actual space required will exceed this estimate because of data set overhead.

If the available space is inadequate, use PROC DATASETS to delete temporary or permanent data sets that are no longer needed for the current execution of a program. Executing PROC DATASETS with a DELETE statement immediately frees space. You can also free space by reusing a data set name, although this method frees space only after successful completion of the step, which requires enough space for both versions of the data set to exist concurrently.

Chapter Summary

Commonly recognized types of programming error are logical and syntactical in nature. Inefficient programming is also considered a type of error. Careful planning and testing during the program development phase leads to successful outcomes. Keeping the program modular facilitates its testing, documentation, and maintenance. Planning for adequate space avoids wasting computer resources.

Table 4: Most Common SAS Errors

Error Message	Explanation	Recommended Action
Statement out of order/ Symbol is not recognized	The SAS compiler has not processed valid statements. Usually a semicolon is missing from a statement which causes the compiler to encounter inappropriate statement order.	Check each statement in the program, look for missing semi-colons, and resubmit.
Character literal exceeds 200	The SAS compiler processed mismatched quote marks. Usually a quoted string is not enclosed with quote marks.	Check each pair of quotes: make sure that all quoted strings begin and end with a single quote mark.
Format XXXXXX is unknown	The SAS compiler does not recognize format specification. Either the format library is not available for access, PROC FORMAT has not executed, or the format name is misspelled.	Check for LIBNAME reference to the format library if that is where formats reside or ensure that PROC FORMAT is part of current execution. Carefully check the format name specification.
Array subscript out of bounds	An array definition does not have the number of elements that the current index value indicates.	Use a PUT statement to print the index value that is causing the error, and check the array definition for the cause.
Apparent symbolic reference XXXXXX not resolved	The SAS compiler encountered a macro variable reference which is not defined.	Check the macro code, ensure that each value is defined for the current execution. Sometimes, because of macro nesting, a global statement is required to have intra-macro reference recognition.

CHAPTER 3

Report Writing Applications

by Sheree H. Andersen

Abstract

The SAS System provides an impressive array of tools for report writing, enough to satisfy even the most discriminating requests. Report specifications ranging from the simplest to the most complex may be developed using reporting procedures (PRINT, TABULATE, REPORT) or FILE and PUT statements in a DATA step. The report procedures included in SAS software are easy to invoke but provide varying degrees of flexibility in the report content and aesthetics. As the flexibility increases, there is a corresponding increase in coding complexity. Report programs that use FILE and PUT statements provide the maximum control over report content and appearance, but consequently they are more difficult to code. This chapter introduces a variety of unrelated applications that have been developed for unique reporting specifications. They can be added to an existing program library or used to start one.

Specifications

The code in this chapter was developed and tested with Release 6.08 of the SAS System under the Windows environment. Use of the code with other releases of the SAS System or other environments may require user modification. Modified code is not supported by the author.

About the Author

Sheree H. Andersen is an independent SAS consultant with 14 years of experience using SAS software. Sheree has a BS degree in Statistics from Brigham Young University and an MS degree in Biostatistics from the University of Utah. Her areas of expertise include base SAS software, report writing, and the SAS macro facility.

Questions and Comments Should be Directed to:

Sheree H. Andersen
1530 E. Deer Haven Drive
North Logan, UT 84321
Telephone: 801-750-0908

Examples from this book are available online, see inside back cover for details.

Report-Writing Applications

Sheree H. Andersen

Introduction

This chapter outlines applications to be used in report writing. It is best understood by users with an intermediate-level of SAS programming experience. The applications were developed to meet specific design criteria including that the code be generalized and reusable. Usually, SAS code that meets these criteria is most valuable because it enables reports of slight variation to be generated easily. You can adapt the applications presented in this chapter to fit a variety of situations. The chapter covers the following topics:

- Report Writing Generalizations
- Application 1: Adding Classification Variables
- Application 2: Logical Spacing within a Report
- Computing Percentiles of Categorical Data with a Macro

Report-Writing Generalizations

To determine which of the many report writing methods is right for your report, a checklist may prove helpful. Some of the questions that need to be answered include:

- Is summary information or observation listing needed?
- Are page breaks or custom line spacing needed?
- Does the report include computed variables, standard statistics, or both?
- Is the report ad-hoc or to be run on a routine basis?
- Is standard SAS output sufficient, or is a customized report design needed?

Once these and other relevant questions are answered, you've narrowed your solution options. If a report needs custom line spacing, the solution must involve use of the FILE and PUT statements in a DATA step. If the report content includes lines that do not fit the natural data set orientation of variables and observations, it will also require custom programming and not the use of SAS procedures. Being aware of the capability and limitations of the various reporting procedures is a prerequisite to quality programming.

The applications presented in this chapter demonstrate how to structure data in commonly requested forms. Advantages, disadvantages, and alternate methods are also addressed. Additionally, sample code is presented with each application.

Application 1: Adding Classification Variables

You will find this application useful if your report:

- has a key variable on each observation
- uses SAS formats for value translation
- needs easy, rapid maintenance
- has storage space limitations, necessitating temporary association of classification variables

The SAS features that are used include:

- PROC FORMAT
- the DATA step SUBSTR function

Description

Through mapping of a key variable that exists on each observation, you can obtain variables which define levels of summary or classification. The classification variables may be temporarily added during processing rather than permanently stored with the data. Maintenance is easily accomplished through format corrections and updates rather than data set revisions. When updates are frequent, the temporary association of classification variables is particularly useful because editing a format file is easier than maintaining a SAS data set that stores the classification relations.

To implement this technique, create a SAS format. The format maps the key variable to a text string which is composed of juxtaposed classification variable values that have a limited domain and are possibly encoded. The text string is then broken down into the respective classification elements using the SUBSTR function. The encoded variable values may be associated with another format which provides additional value translation. The classification elements can be, but are not necessarily, subsumed in each other. For example, if CITY is the detail variable, you can add the following classifications:

CITY ==> STATE ==> REGION ===> COUNTRY ===> SIZE

For the purpose of illustration, the variable SIZE is not subsumed in the COUNTRY classification, as STATE is within REGION, and REGION within COUNTRY.

Example

This example uses CITY as the key variable and adds classification variables by first setting up the format with the text string:

```
proc format;
   value $classvar
   'CARY'    = 'NCEUSA2'
   'DENVER'  = 'COWUSA3'
   'HOUSTON' = 'TXSUSA3'
   .
   .
   .
   ;

/****  Create additional formats to translate the encoded values. ****/
   value $region
   'N' = 'North'
   'S' = 'South'
   'E' = 'East'
   'W' = 'West'
   ;
   value $size
   '1' = 'Small'
   '2' = 'Medium'
   '3' = 'Large';

/**** Use the SUBSTR function to add the classification variables. ****/
data temp;
   set city;
   length region $5 country $3 size $6;
   string  = put(city, $classvar.);
   state   = substr(string,1,2);
   region  = substr(string,3,1);
   country = substr(string,4,3);
   size    = substr(string,7,1);
   drop string;
   format region $region. size $size.;
run;
```

A printing of the output data may contain observations like those shown in Output 1.

Output 1: Printing of SUBSTR Example

CITY	STATE	REGION	COUNTRY	SIZE
CARY	NC	South	USA	Medium
DENVER	CO	West	USA	Large
HOUSTON	TX	South	USA	Large

The DATA step could also incorporate additional SAS functions such as STNAME to expand the value of STATE from the postal abbreviation to its full name. Modifications of this type need corresponding changes to the LENGTH statement so that value truncation is not a problem.

A variation of this technique can also aid in the data processing aspect of report writing. If the key variable has a large domain and the format proves to be cumbersome, diffuse the processing and maintenance tasks by creating multiple formats containing the text string information. For example, you could add classification variables based on ZIP code by making ten separate formats containing the text string information, with each format dependent upon the first character of ZIP code. Using SUBSTR with ZIP code associates the appropriate format. For this example the census entities COUNTY and TRACT compose the text string of classification variables that are to be added.

```
proc format;
   value $zip0fmt
   '00001' = '0011000'
   '00002' = '0011000'
   '00003' = '0011031'
   '00005' = '0011020'
   .
   .
   .
   ;
data temp;
   set zips;
   length zipc $1 county $3 tract $4;
   zipc  = substr(zip,1);
   if (zipc='0') then string = put(zip, $zip0fmt.);
    else if (zipc='1') then string = put(zip, $zip1fmt.);
    else if (zipc='2') then string = put(zip, $zip2fmt.);
    else if (zipc='3') then string = put(zip, $zip3fmt.);
    else if (zipc='4') then string = put(zip, $zip4fmt.);
    else if (zipc='5') then string = put(zip, $zip5fmt.);
    else if (zipc='6') then string = put(zip, $zip6fmt.);
    else if (zipc='7') then string = put(zip, $zip7fmt.);
    else if (zipc='8') then string = put(zip, $zip8fmt.);
    else if (zipc='9') then string = put(zip, $zip9fmt.);
   county   = substr(string,1,3);
   tract    = substr(string,4,4);
```

Alternate Methods

As with most SAS applications, there is more than one way to derive similar results. You should evaluate each of the different methods for its respective advantages and disadvantages. Where efficiency is a key consideration, a benchmark run that is designed to closely approximate the proposed task is recommended.

Similar results to temporarily adding classification variables with formats and substrings can be obtained by a merge. The SAS data set containing detail information can be merged with a SAS data set serving as a table with the appropriate classification variable relations. The drawback with this approach is that a merge requires both data sets to be sorted by the variables used in the merge. For large data sets, a sort with a subsequent merge could prove to be very inefficient.

Another approach uses multiple formats that map the key variable to each of the classification variables individually. However, maintenance would be more difficult because updates to the key variable would require changes wherever it is referenced.

Application 2: Logical Spacing within a Report

Occasionally, report specifications require spacing that is difficult to obtain using the standard SAS report procedures. Sometimes the customization is specific enough to require FILE and PUT statements. A technique to logically determine line spacing or page breaks, with FILE and PUT statements, is presented here. This application is best suited for data that has been summarized by PROC MEANS and transposed by PROC TRANSPOSE.

Description

A standard report with consistent or fixed column headings may require double line spacing or page breaks between groups of related, transposed variables. For this technique to work best, the related variables need identical name roots. Typically, the data to be reported needs to be summarized with standard statistics or percent-of-total information for categorical variables. A modification of this technique, shown in the next section, works well when there is a combination of statistics and other descriptive information requiring different output formats.

Once the data is transposed, the values of the _NAME_ variable are substringed to obtain a logical grouping variable. The common root names of the original, related variables readily lead to the logical grouping variable. If the data is not already organized into the desired report order, a sort, by the grouping variable, must be done. Then FIRST. processing is incorporated with the PUT statement. You can add additional logic to handle specific cases such as checking the lines left on the page.

You will find this technique useful if your report:

- needs logical line spacing or page breaks
- has common root names used for related variables

The SAS features that are incorporated include:

- summarized, transposed data
- PROC FORMAT
- FILE and PUT statements
- LL option on the FILE statement
- FIRST. and LAST. variable processing

Example

This example uses demographic and vehicle buyer data. The demographic variables AGE, EDUC, and MS are categorical. The values of AGE are the midpoint of 5-year intervals with the implied natural boundaries of 'Less than 30' and '65 and Over' for vehicle buyers. The levels of education include: high school graduate, some college, college graduate and technical or other. Marital status has 3 categories: Married, Single, and Other. The desired report shows the percent of total for each category of the demographic variables with double spacing between the related categories. The columns of the report correspond to different vehicle types available for purchase.

The code needed to formulate this report follows:

```
/**** Create a format for related variables. ****/
proc format;
   value $group
   'A' = 'Age of Buyer'
   'E' = 'Education Level'
   'M' = 'Marital Status';

/**** Format original variable names to comply with row descriptions. ****/
   value $rows
   'AGE1' = 'Less than 30'
   'AGE2' = '30-34'
   'AGE3' = '35-39'
   'AGE4' = '40-44'
   'AGE5' = '45-49'
   'AGE6' = '50-54'
   'AGE7' = '55-59'
   'AGE8' = '60-64'
   'AGE9' = '65 and over'

   'ED1'  = 'High School Graduate'
   'ED2'  = 'Some College'
   'ED3'  = 'College Graduate'
   'ED4'  = 'Technical, Other'

   'MS1'  = 'Married'
   'MS2'  = 'Single'
   'MS3'  = 'Other'
  ;
data demo;
   set trucks (keep=age educ ms seg);

/**** Create category frequency variables. ****/
   if (age < 28) then age1 = 1;
    else if (age = 32) then age2 = 1;
    else if (age = 37) then age3 = 1;
    else if (age = 42) then age4 = 1;
    else if (age = 47) then age5 = 1;
    else if (age = 52) then age6 = 1;
    else if (age = 57) then age7 = 1;
    else if (age = 62) then age8 = 1;
    else if (age = 68) then age9 = 1;
   if (educ = '3') then ed1 = 1;
    else if (educ = '4') then ed2 = 1;
    else if (educ = '5') then ed3 = 1;
    else if (educ = '6') then ed4 = 1;
   if (ms = 'M') then ms1 = 1;
    else if (ms = 'S') then ms2 = 1;
    else if (ms = 'O') then ms3 = 1;
   keep age1--ms3 seg;

/**** Summarize the data. ****/
proc means data=demo nway noprint;
   class seg;
   var age1--ms3;
   output out=sdemo sum(age1--ms3)=;
```

```
/**** Compute percents using the category frequencies. ****/
data pct;
   set sdemo;
   array pct age1--ms3;
   do over pct;
      pct = (100 * pct) / _freq_;
      end;

/**** Transpose the data orientation. ****/
proc transpose data=pct out=tdemo;
   id seg;
   var age1--ms3;

/**** Create logical grouping variable and sort if necessary. ****/
data tdemo;
   set tdemo;
   group = substr(_name_,1,1);
data _null_;
   file out ll=lines print header=top;
   set tdemo;
   by group;

/**** Govern spacing between groups with FIRST. processing. ****/
if (first.group) then do;
   if (lines<20) then put _page_;
    else put //;
   put @1 group $group. / @1 15 * '-';
   end;

/**** Write formatted output. ****/
   put @3 _name_ $rows. @23 (bus--utility) (5.1 +3);
   return;
top:
   put 'Demographic Characteristics by Vehicle Type' /
   @15 43 * '-' /
   @24 'BUS    MINIVAN   PICKUP  UTILITY';
   return;
   run;
```

The report is shown in Output 2.

Output 2: Logical Spacing Within a Report

```
            Demographic Characteristics by Vehicle Type
            -----------------------------------------
                            BUS     MINIVAN     PICKUP     UTILITY

Age of Buyer
------------
  Less than 30              2.1       6.6        13.6        15.0
  30-34                     6.9      16.8        12.3        16.3
  35-39                    20.7      22.6        13.1        17.7
  40-44                    18.0      18.8        12.2        16.2
  45-49                    16.7      10.3        13.3        15.4
  50-54                     9.6       6.2        10.5         9.3
  55-59                     6.1       5.2         8.0         4.2
  60-64                     6.9       5.1         8.0         3.2
  65 and over              13.0       8.3         9.1         2.6

Education Level
---------------
  High School Grad          3.1       2.6         9.0         2.8
  Some College             18.8      16.5        36.9        19.5
  College Graduate         30.1      27.3        32.5        33.1
  Technical, Other         47.9      53.6        21.6        44.7

Marital Status
---------------
  Married                  92.3      93.0        77.3        73.7
  Single                    6.1       5.2        20.4        24.0
  Other                     1.7       1.8         2.2         2.4
```

Alternate Methods

Similar results to those shown above can be obtained using PROC TABULATE. Percent-of-total statistics can be computed and placed in the column table dimension with demographic variables concatenated, as shown. Where the proposed technique differs is in the ability to logically place spacing in the report.

Vertically Combining Statistics with Different Formats

The previous report can be enhanced by adding a row with the median, or 50th percentile, of age. Making several adjustments to the program generates a report that includes the median age. Median age is preferred over mean age as a measure of central tendency primarily because it is influenced less by outliers. The macro to compute percentiles for categorical data is included later in this section. It computes a linear interpolation within the categorical interval containing the requested percentile.

For the percentile macro to work properly, the upper limit of the age categories needs to be used. A new variable, AGEM, can be created that has the upper limit as its values instead of the category midpoints. This example places the PCTL macro results in the output data set, MEDAGE. If no output data set macro parameter is specified the results are placed in DATA1, by default. A complete description of the PCTL macro parameters is given later in this chapter.

To add a row for the median age these changes need to be made to the program:

- A macro call that computes the median by each of the vehicle types.
- A merge of the median data set with the data set containing the summarized data.
- A LENGTH statement issued prior to the merge orders the variables such that median age appears after the last age category, '65 and over'.
- The median age is output to the report using a different format than that used for the percents.

The effected lines are highlighted below:

```
/**** Create a format for related variables. ****/
proc format;
   value $group
   'A' = 'Age of Buyer'
   'E' = 'Education Level'
   'M' = 'Marital Status';

/**** Format original variable names to comply with row descriptions. ****/
   value $rows
   'AGE1' = 'Less than 30'
   'AGE2' = '30-34'
   'AGE3' = '35-39'
   'AGE4' = '40-44'
   'AGE5' = '45-49'
   'AGE6' = '50-54'
   'AGE7' = '55-59'
   'AGE8' = '60-64'
   'AGE9' = '65 and over'
   'AGEM' = 'Median Age'

   'ED1'  = 'High School Graduate'
   'ED2'  = 'Some College'
   'ED3'  = 'College Graduate'
   'ED4'  = 'Technical, Other'

   'MS1'  = 'Married'
   'MS2'  = 'Single'
   'MS3'  = 'Other'
  ;
data demo;
   set trucks (keep=age educ ms seg);

/**** Create category frequency variables. ****/
   if (age < 28) then age1 = 1;
    else if (age = 32) then age2 = 1;
    else if (age = 37) then age3 = 1;
    else if (age = 42) then age4 = 1;
    else if (age = 47) then age5 = 1;
    else if (age = 52) then age6 = 1;
    else if (age = 57) then age7 = 1;
    else if (age = 62) then age8 = 1;
    else if (age = 68) then age9 = 1;
   if (educ = '3') then ed1 = 1;
    else if (educ = '4') then ed2 = 1;
    else if (educ = '5') then ed3 = 1;
    else if (educ = '6') then ed4 = 1;


   if (ms = 'M') then ms1 = 1;
    else if (ms = 'S') then ms2 = 1;
    else if (ms = 'O') then ms3 = 1;
   keep age1--ms3 seg agem;

/**** Summarize the data. ****/
proc means data=demo nway noprint;
   class seg;
   var age1--ms3;
   output out=sdemo sum(age1--ms3)=;
```

```
/**** Invoke the Percentile Macro. ****/
%pctl(50,agem,by=seg,out=medage)

/**** Compute percents using the category frequencies. ****/
data pct;
   length age1-age9 agem ed1-ed4 ms1-ms3;
   merge sdemo medage;
   by seg;
   array pct age1-age9 ed1--ms3;
   do over pct;
      pct = (100 * pct) / _freq_;
      end;

/**** Transpose the data orientation. ****/
proc transpose data=pct out=tdemo;
   id seg;
   var age1--ms3;

/**** Create logical grouping variable and sort if necessary. ****/
data tdemo;
   set tdemo;
   group = substr(_name_,1,1);
data _null_;
   file out ll=lines print header=top;
   set tdemo;
   by group;

/**** Govern spacing between groups with FIRST. processing. ****/
if (first.group) then do;
   if (lines<20) then put _page_;
    else put //;
   put @1 group $group. / @1 15 * '-';
   end;

/**** Conditionally output statistics with the appropriate format. ****/
   if (_name_='AGEM') then put
      @3 _name_ $rows. @23 (bus--utility) (5.2 +3);
    else put @3 _name $rows. @23 (bus--utility) (5.1 +3);
   return;
top:
   put 'Demographic Characteristics by Vehicle Type' /
   @15 43 * '-' /
   @24 'BUS    MINIVAN   PICKUP  UTILITY';
   return;
   run;
```

The modified report is shown in Output 3.

Output 3: Vertically Combining Statistics with Different Formats

```
                Demographic Characteristics by Vehicle Type
                -------------------------------------------
                      BUS     MINIVAN     PICKUP    UTILITY

Age of Buyer
------------
  Less than 30        2.1        6.6       13.6       15.0
  30-34               6.9       16.8       12.3       16.3
  35-39              20.7       22.6       13.1       17.7
  40-44              18.0       18.8       12.2       16.2
  45-49              16.7       10.3       13.3       15.4
  50-54               9.6        6.2       10.5        9.3
  55-59               6.1        5.2        8.0        4.2
  60-64               6.9        5.1        8.0        3.2
  65 and over        13.0        8.3        9.1        2.6
  Median age         49.10     43.92      45.83      44.19

Education Level
---------------
  High School Grad    3.1        2.6        9.0        2.8
  Some College       18.8       16.5       36.9       19.5
  College Graduate   30.1       27.3       32.5       33.1
  Technical, Other   47.9       53.6       21.6       44.7

Marital Status
---------------
  Married            92.3       93.0       77.3       73.7
  Single              6.1        5.2       20.4       24.0
  Other               1.7        1.8        2.2        2.4
```

Computing Percentiles of Categorical Data with a Macro

You can use the following macro to calculate percentiles of categorical variables. Percentiles of continuous variables can be done using PROC UNIVARIATE or PROC RANK. This macro computes a value for the percentile variable that is a linear interpolation within the categorical interval that contains the requested percentile. You must use the upper limit of the categories as the values of the variable for which the percentiles are to be calculated, occasionally this may require the recoding of another variable as shown in the example above. The macro has the ability to handle BY-variable processing, weights and named data set input and output. It has the positional and keyword parameters shown in Table 1.

Table 1: Percentile Macro Parameters

Name	Type	Status	Function	Example
PCTL	positional	required	percentile request	25
ON	positional	required	variable name	agem
BY	keyword	optional	by variable	by=state ms educ
IN	keyword	optional	input data set	in=in
OUT	keyword	optional	output data set	out=out
WEIGHT	keyword	optional	weight variable	weight=wt_var

The macro may be invoked by a macro call similar to the one shown below. As many BY variables as needed may be specified, separated by blanks.

```
%pctl(25,agem,by=state ms educ,in=in,out=out,weight=wt_var)
```

Submitting this macro call would calculate a weighted first quartile for each unique combination of the variables STATE, MS, and EDUC in the data set named IN. The output data set containing the results is named OUT.

The PCTL macro follows:

```
/**** Macro for Computing Percentiles of Categorical Data ****/
%macro pctl(pctl,on,by=,in=&syslast,out=data1,weight=);
%if (%str(&by)^=%str()) %then %do;
   %let bystr=&by;
   %let null=%str( );
   %let last=%index(&bystr,&null);
   %do %while (&last^=0);
      %let bystr=%substr(&bystr,&last);
      %let last=%index(&bystr,&null);
      %end;
   %let firstby=first.&bystr;
   %let lastby=last.&bystr;
   %str(proc sort data=&in;);
   %str(by &by;);
   %end;
 %else do;
   %let firstby=_n_=1;
   %let lastby=eof;
   %end;
%str(proc freq data=&in;);
%if (%str(&by)^=%str()) %then %do;
   %str(by &by;);
   %end;
%str(tables &on / noprint out=&out;);
%if (%str(&weight)^=%str()) %then %str(weight &weight;);
data &out;
   set &out(where=(&on^=.)) end=eof;
   keep &on &by;
%if (%str(&by)^=%str()) %then %do;
   %str(by &by;);
   %end;
   laston=lag(on);
   lastpct=lag(percent);
   if (&firstby) then sumpct=0;
   if (sumpct>=&pctl) then delete;
   sumpct + percent;
   if (sumpct>=&pctl) then do;
      if (&firstby | &lastby) then do;
         if (&firstby) then cell='RIGHT';
          else cell='LEFT';
         put ">> Warning: &pctl.th pctl of &on is in " cell $5. "-most cell";
         put '>> for open-ended cells, this may be unreliable';
         put '>> a missing value will be returned';
         %if (%str(&by)^=%str()) %then %do;
            put 'for by values ' &by;
            %end;
         &on=.;
         output;
         end;
```

```
      else do;
        if (sumpct>&pctl) then &on=((&pctl - lastpct) / (sumpct - lastpct))
          * (&on - laston +1) + laston;
        output;
        end;
     end;
  label &on="&on &pctl.th pct est. from cum. dist.";
%mend;
```

Conclusion

This chapter introduces a variety of useful report-writing techniques and gives examples on temporarily adding classification variables to a data set and obtaining logical spacing within a report. Vertical concatenation of statistics requiring different formats is also shown, as well as a macro that produces percentiles for categorical data.

CHAPTER 4

Propagating Documentation

by Laurie Burch

Abstract

Everybody hates documentation – unless it does your work for you. This chapter describes the benefits of documenting SAS data sets and variables. Significant productivity is gained during the programming phase when extensive and thorough documentation has been done as a first step. The user can then take advantage of the detailed documentation stored with data sets throughout all subsequent SAS programming. The same documentation that is used to generate SAS output can also be used for project documentation. Since SAS documentation must be current to have correct output, this makes it superior to manual documentation, which is hard to maintain and often out of date.

Specifications

The code in this chapter was developed and tested with Release 6.08 of the SAS System under the Windows environment. Use of the code with other releases of the SAS System or other environments may require user modification. Modified code is not supported by the author.

About the Author

Laurie Burch is a self-employed computer analyst with over 20 years of experience using SAS software. Her areas of expertise include base SAS software, SAS/AF, SAS/FSP, and SAS/GRAPH software. Laurie has a BA degree in Mathematics from Berea College.

Questions and Comments Should be Directed to:

Laurie Burch
7910 Longbranch Parkway
Takoma Park, MD 20912
Telephone: 301-270-1608

Propagating Documentation

Laurie Burch

Introduction

Tell me when a programmer loves to do documentation. Did you say "never?" If you're an experienced SAS programmer, you said "when it does my work for me!"

Program and database documentation is lengthy and time-consuming. We often put it off as the last task in a project. When it is finally finished, it is placed on a shelf to become almost immediately obsolete as the project it documents takes on a life of its own and starts a career of modifications.

We all intend to update our documentation, but the organization's next deadline is always looming, and documentation is the easiest task to let slide. When a new SAS programmer comes to the project and is asked to make a change, his first task is to find out if the documentation is current and usable. Frequently, the answer is no, and the obsolete documentation is used only as a guide to help him understand what was originally programmed.

We Document Anyway

What a depressing view of work habits! But think for a moment; much of what is required to document files and data is frequently coded into our SAS programs as we write them. For example, SAS software allows you to specify the following information for each variable in a SAS data set:

- meaningful label descriptions
- default formats (numeric or character, length, etc.)
- descriptions for each code or range of codes.

We frequently use these capabilities when we call SAS procedures because we want the output to be as descriptive and readable as possible. This on-the-fly documentation can be placed anywhere in a SAS program. It can be added in a DATA step, in which case it stays with the variable from step to step (propagation). Or it can be added when a SAS procedure is called, in which case it is temporary and stays with the variable only during the execution of that procedure.

Let's Use It

Suppose we use these documentation capabilities in the very first step of a project and store the results in permanent SAS data set(s). We then gain several major benefits.

- Our documentation works for us. Each time we produce a report, table, graph or other analysis, the variables are automatically labeled and the values formatted.
- As new SAS data sets are created from old SAS data sets, the documentation associated with the old data sets will automatically be carried forward to the new data sets (propagation).
- Documentation is always current. You cannot afford to let it get outdated since that would make output incorrect.
- Documentation can be printed, using SAS procedures, in easily readable reports that can be filed as part of project documentation.

This rest of this chapter will show, through an example, how dramatically SAS documentation and the propagation of that documentation can work for you.

The Example

The SAS data set CENSUS.PLACES listed in Ouput 1 lists some of the data taken from the 1990 U.S. Census of Population and Housing for Chevy Chase and Takoma Park, Maryland. These two towns are both in Montgomery County, just outside Washington, D.C., and are representative of the great diversity found in suburbs surrounding a major metropolitan area.

Output 1: SAS Data Set CENSUS.PLACES

```
                  1990 Census of Housing and Population
                  Chevy Chase and Takoma Park, Maryland

OBS  PLACEFP    AREALAND      HU100     POP100    P0020001   P0030001

 1    16620        1211        1005       2675         784        980
 2    16625        6643        3548       8559        2406       3421
 3    16720         271         228        632         183        218
 4    16730        1072         715       2078         586        692
 5    16787         295         272        749         210        267
 6    76650        3074        4938      11544        2582       4705

OBS   P0060001      P0060002      P0060003      P0060004      P0060005

 1        2606            32             2            30             5
 2        7897           352            11           233            66
 3         608             8             1            10             5
 4        2018            18             1            39             2
 5         724            10             2            12             1
 6        6444          4140            52           410           498
```

We don't know what this data is about because the variable names are undocumented and have no meaning. Looking at the values of the variables doesn't help since all values are either coded or represent counts. We need to start at Step 1 and build some documentation.

Step 1: Building the FORMAT Library

It it helpful as a first step in a SAS project to go through all the variables in our data set(s) and look for those with coded values; i.e., each value is a code that has a meaning. We want to store a description of the codes for each of these variables in a format library. PLACEFP is the only coded variable in CENSUS.PLACES. It contains a code representing Census Place, a term used by the Census Bureau to designate an incorporated city or a densely settled population that is identifiable by name. By aggregating the codes, we can define new codes for towns and, in turn, describe the code for each town. The following SAS program builds a permanent format library.

```
libname library 'c:\';
proc format library=library;
   value $place
      '16620' = 'Chevy Chase Town'
      '16625' = 'Chevy Chase CDP'
      '16720' = 'Chevy Chase Section Five Village'
      '16730' = 'Chevy Chase Section Three Village'
      '16787' = 'Chevy Chase Village Town'
      '76650' = 'Takoma Park'
      ;
   value $town
      '1' = 'Chevy Chase'
      '2' = 'Takoma Park'
      ;
   value $conv
     '16620','16625','16720','16730','16787' = '1'
      '76650' = '2'
      ;
run;
```

We want our formats to be permanent. In other words, we want to define them once and store them in a library. Any subsequent use of these formats in DATA or PROC steps will draw upon the library for their definitions.

The LIBNAME statement on the first line of the program associates a libref with the format library. The word LIBRARY is usually used as the libref since the SAS System looks for permanent formats only in the SAS library that has been assigned the LIBRARY libref.

The PROC FORMAT statement uses the LIBRARY= option to associate the format library with the libref. All formats created in this PROC FORMAT step are stored in the format library.

Each format to be defined starts with a VALUE statement that assigns a name to the format. The codes are then listed, along with a description of the meaning of each code. Character formats, which are used with character variables, must start with a $ sign.

We may define as many formats as we wish. They may be for variables already in the SAS data set or they may be used for future variables yet to be created.

Step 2: Adding Labels and Formats

The next step is to add labels and formats for each variable in CENSUS.PLACES. We can do this at the same time we do other DATA step tasks, such as creating new variables. The following SAS code does this.

```
libname census 'c:\';
libname library 'c:\';

data census.sqm (label='Census Places with SQM Calculations');
   set census.places;

   sq_miles = arealand/2.59/1000;
   pop_sqm  = pop100/sq_miles;
   hu_sqm   = hu100/sq_miles;
   fam_hu   = hu100/p0020001;

   label placefp  = 'Place'
         arealand = 'Land Area in Sq Km (1/1000)'
         sq_miles = 'Land Area in Sq Miles'
         pop_sqm  = 'Population Per Square Mile'
         hu_sqm   = 'Housing Units Per Square Mile'
         fam_hu   = 'Families Per Housing Unit'
         hu100    = 'Housing Units'
         pop100   = 'Population'
         p0020001 = 'Families'
         p0030001 = 'Households'
         p0060001 = 'White'
         p0060002 = 'Black'
         p0060003 = 'American Indian, Eskimo, or Aleut'
         p0060004 = 'Asian or Pacific Islander'
         p0060005 = 'Other Race'
         ;

   format placefp $place. arealand sq_miles fam_hu 4.1
      hu100 pop100 p0020001 p0030001 p0060001 p0060002 p0060003
      p0060004 p0060005 pop_sqm hu_sqm comma8.;
run;
```

The program starts with two LIBNAME statements. The CENSUS libref tells us where we will be storing our permanent SAS data sets, and the LIBRARY libref tells us where to find the format library that we created in Step 1.

CENSUS.SQM is created from CENSUS.PLACES. Its purpose is to create four new variables and to document both old and new variables. The entire data set is assigned a descriptive label by using a LABEL= option on the DATA statement. When the documentation is printed for CENSUS.SQM, which we do later in this chapter, this label will appear in the documentation; it describes the contents of the data set.

The number stored in AREALAND is in thousandths (.001) of a square kilometer. SQ_MILES converts AREALAND to square miles. POP-SQM is the population per square mile; HU-SQM is the number of housing units per square mile; and FAM_HU is the number of families per housing unit.

Each variable, from both the CENSUS.PLACES data set and the new CENSUS.SQM data set, is given a meaningful label using the LABEL statement.

The FORMAT statement associates a format with each variable. Notice that each format name ends with a period when used in the FORMAT statement so that the SAS System can distinguish a format name from a variable name. PLACEFP is assigned the $PLACE. format, which is one of the formats we stored in our format library. Our program will have no problem finding this format since we used a LIBNAME statement at the beginning of the program to tell us where we stored our formats.

AREALAND, SQ_MILES, and FAM_HU all use a format of 4.1, which is one of the SAS software built-in formats. This format says that these variables are no greater than 4 numeric digits in length with a decimal point before the last digit. All the other numeric variables have been assigned a format of COMMA8., which is also a SAS software built-in format. COMMA8. says that commas are to be placed in the numbers for readability and that the total length of each variable will be no more than 8 characters, including commas. This format will print the number 100000 as 100,000.

Before and After

We now have two SAS data sets. CENSUS.SQM has been documented; CENSUS.PLACES has not. The following SAS code lists selected variables from CENSUS.PLACES, the undocumented data set.

```
libname census 'c:\';

title '1990 Census of Housing and Population';
title2 'Data Set with No Documentation';
proc print data=census.places;
   var placefp pop100 hu100;
run;
```

The results are shown in Output 2. There is no way to tell what this data is about since there are no meaningful column headings or code descriptions.

Output 2: Listing of Undocumented Data Set

```
                1990 Census of Housing and Population
                    Data Set with No Documentation

               OBS    PLACEFP        POP100        HU100

                1      16620          2675          1005
                2      16625          8559          3548
                3      16720           632           228
                4      16730          2078           715
                5      16787           749           272
                6      76650         11544          4938
```

CENSUS.SQM is the same data set but with documentation added. We can use similar program code to list this data set. We have added some additional options to take advantage of the available documentation.

```
libname census 'c:\';
libname library 'c:\';

title '1990 Census of Housing and Population';
title2 'Data Set with Documentation';
proc print data=census.sqm label;
   var placefp pop100 hu100;
run;
```

We have added a LIBNAME statement to define LIBRARY as the location of our format library. We have also added a LABEL option on the PROC PRINT statement. This tells the SAS System that we wish to use the labels stored with the data set as column headings. The result is shown in Output 3.

Output 3: Listing of Documented Data Set

```
                1990 Census of Housing and Population
                     Data Set with Documentation

                                                                Housing
  OBS      Place                                 Population       Units

    1      Chevy Chase Town                           2,675       1,005
    2      Chevy Chase CDP                            8,559       3,548
    3      Chevy Chase Section Five Village             632         228
    4      Chevy Chase Section Three Village          2,078         715
    5      Chevy Chase Village Town                     749         272
    6      Takoma Park                               11,544       4,938
```

Now we know exactly what data we have. The PLACEFP variable used the codes from the format library to provide meaningful labels for each code. The labels for each variable are used as column headings. The COMMA8. format that is associated with POP100 and HU100 places commas at the appropriate places to make numbers more readable. Very similar code, but dramatically different results.

Propagating Documentation

This is where you really see the power of the SAS software documentation capabilities! When you use an existing SAS data set to create a new SAS data set, all the variables that are written to the new data set carry their documentation with them. The following code gives an example of creating a new SAS data set from an already documented data set.

```
libname census 'c:\';
libname library 'c:\';

data;
   set census.sqm;
   nonwhite=p0060002+p0060003+p0060004+p0060005;
   label nonwhite='Nonwhite';
   format nonwhite comma8.;
run;

proc print label;
   var placefp p0060001 nonwhite;
   title '1990 Census of Population and Housing';
run;
```

In this example, the variable NONWHITE is created, documentation is added for it, and a report is printed. The resulting output is shown in Output 4.

Output 4: Documentation Carried Forward

```
                1990 Census of Population and Housing

   OBS    Place                                  White    Nonwhite

    1     Chevy Chase Town                       2,606          69
    2     Chevy Chase CDP                        7,897         662
    3     Chevy Chase Section Five Village         608          24
    4     Chevy Chase Section Three Village      2,018          60
    5     Chevy Chase Village Town                 724          25
    6     Takoma Park                            6,444       5,100
```

Notice that the documentation for the P0060001 variable has been carried forward into the new SAS data set. We added the documentation for the NONWHITE variable in the DATA step. If we were to use this data set to create still another data set, the documentation for both would be carried forward.

Recoding Values

Formats can also be used to recode variable values and place them into new variables. The new variables can then be assigned formats just as any other variable. The following code shows an example of how to do this.

```
libname census 'c:\';
libname library 'c:\';

data;
   set census.sqm;
   nonwhite=p0060002+p0060003+p0060004+p0060005;
   label nonwhite='Nonwhite';
   format nonwhite comma8.;
   town=put(placefp,$conv.);
   label town='Town';
   format town $town.;
run;

proc sort;
   by town;
run;

proc print uniform label;
   by town;
   var placefp p0060001 nonwhite;
   sum p0060001 nonwhite;
   title '1990 Census of Population and Housing';
run;
```

The PUT function uses the $CONV. format, which is stored in our format library, to translate the codes in the PLACEFP variable into a new set of codes that are stored in the variable TOWN. The PUT function enables you to write the value of PLACEFP with the $CONV. format into a new character variable.

The $TOWN. format, also stored in our format library, is then used to label the new codes when they are printed. The result is shown in Output 5.

Output 5: Recoding to Create a New Variable

```
               1990 Census of Population and Housing

------------------------- Town=Chevy Chase -------------------------

  OBS    Place                                White    Nonwhite

    1    Chevy Chase Town                     2,606          69
    2    Chevy Chase CDP                      7,897         662
    3    Chevy Chase Section Five Village       608          24
    4    Chevy Chase Section Three Village    2,018          60
    5    Chevy Chase Village Town               724          25
                                           --------    --------
 TOWN                                        13,853         840


------------------------- Town=Takoma Park -------------------------

  OBS    Place                                White    Nonwhite

    6    Takoma Park                          6,444       5,100
                                           ========    ========
                                             20,297       5,940
```

This example also shows the use of the BY and SUM statements in the PRINT procedure. The BY statement asks that there be a line break each time the value of the BY variable changes. It requires that the data set be sorted by the BY variable, which we have done in this example. SUM asks that totals be calculated, and since there is also a BY statement, the totals will be calculated for each BY group as well as for all observations.

The UNIFORM option on the PROC PRINT statement tells the SAS System that we want all listings for all BY groups to be printed uniformly; i.e., that there not be any variation in print line length between BY groups.

We can also define formats that are not stored in a permanent format library, as shown in this example code.

```
libname census 'c:\';
proc format;
   value race 1='White'
              2='Nonwhite'
              ;
run;

data;
   set census.sqm;
   keep town race pop;
   town=put(placefp,$conv.);
   label pop='Population';
   format race race. pop comma8. town $town.;
   race=1;
   pop=p0060001;
   output;
   race=2;
   pop=p0060002+p0060003+p0060004+p0060005;
   output;
run;
```

We have reshaped the data and kept only a few variables. Each time the OUTPUT statement is executed, a new observation is placed in the data set. The RACE variable codes are defined in the FORMAT procedure, but since the LIBRARY= option is not used, the format is only temporary. Any SAS program that associates values to the RACE codes must include the FORMAT procedure in the code. The reshaped data looks like this.

OBS	TOWN	POP	RACE
1	Chevy Chase	2,606	White
2	Chevy Chase	69	Nonwhite
3	Chevy Chase	7,897	White
4	Chevy Chase	662	Nonwhite
5	Chevy Chase	608	White
6	Chevy Chase	24	Nonwhite
7	Chevy Chase	2,018	White
8	Chevy Chase	60	Nonwhite
9	Chevy Chase	724	White
10	Chevy Chase	25	Nonwhite
11	Takoma Park	6,444	White
12	Takoma Park	5,100	Nonwhite

We can now use the FREQ procedure to get column and row totals and to get percentages for rows, columns and the overall table. The following code shows how to do this.

```
proc freq;
   tables town*race;
   weight pop;
   title '1990 Census of Population and Housing';
run;
```

The WEIGHT statement instructs the FREQ procedure to weight the frequencies by the values of the POP variable. The output is shown in Output 6.

Output 6: Using a Temporary Format with a Frequency Table

```
               1990 Census of Population and Housing

                         TABLE OF TOWN BY RACE

                 TOWN         RACE

                 Frequency   |
                 Percent     |
                 Row Pct     |
                 Col Pct     |White   |Nonwhite|  Total
                 ------------+--------+--------+
                 Chevy Chase |  13853 |    840 |  14693
                             |  52.80 |   3.20 |  56.00
                             |  94.28 |   5.72 |
                             |  68.25 |  14.14 |
                 ------------+--------+--------+
                 Takoma Park |   6444 |   5100 |  11544
                             |  24.56 |  19.44 |  44.00
                             |  55.82 |  44.18 |
                             |  31.75 |  85.86 |
                 ------------+--------+--------+
                 Total          20297     5940    26237
                                77.36    22.64   100.00
```

This is a format that some people find more useful. Note that the population numbers do not make use of the COMMA8. format. This is peculiar to the FREQ procedure; most procedures do make use of it.

Overriding the Documentation

Sometimes you will not want to use a format or label that you have stored for a variable in the data set. You can override it simply by defining a new format or a new label at the time you use it, as shown in this example.

```
libname census 'c:\';
libname library 'c:\';

proc print data=census.sqm label;
   var placefp pop100 sq_miles pop_sqm;
   format sq_miles 5.3;
   label sq_miles='Square Miles';
   title '1990 Census of Population and Housing';
run;
```

The FORMAT statement is instructing the SAS System to print SQ_MILES with a 5.3 format rather than the 4.1 format assigned when we created our data set. The LABEL statement changes the label for SQ_MILES to 'Square Miles' from the 'Land Area in Sq Miles' label originally given to it. The resulting output is shown in Output 7.

Output 7: Overriding a Permanent Format and Label

```
              1990 Census of Population and Housing

                                                                   Population
                                                           Square  Per Square
OBS  Place                                     Population  Miles      Mile

 1   Chevy Chase Town                               2,675  0.468      5,721
 2   Chevy Chase CDP                                8,559  2.565      3,337
 3   Chevy Chase Section Five Village                 632  0.105      6,040
 4   Chevy Chase Section Three Village              2,078  0.414      5,021
 5   Chevy Chase Village Town                         749  0.114      6,576
 6   Takoma Park                                   11,544  1.187      9,726
```

The new format and label lasts only for the duration of the procedure; it does not change what is permanently stored with the SAS data set.

There will be times that you will *not* want to use a format with a variable. The way to do this is to specify the variable name in a FORMAT statement without a format. This code provides an example.

```
libname census 'c:\';
libname library 'c:\';

proc print data=census.sqm label;
   var placefp pop100 sq_miles pop_sqm;
   format placefp;
   title '1990 Census of Population and Housing';
run;
```

The FORMAT statement lists the variable PLACEFP but does not specify a format. PLACEFP is printed as it is stored internally, with no format specified, as shown in Output 8.

Output 8: Printing without a Format

```
              1990 Census of Population and Housing

                                     Land Area
                                       in Sq          Pop/Sq
           OBS    Place    Population  Miles            Mile

            1     16620       2,675     0.5            5,721
            2     16625       8,559     2.6            3,337
            3     16720         632     0.1            6,040
            4     16730       2,078     0.4            5,021
            5     16787         749     0.1            6,576
            6     76650      11,544     1.2            9,726
```

Modifying the Documentation

You may want to make permanent changes to your documentation if you find yourself frequently overriding it. You can do this with a DATA step, by creating a new data set or overwriting the old data set, or you can use the DATASETS procedure to make the changes in place.

The following example makes changes to the CENSUS.SQM data set using the DATASETS procedure and prints the results.

```
libname census 'c:\';
libname library 'c:\';

proc datasets library=census;
   modify sqm (label='Census Places');
   rename sq_miles=sqmiles;
   label pop_sqm='Pop/Sq Mile';
run;

proc print data=census.sqm label;
   var placefp pop100 sqmiles pop_sqm;
   title '1990 Census of Population and Housing';
run;
```

The SQ_MILES variable has been renamed SQMILES by removing the hyphen from its name, and the POP_SQM variable has been given a new label. The new variable SQMILES is specified in the VAR statement of the PRINT procedure. Its new label automatically appears in the output, shown in Output 9.

Output 9: Printing the Modified Data Set

```
                1990 Census of Population and Housing

                                                 Land Area
                                                   in Sq      Pop/Sq
OBS  Place                            Population   Miles       Mile

  1  Chevy Chase Town                      2,675     0.5       5,721
  2  Chevy Chase CDP                       8,559     2.6       3,337
  3  Chevy Chase Section Five Village        632     0.1       6,040
  4  Chevy Chase Section Three Village     2,078     0.4       5,021
  5  Chevy Chase Village Town                749     0.1       6,576
  6  Takoma Park                          11,544     1.2       9,726
```

Documenting the Documentation

All the hard work we did when we first created the CENSUS.SQM data set can now be printed out and filed as part of the project documentation by using the following code.

```
libname census 'c:\';
libname library 'c:\';

proc contents data=census.sqm position; run;
proc format library=library fmtlib page; run;
```

The CONTENTS procedure lists all the variables in the data set, in alphabetical order and then positional order. The FORMAT procedure, with the FMTLIB option, lists all the formats stored in the format library. The output for the CONTENTS procedure is shown in Output 10.

Output 10: The CONTENTS Procedure

```
                              CONTENTS PROCEDURE

Data Set Name: CENSUS.SQM                          Observations:          6
Member Type:   DATA                                Variables:             15
Engine:        V608                                Indexes:               0
Created:       1:16 Wednesday, May 18, 1994        Observation Length:    117
Last Modified: 15:43 Wednesday, May 18, 1994       Deleted Observations:  0
Protection:                                        Compressed:            NO
Data Set Type:                                     Sorted:                NO
Label:         Census Places

          -----Alphabetic List of Variables and Attributes-----

 #   Variable    Type   Len   Pos   Format     Label
--------------------------------------------------------------------------------
 2   AREALAND    Num      8     5   4.1        Land Area in Sq Km (1/1000)
15   FAM_HU      Num      8   109   4.1        Families Per Housing Unit
 3   HU100       Num      8    13   COMMA8.    Housing Units
14   HU_SQM      Num      8   101   COMMA8.    Housing Units Per Square Mile
 5   P0020001    Num      8    29   COMMA8.    Families
 6   P0030001    Num      8    37   COMMA8.    Households
 7   P0060001    Num      8    45   COMMA8.    White
 8   P0060002    Num      8    53   COMMA8.    Black
 9   P0060003    Num      8    61   COMMA8.    American Indian, Eskimo, or Aleut
10   P0060004    Num      8    69   COMMA8.    Asian or Pacific Islander
11   P0060005    Num      8    77   COMMA8.    Other Race
 1   PLACEFP     Char     5     0   $PLACE.    Place
 4   POP100      Num      8    21   COMMA8.    Population
13   POP_SQM     Num      8    93   COMMA8.    Pop/Sq Mile
12   SQMILES     Num      8    85   4.1        Land Area in Sq Miles

                              CONTENTS PROCEDURE

                     -----Variables Ordered by Position-----

 #   Variable    Type   Len   Pos   Format     Label
--------------------------------------------------------------------------------
 1   PLACEFP     Char     5     0   $PLACE.    Place
 2   AREALAND    Num      8     5   4.1        Land Area in Sq Km (1/1000)
 3   HU100       Num      8    13   COMMA8.    Housing Units
 4   POP100      Num      8    21   COMMA8.    Population
 5   P0020001    Num      8    29   COMMA8.    Families
 6   P0030001    Num      8    37   COMMA8.    Households
 7   P0060001    Num      8    45   COMMA8.    White
 8   P0060002    Num      8    53   COMMA8.    Black
 9   P0060003    Num      8    61   COMMA8.    American Indian, Eskimo, or Aleut
10   P0060004    Num      8    69   COMMA8.    Asian or Pacific Islander
11   P0060005    Num      8    77   COMMA8.    Other Race
12   SQMILES     Num      8    85   4.1        Land Area in Sq Miles
13   POP_SQM     Num      8    93   COMMA8.    Pop/Sq Mile
14   HU_SQM      Num      8   101   COMMA8.    Housing Units Per Square Mile
15   FAM_HU      Num      8   109   4.1        Families Per Housing Unit
```

The POSITION option on the PROC CONTENTS statement tells the SAS System to print a second list of variable names in the order of their position in the data set; this may be helpful when trying to fix a problem in the raw data file. By default, variables are listed alphabetically.

The first section of the report gives information about the data set itself. This includes the data set name, when it was created, and the last time it was modified. Since we used the DATASETS procedure to modify a format and label in the CENSUS.SQM data set, we see a modified date that is different from the creation date.

We can also see how many observations and variables are in the data set, as well as whether there are any indexes associated with the data set and whether the data set is compressed.

Each of the variable listings, both alphabetical and positional, give information about each variable as follows:

- the position of the variable in the data set
- the variable's name
- whether the variable is character or numeric
- the length of the variable
- the starting position of the variable in the observation
- the variable's format
- the variable's informat
- the variable's label

Output 11 shows the output for the FORMAT procedure.

Output 11: The FORMAT Procedure

```
 ----------------------------------------------------------------------------
|       FORMAT NAME: $CONV     LENGTH:     1   NUMBER OF VALUES:    6        |
|   MIN LENGTH:   1  MAX LENGTH:  40  DEFAULT LENGTH   1  FUZZ:         0    |
|----------------------------------------------------------------------------|
|START           |END             |LABEL  (VER. 6.08    18MAY94:14:35:36)    |
|----------------+----------------+------------------------------------------|
|16620           |16620           |1                                         |
|16625           |16625           |1                                         |
|16720           |16720           |1                                         |
|16730           |16730           |1                                         |
|16787           |16787           |1                                         |
|76650           |76650           |2                                         |
 ----------------------------------------------------------------------------


 ----------------------------------------------------------------------------
|       FORMAT NAME: $PLACE    LENGTH:    33   NUMBER OF VALUES:    6        |
|   MIN LENGTH:   1  MAX LENGTH:  40  DEFAULT LENGTH  33  FUZZ:         0    |
|----------------------------------------------------------------------------|
|START           |END             |LABEL  (VER. 6.08    18MAY94:14:35:35)    |
|----------------+----------------+------------------------------------------|
|16620           |16620           |Chevy Chase Town                          |
|16625           |16625           |Chevy Chase CDP                           |
|16720           |16720           |Chevy Chase Section Five Village          |
|16730           |16730           |Chevy Chase Section Three Village         |
|16787           |16787           |Chevy Chase Village Town                  |
|76650           |76650           |Takoma Park                               |
 ----------------------------------------------------------------------------
```

Output 11: The FORMAT Procedure (continued)

```
---------------------------------------------------------------------------
|       FORMAT NAME: $TOWN     LENGTH:    11    NUMBER OF VALUES:     2    |
|   MIN LENGTH:    1  MAX LENGTH:  40  DEFAULT LENGTH  11  FUZZ:         0 |
|--------------------------------------------------------------------------|
|START           |END             |LABEL  (VER. 6.08    18MAY94:14:35:36)  |
|----------------+----------------+----------------------------------------|
|1               |1               |Chevy Chase                             |
|2               |2               |Takoma Park                             |
---------------------------------------------------------------------------
```

The output is a table for each format in the library. Detailed information is given about each code defined in the format. The following information is seen in our example:

- FORMAT NAME is the name of the format.
- LENGTH is the length of the longest label.
- NUMBER OF VALUES specifies the number of codes for the format.
- MIN LENGTH is the length of a value specified in the LABEL field.
- MAX LENGTH is the length of the longest value in the LABEL field.
- DEFAULT LENGTH is the length of the longest value in the label field.
- START and END are the beginning and ending values for a range specification.
- LABEL is the description of the code.

Our example used the FORMAT procedure to document coded values, so some of the information in this report is not applicable to the way we have used the procedure.

Conclusion

Document first (not last) and document extensively. Reap the productivity gains during the life of your project; then file your documentation at the conclusion of your project. Have confidence that your documentation is correct since it is used in your SAS programs.

References

SAS Institute Inc., *SAS Language: Reference, Version 6, First Edition*, Cary, NC: SAS Institute Inc., 1990.

SAS Institute Inc., *SAS Procedures Guide, Version 6, Third Edition*, Cary, NC: SAS Institute Inc., 1990.

CHAPTER 5

A Stepwise Approach to Using PROC TABULATE

by Michele M. Burlew

Abstract

The TABULATE procedure is useful for producing presentation-quality reports. SAS users who find it difficult to write PROC TABULATE programs may find that the stepwise approach presented in this chapter simplifies the process. This stepwise approach breaks up the process of report writing with PROC TABULATE into manageable steps. In this chapter, these steps are illustrated by writing two reports summarizing results from a community health assessment program.

Specifications

The code in this chapter was developed and tested with Release 6.08 of the SAS system under the Windows environment. Use of the code with other releases of the SAS System or other environments may require user modification. Modified code is not supported by the author.

About the Author

Michele Burlew is President of Episystems, Inc. and has over 14 years of experience using SAS software. She has a BS degree in Biology from Cornell University and an MS degree in Biomedical Engineering from the University of Wisconsin-Madison. Michele's areas of expertise include base SAS software, DATA step programming, SAS macros, SAS Screen Control Language, and SAS/AF, SAS/FSP, SAS/GRAPH, and SAS/STAT software.

Questions and Comments Should be Directed to:

Michele Burlew
Episystems Inc.
13 Red Fox Road
St. Paul, MN 55127

Examples from this book are available online, see inside back cover for details.

A Stepwise Approach to Using PROC TABULATE

Michele M. Burlew

Introduction

The TABULATE procedure is useful for producing presentation-quality reports. SAS users who find it difficult to write PROC TABULATE programs may find that the stepwise approach presented in this chapter simplifies the process.

The steps in report writing with PROC TABULATE are illustrated in this chapter by writing two reports summarizing results from a community health assessment program. The chapter discusses each step used in building the first report, which summarizes all variables for assessment participants. The second, shorter report is then constructed focusing on the cholesterol variables.

The following list of steps to use in report writing with PROC TABULATE begins with three basic steps. The first is to understand the basic syntax of PROC TABULATE. The next is to run other, simpler SAS procedures to understand the structure and contents of the data set that will be processed to produce the report. The third step is to state what the report will present and to mock up a sample report. At this point, the next steps to take involve writing increasingly more complex and detailed PROC TABULATE programs in order to produce the final report.

Note: It is assumed that the reader of this chapter has basic SAS programming skills and some familiarity with PROC TABULATE.

List of Steps in Report Writing with PROC TABULATE

Step 1: Understand the basic syntax of PROC TABULATE.
Step 2: Understand the data set used to generate the report.
Step 3: Determine what the report should present.
Step 4: Identify the dimension - page, row, column - of each variable.
Step 5: Determine the classification variables, the analysis variables, and the statistics.
Step 6: Determine the relationships among the variables and statistics; determine the operators needed to represent the relationships.
Step 7: Identify the variables to be summarized and the dimension of the summary information.
Step 8: Identify the variables to be used in computing percentages.
Step 9: Determine how missing values should be handled in the report.
Step 10: Improve the readability of the report.

Building the First Report

Step 1: Understand the basic syntax of PROC TABULATE.

An overview of commonly used PROC TABULATE statements and options is presented here. Note: Angle brackets indicate optional arguments in the syntax. Refer to *the SAS Guide to TABULATE Processing, Second Edition* and the *SAS Procedures Guide, Version 6, Third Edition* for complete information.

```
PROC TABULATE <options>;
    CLASS classification-variables;
    VAR  analysis-variables;
    TABLE  <<page-dimension-expression>,
            <row-dimension-expression>>,
            column-dimension-expression  /
            <options> ;
    BY by-variables;
    KEYLABEL  keyword-1='label-1'  <<keyword-2='label-2'> ...
              <keyword-n='label-n'>>;
    LABEL  variable-1='label-1'     <<variable-2='label-2> ...
            <variable-n='label-n'>>;
    FORMAT  variable-list-1 format-1 <<variable-list-2 format-2> ...
             <variable-list-n format-n>>;
RUN;
```

The PROC TABULATE statement:

```
PROC TABULATE <options>;
```

The PROC TABULATE statement starts the PROC TABULATE step. A description of some of the options that can be specified on the PROC TABULATE statement follows. These options, when specified, are in effect for all reports requested in the step.

- DATA=*SAS-data-set-name*

  As with most SAS procedures, the DATA=*SAS-data-set-name* option can be specified to indicate which data set to process in the PROC TABULATE step.
- FORMAT=*format-name*

  By default, PROC TABULATE displays statistic values with the format BEST12.2. One way to override the SAS default is to specify your own default format with the FORMAT= option.
- MISSING

  By default, missing values are not considered as valid classification levels when a PROC TABULATE report is constructed. To override this default and allow missing values to be considered as valid classification levels in the reports generated in a PROC TABULATE step, specify the MISSING option on the PROC TABULATE statement.

Either a CLASS statement or a VAR statement or both must be included in the PROC TABULATE step. A variable may be specified on the CLASS statement or the VAR statement, but not on both.

The CLASS statement:

```
CLASS classification-variables;
```

The CLASS statement specifies the classification variables in the reports generated in a PROC TABULATE step. The values of the classification variables define the categories for which statistics are computed. The classification variables can be character or numeric. If the classification variable is numeric and continuous over a large range, a user-defined format may be useful to group the values of the variable and reduce the size of the report. The CLASS statement is specified once in the PROC TABULATE step and is in effect for all reports specified in the step.

The VAR statement:

```
VAR analysis-variables;
```

Use the VAR statement to specify the analysis variables in your report. Analysis variables are numeric and are the variables for which you want to compute statistics like mean or standard deviation. The VAR statement is specified once in the PROC TABULATE step and is in effect for all reports specified in the step.

The TABLE statement:

```
TABLE <<page-dimension-expression>,
        <row-dimension-expression>>,
        column-dimension-expression / <options>;
```

The TABLE statement defines the layout of the report. At least one TABLE statement must be specified in a PROC TABULATE step. Multiple TABLE statements in a PROC TABULATE step may also be specified, with each TABLE statement producing a separate report.

The report specified by the TABLE statement can have up to three dimensions: page, row, and column. The combination of variable names, statistics keywords, operators, and formatting instructions used to describe the layout of each dimension is called a dimension expression. Dimension expressions are separated by commas on the TABLE statement.

Every report has a column dimension. Row and page dimensions are optional. The rightmost dimension expression is always the column dimension. The second dimension expression from the right is always the row dimension. The third dimension expression from the right is always the page dimension.

All variables used in the TABLE statement must be specified in either the CLASS or the VAR statement. In addition, a reserved class variable is provided in PROC TABULATE to summarize classifications. This variable, called the universal class variable ALL, can be included in the TABLE statement to summarize classifications. The universal class variable ALL is not specified on either the CLASS or the VAR statement.

Operators are used as a shorthand notation to represent the relationships among the variables, the statistics, the universal class variable ALL, and the formatting instructions. These relationships define the layout of the report. There are six operators (five symbols and a blank space) that may be used in a TABLE statement:

- The comma (,) is used to separate two dimension expressions.
- A blank space is used to concatenate variables or statistics. The output for a variable or statistic placed after the blank space appears after the output for the variable before the blank space.
- An asterisk (*) is used to cross variables or statistics. If two class variables are joined by an asterisk, or crossed, categories are formed from the combination of the values of the two class variables. If a class variable and an analysis variable are crossed, statistics are computed for the groups defined by the values of the class variable. Formatting instructions can be crossed with a statistic or variable as well. These formatting instructions are applied to the variable or statistic preceding the asterisk.
- Parentheses ( ) are used to group variables and statistics. Grouping variables and statistics allows you to reduce the amount of code you write by applying an operator to the group rather than by applying the operator to each variable or statistic separately.
- Angle brackets <> are used to specify denominators for percent computations. The denominator definitions are enclosed within the brackets.
- Equal signs (=) are used to assign labels or formats to variables or statistics.

You can specify several statistics on the TABLE statement. Table 1 lists selected statistics and their keywords.

Table 1. A list of selected PROC TABULATE statistics and keywords

Statistic	Keyword
Number of observations without missing analysis values	N
Number of observations with missing analysis values	NMISS
Mean	MEAN
Standard deviation	STD
Minimum value	MIN
Maximum value	MAX
Frequency count percentage	PCTN

Some of the more useful options that can be added to the TABLE statement are

- BOX=*value*

  The BOX=*value* option places text in the empty box in the upper left of a two- or three- dimensional table where *value* can be one of three choices:

  *_PAGE_* puts the page dimension text in the box instead of above the table
  'text' puts quoted *text* in the box
  variable puts the variable name or variable label in the box.

- MISSTEXT=*'text'*

  The MISSTEXT=*'text'* option is used to replace the default missing value representation in empty cells in the report with up to 20 characters of text.
- PRINTMISS

  This option specifies that all possible values for a class variable are printed whenever headings for that variable are printed. This gives the report a uniform appearance by making the row and column headings the same on all logical pages of the report.
- RTSPACE=*number*

  RTS=*number*

  The RTS=*number* option is used to override the default width for row headings with the width you prefer.

The BY statement:

BY *by-variables*;

As with many other SAS procedures, the BY statement can be used with PROC TABULATE to obtain separate tables for each group defined by the values of the variables on the BY statement.

The KEYLABEL statement:

KEYLABEL *keyword-1='label-1'*
<<keyword-2='label-2'> ...
<keyword-n='label-n'>>;

The KEYLABEL statement provides labels for the statistics specified in the TABLE statement and for the universal class variable ALL.

The LABEL statement:

LABEL *variable-1='label-1'*
<<variable-2='label-2' > ...
<variable-n='label-n'>>;

As with many other SAS procedures, the LABEL statement may be used in a PROC TABULATE step to assign labels to variables.

The FORMAT statement:

FORMAT *variable-list-1 format-1*
<<variable-list-2 format-2> ...
<variable-list-n format-n>>;

The FORMAT statement can be used in a PROC TABULATE step to associate SAS formats and user-defined formats to the class variables which are used as page, row, and column headings.

Step 2: Understand the data set used to generate the report.

To understand the structure and contents of your data set, it is a good idea to use other procedures before you construct your report. For example, run PROC CONTENTS or PROC DATASETS to determine the variable names, variable types (character or numeric), and variable formatting. List a few of the observations with PROC PRINT. To find out counts and ranges of numeric values, run PROC MEANS. Run PROC FREQ on the classification variables to quickly find frequency counts of classification variables. The output from these procedures gives you an idea of the size of your reports and whether formatting may make the final PROC TABULATE report more readable.

The data set used in this chapter is named REPWRITE.HEALTH. This data set contains measurements for 110 adult participants in a community health assessment program for two years. Each observation contains information for one person for one year. See Output 1 for details. The cholesterol status variable indicates whether the participant has a cholesterol value greater than or equal to 200 for that year of assessment. The goal for the participants was to reduce weight, blood pressure, and cholesterol values.

Output 1 contains the PROC CONTENTS listing for the data set REPWRITE.HEALTH. The PROC CONTENTS output shows that AGE, CHOL, DIAST, ID, SYSTOL, WEIGHT, and YEAR are numeric variables and that CHOL200, EXERCISE, GENDER, and SMOKER are character variables. Numeric formats have been assigned to the numeric variables. Labels have been assigned to the variables to provide additional information about the variables. Output 2 shows the PROC PRINT listing of the first 15 observations in REPWRITE.HEALTH. The PROC MEANS output is displayed in Output 3.

Output 1. PROC CONTENTS of REPWRITE.HEALTH

```
Data Set Name: REPWRITE.HEALTH2                          Observations:          220
Member Type:   DATA                                      Variables:             11
Engine:        V608                                      Indexes:               0
Created:       13:49 Saturday, February 12, 1994         Observation Length:    31
Last Modified: 14:16 Saturday, February 12, 1994         Deleted Observations:  0
Protection:                                              Compressed:            NO
Data Set Type:                                           Sorted:                NO
Label:

                 -----Engine/Host Dependent Information-----
                     Data Set Page Size:          4096
                     Number of Data Set Pages:    3
                     File Format:                 607
                     First Data Page:             1
                     Max Obs per Page:            131
                     Obs in First Data Page:      77

            -----Alphabetic List of Variables and Attributes-----
  #  Variable   Type  Len  Pos  Format  Label
 -----------------------------------------------------------------------
  4  AGE        Num     3    8  2.      Age at Exam
  9  CHOL       Num     3   26  3.      Cholesterol
 11  CHOL200    Char    1   30          Cholesterol => 200?
  7  DIAST      Num     3   22  3.      Diastolic Pressure
 10  EXERCISE   Char    1   29          Participate in Exercise Program?
  3  GENDER     Char    1    7          Gender
  2  ID         Num     4    3  4.      Participant ID Number
  8  SMOKER     Char    1   25          Smoker?
  6  SYSTOL     Num     3   19  3.      Systolic Pressure
  5  WEIGHT     Num     8   11  5.1     Weight (pounds)
  1  YEAR       Num     3    0  4.      Year of Exam
```

Output 2. PROC PRINT of first 15 observations of REPWRITE.HEALTH

```
OBS YEAR   ID GENDER AGE WEIGHT SYSTOL DIAST SMOKER CHOL EXERCISE CHOL200
  1 1991   53   F     43  136.0   164   103    N     184     N        N
  2 1992   53   F     44  143.0   163   111    N     191     N        N
  3 1991   63   F     58  175.0   117    66    Y     191     N        N
  4 1992   63   F     59  167.0   111    62    Y     162     Y        N
  5 1991  100   M     51  212.0   133    84    N     292     N        Y
  6 1992  100   M     52  221.0   132    90    N     304     N        Y
  7 1991  167   F     38  163.0   136    85    Y     228     Y        Y
  8 1992  167   F     39  165.0   129    80    Y     194     Y        N
  9 1991  370   M     55  181.0   126    80    N     223     N        Y
 10 1992  370   M     56  199.0   113    76    N     194     Y        N
 11 1991  381   F     27  161.0   134    91    Y     198     N        N
 12 1992  381   F     28  177.0   121    86    Y     193     N        N
 13 1991  414   M     57  228.0   135    80    Y     215     N        Y
 14 1992  414   M     58  251.0   122    76    N     226     N        Y
 15 1991  524   M     48  211.0   127    78    Y     270     Y        Y
```

Output 3. PROC MEANS of numeric variables, excluding the variables ID and YEAR

```
Variable  Label                 N         Mean       Std Dev       Minimum       Maximum
-----------------------------------------------------------------------------------------
AGE       Age at Exam         220   44.5363636    11.1410035    21.0000000    71.0000000
WEIGHT    Weight (pounds)     220  174.7863636    35.3883194    96.0000000   294.0000000
SYSTOL    Systolic Pressure   220  122.3727273    17.2811081    84.0000000   183.0000000
DIAST     Diastolic Pressure  220   79.0818182    10.6351977    57.0000000   111.0000000
CHOL      Cholesterol         220  203.4227273    39.2784049   121.0000000   314.0000000
-----------------------------------------------------------------------------------------
```

Output 4 shows the PROC FREQ tables of character variables and the numeric variables AGE and YEAR. These tables show that there are two years of data in the data set and that the age of the employees ranges from 21 to 71.

The PROC FREQ output and the PROC PRINT output show that the GENDER variable values are recorded as either "F" or "M". The listings also show that the SMOKER variable, the CHOL200 variable, and the EXERCISE variable have values of either "N" or "Y".

Output 4. PROC FREQ of selected variables

```
                        Year of Exam
                                 Cumulative  Cumulative
      YEAR   Frequency   Percent   Frequency    Percent
      ---------------------------------------------------
      1991        110      50.0         110       50.0
      1992        110      50.0         220      100.0


                           Gender
                                 Cumulative  Cumulative
     GENDER   Frequency   Percent   Frequency    Percent
     ----------------------------------------------------
     F              106      48.2         106       48.2
     M              114      51.8         220      100.0


                        Age at Exam
                                 Cumulative  Cumulative
       AGE   Frequency   Percent   Frequency    Percent
       --------------------------------------------------
        21          1      0.5           1        0.5
        22          1      0.5           2        0.9
        23          1      0.5           3        1.4
        24          2      0.9           5        2.3
        25          4      1.8           9        4.1
...(ages 26 to 65 omitted)...
        66          1      0.5         217       98.6
        67          1      0.5         218       99.1
        70          1      0.5         219       99.5
        71          1      0.5         220      100.0


                          Smoker?
                                 Cumulative  Cumulative
     SMOKER   Frequency   Percent   Frequency    Percent
     ----------------------------------------------------
     N              162      73.6         162       73.6
     Y               58      26.4         220      100.0


                    Cholesterol => 200?
                                  Cumulative  Cumulative
     CHOL200   Frequency   Percent   Frequency    Percent
     -----------------------------------------------------
     N               124      56.4         124       56.4
     Y                96      43.6         220      100.0


              Participate in Exercise Program?
                                  Cumulative  Cumulative
    EXERCISE   Frequency   Percent   Frequency    Percent
    ------------------------------------------------------
    N                150      68.2         150       68.2
    Y                 70      31.8         220      100.0
```

Step 3: Determine what the report should present.

In the example used here, the first report is an annual summary of the results of the health assessment program. Test results should be summarized in this report for each year and broken down by gender and age. A mock up of this report is shown in Figure 1.

Results for one year per table		Weight	Diastolic Blood Pressure	Systolic Blood Pressure	Cholesterol		Cholesterol => 200?		Smoker?		Participate in Exercise Program?	
	N	Mean	Mean	Mean	Mean	Max	% No	% Yes	% No	% Yes	% No	% Yes
All Participants												
Females Age groups...												
All Females												
Males Age groups...												
All Males												

- Each table should present the information collected for one year.
- The frequency percentages should sum to 100% for each variable on each row classification.

Figure 1. Mock up of annual summary report

At this point, the preliminary steps are completed. Now begins the stepwise process of writing increasingly more complex and detailed PROC TABULATE programs to produce the final report.

Step 4: Identify the dimension -- page, row, column -- of each variable.

Recall that one table is to be produced for each year. To make this report readable, you want to put each year's summary on a separate page and not combined on one page. Therefore, the variable YEAR is a page dimension variable.

The rows of the table are defined by gender and age. Therefore, the row dimension variables are GENDER and AGE. Also in the row dimension is the summary of participants overall and by gender. The universal class variable ALL is needed in the row dimension to produce these summaries.

The columns of the table are made up of statistics and frequency counts. The variables used to compute statistics and frequency counts are WEIGHT, DIAST, SYSTOL, CHOL, CHOL200, SMOKER, and EXERCISE. These variables, as well as the statistic N, are in the column dimension.

Step 5: Determine the classification variables, the analysis variables, and the statistics.

Referring to Figure 1, you see that the following variables are used to define the categories for which statistics are computed: YEAR, GENDER, AGE, CHOL200, SMOKER, and EXERCISE. Therefore, these variables are classification variables and are specified on the CLASS statement.

The variables for which statistics are computed are WEIGHT, DIAST, SYSTOL, and CHOL. These analysis variables are specified on the VAR statement.

The statistics computed in the report are N, mean, maximum, and frequency percentages.

Step 6: Determine the relationships among the variables and statistics; determine the operators needed to represent the relationships.

Now, review the report mock up to note the relationships among the variables and statistics and determine the operators needed to represent these relationships.

In the annual summary report, note the following relationships:

- Ignoring the summary rows temporarily, the rows of the report are the combinations of the values of GENDER and AGE for a given value of YEAR. Therefore, the variables GENDER and AGE are crossed in the row dimension. YEAR is in the page dimension.
- The analysis variables, WEIGHT, DIAST, SYSTOL, and CHOL, and the classification variables CHOL200, SMOKER, and EXERCISE are arranged in columns side by side. Therefore, these column

dimension variables are concatenated and are separated from each other in the TABLE statement with a blank space.

- The statistics, mean, maximum, and frequency percentages are shown beneath their respective analysis variable or their classification variable value. Therefore, each statistic is crossed with its respective analysis variable or its classification variable. Two statistics are computed for CHOL. These statistics are shown side by side. These two statistics are concatenated and separated from each other in the TABLE statement with a blank space.
- The statistic N is concatenated to the variable WEIGHT. In the TABLE statement, N is separated from WEIGHT with a blank space.
- The summary rows, "All Participants", "All Females", and "All Males", are concatenated to the rows that are defined by the combination of values of GENDER and AGE. The universal class variable ALL is used to produce these summary rows.

It is sometimes easier to start writing a report with just the classification variables. After that is done, include the analysis variables in the report. Last, add the statistics.

The following code produces a report with just the classification variables. An excerpt of the report is presented in Output 5.

```
proc tabulate data=repwrite.health;
   class year gender age smoker chol200 exercise;
   table year, gender*age, chol200 smoker exercise;
run;
```

Output 5. Excerpt of output from PROC TABULATE program with classification variables

The SAS System

Year of Exam 1991

		Cholesterol => 200?		Smoker?		Participate in Exercise Program?	
		N	Y	N	Y	N	Y
Gender	Age at Exam	N	N	N	N	N	N
F	23	1.00	.	1.00	.	.	1.00
	25	1.00	.	1.00	.	.	1.00
...(ages 26 to 65 omitted)...							
	66	.	1.00	1.00	.	1.00	.
M	21	1.00	.	1.00	.	.	1.00
	24	1.00	.	1.00	.	1.00	.
	25	2.00	.	2.00	.	1.00	1.00

(CONTINUED)

The following code adds the analysis variables to the report. An excerpt of the report is presented in Output 6. Note that the default statistic for the analysis variables is SUM and the default statistic computed for each value of the classification variables is N.

```
proc tabulate data=repwrite.health;
  class year gender age smoker chol200 exercise;
  var weight systol diast chol;
  table year,
        gender*age,
        weight systol diast chol chol200 smoker exercise;
run;
```

Output 6. Excerpt of output from PROC TABULATE program with classification variables and analysis variables

The SAS System

Year of Exam 1991

Gender	Age at Exam	Weight (pounds)	Systolic Pressure	Diastolic Pressure	Cholesterol	Cholesterol => 200? N	Cholesterol => 200? Y
		SUM	SUM	SUM	SUM	N	N
F	23	158.00	126.00	70.00	188.00	1.00	.
	25	145.00	128.00	89.00	160.00	1.00	.
...*(ages 26 to 65 omitted)*...							
	66	175.00	148.00	101.00	201.00	.	1.00
M	21	154.00	103.00	68.00	162.00	1.00	.
	24	146.00	116.00	67.00	191.00	1.00	.
	25	385.00	233.00	146.00	357.00	2.00	.

(CONTINUED)

The SAS System

Year of Exam 1991

Gender	Age at Exam	Smoker? N	Smoker? Y	Participate in Exercise Program? N	Participate in Exercise Program? Y
		N	N	N	N
F	23	1.00	.	.	1.00
	25	1.00	.	.	1.00
..*(ages 26 to 65 omitted)*...					
	66	1.00	.	1.00	.
M	21	1.00	.	.	1.00
	24	1.00	.	1.00	.
	25	2.00		1.00	1.00

(CONTINUED)

The last program in this step adds the statistics to the report. The following code produces the report excerpt presented in Output 7. Note in Output 7 that the frequency percentages are computed as a percentage of the total number of observations in the data set.

```
proc tabulate data=repwrite.health;
   class year gender age smoker chol200 exercise;
   var weight systol diast chol;
   table year,
          gender*age,
          n weight*mean systol*mean diast*mean
          chol*mean chol*max
          chol200*pctn smoker*pctn exercise*pctn;
run;
```

Output 7. Excerpt of output from PROC TABULATE with classification variables, analysis variables, and statistics

The SAS System

Year of Exam 1991

Gender	Age at Exam	N	Weight (pounds) MEAN	Systolic Pressure MEAN	Diastolic Pressure MEAN	Cholesterol MEAN	Cholesterol MAX
F	23	1.00	158.00	126.00	70.00	188.00	188.00
	25	1.00	145.00	128.00	89.00	160.00	160.00
...(ages 26 to 52 omitted)...							
	66	1.00	175.00	148.00	101.00	201.00	201.00
M	21	1.00	154.00	103.00	68.00	162.00	162.00
	24	1.00	146.00	116.00	67.00	191.00	191.00
	25	2.00	192.50	116.50	73.00	178.50	185.00

(CONTINUED)

The SAS System

Year of Exam 1991

Gender	Age at Exam	Cholesterol => 200? N PCTN	Cholesterol => 200? Y PCTN	Smoker? N PCTN	Smoker? Y PCTN	Participate in Exercise Program? N PCTN	Participate in Exercise Program? Y PCTN
F	23	0.45	.	0.45	.	.	0.45
	25	0.45	.	0.45	.	.	0.45
...(ages 26 to 52 omitted)...							
	66	.	0.45	0.45	.	0.45	.
M	21	0.45	.	0.45	.	.	0.45
	24	0.45	.	0.45	.	0.45	.
	25	0.91	.	0.91	.	0.45	0.45

(CONTINUED)

This nearly completes the basic program to create the annual summary report. Three additions are needed: the summary for each year, the summary by gender and year, and the frequency percentage denominator definitions for the three classification variables, CHOL200, SMOKER, and EXERCISE. The next two steps discuss how to add the summaries and the denominator definitions.

Step 7: Identify the variables to be summarized and the dimension of the summary information.

Referring to the mock up of the annual summary report in Figure 1, note that a summary of all of the participants' information for each year is specified on the first row of the report. This summary is in the row dimension of the report. A summary is also specified for each gender. Again, the summary is in the row dimension of the report.

These summaries look like classification variables in the report. They are specified in the TABLE statement like classification variables and are indicated by the universal class variable ALL. The program that includes these summaries follows. An excerpt of the report appears in Output 8 which includes changes made in Step 8 as well.

```
proc tabulate data=repwrite.health;
   class year gender age smoker chol200 exercise;
   var weight systol diast chol;
   table year,
        all gender*(age all),
        n weight*mean systol*mean diast*mean
        chol*mean chol*max
        chol200*pctn smoker*pctn exercise*pctn;
run;
```

The preceding code adds the following to the program given in Step 6:

- The universal class variable ALL is added as the first item in the row dimension. This requests an overall summary of the data for each year on the first row of each year's table.
- The universal class variable ALL is grouped with AGE and the group is joined to GENDER with an asterisk. This requests an overall summary for each combination of YEAR and GENDER values. This summary for a specific value of GENDER is printed after computations for the categories defined by the crossing of that value of GENDER with AGE. If AGE and ALL were not grouped, the summaries by GENDER would appear at the end of the report rather than at the end of each GENDER section.

Step 8: Identify the variables to be used in computing percentages.

If percentages based on frequency counts or percentages based on sums are to be computed in the report, identify the variables used to compute the percentages. It may also be necessary to define the denominator for computing the percentages.

In Figure 1, note that frequency count percentages of each of the values of the three variables, CHOL200, SMOKER, and EXERCISE, are computed for each combination of YEAR, GENDER, and AGE. These percentages are in the column dimension.

The statistic to use to request percentages based on frequency counts is PCTN. (When computing percentages based on sums, use PCTSUM.) In the mock up, the percentages for each variable sum to 100 within each row. This is not the default computation of percentages in PROC TABULATE as was seen in Output 7. The default is to compute the percentage for each cell such that the sum of all the cell percentages for a variable is 100. You may change the basis of the computation of percentages by specifying a denominator definition in angle brackets after the PCTN keyword. In the example of CHOL200, the goal is to use as denominator for each combination of YEAR, GENDER, and AGE, the sum of the frequency of all occurrences of CHOL200 in that combination. This is indicated by enclosing CHOL200 in brackets and placing this expression next to the PCTN keyword.

Further discussion of denominator definitions is beyond the scope of this chapter. Refer to the *SAS Guide to TABULATE Processing* for an in-depth discussion of specifying denominators.

The code that follows includes percentages with denominator definitions. An excerpt of the report is in Output 8.

```
proc tabulate data=repwrite.health;
  class year gender age smoker chol200 exercise;
  var weight systol diast chol;
  table year,
        all gender*(age all),
        n weight*mean systol*mean diast*mean
        chol*mean chol*max
        chol200*pctn<chol200> smoker*pctn<smoker>
        exercise*pctn<exercise>;
run;
```

Output 8. Excerpt of output from PROC TABULATE with totals and frequency percentages

The SAS System

Year of Exam 1991

			Weight (pounds)	Systolic Pressure	Diastolic Pressure	Cholesterol	Cholesterol
		N	MEAN	MEAN	MEAN	MEAN	MAX
ALL		110.00	173.59	125.75	79.80	206.02	314.00
Gender	Age at Exam						
F	23	1.00	158.00	126.00	70.00	188.00	188.00
	25	1.00	145.00	128.00	89.00	160.00	160.00
...(ages 26 to 52 omitted)...							
	66	1.00	175.00	148.00	101.00	201.00	201.00
	ALL	53.00	149.91	126.85	80.68	193.85	273.00
M	Age at Exam						
	21	1.00	154.00	103.00	68.00	162.00	162.00
	24	1.00	146.00	116.00	67.00	191.00	191.00
	25	2.00	192.50	116.50	73.00	178.50	185.00

(CONTINUED)

The SAS System

Year of Exam 1991

		Cholesterol => 200?		Smoker?		Participate in Exercise Program?	
		N	Y	N	Y	N	Y
		PCTN	PCTN	PCTN	PCTN	PCTN	PCTN
ALL		50.91	49.09	69.09	30.91	74.55	25.45
Gender	Age at Exam						
F	23	100.00	.	100.00	.	.	100.00
	25	100.00	.	100.00	.	.	100.00
...(ages 26 to 52 omitted)...							
	66	.	100.00	100.00	.	100.00	.
	ALL	62.26	37.74	64.15	35.85	73.58	26.42
M	Age at Exam						
	21	100.00	.	100.00	.	.	100.00
	24	100.00	.	100.00	.	100.00	.
	25	100.00	.	100.00	.	50.00	50.00

(CONTINUED)

Step 9: Determine how missing values should be handled in the report.

The functions of the three missing values options -- MISSING, MISSTEXT, and PRINTMISS -- were described in Step 1. The questions to ask at this point are the following:

- Should classifications that contain missing values be included in the report? If so, add the MISSING option to the PROC TABULATE statement.
- If a table cell is empty, should the default missing value representation be replaced in the empty cell with a specified string of text? If so, add the MISSTEXT=*'text'* option to the TABLE statement. Note that in this sample data set there are no females under 36 with cholesterol greater than or equal to 200. The MISSTEXT=*'0'* option is used for that classification.
- Should the headings be the same on every table of a report defined in a TABLE statement? If so, add the PRINTMISS option to the TABLE statement.

The two options, MISSING and MISSTEXT=*'0'* are included in the final report program. The third option, PRINTMISS, is not needed. The final report program is shown at the end of Step 10.

At this point, the basic report program is complete. The last step improves the readability of the report by adding titles, footnotes, labels, and formatting.

Step 10: Improve the readability of the report.

The following statements and options can be included in a PROC TABULATE program to make the report more meaningful and easier to read. Some of the changes to be made to the annual summary report are included with the description of the statements and options.

- Add titles and footnotes to the report.
- Specify formats for variables and statistics.

  The default format for statistics in PROC TABULATE is BEST12.2. Often this format is wider than is needed. Formats for several of the statistics in the report are specified.

  Associating user-defined formats to the classification variables often makes a report more readable. In the mock up of the report, AGE was listed as AGE groups. A format is defined to group the ages into three levels: 21-35, 36-55, and 56 and older. User-defined formats are also associated with the classification variables GENDER, CHOL200, SMOKER, and EXERCISE.

  To change the format of a statistic, use the F=*format* modifier in the TABLE statement. The F=*format* modifier is joined by an asterisk to the statistic whose format you want to change. Formats for class variables are changed with the FORMAT statement.
- Define labels for variables and statistics.

  To change the label of a variable or statistic, specify the label after the variable name. Labels for variables may also be changed with the LABEL statement.

  Use the KEYLABEL STATISTIC=*'text'* statement to change the default label for a statistic or the class variable ALL for all reports in the PROC TABULATE step.
- Specify SAS System options such as PAGENO, PAGESIZE, LINESIZE, DATE, and CENTER to improve the look of the report.
- Change the width of the space allocated to print the row classifications with the RTS=*number* option on the TABLE statement.
- Add text in the box in the upper left of the table by using the BOX= option on the TABLE statement.

The code for the final report program follows. This program includes many of the above enhancements. The final report is in Output 9.

```
title1 'ANNUAL SUMMARY OF HEALTH ASSESSMENT PROGRAM';
title2 'BY GENDER AND AGE';
options pageno=1 ls=117 ps=45 center;

proc format;
  value agefmt    21-35='21-35'
                  36-55='36-55'
                  56-high='56+';
  value $gendfmt  'F'='Female'
                  'M'='Male';
  value $ynfmt    'N'='No'
                  'Y'='Yes';
run;

proc tabulate data=repwrite.health missing;
  class year gender age smoker chol200 exercise;
  var weight systol diast chol;

  table   year,
          all gender*(age all),
          n*f=4.
          (weight systol diast)*mean='Mean'*f=9.
          chol*(mean='Mean'*f=7. max='Maximum'*f=7.)
          chol200*pctn<chol200>*f=7.1 smoker*pctn<smoker>*f=7.1
          exercise*pctn<exercise>*f=7.1    /
          box=_page_ rts=18 misstext='0';
  keylabel   all='Total'
             pctn='Percent';
  format age agefmt. gender $gendfmt. chol200 smoker exercise
          $ynfmt.;
run;
```

The following changes were made to the preceding code:

- The MISSING and MISSTEXT= options were added as described in Step 9.
- Titles were added.
- The OPTIONS statement was used to improve the layout of the report.
- User-defined formats were created and associated with several classification variables.
- Labels and formats were added to the statistics.
- Coding on the TABLE statement was shortened by grouping variables and statistics within parentheses.
- The KEYLABEL statement was included to change the label for ALL and PCTN.

Output 9. Complete annual summary report

ANNUAL SUMMARY OF HEALTH ASSESSMENT PROGRAM
BY GENDER AND AGE

1

Year of Exam 1991			Weight (pounds)	Systolic Pressure	Diastolic Pressure	Cholesterol		Cholesterol => 200?		Smoker?		Participate in Exercise Program?	
								No	Yes	No	Yes	No	Yes
		N	Mean	Mean	Mean	Mean	Maximum	Percent	Percent	Percent	Percent	Percent	Percent
Total		110	174	126	80	206	314	50.9	49.1	69.1	30.9	74.5	25.5
Gender	Age at Exam												
Female	21-35	13	147	122	78	168	198	100.0	0	69.2	30.8	61.5	38.5
	36-55	32	145	128	81	201	273	50.0	50.0	62.5	37.5	75.0	25.0
	56+	8	172	132	83	208	249	50.0	50.0	62.5	37.5	87.5	12.5
	Total	53	150	127	81	194	273	62.3	37.7	64.2	35.8	73.6	26.4
Male	Age at Exam												
	21-35	14	184	117	73	190	273	71.4	28.6	78.6	21.4	64.3	35.7
	36-55	32	196	123	80	223	314	34.4	65.6	71.9	28.1	81.3	18.8
	56+	11	209	139	85	236	306	18.2	81.8	72.7	27.3	72.7	27.3
	Total	57	196	125	79	217	314	40.4	59.6	73.7	26.3	75.4	24.6

ANNUAL SUMMARY OF HEALTH ASSESSMENT PROGRAM
BY GENDER AND AGE

2

Year of Exam 1992			Weight (pounds)	Systolic Pressure	Diastolic Pressure	Cholesterol		Cholesterol => 200?		Smoker?		Participate in Exercise Program?	
								No	Yes	No	Yes	No	Yes
		N	Mean	Mean	Mean	Mean	Maximum	Percent	Percent	Percent	Percent	Percent	Percent
Total		110	176	119	78	201	306	61.8	38.2	78.2	21.8	61.8	38.2
Gender	Age at Exam												
Female	21-35	12	151	118	77	170	195	100.0	0	66.7	33.3	58.3	41.7
	36-55	33	149	119	79	198	263	66.7	33.3	75.8	24.2	63.6	36.4
	56+	8	166	128	84	192	218	75.0	25.0	62.5	37.5	62.5	37.5
	Total	53	152	120	79	190	263	75.5	24.5	71.7	28.3	62.3	37.7
Male	Age at Exam												
	21-35	14	184	110	71	180	232	78.6	21.4	85.7	14.3	57.1	42.9
	36-55	30	201	117	79	219	304	43.3	56.7	80.0	20.0	66.7	33.3
	56+	13	205	128	81	223	306	30.8	69.2	92.3	7.7	53.8	46.2
	Total	57	198	118	77	211	306	49.1	50.9	84.2	15.8	61.4	38.6

Building the Second Report

A second, shorter report is now built focusing on the cholesterol variables. Since the information gathered previously in steps 1 and 2 can be used in building the second report, this section starts with Step 3.

Step 3: Determine what the report should present.

The second report is a one-page comparison of cholesterol values by year, gender, and age. A mock up of this report is shown in Figure 2.

Cholesterol Results by Year						
	Year		Year			
	1991	1992	1991		1992	
	Mean Cholesterol	Mean Cholesterol	Percent with Cholesterol <200	Percent with Cholesterol =>200	Percent with Cholesterol <200	Percent with Cholesterol =>200
All Participants						
Females						
Age Groups...						
All Females						
Males						
Age Groups...						
All Males						
• For each year, the frequency percentages should sum to 100% on each row classification.						

Figure 2. Mock up of cholesterol results report

Step 4: Identify the dimension -- page, row, column -- of each variable.

The entire report is on one page. Therefore, there is no page dimension in this report.

The rows of the table are defined by gender and age as in the annual summary report. Therefore, the row dimension variables are GENDER and AGE. Also in the row dimension is the summary of all participants for the year and summaries by gender. The universal class variable ALL is needed in the row dimension.

The columns of the table are made up of statistics and frequency percentages by year. The variables used to compute statistics and frequency percentages in the column dimension are CHOL and CHOL200. The variable YEAR is also used. CHOL, CHOL200, and YEAR are in the column dimension.

Step 5: Determine the classification variables, the analysis variables, and the statistics.

In Figure 2, the following variables are used to define the categories for which statistics are computed: YEAR, GENDER, AGE, and CHOL200. Therefore, these variables are the classification variables and are specified on the CLASS statement.

The variable for which statistics are computed is CHOL. Therefore, CHOL is an analysis variable and specified on the VAR statement. The statistics computed in the report are mean and frequency percentages.

Step 6: Determine the relationships among the variables and statistics; determine the operators needed to represent the relationships.

GENDER and AGE are in the row dimension. Each row is to be a combination of the values of the two variables. Therefore, GENDER and AGE are crossed and joined by an asterisk in the row dimension.

YEAR, CHOL, and CHOL200 are in the column dimension with YEAR being used twice. The mean cholesterol for each value of YEAR is computed. YEAR is crossed with the analysis variable CHOL and the statistic MEAN is specified by joining the keyword MEAN to CHOL with an asterisk. The frequency percentages of participants with cholesterol more than or equal to 200 for each value of YEAR, GENDER, and AGE is computed. YEAR is crossed with the classification variable CHOL200 and the statistic PCTN is joined to CHOL200 with an asterisk.

The following code produces a report with the classification variables, the analysis variables, and the statistics. An excerpt of the report is presented in Output 10.

```
proc tabulate data=repwrite.health;
   class year gender age chol200;
   var chol;
   table gender*age, year*chol*mean year*chol200*pctn;
run;
```

Output 10. Excerpt of output with classification variables, analysis variables, and statistics

```
                                        The SAS System
-------------------------------------------------------------------------------------------------------------
|                          |                           |                      Year of Exam                  |
|                          |                           |----------------------------------------------------|
|                          |       Year of Exam        |           1991           |          1992           |
|                          |---------------------------+--------------------------+-------------------------|
|                          |    1991     |    1992     |  Cholesterol => 200?     |  Cholesterol => 200?    |
|                          |-------------+-------------+--------------------------+-------------------------|
|                          |Cholesterol  |Cholesterol  |      N      |     Y      |      N     |     Y      |
|                          |-------------+-------------+-------------+------------+------------+------------|
|                          |    MEAN     |    MEAN     |    PCTN     |    PCTN    |    PCTN    |    PCTN    |
|--------------------------+-------------+-------------+-------------+------------+------------+------------|
|Gender      |Age at Exam  |             |             |             |            |            |            |
|------------+-------------|             |             |             |            |            |            |
|F           |23           |       188.00|            .|         0.45|           .|           .|           .|
|            |-------------+-------------+-------------+-------------+------------+------------+------------|
|            |24           |            .|       160.00|            .|           .|        0.45|           .|
|            |-------------+-------------+-------------+-------------+------------+------------+------------|
|            |25           |       160.00|            .|         0.45|           .|           .|           .|
|            |-------------+-------------+-------------+-------------+------------+------------+------------|
...(ages 26 to 65 omitted)...
|            |-------------+-------------+-------------+-------------+------------+------------+------------|
|            |66           |       201.00|            .|            .|        0.45|           .|           .|
|            |-------------+-------------+-------------+-------------+------------+------------+------------|
|            |67           |            .|       199.00|            .|           .|        0.45|           .|
|------------+-------------+-------------+-------------+-------------+------------+------------+------------|
|M           |21           |       162.00|            .|         0.45|           .|           .|           .|
|            |-------------+-------------+-------------+-------------+------------+------------+------------|
|            |22           |            .|       138.00|            .|           .|        0.45|           .|
|            |-------------+-------------+-------------+-------------+------------+------------+------------|
|            |24           |       191.00|            .|         0.45|           .|           .|           .|
|            |-------------+-------------+-------------+-------------+------------+------------+------------|
|            |25           |       178.50|       191.00|         0.91|           .|        0.45|           .|
-------------------------------------------------------------------------------------------------------------
(CONTINUED)
```

Step 7: Identify the variables to be summarized and the dimension of the summary information.

In Figure 2, a summary of all the participants' information is specified on the first row of the report. This summary is in the row dimension of the report. A summary is also specified for each gender. Again, the summary is in the row dimension of the report.

The universal class variable ALL is added to the program to produce these summaries. The code follows. An excerpt of the report is in Output 11 which includes changes made in Step 8 as well.

```
proc tabulate data=repwrite.health;
   class year gender age chol200;
   var chol;
   table all gender*(age all),
         year*chol*mean year*chol200*pctn;
run;
```

Step 8: Identify the variables to be used in computing percentages.

In Figure 2, note that the frequency count percentages for CHOL200 for each combination of YEAR, GENDER, and AGE are in the column dimension, and the percentages for each YEAR sum to 100. Because this is not the default computation of percentages in PROC TABULATE, a denominator definition is added to the PCTN keyword. This denominator definition is derived the same way as in the annual summary report.

The following code includes the PCTN denominator definition. An excerpt of the output is in Output 11.

```
proc tabulate data=repwrite.health;
  class year gender age chol200;
  var chol;
  table  all gender*(age all),
         year*chol*mean year*chol200*pctn<chol200>;
run;
```

Output 11. Excerpt of output with totals and frequency percentages

The SAS System

		Year of Exam		Year of Exam			
				1991		1992	
		1991	1992	Cholesterol => 200?		Cholesterol => 200?	
		Cholesterol	Cholesterol	N	Y	N	Y
		MEAN	MEAN	PCTN	PCTN	PCTN	PCTN
ALL		206.02	200.83	50.91	49.09	61.82	38.18
Gender	Age at Exam						
F	23	188.00	.	100.00	.	.	.
	24	.	160.00	.	.	100.00	.
	25	160.00	.	100.00	.	.	.
...(ages 26 to 65 omitted)...							
	66	201.00	.	.	100.00	.	.
	67	.	199.00	.	.	100.00	.
	ALL	193.85	190.40	62.26	37.74	75.47	24.53
M	Age at Exam						
	21	162.00	.	100.00	.	.	.
	22	.	138.00	.	.	100.00	.
	24	191.00	.	100.00	.	.	.
	25	178.50	191.00	100.00	.	100.00	.

(CONTINUED)

Step 9: Determine how missing values should be handled in the report.

In the cholesterol results report, the PRINTMISS option is not included since the report has no page dimension.

The other two options MISSING and MISSTEXT=*'0'* are included for the same reasons as in the annual summary report.

Step 10: Improve the readability of the report.

The following changes are made to the cholesterol results report program to improve the readability of the report.

- Titles are specified.
- Formats for several of the variables and statistics in the report are specified. User-defined formats are associated with the classification variables AGE, GENDER, and CHOL200.
- The KEYLABEL statement is used to change the default labels for the MEAN and PCTN statistics and for the universal class variable ALL throughout the report. MEAN is set to a character blank in order to suppress the line that prints the statistic label. A complete label for mean cholesterol is specified in the row dimension expression.
- The SAS System options PAGENO, PAGESIZE, LINESIZE, and CENTER are specified to improve the layout of the report.
- The width of the space allocated to print the row classifications is specified with the RTS=*number* option on the TABLE statement.

The following code produces the final report program which includes many of the above-mentioned enhancements. The final report is in Output 12.

```
title 'CHOLESTEROL RESULTS BY YEAR FOR HEALTH ASSESSMENT PROGRAM';
options pageno=1 ls=110 ps=45 center;

proc format;
  value agefmt  21-35='21-35'
                36-55='36-55'
                56-high='56+';
  value $gendfmt  'F'='Female'
                  'M'='Male';
  value $ynfmt  'N'='No'
                'Y'='Yes';
run;

proc tabulate data=repwrite.health;
      class year gender age chol200;
      var chol;
      table all gender*(age all),
         year*chol='Mean Cholesterol'*mean*f=12.
         year*chol200*pctn<chol200>*f=9.1 /
         rts=21 misstext='0';
      format gender $gendfmt. age agefmt. chol200 $ynfmt.;
      keylabel  pctn='Percent'
                mean=' '
                all='Total';
run;
```

Output 12. Final cholesterol results report

CHOLESTEROL RESULTS BY YEAR FOR HEALTH ASSESSMENT PROGRAM

		Year of Exam		Year of Exam			
		1991	1992	1991		1992	
				Cholesterol => 200?		Cholesterol => 200?	
				No	Yes	No	Yes
Gender	Age at Exam	Mean Cholesterol	Mean Cholesterol	Percent	Percent	Percent	Percent
Female	21-35	168	170	100.0	0	100.0	0
	36-55	201	198	50.0	50.0	66.7	33.3
	56+	208	192	50.0	50.0	75.0	25.0
	Total	194	190	62.3	37.7	75.5	24.5
Male	Age at Exam						
	21-35	190	180	71.4	28.6	78.6	21.4
	36-55	223	219	34.4	65.6	43.3	56.7
	56+	236	223	18.2	81.8	30.8	69.2
	Total	217	211	40.4	59.6	49.1	50.9
Total		206	201	50.9	49.1	61.8	38.2

Conclusion

When selecting a report-writing tool, PROC TABULATE may be overlooked or under utilized because of its complexity. However, PROC TABULATE is an excellent choice for producing presentation-quality reports. By breaking up the process of writing a report with PROC TABULATE into the manageable steps presented in this chapter, it becomes easier to take full advantage of the features of PROC TABULATE.

Before beginning to write your PROC TABULATE program, it is important to understand basic PROC TABULATE syntax, to examine the data in your data set, and to know what your report should present. Procedures other than TABULATE are easier to use to examine the contents of your data set. A written mock up of your final report can be referred to as you progress through the steps of writing your PROC TABULATE program. The initial versions of your program should be written to develop the basic structure of the report and should include few options. After programming the basic structure, incorporate in your program the options and statements that make your report more readable and of presentation quality.

References

SAS Institute Inc. *SAS Guide to TABULATE Processing, Second Edition,* Cary, NC: SAS Institute Inc., 1990. This manual is a comprehensive reference and usage guide for PROC TABULATE. A tutorial on using PROC TABULATE is presented in this manual. Two sample applications are used to illustrate several of the features of PROC TABULATE.

SAS Institute Inc., *SAS Procedures Guide, Version 6, Third Edition*, Cary, NC: SAS Institute Inc., 1990. Complete reference information for PROC TABULATE is presented in Chapter 37.

For Further Reading

SAS Institute Inc., *SAS Guide to Report Writing: Examples, Version 6, First Edition*, Cary, NC: SAS Institute Inc., 1994. This book provides realistic programs to show users the range of reports that is possible with SAS report-writing tools. Five PROC TABULATE examples are included.

SAS Institute Inc., *SAS Language and Procedures: Usage, Version 6, First Edition*, Cary, NC: SAS Institute Inc., 1989. In Chapter 25, basic PROC TABULATE syntax is described and several examples are presented to illustrate how you can use PROC TABULATE to summarize information about your data.

SAS Institute Inc., *SAS Language and Procedures: Usage 2, Version 6, First Edition*, Cary, NC: SAS Institute Inc., 1991. Chapter 13 contains a description of using PROC TABULATE to create simple reports. The emphasis in this chapter is on formatting data values to create meaningful reports.

The technical journal *Observations* published by SAS Institute often prints articles about PROC TABULATE. A list of some of the articles follows:

Gibes, Kernon M. "Customizing TABULATE Procedure Output for DEC Laser Printers", *Observations: The Technical Journal for SAS Software Users*, Third Quarter 1993, 13-23. This article describes changing the default box characters for PROC TABULATE when printing on DEC Laser Printers.

Keene, Tina, "Computing Percentages with the TABULATE Procedure", *Observations: The Technical Journal for SAS Software Users*, Fourth Quarter 1991, 5-17. This article is an advanced discussion of computing percentages with PROC TABULATE.

Sharpe, Jason and Lopes, Jeff, "Input/Output", *Observations: The Technical Journal for SAS Software Users*, Third Quarter 1992, 67-69. This article discusses reformatting a SAS data set in conjunction with building a PROC TABULATE report.

Sharpe, Jason and Lopes, Jeff, "Input/Output", *Observations: The Technical Journal for SAS Software Users*, Fourth Quarter 1992, 64-69. This article continues the discussion in the article cited in the previous reference.

The *SAS Users Group International Conference Proceedings*, published every year, provides an additional source of PROC TABULATE programming information.

CHAPTER 6

Creating Customized Reports Using the DATA _NULL_ Step

by Arthur L. Carpenter

Abstract

The DATA _NULL_ step is a very flexible report writing tool. It provides a level of control that is not available with other report writing methods within the SAS System. The techniques described in this chapter show you how to use the DATA _NULL_ step to produce a variety of reports. These techniques will allow you to precisely place information on a page, control the destination of the report, create multiple reports from a single pass of the data, and create phone book style reports. The primary DATA step statements used in report writing are described. Examples demonstrate the major options. If you apply the elements presented in this chapter, you too will be able to create customized reports.

Specifications

The code in this chapter was developed and tested with Release 6.08 of the SAS System under the Windows environment. Use of the code with other releases of the SAS System or other environments may require user modification. Modified code is not supported by the author.

About the Author

Arthur L. Carpenter is a senior consultant with California Occidental Consultants, CALOXY, with over 17 years of experience as a statistician and data analyst. He has developed and presented courses and seminars on statistics and SAS programming and has taught for Colorado School of Mines, the University of Redlands, and the University of California at San Diego. Art has served as President of the Southern California SAS User's Group, as a Section Chair at the Western Users of SAS Software regional conference, and in various positions at SUGI. He is currently co-authoring a book with Charlie Shipp on SAS/GRAPH software, which is to be published by SAS Institute's Books by Users program in late 1994.

Questions and Comments Should be Directed to:

Arthur Carpenter
CALOXY
4239 Serena Avenue
Oceanside, CA 92056-5018
Telephone: 619-724-8579

Examples from this book are available online, see inside back cover for details.

Creating Customized Reports Using the DATA _NULL_ Step

Arthur L. Carpenter

Introduction

The generation of customized reports is an important and often frustrating task. Although most procedures provide some ability to modify or control what the output will look like and how it will be laid out, the level of control available can often be inadequate. One tool that does give you control over your report is the DATA _NULL_ step. The DATA _NULL_ step is not a special tool, but rather an ordinary DATA step that takes advantage of the large number of statements in the SAS programming language. These statements provide the flexibility to create virtually any report.

The techniques highlighted in this chapter describe one of a number of report-writing tools that are available within the SAS System (Linden, 1994). The DATA step is the most flexible of the report-writing tools; however, it requires you to do more of the work. When you find that the report-writing procedures such as PROC REPORT do not provide the level of control required, consider the DATA step as a reporting tool. The DATA step is often the best (or only possible) report-writing tool when

- there are multiple sources of data (more than one dataset).
- you require complete control over the exact placement of information (as in a preprinted form).
- you need to create a report that requires multiple observations to be placed on each line (for example, a phone book).
- the report does not follow the usual tabular (rows and columns) format used by most procedures.

The preceding list reflects a wide range of complexity. The DATA_NULL_ step is so flexible that it can be used to create many types of reports. These include reports

- where one observation completely defines an output page
- that contain multiple columns for each variable (like a phone book)
- where multiple reports are generated from each observation
- that require data dependent headers and titles
- that are completely customized.

By discussing DATA step statements that are uniquely suited to creating the types of reports that you wish to produce, this chapter will show you

- how to precisely place data values and character strings
- how to control the output destination for your report

- methods for controlling the report titles and headers
- techniques suited for reports in which one data observation describes one full report page
- ways to generate multiple reports with a single pass of the data
- how to create multi-column reports
- a number of special techniques and options that make the process of report generation easier.

The phrase "DATA _NULL_ step," through tradition and practice, embraces a collection of techniques that are used to write customized reports and to generate code. Traditionally these techniques have been used to create tables, listings, and presentations of data in formats that are unachievable by other means such as PROC PRINT.

DATA _NULL_

The DATA _NULL_ step takes its name from the use of the _NULL_ keyword in the DATA statement. A DATA statement of the form

```
DATA _NULL_ <(options)>;
```

does not produce a data set with the name of _NULL_, but rather produces no data set at all.

There are several advantages to the use of the DATA _NULL_ step (Linden, 1994):

- Control of the page layout.
- Full functionality and power of the DATA step.
- Multiple output tables can be created in one step (one pass of the data).
- Unlike other SAS reporting tools, it is not necessary to first create a SAS dataset, thereby minimizing data storage requirements.

There are two statements especially suited for use with the DATA _NULL_ step: FILE and PUT. These two statements are analogous to the INFILE and INPUT statements used to read raw data. The FILE statement is used to direct the output file to a particular destination, while the PUT statement determines what is to be written to the page and how it is to be written.

The general form of the DATA _NULL_ step is

```
data _null_;
file fileref<options>;
put <statement modifiers>;
run;
```

Since the FILE statement is executable it should precede the PUT statement to which it applies. Although a single DATA _NULL_ step can be used to create multiple reports by using two or more different FILE statements this is rarely necessary and generally there will be only one FILE statement followed by one or more PUT statements.

Designing the Page Layout

Since the DATA _NULL_ step depends heavily on position (row and column) to place information on the page, the coding process can be greatly facilitated by creating a report layout page. Coding sheets work well, but any graph paper with spaces large enough to hold letters can be used. The layout page can be used to precisely determine the row and column for character placement.

Writing Information Using the PUT Statement

Using the PUT Statement to Write Character Strings

The PUT statement is used to control what is to be written and where on the page it will be placed. The general form of the PUT statement is

```
put <modifiers>;
```

where the *modifiers* may include pointer controls, variable names, formats, and character strings. The simplest form of the statement is

```
put;
```

which just writes a blank line.

Since SAS automatically keeps track of pointers to the current row and column, you really only need to specify these pointers when they need to be changed prior to writing. Column control can be achieved through the use of the @ sign. The statement

```
put @5 '** ANNUAL REPORTS **';
```

writes the stated character string on the current line (row) starting at column 5. Column control can also be specified by the use of the plus sign (+), which is used to specify an absolute displacement. The following statement

```
put @5 'AA' +5 'BB';
```

writes the string 'AA' in columns 5 and 6 which leaves the column pointer pointing to column 7. The +5 adds five to the column location so the 'BB' will start in column 12.

You can jump the pointer to the next or successive lines by including a slash ('/') in the PUT statement. When a slash is encountered SAS moves the line pointer to the next line and the column pointer to column 1. The statement

```
put @5 '** ANNUAL **' / @5 '** REPORT **';
```

produces the stacked label:

```
    ** ANNUAL **
    ** REPORT **
```

Most of the options and statement modifiers used with the INPUT statement can also be used with the PUT statement. While INPUT reads a flat file into SAS variables, PUT has the capability of directly writing character strings that are not contained in a variable. This is a very important feature because it allows you to easily control the text portions of the page. The trailing @ and trailing @@ options are discussed below and behave somewhat differently for the INPUT and PUT statements.

Using Character Strings to Separate Text

In addition to generating labels, one of the more common uses of character strings is to place lines as text separators. A series of underscores produce this effect. The following PUT statement requires SAS to compile and store a large character string which could be more efficiently written by repeating a shorter string.

```
put @4 '__________________________________________________';
```

The following statement repeats a five character string 10 times, for the same result as shown in the previous statement:

```
put @4 10*'_____';
```

Vertical lines can be generated by using the vertical bar (¦) on successive lines. The following PUT statement:

```
put @5 '__________' / @5 '¦ line 1'
  / @5 '¦ line 2' / @5 '__________';
```

produces

```
 __________
 ¦ line 1
 ¦ line 2
 __________
```

Other operating system and printer-specific characters are often available. Since these usually involve the use of nonstandard keystrokes, consult the documentation for your operating system and printer. The constructed character is then surrounded with quotes and treated like any other character (McDonald, 1993).

Displaying Variable Values

Like character strings the values associated with variables can also be written to the report. For example, the following PUT statement writes the value of a calculated variable:

```
total = total + amntpd;
if last.client then
      put @14 total;
```

Usually many of the variables are brought into the DATA _NULL_ step with a SET, MERGE, or INPUT statement, and these are directly written or manipulated to create new variables.

As shown above, character variables can be used to store strings such as underlines, and the REPEAT function is especially useful for this task. Notice that the REPEAT function's second argument is the number of times the first will be repeated; consequently an underline of length 50 uses 49 as the second argument. The following PUT statement generates the same underline as shown in the two previous examples concerning underlines; however, if the same line is to be written several times processing can be speeded up by using the repeat function.

```
undl = repeat('_',49);
put @4 undl;
```

Functions cannot be used in the PUT statement so a separate variable, UNDL, is created and its value written using the PUT.

Controlling the Output Destination

The PUT statement directs where on the page the information will be written, and the FILE statement determines the destination of the written page.

Using the FILE Statement

The keyword FILE is usually followed by the file designation. This can either be a fileref or the actual file name. It is easier to create a more portable and generalizable program by using a fileref that has been previously defined through either a FILENAME statement or for some operating systems by the operating system itself.

This is an executable statement. Consequently it should precede the PUT statement(s) in the DATA _NULL_ step. As is shown in the following DATA step, multiple output destinations can be specified by using multiple FILE statements each pointing to different filerefs.

```
filename inv 'invoice';
filename sales 'rpt';

data _null_;

name = 'Jones';
code = '123';
cost = 4285.32;

file inv;
put @4 'Buyer ' name  cost;

file sales;
put @2 'item code ' code 'cost' cost;
run;
```

The DATA step produces the following LOG which provides information about the file names and record counts for the files indicated in the FILE statements.

```
NOTE: The file INV is:
      FILENAME=C:\WINSAS\invoice,
      RECFM=V,LRECL=132

NOTE: The file SALES is:
      FILENAME=C:\WINSAS\rpt,
      RECFM=V,LRECL=132

NOTE: 1 record was written to the file INV.
      The minimum record length was 22.
      The maximum record length was 22.
NOTE: 1 record was written to the file SALES.
      The minimum record length was 19.
      The maximum record length was 19.
NOTE: The DATA statement used 1.87 seconds.
```

Specification of the FILEREF

The FILE statement may either use a fileref as in the above example or may point directly to the file. When the full file designation is used, it is surrounded by quotes, and this quoted string is passed to the operating system for processing. Filerefs are not surrounded by quotes. The use of filerefs is usually preferable to hard coding the file designation in the program.

Two filerefs, PRINT and LOG, are automatically defined by SAS when the system is invoked. PRINT directs the output stream directly to the default printer or to the OUTPUT window when in the Display Manager. The LOG fileref writes the output to the SAS LOG or to the LOG window (this is the default if no fileref is specified).

Using Specialized Functionality

In addition to the options shown above both the FILE and PUT statements have a number of options that allow even better control over the printed page.

Using Pointer Controls (Trailing @)

By default each successive PUT statement writes to a new line. It is possible to hold a line by ending the PUT statement with either an @ or @@ (unlike the INPUT statement, there is no difference between the two). The first statement below produces exactly the same result as the next two.

```
put @2 'item code ' code 'cost' cost;

put @2 'item code ' code @;
put 'cost' cost;
```

The trailing @ is especially useful when there is more than one possible ending for the line to be written and the appropriate ending has not yet been determined when the first part is written. A somewhat simplistic example might be

```
put 'The Total Annual Expenditures are in ' @;
if country='US' then put 'Dollars';
else if country='FRANCE' then put 'Francs';
```

When the variable COUNTRY is equal to 'US', this code produces

```
The Total Annual Expenditures are in Dollars
```

Using Formats

Formats can be associated with variables either with the FORMAT statement or by following the variable name with the appropriate format in the PUT statement.

The statement

```
put @5 'Invoice Date: ' date worddate18.;
```

produces

```
Invoice Date:          June 4, 1978
```

The use of the PUT and LEFT functions can eliminate the leading blanks before the date. The PUT function cannot be used inside the PUT statement, so a new variable, STRING, is created and then written using the PUT statement. The statements

```
string =  left(put(date,worddate18.));
put @5 'Invoice Date: ' string;
```

produce

```
Invoice Date: June 4, 1978
```

Placing and Centering Titles

When you use the DATA _NULL_ step, footnotes never appear on the output page. By default titles defined with the TITLE statement are automatically used when the fileref is PRINT. Usually you would rather control all title and footnotes yourself, and the FILE statement option NOTITLES ensures that previously defined titles are not used. You can then define your own titles and footnotes by using character variables (Emmrich, 1986).

Instead of using the title statement

```
title1 'Western States Air Pollution Study';
```

you can define a variable, TITLEA (the variable name TITLE1 might have been confusing).

```
titlea = 'Western States Air Pollution Study';
```

Titles are usually centered so you need a mechanism to dynamically center the title string held in variable TITLEA. This is done fairly easily if you know how wide the page is and the length of the string to be centered. The page width is controlled by the LINESIZE option, which can be set either in the OPTION statement, OPTION Window, or more conveniently on the FILE statement, as follows:

```
file annreprt notitles linesize=133;
```

The centering of the title is done by shifting the title by half of the space not used by the title. The LENGTH function returns the number of characters in the variable and this can be subtracted from the total available to determine the number not used. For example,

```
centera = (133-length(titlea))/2;
put @centera titlea;
```

Notice that instead of a number following the @ sign, the variable CENTERA that resolves to a number is used. This shifts the title by half of the unused space. As is shown in the next section, footnotes can be handled in the same way.

Preparing Special Types of Reports

There are several ways to construct a particular report. For some reports a single observation can complete the entire page. At other times one page contains information from several observations and perhaps from more than one data set. Page layout control can be specified such that the user has control of both the line and column pointers, so that it is possible to create multi-column reports. A page from a telephone book would be an example of a multi-column report.

Creating Reports with One Observation Per Page

At times a single observation in the data set may contain all the information which is to be written to a page of the report. This may be the case when the data are summarized with a BY statement, and the key fields form unique combinations. This can actually simplify the generation of the report because one pass of the DATA step corresponds to one data observation and to one page in the report.

The _PAGE_ modifier can be used in the PUT statement to signal SAS that the current page is complete and should be written to the fileref. The form of the statement is

```
put _page_;
```

Be sure not to use _page_ as a variable name, since unanticipated results could occur.

When you generate this kind of report you will generally have a series of PUT statements within the DATA _NULL_ step. In the following example a medical insurance claims summary is produced for the company "Industrial Hardware". In the program segment the entire page is created from a single observation. Notice that the title and footnote are generated in separate segments that are called with the LINK statement.

```
data _null_;
set claims;

file print;

link title;

put // 'Summary of all Cases';

put / @5 'Number of claims: ' @25 cases;
put   @10 'Claim amount: ' @25 clchrg dollar11.0;
put   @10 'Allowed amount: ' @25 allowed comma11.0;
put   @10 'Savings: ' @25 savings dollar11.0;
```

```
link foot;
return;

title:
offset = (60-length(client))/2;
put @offset client //;
return;

foot:
string = 'Savings realized during 1994';
offset = (60-length(string))/2;
put // @offset string _page_;
return;
run;
```

The program produces the following output for one observation in the data set CLAIMS:

```
                    Industrial Hardware



Summary of all Cases

    Number of claims:    437
         Claim amount:        $42,798
         Allowed amount:       36,731
         Savings:              $6,067

                 Savings realized during 1994
```

In this example the page is written just after the footnote, that is, as soon as _PAGE_ is encountered.

Producing Multiple Reports in One Step

In the above example one observation created a single page. At times that one observation may contain information that is to appear in two or more separate reports. One way to accomplish this would be to use separate DATA _NULL_ steps for each report; however, this is not very efficient. It is easy enough to read the observation once and then direct the appropriate parts to different reports by using more than one FILE statement. Since FILE statements are executable, the PUT statements direct output to the destination designated in the most recently executed FILE statement.

The following DATA step creates two reports: the one shown above and another for outpatients. Notice that both are now being directed to filerefs that must have been defined earlier in the job stream.

```
data _null_;
set claims;

file allcase;

link title;
put // 'Summary of all Cases';
put / @5 'Number of claims: ' @25 cases;
put   @10 'Claim amount: ' @25 clchrg dollar11.0;
put   @10 'Allowed amount: ' @25 allowed comma11.0;
put   @10 'Savings: ' @25 savings dollar11.0;
link foot;

file opcase;
link title;
put // 'Summary of outpatient cases';
put / @5 'Outpatient claims: ' @25 opcases;
put   @10 'Claim amount: ' @25 opchrg dollar11.0;
put   @10 'Allowed amount: ' @25 opallow comma11.0;
put   @10 'Savings: ' @25 opsav dollar11.0;
link foot;
return;

title:
offset = (60-length(client))/2;
put @offset client //;
return;

foot:
string = 'Savings realized during 1994';
offset = (60-length(string))/2;
put // @offset string _page_;
return;
run;
```

As is shown in the following output, this code produces two pages (one in each report) for each observation:

```
                    Industrial Hardware



Summary of all Cases

    Number of claims:   437
         Claim amount:       $42,798
         Allowed amount:      36,731
         Savings:             $6,067


                Savings realized during 1994
```

```
                    Industrial Hardware



Summary of outpatient cases

    Outpatient claims: 153
         Claim amount:       $15,364
         Allowed amount:      14,871
         Savings:                $493

              Savings realized during 1994
```

Creating Multi-column Reports

One of the very useful features of the DATA _NULL_ step is the ability to write to any location on the page. In each of the previous examples, once a given line on the page has been left it was not possible to go back to it. This need not be the case. The above examples all write a line at a time and the process is geared to the line rather than to the page. Writing to the entire page enables you to create pages such as a phone book where the same variable appears in multiple columns.

The pointers for the entire page can be accessed by specifying the N=PAGESIZE (or N=PS) option in the FILE statement. This option is used in conjunction with a line pointer in the PUT statement. Just as the @ sign is used to designate a column, the # sign is used to designate a row. The following two statements could be used to write the variable NAME starting on line 5 column 10, and the variable NUMBER on line 5 column 30:

```
file phonelst n=ps;
put #5 @10 name @30 number;
```

The power of this technique is fully realized when the row and column pointers are actually variables that are driven either by the data or perhaps through a pair of nested DO loops. The following code generates a list of employees and their telephone extension numbers.

```
data _null_;
 file phonelst n=ps ls=65 notitle;

 string = 'Employee Extensions';
 center=(60-length(string))/2;
 put @center string;

 do col = 1, 31;
    do row=4 to 40;
       set phnums;
       name = trim(lname) ||', '|| fname;
       put #row @col ext  name;
    end;
 end;
 put _page_;
 run;
```

In the preceding code, the SET statement is contained within the nested DO loops. Since it is an executable statement, one observation will be read (and written) for each unique value of the DO loop variables ROW and COL. The page title is written at the top of each page just before control passes to the DO loops. When the last observation is read, processing stops for the DATA step. If the DO loops are satisfied (there must be another observation), the page is written using _PAGE_, and control is passed back to the start of the step where the next page is started with a new title.

A portion of the telephone list produced by this code is shown below.

```
                   Employee Extensions


0799 Adams, Mary                 0753 Lawless, Henry
0115 Adamson, Joan               0753 Leader, Zac
7435 Alexander, Mark             3762 Little, Sandra
4897 Antler, Peter               5318 Long, Margot
0664 Atwood, Teddy               3667 Manley, Debra
3682 Banner, John                4899 Mann, Steven
1894 Baron, Roger                6389 Marks, Gerald
3109 Batell, Mary                6347 Marksman, Joan
5490 Block, Will                 4890 Marshall, Robert
4687 Candle, Sid                 0298 Masters, Martha
5788 Carlile, Patsy              4687 Maxim, Kurt
5398 Chang, Joseph               1357 Maxwell, Linda
1983 Chang, Tim                  1904 Mercy, Ronald
3109 Chou, John                  3753 Moon, Rachel
7845 Chu, David                  1092 Most, Mat
3276 Cordoba, Juan               3457 Nabers, David
1536 Cranberry, David            2984 Nolan, Terrie
2874 Cranston, Rhonda            7438 Olsen, June
5789 Dandy, Martin               3875 Panda, Merv
5241 Davidson, Mitch             5782 Perez, Mathew
8425 East, Clint                 8324 Pope, Robert
0863 East, Jody                  4765 Reilly, Arthur
2190 Haddock, Linda              7437 Robertson, Adam
5890 Halfner, John               3276 Rodgers, Carl
```

Additional examples of multi-column reports can be found in the SAS Applications Guide.

Interestingly, the OVERPRINT option cannot be used when using line pointers (ps=n and the #).

Finesse

The above examples, options, and statements should be sufficient to get you started with the process of generating reports. There are, however, a number of things that can be done to further dress up your report. These include additional options as well as 'tricks of the trade.'

Taking Advantage of Special Features of the PUT Statement

controlling hardware options

Most modern printers (especially those that are graphics capable) have built-in hardware capabilities and features that can be used to advantage when generating a customized report. While there is no facility within the DATA _NULL_ step to directly control printer options, you can achieve some control for certain printers.

When a print file is sent to a printer the characters are interpreted by the printer which translates them into print. For some printers, however, not all characters are printed. Instead some very specific characters are interpreted as hardware commands. Characters known as escape sequences can be used to alert the printer to change fonts, margins, character size and so on. McDonald (1993) included several examples of many of the common escape sequences used for an HP LaserJet.

OVERPRINT

The overprint option allows SAS, through the use of printer carriage controls, to rewrite to the same line a second time without replacing the original characters. This feature is most often used to underline portions of text. OVERPRINT can only be used if the file to be created is a print file, and the printer itself allows overprinting. Consider the following DATA step:

```
data _null_;
file annrpt print;

put @5 'ANNUAL REPORT' overprint
    @5 '_____________';
run;
```

The OVERPRINT option resets the column pointer to 1, and uses printer carriage control characters ('+' is used for overprinting) to prevent the overwriting of the previous characters. The PRINT option in the FILE statement (don't confuse it with the PRINT fileref) lets SAS know that the output file should contain carriage control characters. The PRINT option is assumed if the fileref is PRINT.

ALL

Although usually not needed for report writing, the _ALL_ option can be handy during the debugging phases of the coding process. The statement

```
put _all_;
```

writes in named format the value of all of the variables currently stored in the program data vector, PDV. This is a real easy way to see what all of the current settings are for various counters, flags, and variables used for branching.

Special Options of the FILE Statement

The FILE statement has a number of useful options. Two of the most commonly used of these are HEADER= and LINESLEFT=.

LINESLEFT=

This option is used to designate a variable which holds the number of remaining available lines on the page. Often while you are writing a page you need to leave room at the bottom of the page for the margin or footnote, or just to keep groups of information intact. Although LINESLEFT= can be abbreviated as ll=, I usually leave it unabbreviated because ll= looks too much like the number 11 (eleven). The following portion of code will write two lines at the bottom of each page:

```
file annrpt linesleft=lleft;

if lleft=5 then do;
      put 'SIM is a registered trademark of';
      put 'of SIM Construction, Simi Valley, CA.';
      put _page_;
      end;
```

Usually the variable containing the number of remaining lines is queried in an IF statement and some action taken when the number of remaining lines drops below some threshold.

HEADER=

The HEADER= option designates a label in the DATA _NULL_ step. The code associated with this label is automatically executed whenever SAS first writes to a new page. Using this option is an easy way to provide titles, column headers, and page layout for each page.

Obviously header information can be written without using this option and indeed all of the previous examples did not use it. For simple DATA _NULL_ steps it is often easier to allow the automatic generation of the header. The following code shows a sample labeled section:

```
file annrpt header=hdr;

... more SAS statements ...

return;
hdr:
put @25 'Annual Report for XYZ Company';
return;
```

The RETURN statement is used before the HDR: label to isolate this section from the main portion of the DATA _NULL_ step.

At times the use of the HEADER= option produces some unanticipated results and is not always the best way to generate a header. This can especially be true when writing the value of a variable in the header. Unfortunately the header is written to the new page as soon as the previous page has been completed and this is usually before the next observation has been read. Consequently the data used in the header may not match that which is used in the body of the report. When this happens it may be easier to use counters or flags to branch to the appropriate section after the data are read. In the following code, FIRST.CLIENT is used as a flag that identifies when the header section (HDR) is executed:

```
data _null_;
file annrpt;
set summary;
by client;
if first.client then link hdr;
... SAS statements ...
if last.client then put _page_;
return;
hdr:
... more SAS statements ...
return;
run;
```

The use of the HEADER= option is an easy way to place information at the top of each page; however, there are times when it is just not flexible enough.

Using Formats

Formats provide an easy way modify the presentation of numbers and character strings. An extensive collection of formats is provided with the base SAS software and additional formats can be created by using PROC FORMAT.

As in any DATA step, formats can be associated with a variable through the use of the FORMAT statement. The designated format is then used whenever that variable appears in a PUT statement. For example, the following code

```
clmdate = '05apr78'd;
put @12 clmdate;
format clmdate mmddyy10.;
```

produces the date

```
04/05/1978
```

Notice that since the FORMAT statement is not executable, it can appear anywhere in the DATA step and does not need to be placed before the PUT statement.

Formats can also be used on the PUT statement and can be used to replace any existing format definitions. As shown in the following program fragment, formats immediately follow the variable name:

```
clmdate = '05apr78'd;
put @12 clmdate date7.;
format clmdate mmddyy10.;
```

The DATE7. format replaces the MMDDYY10. format and the following is displayed:

```
05APR78
```

Variable and format lists can be used as a shorthand by placing the variables in one set of parentheses followed by the formats and pointer controls inside a second set of parentheses. The following two PUT statements

```
data _null_;
date = '04jun78'd;
name = 'Jones';
cost = 4285.32;
put @2 name $5.+2 date date7. cost dollar10.2;
put (name date cost) (@2 $5.+2 date7. dollar10.2);
run;
```

produce the same result, as follows:

```
Jones  04JUN78 $4,285.32
Jones  04JUN78 $4,285.32
```

SAS will step through the two sets of parentheses at the same time. Consequently, position is very important. When there are fewer formats than variables, the list of formats and pointer controls will be reused as required. The following code

```
data _null_;
hum1 = .20;
hum4 = .40;
hum7 = .30;
hum10 = .18;
hum13 = .15;

put (hum1 hum4 hum7 hum10 hum13) (percent6.2);
run;
```

produces the following line in the output:

```
20%    40%    30%    18%    15%
```

Conclusion

The DATA _NULL_ step is a flexible tool for producing customized reports and output. The full power of the SAS programming language is combined with control over the line and column pointers in the PUT statement. Special options in the FILE statement such as HEADER=, PS=N, and LINESLEFT= allow the user to monitor the process of generating a page.

References

Emmrich, D. (1986), "SAS Report Writing: Generation of Statistical Tables Using PROC PRINTTO and the DATA _NULL_ Step," *Proceedings of the Eleventh Annual SAS Users Group International Conference, 11,* 652-656. A report writing example of the DATA _NULL_ step includes several tips and techniques.

Linden, C. and J. Green III, "Writing Reports with SAS Software: What Are Your Options?," *Observations: The Technical Journal for SAS Software Users*, First Quarter 1994, 10-42. This is a very complete review of various report writing options within the SAS system.

McDonald, M. (1993), "Publication Quality Output from the SAS System", *Proceedings of the Eighteenth Annual SAS Users Group International Conference*, 18, 847-852. Discusses the use of imbedded printer specific escape sequences in a DATA _NULL_ step.

SAS Institute Inc. (1987), *SAS Applications Guide*, 1987 Edition, Cary, NC: SAS Institute Inc. Pages 152 through 163 deal with report writing issues using the DATA _NULL_ step.

For Further Reading

Aster, R. and R. Seidman (1991) *Professional SAS Programming Secrets*, Blue Ridge Summit, PA: Windcrest Books, 582 pp. Tips are spread throughout this excellent book; however, pp. 168-177 specifically address issues related to writing to text files.

Barlow, G. and A. Ringelberg (1992), "Dances With Data," *Proceedings of the Seventeenth Annual SAS Users Group International Conference, 17,* 762-767. An overview of the DATA _NULL_ step is given along with example code.

Cannon, W. and J. Bullard (1989), "Using SAS/AF to Generate the DATA _NULL_ Statements Commonly Used in Custom Report Writing," *Proceedings of the Fourteenth Annual SAS Users*

Group International Conference, 14, 1112-1118. A short DATA _NULL_ example is included that writes a data table.

Freeman, K. (1990), "Using SAS/AF Software to Transport SAS Data Files from the VMS Environment to the OS Environment," *Proceedings of the Fifteenth Annual SAS Users Group International Conference*, 15, 1188-1195. The DATA _NULL_ step is used to generate DCL, JCL, and SAS code.

Jaffe, J. (1989), *Mastering the SAS System*, New York, NY: Van Nostrand Reinhold, 629 pp. Chapter 18 (pp. 431-454) discusses in detail many of the same concepts covered in this chapter. The text includes a number of good examples.

Olszewski, L., "Managing Text with Base SAS Software," *Observations: The Technical Journal for SAS Software Users*, First Quarter 1993, 38-44. A variety of examples show how the data _NULL_ step is used for just about everything except report writing.

SAS Institute Inc. (1989), *SAS Language and Procedures: Usage, Version 6, First Edition*, Cary, NC: SAS Institute Inc. Two different chapters deal with customized report writing using the DATA _NULL_ step. Chapter 29, pp. 441-455, concentrates on the PUT and FILE statements. Chapter 30, pp. 457-469, concentrates on the customization of reports using some of the more common options.

SAS Institute Inc. (1991) *SAS Language and Procedures: Usage 2, Version 6, First Edition*, Cary, NC: SAS Institute Inc. An example in Chapter 15, pp. 286-290, uses the DATA _NULL_ step to detect and report on errors. Chapter 20, pp. 407-439, includes examples showing the use of the FILE and PUT statements in a DATA _NULL_ step to write and copy files.

Saxe, R. (1989), "Using DATA _NULL_ and STOP Statements to Ease the Transition to the SAS System," *Proceedings of the Fourteenth Annual SAS Users Group International Conference*, 14, 559-560. A short example of the DATA _NULL_ step that does not generate a report.

CHAPTER 7

Creating Customized Reports Using Screen Control Language

by Arthur L. Carpenter

Abstract

Customized reports can be generated from within the Screen Control Language environment. Although not as easy to use as the PUT statement in the DATA step, SCL functions provide all of the control that you might need to generate a fully customized report.

This chapter presents the five primary SCL functions that are required to create a customized report. Their options are discussed and examples are given that show how they are used. SCL report writing techniques are contrasted to similar techniques used in the DATA _NULL_ step. After completing this chapter you will have been introduced to all of the major components of report writing within the SCL environment.

Specifications

The code in this chapter was developed and tested with Release 6.08 of the SAS System under the Windows environment. Use of the code with other releases of the SAS System or other environments may require user modification. Modified code is not supported by the author.

About the Author

Arthur L. Carpenter is a senior consultant with California Occidental Consultants, CALOXY, with over 17 years of experience as a statistician and data analyst. He has developed and presented courses and seminars on statistics and SAS programming and has taught for Colorado School of Mines, the University of Redlands, and the University of California at San Diego. Art has served as President of the Southern California SAS User's Group, as a Section Chair at the Western Users of SAS Software regional conference, and in various positions at SUGI. He is currently co-authoring a book with Charlie Shipp on SAS/GRAPH software, which is to be published by SAS Institute's Books by Users program in late 1994.

Questions and Comments Should be Directed to:

Arthur Carpenter
CALOXY
4239 Serena Avenue
Oceanside, CA 92056-5018
Telephone: 619-724-8579

Examples from this book are available online, see inside back cover for details.

Creating Customized Reports Using Screen Control Language

Arthur L. Carpenter

Introduction

Screen Control Language, SCL, can be used to generate customized reports in much the same way as in the DATA _NULL_ step. The SCL statements do not have all of the functionality of the FILE and PUT statements; however, similar types of reports can be generated. This can be a big advantage to developers of SAS/AF and SAS/FSP systems, because they can utilize the full functionality of SCL without stepping out of the SCL environment (as must be done when using a SUBMIT block).

Although the steps used in SCL report generation are similar to those used in a DATA _NULL_ step, you as a programmer must be responsible for details that are often automatically taken care of in the DATA step. As in DATA _NULL_ processing, it is possible to gather information from a number of sources and then to write to one or more output locations.

This chapter outlines five SCL functions used specifically to write information to a file, and demonstrates through examples their use in an SCL program.

SCL Functions

The operations associated with writing a file are each accomplished by an SCL function. As a point of interest, each of the functions associated with writing to (and reading from) a text file starts with the letter f. The steps and their accompanying functions are

- FOPEN identify and open a file for output
- FPOS determine the position to write
- FPUT write information to a buffer
- FWRITE write the contents of the buffer to the file
- FCLOSE close the output file

FOPEN

This function is roughly analogous to the FILE statement in the DATA _NULL_ step. Generally only one report is generated at a time; however, it is certainly possible to open several output locations at one time. The FOPEN function returns a fileid which is stored in a numeric variable. This fileid is then used in each of the remaining functions to identify to which file you want to write. The general form of the function is

fileid = fopen(*fileref*, 'u');

where the fileref was previously created by the system, by using a FILENAME statement, or through the use of the FILENAME SCL function. The 'u' opens the file in update mode.

FPOS and FCOL

Unlike the PUT statement in the DATA _NULL_ step, you cannot specify both the position and what you want to write in the same statement in SCL. Also you do not have control over the line pointer. Once a line is written the pointer is moved ahead and you cannot go back.

After the output file has been opened, you need to identify where on the current line you would like to write. The FPOS function is analogous to the *@n* in the PUT statement; it moves the column pointer to the desired location.

In the following statement, the fileid is the same variable that was created by the FOPEN function. The second argument is the column at which you would like to start writing.

```
rc = fpos(fileid,col);
```

The FCOL function is the opposite of the FPOS in that it returns the value of the pointer to a SCL variable. At times you may want to determine the current position of the pointer. This happens often when you want to write a second value on the same line, and you need to specify an offset or space between the two. This is shown in the following example. The variable NEXTCOL contains the starting position for the second variable.

```
nextcol = fcol(fileid) + 3;
rc = fpos(fileid,nextcol);
```

FPUT

The text is written at the current pointer location using the FPUT function. Only one variable is written at a time and only character strings are written. Numeric variables should be converted to a text string before you use the FPUT function.

The following statement writes the value of the character variable NAME to the File Data Buffer (FDB) for the file identified by the value of the variable FILEID.

```
rc = fput(fileid,name);
```

Since the FPUT function writes only character variables, numeric variables must first be converted to character strings. The PUTN function is similar to the PUT function available in the DATA step, and is very useful for this conversion. The following statements convert a SAS date value to a character string:

```
string = left(putn(date,'mmddyy10.'));
rc = fput(fileid,string);
```

Thus for the date September 27, 1994 these statements produce

```
09/27/1994
```

Take care to make sure that the string length and its offset (FPOS) do not exceed the file width specified in the FOPEN function. If they do, the generated line will be blank.

Since FPUT writes only one variable at a time, a series of FPOS and FPUT function calls may be required to write each line. The following example combines FPUT, FPOS, and FCOL to write the first (FNAME) and last (LNAME) name separated by three spaces on the same line.

```
rc = fpos(fileid,1);
rc = fput(fileid,fname);
```

```
nextcol = fcol(fileid) + 3;
rc = fpos(fileid,nextcol);
rc = fput(fileid,lname);
```

When FNAME = 'Laura' and LNAME = 'Jones', this produces the following line:

```
Laura    Jones
```

FWRITE

When the line has been completed, it needs to be transferred from the buffer and written to the output file. The FWRITE function performs this operation. Remember that it transfers one line at a time to the output file. In the following code, the first argument is the fileid associated with the file in the FOPEN, and the second is either a character variable or a character string, and it gives us the opportunity to insert carriage control information into the output file.

```
rc = fwrite(fileid,cc);
```

When this option is used, you can jump to a new page, underline using overprinting, and so on.

This is demonstrated in the following program fragment which assumes that the variable COMPANY = 'ABC Manufacturing'. The first statement determines the length of the name of the company. A variable (UNDL) of the same length is then created using the REPEAT function to use as the underline. The second FPOS is required to reposition the pointer after the first FWRITE. Then the underline is written (UNDL) to the buffer. The second FWRITE transfers the buffer contents to the page with the '+' carriage control, which causes the printer not to advance to the next line before printing.

```
len = length(company);
undl = repeat('_', len-1);
rc = fpos(fileid,5);
rc = fput(fileid,company);
rc = fwrite(fileid);
rc = fpos(fileid,5);
rc = fput(fileid,undl);
rc = fwrite(fileid,'+');
```

This code produces

```
    ABC Manufacturing
```

FCLOSE

After all information has been written to the output file, close the file by using the FCLOSE function, as shown below. If the file is not closed it will remain open until the application terminates, and this is not always desirable.

```
rc = FCLOSE(fileid);
```

Return Codes

Most of the functions shown above return a value (in the above examples to a variable called RC) that indicates the success or failure of the operation. Well-written programs check the status of the return codes to make sure that the program is doing what is anticipated.

Using SCL Statements to Write Reports

The examples shown in this section are part of a program used to generate a one-page report. The incoming data set has already been constructed to have the necessary variables and its single observation is used to generate a single page. This example was constructed around a method block; however, a CALL DISPLAY could also be used. For clarity, a great deal of the code has been eliminated and only a portion of the report is shown.

The first step is to open the output file using the fileref CLMRPT in output mode and create records with a length of 81 characters and containing carriage controls. The fileref could be defined either by using the FILENAME statement elsewhere in the application or by using the FILENAME function shown here.

```
rc = filename('clmrpt','<user path information>');
flout = fopen('clmrpt','o',81,'p');
```

It is possible to center strings and headings. The following code centers the variable COMPANY within the space of 50 columns (with an additional 10 used for the left margin). Since this is the first line of a new page, the FWRITE contains a carriage control of '1'. Notice that there are two FWRITE functions. The second will write a blank line.

```
pad = int((50-length(company))/2);
if pad lt 0 then pad=0;
rc = fpos(flout,pad+10);
rc = fput(flout,company);
rc = fwrite(flout,'1');
rc = fwrite(flout,' ');
```

This code produces the following centered title. The 1 is the carriage control character that is inserted in the text file. The character itself could be different for your operating system.

```
1                                  ABC Manufacturing
```

You can construct a line of output from combinations of variables. As is shown below, several variables can be combined into one, which can then be written using a single FPUT.

```
if lname = ' ' then line1=' ';
else line1 = trim(fname) ||' '|| lname;
rc = fpos(flout,5);
rc = fput(flout,line1);
rc = fwrite(flout, ' ');
```

For LNAME = 'Jones' and FNAME = 'Laura' these lines produce the following line in the text file.

```
Laura Jones
```

Two separate pieces of information can be placed on one line without first concatenating them into a single string. This is done in the following code with separate FPUTs and one FWRITE.

```
rc = fpos(flout,10);
rc = fput(flout,'Completed By: ');
rc = fpos(flout,27);
rc = fput(flout,reviewer);
rc = fwrite(flout,' ');
```

For the reviewer Clint Smith the above lines produce

```
    Completed By:     Clint Smith
```

After everything has been written to the file and before returning to the calling program, close the file by using the FCLOSE function.

```
rc = fclose(flout);
```

The entire program for this example is contained in the following method block. Data assignment statements have been added for clarity.

```
client:
method;

lname='Jones';
fname='Laura';
date = '27sep94'd;
reviewer = 'Clint Smith';
company  = 'ABC Manufacturing';

rc = filename('clmrpt','<system dependent information>');
flout = fopen('clmrpt','o',81,'p');

pad = int((50-length(company))/2);
if pad lt 0 then pad=0;
rc = fpos(flout,pad+10);
rc = fput(flout,company);
rc = fwrite(flout,'1');
rc = fwrite(flout,' ');

rc = fpos(flout,5);
rc = fput(flout,'Client name');
rc = fwrite(flout, ' ');

if lname = ' ' then line1=' ';
else line1 = trim(fname) ||' '|| lname;
rc = fpos(flout,5);
rc = fput(flout,line1);
rc = fwrite(flout, ' ');
rc = fwrite(flout, ' ');
```

```
rc = fpos(flout,10);
rc = fput(flout,'Completed By: ');
rc = fpos(flout,27);
rc = fput(flout,reviewer);
rc = fwrite(flout,' ');

rc = fclose(flout);
endmethod;
```

One page of the report is shown below.

```
                    ABC Manufacturing

   Client name
   Laura Jones

        Completed By:     Clint Smith
```

Conclusion

SCL statements can be used to generate many of the same types of customized reports as can also be created by the DATA _NULL_ step. Although there are fewer options to learn, the task of mastering and manipulating the SCL functions is not necessarily easier. The available statements are not as complex, but usually more statements are required and their placement can be tedious. In the DATA _NULL_ step a single PUT statement may position and write a number of variables, while in SCL each variable may require two or three statements. However, for the SAS/AF and SAS/FSP developer, using SCL statements to generate a report can be an advantage because they can use the full functionality of the SCL without stepping out of the SCL environment.

For Further Reading

SAS Institute Inc. (1990), *SAS Screen Control Language: Reference*, Version 6, First Edition, Cary, NC: SAS Institute Inc. Each of the functions mentioned in this chapter is described in Chapter 8. A section, "Manipulating External Files," pp. 46-50, provides an overview of the process.

SAS Institute Inc. (1991), *SAS Screen Control Language: Usage*, Version 6, First Edition, Cary, NC: SAS Institute Inc. Part 4 deals with "Accessing and Manipulating External Files," and while all of the examples deal with reading external files, the section, "Writing Modified Values to Files," pp. 425-429, has information concerning the topic of report writing.

CHAPTER 8

PROC TABULATE in Simple Terms

by Alan Davis

Abstract

In PROC TABULATE, the user will find a powerful ally in the summary of data for tabular display. This chapter shows the general characteristics of PROC TABULATE and shows the minimum required commands to produce several major types of tables. Additionally, several OPTIONS, KEYWORDS and STATEMENTS are presented which circumvent common obstacles in the way of table production.

Specifications

The code in this chapter was developed and tested with Versions 5 and 6 of the SAS System under the DOS environment. Use of the code with other releases of the SAS System or environments may require user modification. Modified code is not supported by the author.

About the Author

Alan Davis is an Instructor in the Department of Family Medicine at the University of Oklahoma. He has been a SAS software user for 14 years. His areas of expertise include base SAS, SAS/STAT, and SAS/GRAPH software. Alan has a BA degree in Mathematics from the University of Houston, an MA degree in Physics from Vanderbilt University, and MPH and Ph.D. degrees in Biostatistics from the University of Oklahoma.

Questions and Comments Should be Directed to:

Alan Davis
705 NW 16th Street
Oklahoma City, OK 73103
Telephone: 405-525-2421

Examples from this book are available online, see inside back cover for details.

PROC TABULATE in Simple Terms

Alan Davis

Introduction

Consider, if you will, the statistical table. It stands somewhere between text and graphics in its ability to summarize data. In text, when the numbers become too numerous, authors are encouraged to summarize them in a table. Tables can be more concise than graphics, and also more precise when specific numbers need to be reported.

A table consists of one or more rows of numbers. Each row falls on one printed line; table entries which are vertically aligned are referred to as columns. Tables may be numbered in their order of reference in a text. The title of a table describes its contents, and should make clear which set of data is being summarized, and the meaning of the numbers in the table. For the sake of clarity, units should be presented explicitly in the body of the table if they cannot be summarized in the title, row, or column label.

This chapter gives directions for producing several kinds of statistical tables within the TABULATE procedure. The sections of this chapter are meant as an introduction to PROC TABULATE, including enough information to easily produce tables which I have found very useful. Each section describes a particular type of table, then shows how to generate it by using PROC TABULATE.

PROC TABULATE is an extremely useful procedure because it allows convenient construction of tables for publication, or for a quick review of data. The user can see, all on one page, summaries that other procedures may require several pages and more effort to produce. Data do not have to be presented to TABULATE in sorted order. The procedure produces a customized report which puts together the statistics for the variables of interest. Since the process is automated there is no chance of introducing errors by scanning over several pages of printout and manually filling in a table.

PROC TABULATE can present statistics in any form from any number of variables. The body of the table may represent statistics such as counts, percentages, sums, percent of sums, means, variances, and formatted values such as dollars, dates, and discrete intervals.

Language syntax with PROC TABULATE is the same as with other procedures in SAS. PROC TABULATE reads a SAS data set and prints a table in the output stream. Statements in PROC TABULATE include VAR, which identifies quantitative variables, and CLASS, which identifies categorical variables. VAR variables are those which are to be analyzed for mean or other characteristics of a continuous distribution, whereas CLASS variables designate distinct classes for categorization.

The TABLE statement determines the actual content of the table. SAS FORMATS are also very important in the creation of useful tables.

Comparing Group Means With Overall Mean

A very common example of the TABULATE output is a side-by-side comparison of group means with an overall mean of a variable. For instance, if you have three levels of a stimulus and want to compare mean response with the overall mean for three groups, the following table would suffice:

Table 1. Comparison of responses for each level with overall mean RESPONSE, msec.

	RESPONSE
	MEAN
LEVEL	
1	22.00
2	46.00
3	31.00
ALL	33.00

The SAS statements required to do this are:

```
PROC TABULATE;
VAR RESPONSE;
CLASS LEVEL;
TABLE LEVEL ALL, RESPONSE * MEAN;
RUN;
```

The second statement is the VAR statement; it designates RESPONSE as the variable to be analyzed. The next is a CLASS statement used to identify variables having categorical values. The LEVEL variable indicates which level of stimulus has been applied. The TABLE statement defines the operations to be done and defines the rows and columns. The keyword ALL indicates that the overall mean is printed following the means for each level. The comma separates the row from the column definition. The column for this table is the mean of the response variable.

To produce the result shown in Table 1, use your own data set or key in the following DATA step and then use the TABULATE statements.

```
DATA A;
INPUT LEVEL RESPONSE;
CARDS;
1 21
1 23
2 41
2 51
3 33
3 29
;
```

Obtaining Counts and Percents of a Sample

Suppose you have a set of data in which people are classified by age and skill. The variable AGE consists of three categories, 9, 10, and 11, and SKILL consists of levels A for above average and B for below average.

You want to show the trend of skill with age and the number and percent of people in each category, with age going down the column and skill going across. The table would appear as:

Table 2. Number and percent in each category.

	SKILL			
	A		B	
	N	PCTN	N	PCTN
AGE				
9	3.00	9.09	8.00	24.24
10	4.00	12.12	7.00	21.21
11	5.00	15.15	6.00	18.18

The SAS statements that create this table are included as follows:

```
DATA B;
DO SKILL= 'A' , 'B';
DO AGE= 9 TO 11;
INPUT WT @@;
OUTPUT;
END;
END;
CARDS;
  3 4 5 8 7  6
PROC TABULATE;
FREQ WT;
CLASS SKILL AGE;
TABLE AGE, SKILL*(N PCTN);
RUN;
```

In PROC TABULATE, the FREQ statement is used to identify WT as a variable that determines the frequency of each observation. The key words N and PCTN request that the statistics COUNT and percent of TOTAL N be presented for each category.

You can modify the above code to produce column percent with the following:

```
TABLE AGE, SKILL*(N PCTN<SKILL>);
```

Then modify the code to produce row percent with the following:

```
TABLE AGE, SKILL*(N PCTN<AGE>);
```

Producing Statistical Summaries of Subgroups (Ranges)

The previous sections have shown how to present means and percentages using PROC TABULATE. Often, however, the variable's range (variance, standard deviation, standard error of the mean) is of interest. Remembering that the purpose of a table is to be concise yet adequate in summarizing data, suppose you want to know the variability of a sample, and that you want to present its standard deviation, minimum and maximum, along with its mean and sample size. Suppose that the variables are systolic and diastolic blood pressure. Here is a table showing those ranges.

Table 3. A table describing mean and variability of blood pressure in mm Hg.

	N	MEAN	STD	MIN
SBP	2.00	135.50	19.09	122.00
DBP	2.00	84.50	4.95	81.00

(Continued)

	MAX
SBP	149.00
DBP	88.00

The following code produces Table 3:

```
DATA BPRESS;
INPUT DBP SBP;
CARDS;
88 149
81 122
PROC TABULATE;
VAR SBP DBP;
TABLE SBP DBP, N MEAN STD MIN MAX;
RUN;
```

Note that Table 3 is continued because of lack of space to print all of the columns in the table. To remedy this use the RTS Row Title Space option of the TABLE statement to get all the column on one line. Since the variable names DBP and SBP are three characters long, use RTS=5 to adequately fit the row titles. Furthermore, you can expand the column headers using the KEYLABEL statement, which assigns labels to keywords and in the TABLE statement. The following table results:

Table 4. An improvement on Table 3.

	SAMPLE SIZE	MEAN	STANDARD DEVIATION	MINIMUM	MAXIMUM
SBP	2.00	135.50	19.09	122.00	149.00
DBP	2.00	84.50	4.95	81.00	88.00

The SAS statements that produce this table are:

```
PROC TABULATE;
VAR SBP DBP;
KEYLABEL N='SAMPLE SIZE' STD='STANDARD DEVIATION' MIN='MINIMUM'
MAX='MAXIMUM';
TABLE SBP DBP, N MEAN STD MIN MAX/RTS=5;
RUN;
```

The data set is the same used to produce Table 3.

Assume that the table is to go into a report and the table rule lines are to be eliminated. The FORMCHAR= option in the PROC TABULATE statement will allow you to specify the vertical and horizontal lines and the corner characters used in tables. This is well described in Chapter 37, "The TABULATE Procedure," in SAS Procedures Guide, Version 6, Third Edition. In this case we want simply to eliminate the rule lines, and designate these characters as blanks. In the PROC statement insert 11 blanks for the option:

```
PROC TABULATE FORMCHAR='
```

Now the table appears as follows:

Table 5. Table 4 without ruled lines.

	SAMPLE SIZE	MEAN	STANDARD DEVIATION	MINIMUM	MAXIMUM
SBP	2.00	135.50	19.09	122.00	149.00
DBP	2.00	84.50	4.95	81.00	88.00

Finally, the table can be improved using LABEL statements to better describe variables. For instance, you can use LABEL SBP='Systolic' DBP='Diastolic'; however, you will then need to adjust RTS to 11.

Dealing With Missing Data

Users often ask, "What happened to my data? I have 100 observations and the table shows only 80!" If some of the variables in your CLASS statement have missing values, TABULATE considers the whole observation to be missing. Thus, even if the particular table does not contain this variable, the table is affected.

This situation is remedied by excluding these variable names on the CLASS statements. A simple rule to follow is: "If it's not on the table statement, don't put it on the CLASS statement." Missing values for VAR variables can be reported with one of the options of the TABLE statement, NMISS.

If you want to know how many observations have the missing value for a CLASS variable, use the MISSING option in the PROC TABULATE statement. The following table shows an example of a cross-tabulation of CLASS variables DISEASE and RISK. Because of missing values of a third variable X which is included in the CLASS statement, the table appears to summarize only three observations.

Table 6. A table depleted by missing values.

	RISK	
	0	1
	N	N
DISEASE		
0	1.00	1.00
1	1.00	

Actually the data set contains nine observations:

```
DATA MISS;
INPUT DISEASE RISK X @@;
CARDS;
0 1 1   1 0 1  0 0 1
1 1 .   0 1 .  1 1 .
1 0 .   0 0 .  1 1 .

PROC TABULATE;
CLASS DISEASE RISK X;
TABLE DISEASE, RISK;
RUN;
```

If you remove X from the CLASS statement and submit the code, Table 7 results. The table reveals the correct classification of the nine observations:

Table 7. The missing observations restored.

	RISK	
	0	1
	N	N
DISEASE		
0	2.00	2.00
1	2.00	3.00

Table 8. Missing categories included using MISSING option.

	RISK	
	0	1
	N	N
DISEASE		
.		1.00
0	2.00	1.00
1	2.00	3.00

In Table 8 a missing classification is shown for the variable disease. This is reported by the following example, which shows the MISSING option in the PROC TABULATE statement:

```
DATA MISS;
INPUT DISEASE RISK X @@;
CARDS;
. 1 3.   1 0 2. 0 0 1.
1 1 .   0 1 . 1 1 .
1 0 .   0 0 . 1 1 .
PROC TABULATE MISSING;
CLASS DISEASE RISK X ;
TABLE DISEASE, RISK;
RUN;
```

Creating Cutpoints For Classifying A Sample

It is often necessary to form groups from an essentially continuous variable. Table 9, for instance, compares counts of the sample divided into 4 age groups. Since AGE is a quantitative variable, it is assigned cutpoints by PROC FORMAT so that the desired grouping is achieved.

Table 9. Formatted values of AGE produce categories for analysis.

AGE			
10 to 20	20 to 40	40 to 65	65 and up
N	N	N	N
3.00	9.00	11.00	4.00

The following SAS statements create Table 9:

```
DATA AGEDIST;
INPUT AGE WT @@;
CARDS;
19 3 27 4 33 5 54 4 59 3 63 4 74 3 83 1
PROC FORMAT;
VALUE AGE 10-<20 = '10 TO 20'
                   20-<40 = '20 TO 40'
                   40-<65 = '40 TO 65'
                   65-<999= '65 AND UP'

;
PROC TABULATE;
CLASS AGE;
FORMAT AGE AGE.;
TABLE AGE;
FREQ WT;
```

The variable WT is used as a frequency variable, and its presence in the FREQ statement causes the value to be repeated that number of times. Note: WEIGHT statement is also available to allow for determination of weighted mean, or standard deviation.

The table also illustrates that the FORMAT procedure is indispensable in making TABULATE's tables more readable. Table 9 has the simplest of all table statements. It puts the age categories along columns. To designate a row, you specify a second dimension in the TABLE statement. The following statement designates AGE to divide the table into rows, and specifies N to occupy the columns.

```
TABLE AGE,N ;
RUN;
```

Table 10 results:

Table 10. A simple columnar table.

	N
AGE	
10 to 20	3.00
20 to 40	9.00
40 to 65	11.00
65 and up	4.00

When the Units are Dollars

Financial data needs to be reported in a form that puts in commas to make the numbers easier to read. SAS formats include both COMMA w.d. and DOLLAR w.d. to do just this. The following table uses the same data set used in Table 10 to present mean values of budgets:

Table 11. Formatting to make a more readable display.

	WT
	MEAN
AGE	
10 to 20	$300,000.00
20 to 40	$450,000.00
40 to 65	$366,666.67
65 and up	$200,000.00

The following SAS statements use the AGEDIST data set to create Table 11:

```
DATA;
SET;
WT=WT*100000;
PROC TABULATE;
VAR WT;
CLASS AGE;
FORMAT AGE AGE.;
TABLE AGE, WT*MEAN*F=DOLLAR12.2;
RUN;
```

Summary

This chapter has shown only a few examples of how to use the TABULATE procedure to produce statistical tables. Many more features of this useful procedure remain for you to explore after you have tried these examples. See the references in the next section for some starting points.

References

SAS Institute Inc. (1988), SAS Procedures Guide, Version 6, Third Edition, Cary, NC: SAS Institute Inc.

SAS Institute Inc. (1990), SAS Guide to Tabulate Processing, Second Edition, Cary, NC: SAS Institute Inc.

For Further Reading

The American Psychological Association Publications Manual, (1983), Washington DC.

Braverman, J.D., and Stewart, W.D. (1973), Statistics for Business and Economics, Ronald Press. This is a good source for reading about tables.

Brusaw, C.T., Alred, G. J., and Oliu, W.E. (1982), Handbook of Technical Writing, New York, NY: St. Martin's Press.

Iverson, Cheryl (1989), American Medical Association Manual of Style, Chicago, IL: American Medical Association.

CHAPTER 9

Character-Based Graphics: New Uses for Old Technologies

by Frank C. DiIorio

Abstract

"Graphics" has come to be synonymous with high-resolution, bit-mapped images. Colorful and informative, they often carry a steep price in terms of computer resources and programmer expertise. A simpler form of graphic display often falls in the shadow of high-resolution images. These are character-based graphics displayable on line and page-printing devices. This class of graphic presentation has much to recommend from the viewpoint of computer resource utilization and effective communication of ideas. This chapter discusses the effective use of character-based graphics. It describes the tool set required for their use and provides many examples of how to design and code attractive, informative reports.

Specifications

The code in this chapter was developed and tested with Releases 6.07 and 6.08 of the SAS System under the Windows environment. Use of the code with other releases of the SAS System or other environments may require user modification. Modified code is not supported by the author.

About the Author

Frank C. DiIorio is Director of Systems Development for ASG, Inc. in Cary, North Carolina. He has a BA degree in Sociology/Economics from the University of Pennsylvania and an MRP degree in City Planning from the University of North Carolina, Chapel Hill. A SAS user for over 19 years, his areas of expertise include data management, program/system tuning, user interface development, and macro language. He is the author of *SAS Applications Programming: A Gentle Introduction*, which presents the basics of the SAS System for the beginning or intermediate user. His second book, *Statistical Computing: An Introduction Using SAS*, is scheduled for publication in early 1995. Currently Frank is co-chair of the 1994 SouthEast SAS Users Group Conference.

Questions and Comments Should be Directed to:

Frank C. DiIorio
ASG, Inc.
2000 Regency Parkway, Suite 355
Cary, NC 27511
Telephone: 919-467-0505

Character-Based Graphics: New Uses for Old Technologies

Frank C. DiIorio

Introduction

The term "computer graphics" has become synonymous with colorful, high-resolution images. These images are often informative and usually carry a steep price in terms of computer hardware and user expertise. Lost in the bit-mapped blizzard of information is a traditional display medium, that of character-based graphics (versus pixel-based graphics) displayable on line or page-printing devices. This class of graphic presentation still has much to offer and may be crafted with a small and straightforward set of base SAS software tools.

This chapter discusses the effective use of character-based graphics. It identifies the benefits of their use, notes the tasks for which they are most appropriate, and describes the toolset required to use them. Program fragments and several comprehensive examples illustrate a variety of simple but powerful techniques for presenting a variety of data. You should come away from this discussion with a clear understanding of the advantages of character-based graphics, how to integrate them into a report generated by SAS, and how to best use the tools available in base SAS.

Graphic Benefits

The ideal graphic presentation, be it bit-mapped or character-based, has several advantages over its numbers and text counterpart. Edward Tufte, in his classic *The Visual Display of Quantitative Information,* succinctly summarizes the strengths of graphical displays and, indirectly, identified the deficiencies of traditional number and text reports. Graphics, says Tufte, should present many numbers in a small space, make large sets of data coherent, encourage comparison of different data items, and serve the purposes of data description, exploration, tabulation, and decoration. Presentation technique is important. Tufte notes that the display should avoid distorting the data and should focus the reader's attention on the *substance* of the chart rather than its *technique* (1983, pages 13-15). Good graphic technique is like a good waiter in a restaurant: effective yet not obtrusive.

Even if a picture is worth a thousand words, however, most people still feel some degree of comfort when presented with a picture *and* some supplemental text or numbers. In the ideal report, you would be able to spot a trend or an anomaly quickly by referring to a graphic and supplement this information with the underlying data values. Consider the case of a report summarizing financial activity for a branch of a bank. It might contain bar charts of key indicators for the last "x" weeks, the numeric values of the indicators, and background information. The bar charts facilitate a quick, visual comparison of the indicators, the numbers lend precision to the bars, and the background information such as historical trends and competitor information give context to the indicators.

Why Character-Based Graphics?

But isn't SAS/GRAPH software the proper vehicle for graphics? Often it is, and it posesses capabilities with respect to color and drawing which are simply not possible with character-based graphics. However, SAS/GRAPH and the Data Step Graphics Interface (DSGI) have several potential pitfalls:

- Difficult to use. The syntax of SAS/GRAPH, the DSGI, and annotation data sets is nonintuitive and complex. Even simple displays can require significant programmer resources. SAS/ASSIST software simplifies the process somewhat, but at the cost of reduced control over the display.
- Limited availability. SAS/GRAPH is a supplemental product and may not be licensed in all installations.

- Resource intensive. Graphics are, by nature, resource intensive. The sheer speed of production of hard copy may be a limiting factor when large numbers of charts are being created.
- Potential overkill. If all that is needed is a quick visual take on what is happening with the data, elaborate graphic displays may be overkill. Many "real world" scenarios may need only simple base SAS procedure output or basic DATA step programming.

Character-based graphics address some of these liabilities and offer some incentives of their own:

- Suited to the task. Character-based graphics may be sufficient for many analysis needs. Indeed, they are well suited for implementation of displays that are not readily duplicated in the graphics environment.
- Universal. One of the strengths of the character-based graphic approach is its simplicity. The techniques may be implemented on any SAS platform and version and displayed on any line or page printer. In a similar vein, the output may be viewed with any text file viewer or editor. No special graphic translation programs are required. This device independence ensures portability of code.
- Effective. Many graphic elements can be attractively displayed with a minimum of coding. Large reports can be produced with little programmer or hardware resource consumption.

Coding Strategy

The techniques described later in this chapter require DATA step coding. Whenever such coding is required you are well advised to avoid the impulse to jump into the task and begin coding. Consider two basic features of your task as a conveyor of information. Specifically, *what* you want to communicate and *how* it should appear in printed form. *What* does the report need to communicate? The value of a variable for the current month? The current month and several preceding months? The change between the months? The deviation between actual and projected values?

How should these values be presented? As bar charts? As a date-oriented "time line"? With both the graphic element and the actual number present? If possible, look to, but don't be constrained by existing reports for presentation ideas.

Once the general format has been determined, it is always prudent to evaluate SAS procedures to see if they produce all or part of the report. Procedures such as CHART, REGRESSION, FREQ, and TIMEPLOT integrate numeric and graphic elements. If your reporting needs are met by the procedures or if you can adjust them to meet the procedures' capabilities, you have saved yourself some work. If not, it's time to start coding the report.

At the most basic level, a report-writing DATA step simply passes a SAS data set through a "filter" (PUT statements) which makes it presentable to the reader. Separate these aspects of the report-writing process. First, sketch the report. Identify headers, footers, subtotals, and detail lines. Consider how the detail lines will be presented. Will more than one observation from the analysis data set contribute to a line in the report? Will the reverse occur? That is, will a single observation from the data set require multiple lines? If either answer is yes, the report's code will likely need to use DATA step features which, among other activities, retain observations' values across observations and keep track of line numbers. These features are discussed and used in examples below.

Next, consider what data preparation needs to be done. In the ideal case, all data "massaging" should be done in previous DATA steps and procedures. For example, the data may need to be sorted. The report may require comparison of individual observations with population or group statistics. These activities are readily handled by procedures such as SORT, SQL, MEANS, and UNIVARIATE. Such preprocessing of the data focuses the work being done in the report-writing DATA step and ultimately makes the program easier to debug and enhance, since the code is less cluttered.

The actual coding and debugging of the DATA step can be simplified if the program handles the report elements separately and in the correct sequence. Timing, critical in traditional reports, is even more important here. Processing at the start of the data set (_N_ = 1) should be performed first, followed by any BY-group processing. If a background graphic element such as a row of dashes is being displayed for the observation, it should be printed or initialized before writing the actual graphic elements. The actual data points, or graphic elements, should be displayed. Writing them last ensures that they will not be overwritten by other graphics. Finally, BY group and end-of-file processing should take place.

The Report-Writing Toolset

Relatively few tools are needed to produce a wide variety of reports. This section presents a brief overview of these DATA step statements and then briefly addresses some pertinent printer-related issues. Space considerations require that the section simply identify the statements, options, and features. It is not meant to be an exhaustive description of the syntax or the feature's use in non-graphic applications. For more detailed treatment of the material, refer to *SAS Language and Procedures: Usage, Version 6, First Edition* and *SAS Language: Reference, Version 6, First Edition.*

FILE Statement Options

The FILE statement identifies the location of the report and specifies options which control the report's appearance. A few options especially useful for graphic report writing are described in the following table:

Table 1: FILE Statement Report-Writing Options

Option	Syntax	Usage
N	N=nlines N=PS	Makes "nlines" lines available to PUT statement line pointer. A value of PS allows PUT to reference any location on the page. Helpful when you need to write "snaking" or newspaper-style columns or when exact print locations are determined at run time.
LINESLEFT LL	LL=var	Stores remaining lines to print on the page in variable "var." Use this when a graphic element contains more than one line and cannot be split across pages.
PS	PS=num	Sets the number of lines available for printing on a page to "num" lines. The number can be a numeric constant or a macro variable which resolves to a positive number.
LS	LS=num	Sets the number of columns available for printing on a page to "num" positions. Like the "num" value for PS above, it may be a numeric constant or macro variable value.
PRINT	PRINT	Gives the report file print file characteristics such as page feeds. This option can only be used when N is 1 or PS.

PUT Statement Features

The PUT statement writes ("puts") characters to the file or device specified by the FILE statement. Some of its features especially relevant to graphic report writing are summarized in the following table:

Table 2: PUT Statement Report-Writing Features

Feature	Syntax	Usage
Trailing @	@ ;	Prevents SAS from releasing the current line once the PUT statement completes execution. Useful when more than one PUT statement is needed to write a single line.
@ column pointer	@col @(expression)	Positions the column pointer to a predetermined column ("col") or to the column which is the result of "expression". Only the integer portion of the value is used. Thus values of 17.01 and 17.87 would each result in the pointer being moved to column 17. No message is written to the SAS Log if truncation of the value occurs.

Table 2: PUT Statement Report-Writing Features *(continued)*

Feature	Syntax	Usage
# line pointer	#line #(expression)	Analagous to the @ pointer, but for the vertical, line number orientation of the report. The value of "line" or "expression" should be greater than 0 and less than the value of PS specified in the FILE statement (see the preceding section, "FILE Statement Options").
Repetition factor	n*"char"	Writes "n" repetitions of the character "char." Useful when you need to write background graphic elements or borders (such as a line of dashes or underscores). The following PUT statement, for example, writes a line of 6 underscores: `put 6*"_";`
OVERPRINT	OVERPRINT	Rather than *replacing* a character at a given position by writing on top of it, OVERPRINT indicates that the character be written *in addition to* any existing characters. The result is useful for creating darkened print cells and other effects not readily available in the standard operating system character sets.

Functions

In many situations the majority of the report-writing task is consumed by calculating the location of the display's symbols. Bars in charts need to fit in the available display space, data points need to be assigned to row and column locations by use of truncation or rounding, and so on. This section describes some of the numeric and character functions which can be used for graphic report writing:

Table 3: Functions for Graphic Report Writing

Option	Syntax	Usage
REPEAT	REPEAT(pattern, #times)	Repeats character variable or constant "pattern" "#times," yielding a string of "#times" plus the original string. Useful for writing background graphic elements in a chart.
SUBSTR	SUBSTR(var, st, count)	SUBSTR can be used to replace a portion of a string. Useful when the report row is contained in a character variable and the observation's data point of interest needs to be set to a specified character. The SUBSTR function can change position "st" for "count" of 1 position to the required character.
INT	INT(var)	Extracts the integer portion of a floating point number. Useful when you want to highlight the implicit truncation of the @ and # pointers.
MIN, MAX, RANGE	MIN(varlist) MAX(varlist) RANGE(varlist)	Identifies the minimum, maximum, and range of values for variables "varlist" in an observation. Useful when you need to determine the bounds of a display on an observation-by-observation basis.

Other DATA Step Features

Virtually any DATA step statement can be found in a report-writing program, especially those which are complex. Some statements and features, however, tend to be used in all but the most basic reports. They are described below.

Table 4: Common DATA Step Features for Report Writing

Feature	Usage
_N_	Automatic variable containing the number of times the DATA statement has been executed (usually equals the observation number being processed). Especially useful at the beginning of the DATA step (_N_ = 1), when you need to initialize values and assign values which will not change during execution of the DATA step.

Table 4: Common DATA Step Features for Report Writing *(continued)*

Feature	Usage
END=eof_var	As either a SET, MERGE, UPDATE or INFILE option, sets "eof_var" to 1 when the end of the SAS data set or raw data set has been reached. Useful when you need to display text and graphics to a report.
RETAIN	Prevents the default reset to "missing" of a variable at the beginning of execution of the DATA step for an observation. Useful when you need to accumulate values across observations (counters, flags, and the like).

PROCs

The majority of the graphic report-writing task takes place in DATA steps. However, as previously noted, the ideal situation for the programmer writing the report is that the DATA step need only concern itself with the actual writing of the report. That is, all necessary data manipulation and summary statistics are already calculated. Several SAS procedures (PROCs) can perform data summarization and create macro variables and output data sets. They are described in the following table:

Table 5: PROCS for Report Writing

PROC	Usage
MEANS	Creates an output data set containing summary statistics for one or more variables. User has the ability to specify summarization for one or more classification variables. The summarized, MEANS output data set can be used for the report writing. It can also be merged with individual observations to determine deviation from a group statistic (e.g., individual's income versus average income for that person's sex and age).
UNIVARIATE	Similar to MEANS, but with a somewhat greater variety of statistics which can be output (notably median and percentiles).
SQL	(Version 6.06 or later.) Structured Query Language. Can perform complex data manipulation with relatively few statements. Output can be SAS data sets or, unlike MEANS and UNIVARIATE, macro variables.

FORMAT	Custom formats can be used to map character and numeric values to a graphic equivalent. Values can be mapped one-to-one or many-to-one, the formatted value equal to a graphic element such as a histogram bar. The following code fragment illustrates this technique:
	`proc format;`
	`value hist  0-10 = '*---'`
	`           11-20 = '**--'`
	`           21-30 = '***-' ;`
	When the HIST format is assigned to the analysis variable, values are displayed as the graphic elements to the right of the equals sign. PICTURE formats may, in some circumstances, be preferable, since they can display the graphic and the actual data value.

Macros and Macro Variables

Reports are rarely static, once-used entitites. Data and the handling of the display space usually vary over time. For example, background data may enhance and give context to a report describing financial trends. You may want to constrain the display of data to a specified range. The report may contain several elements (bar charts summarizing data for a subject and separate displays for each transactionfor a subject).

The obvious, but brute force and error-prone way to vary the presentation of the report is to modify the program code in the DATA step and any associated procedures used to write the report. A more palatable alternative is to use macros and macro variables. Their use can be simple: a macro variable can be used repeatedly through the report-writing code to specify the month for which the report is written. The use of the macro facility can become far more complex: portions of the report can be selectively included and use of printer-dependent features such as shading and bolding can be requested. A few high-level examples here and in the longer examples later in this chapter should give a hint of their usage and power.

Example

Suppose a report is run periodically and uses data for the current month. By default, it displays data points along a horizontal line whose endpoints are the minimum and maximum values for an analysis variable. This display line is, by default, 50 columns long.

Each of these aspects of the report may need to be changed: it could be run against data for a user-specified month; the display may need to be constrained to a particular range of values; the line used for the display may need to be more than the default of 50 print positions to display the data in greater detail. The macro language provides a convenient and relatively straightforward means to make these changes without continual modification to the code. The abstracted program follows. Actions described but not actually coded are displayed in *italics*:

```
%macro rpt(month=, min=, max=, width=50);

parameter checking - both min and max should be either
                     present or missing
                   - width should be in range

%if &min ^= %str( ) %then %do;
    execute SQL procedure to write macro variables MIN
    and MAX
    %end;

data _null_;
%if &month ^= %str( ) %then %do;
    set sasdata.tran&month.;
    %end;
    %else %do;
          %let curr = %substr(&sysdate., 3);
          set sasdata.tran&curr.;
          %end;

retain displine $ &width;

if _n_ = 1 then displine = repeat('-', &width.-1);

if &min. <= analysis_variable <= &max. then do;
   display area &WIDTH print positions long
   end;

run;
%mend;

%rpt(month=0394, min=120, max=250, width=60);
```

The power of the macro language becomes evident even with this simple example. If you specify the range of values to plot (MIN and MAX parameters) you avoid the potentially costly and time-consuming execution of the SQL procedure. The program automatically selects the current month if none is explicitly specified. The display line variable DISPLINE is created and retained using a default width of 50 or the override value supplied by the user. All references to the line width (the RETAIN and DISPLINE assignment statements) use the correct line size -- if the values were coded and changed manually, there would be the possibility of a change being made in the RETAIN statement but not in the assignment. Using macro variables ensures consistency and accuracy.

Printer and System-Dependent Features

One of the attractions of character-based graphics noted earlier in the chapter was device independence. Reports can be as readily printed on a 9-pin dot matrix printer as a high-end mainframe laser printer.

There are situations, however, which call for exploiting the talents and capabilities of a specific printer. These capabilities vary significantly from printer to printer. The command languages usually let you perform activities such as bolding, italicizing, font changing. This is done via transmission of an “escape sequence,” an escape character (Hex 1B or decimal 27) followed by a string of command codes and, possibly, data values describing the activity. Some codes are typically turned on at the beginning of a program and never reset (page orientation, for example), while others are usually turned on, followed by some text, and turned off again (such as bolding).

Writing programs which use the printer's commands sacrifices portability. A program which produces boldface output on a Hewlett Packard LaserJet IIP will not produce the same output on an Epson dot matrix printer unless the control codes for bolding are rewritten in the Epson's control language. A complete treatment of the different command sets is beyond the scope of this chapter, but the following section illustrates the implementation of a common task using a popular printer's command language. You will see that a properly constructed program can use escape sequences effectively with minimal loss of device independence.

The LaserJet IIP Example

The following program demonstrates the implementation of bolding for a Hewlett Packard IIP laser printer. The technique is straightforward: variables containing escape sequences are defined at the beginning of the DATA step (_N_ = 1) and retained. In this case, boldface on and boldface off variables are used (BOLDON and BOLDOFF).

The entire report-writing DATA step is contained in a macro. Macro IF-THEN logic allows selective inclusion of the escape sequences: if no printer is specified, the codes are not included in the PUT statement. This takes more time to code, but allows the report to be sent to *any* printer (minus, of course, the bold printing). As more printers need to be supported, the IF-THEN logic at the top of the program can be extended.

```
%macro rpt(device=);
%let device = %upcase(&device.);
data _null_;
set rpt;
file "esc_seq.lis" print notitles;
%if &device. = IIP %then %do;
     boldon  = '1b'x || "(s3B";     Hex 1B = escape
     boldoff = '1b'x || "(s0B";
     %end;

put low_ok 5. +2 high_ok 5. +2 actual @;
if actual < low_ok | actual > high_ok then put @20
   %if &device. ^= %str() %then boldon ;
   "<== value out of range!"
   %if &device. ^= %str() %then boldoff ;
   ;
   else put;
run;
%mend;

%rpt(device=IIP);
```

Coding Techniques

It would be a disservice to try in the space of one chapter to try to be comprehensive with a subject as broad in scope as graphics. What *can* be accomplished, though, is to give an idea of what's possible, particularly for displays not readily produced by standard graphics procedures. The following sections do that and also show how the tools described in the previous section may be applied.

Bear in mind that the code fragments shown below fall short of being complete, production-quality programs. Items such as column headings, footnotes, and supporting text and numbers are omitted. No checking is performed to test for conflict of parameters. *The focus is on code required to produce the graphic.*

Setup

Several small data sets were used for the examples. The following code shows the DATA steps for all the examples in the rest of this chapter.

```
Examples 1 through 7, 13
data one;
input size @@;
datalines;
10 8 9 12 13 14 15 16 40 30 150 130 120 120 125 .
run;

Examples 8 through 11
data dates;
input subject date date7. value value2;
datalines;
1 01jan94 12 15
1 12jan94  8  6
1 13jan94 20 10
1 15may94  8  5
2 11nov94 10  8
2 15mar94 30 15
2 20may94 25 20
2 02jul94  2  6
2 18sep94  4 10
2 20sep94  6 14
run;

Example 12
data case1;
infile cards;
length event $30;
input id date : date7. t0 t2 t4 event $ &;
datalines;
1 01jan94 5 4 . headache
1 15jan94 4 4 3 nausea
1 10feb94 5 3 1 severe cluster headaches
1 01mar94 3 3 2 headache
1 15mar94 4 2 1
1 17mar94 5 4 1 head hurts
1 02apr94 3 3 2 dizziness
1 10apr94 5 5 2 cramps
1 01jan95 5 4 . cramps
1 15jan95 4 4 3
1 10feb95 5 3 1 vertigo
1 01mar95 3 3 2
1 15mar95 4 2 1 head ache
1 17mar95 5 4 1
1 02apr95 3 3 2
1 10apr95 5 5 2
2 01jan94 5 5 4 dizziness
2 05jan94 . 5 3 felt dizzy
2 10jan94 . . 1 headache
2 15jan94 5 . 3
2  2feb94 2 2 4
2  1apr94 . . . unknown
run;
```

Several examples use macro variables containing descriptive statistics for the analysis data set (minimum, maximum, mean, range, standard deviation). Rather than compute these with the MEANS or UNIVARIATE procedures, the examples use the SQL procedure to create macro variables. This is the more elegant solution since it involves less coding (no merge of analysis and summary data sets is required) and is more efficient (macro variables are simply treated as constants in the DATA step). The SQL code follows:

```
MN: ex 1, 2
MX: ex 1, 2, 4, 5, 6, 7
MEAN: ex 4, 5, 6
RANGE: ex 1, 2, 4, 5, 6, 7
```

```
STD: ex 6 ;

proc sql noprint;
select min(size), max(size), range(size), mean(size), std(size)
  into :mn,        :mx,        :range,      :mean,       :std
  from one;
quit;
%put MN: &mn.  MX: &mx. RANGE: &range. MEAN: &mean. STD: &std. ;

Examples 8 and 10
proc sql noprint;
select min(date), max(date), range(date)
  into :datemin,  :datemax,  :daterng
  from dates;
quit;
%put DATEMIN: &datemin.  DATEMAX: &datemax.  DATERNG: &daterng. ;
```

Example 1

The value of a variable is displayed along a horizontal line. The line's endpoints are determined by an earlier invocation of the SQL procedure and represent the minimum and maximum values in the data set. The plot symbol, an asterisk (*), indicates the location along the minimum-maximum axis for an observation. Since we know the minimum and maximum values in the data set, we can display text to the right of the graph which highlights the extreme values. The length of the display line and its starting location are expressed as numeric constants. The location of the plot symbol is a fraction of the observation's value for the analysis variable relative to the range of the variable in the data set.

```
data _null_;
set one;
file 'ex01.txt' notitles;

if size ^= . then do;
   The obs is FRACT (.xx) of the length of the bar.
   fract = ((&range. - (&mx. - size)) / &range.);

   Now that we know how far along the bar, we can calculate
   the actual print location.
   loc = 10 + (fract * 49);

   put @1 size 5.    @10 50*'_'    @loc '*' @;
   if size = &mn.    then put @63 '<= min' @;
   if size = &mx.    then put @63 '<= max' @;
   if size = &mx. &
      size = &mn.    then put @63 '<= min/max' @;

   Release the pointer
   put;
   end;
run;
```

Output 1: Display Individual, Minimum and Maximum Values

```
   10    *_________________________________________________
    8    *_________________________________________________   <= min
    9    *_________________________________________________
   12    _*________________________________________________
   13    _*________________________________________________
   14    __*_______________________________________________
   15    __*_______________________________________________
   16    __*_______________________________________________
   40    ___________*______________________________________
   30    _______*__________________________________________
  150    _________________________________________________*   <= max
  130    __________________________________________*_______
  120    ______________________________________*___________
  120    ______________________________________*___________
  125    ________________________________________*_________
```

Example 2

Similar to Example 1, but more robust. Rather than express the display line size and starting location as constants, we assign them to variables and retain them using the RETAIN statement. This approach is simpler and less error prone than the original since changes only need to be made once, at the top of the program. Example 13, later in this chapter, uses macro variables to achieve the same effect. The advantage of using RETAIN becomes more apparent when writing long DATA steps.

The output is similar to Example 1 and does not need to be displayed again.

```
data _null_;
set one;
file 'ex02.txt' notitles;

RETAIN variables for display width and starting column
retain bar_size 50 st_col 10;
bar = repeat('_', bar_size-1);

if size ^= . then do;
   fract = ((&range. - (&mx. - size)) / &range.);
   loc = st_col + (fract * (bar_size -1));

   put @1 size 5.   @(st_col) bar @loc '*'
       @(st_col+bar_size+3) ' ' @;
   if size = &mn.   then put '<= min' @;
   if size = &mx.   then put '<= max' @;
   if size = &mx. &
      size = &mn.   then put '<= min/max' @;
   put;
   end;
run;
```

Example 3

Rather than let the program determine the minimum and maximum values for the display area, we manually set the boundaries. These are specified by variables in a RETAIN statement. If a variable has a value which falls outside the specified range, the special plot symbols "<" and ">" are displayed at the minimum and maximum plot positions, respectively. Unlike in Examples 1 and 2, in this example we need to calculate the range of the data in the DATA step. This needs to be done only once, in the "if _n_ = 1" DO group. This example is revisited in Example 13, which expands its capability by using a macro.

```
data _null_;
set one;
file 'ex03.txt' notitles;

retain bar_size 50 st_col 10;
RETAIN minimum and maximum values. These are the endpoints of the
display area (earlier examples had endpoints determined by the
data.
retain min 10 max 120  _range;

Range will be the same for each observation, so just calculate it at
the top of the data set. It will be RETAINed.
if _n_ = 1 then do;
   _range = max - min;
   end;

Create the bar
bar = repeat('_', bar_size-1);

if size ^= . then do;
   if size < min then do;
      If obs has a value below minimum allowed, set print position to
      first column of display area and use a special print symbol.
      loc = st_col;
      symbol = '<';
      end;
      else if size > max then do;
           If obs has a value above maximum allowed, set print pos.
```

```
            to last column of display area and use a special print
            symbol.
            loc = st_col + (bar_size - 1);
            symbol = '>';
            end;
        else do;
            If here, we have a valid (in-range) value of analysis
            variable SIZE.
            fract = (_range - (max - size)) / _range;
            loc   = st_col + (fract * (bar_size - 1)) ;
            symbol= '*';
            end;

    put @1 size 5.  @(st_col) bar   @loc symbol;
    end;
run;
```

Output 2: Restrict Range of Plotted Variables

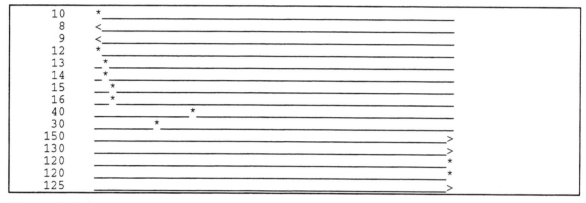

```
   10     *_________________________________________________
    8     <_________________________________________________
    9     <_________________________________________________
   12     *_________________________________________________
   13     _*________________________________________________
   14     _*________________________________________________
   15     __*_______________________________________________
   16     __*_______________________________________________
   40     ________________*_________________________________
   30     __________*_______________________________________
  150     _________________________________________________>
  130     _________________________________________________>
  120     _________________________________________________*
  120     _________________________________________________*
  125     _________________________________________________>
```

Example 4

Two variables are printed per observation. The first variable is the mean of a variable across the entire data set, calculated earlier in the SQL procedure. It is displayed with the plot symbol “P”. The other variable is the individual observation's value of the variable, displayed with an “O”. Since the population value's print location will be the same for each observation, we calculate it when _N_ is 1 and retain the value (variable LOC_P). Note the sequence of writing the variables. “P” is displayed first, thus giving an “O” value the chance to overwrite it.

```
data _null_;
set one;
file 'ex04.txt' notitles;

retain bar_size 50 st_col 10;
LOC_P is the print location of the population mean.
retain loc_p;

Calculate print location of population mean only once. Do it at the
top of the data set and RETAIN it.
if _n_ = 1 then do;
   fract_p = ((&range. - (&mx. - &mean.)) / &range.);
   loc_p   = st_col + (fract_p * (bar_size -1));
   end;

bar = repeat('_', bar_size-1);

if size ^= . then do;
   fract_o = ((&range. - (&mx. - size))   / &range.);
   loc_o   = st_col + (fract_o * (bar_size -1));
   put @1        size 5.
       @(st_col) bar
       @loc_p    'P'
       @loc_o    'O' ;   by writing obs. value after population
                         value, we give it the opportunity to
                         overwrite it
   end;
run;
```

Output 3: Display Two Variables Per Observation

```
   10   O_______________P______________________________________
    8   O_______________P______________________________________
    9   O_______________P______________________________________
   12   _O______________P______________________________________
   13   _O______________P______________________________________
   14   __O_____________P______________________________________
   15   __O_____________P______________________________________
   16   __O_____________P______________________________________
   40   ____________O___P______________________________________
   30   _______O________P______________________________________
  150   ________________P______________________________________O
  130   ________________P__________________________________O______
  120   ________________P__________________________O______________
  120   ________________P__________________________O______________
  125   ________________P______________________________O__________
```

Example 5

This example resembles Example 4, but emphasizes the difference between the mean and individual observations. We calculate the difference between the mean and the observation's value of the analysis variable. Then we express the difference in print positions (variable OBSBARSZ). Finally, we display the bar to the right or left of the population print position if the observation's value is greater than or less than the mean. The population indicator, a vertical bar (|), is printed last to emphasize the focus of the chart. This technique is a simple, visually appealing way to highlight differences from a reference point. Notice that rather than the mean, the reference point could have been an expected value or a range of values.

```
data _null_;
set one;
file 'ex05.txt' notitles;

length obs_bar $50;
retain bar_size 50 st_col 10 loc_p;
if _n_ = 1 then do;
   fract_p = ((&range. - (&mx. - &mean.)) / &range.);
   loc_p   = floor(st_col + (fract_p * (bar_size -1)));
   end;

if size ^= . then do;
   bar = repeat('_', bar_size-1);

   fract_o = ((&range. - (&mx. - size))   / &range.);
   loc_o   = floor(st_col + (fract_o * (bar_size -1)));

   How many print positions is the bar?
   obsbarsz = abs(loc_p - loc_o);
   Create the bar
   obs_bar  = repeat('*', obsbarsz - 1);
   Leave print position of the observation bar alone if less than
   population print location. Otherwise, adjust the print location so
   that it starts immediately after the population print location.
   That is, does the bar go to the left or right of the population
   print symbol? ;
   if loc_o > loc_p then loc_o = loc_p + 1;

   put @1        size 5.
       @(st_col) bar
       @loc_o    obs_bar
       @loc_p    '|'
       ;
   end;
run;
```

Output 4: Display Emphasizes Difference Between Mean and Observation

```
     10     ***************|__________________________________
      8     ***************|__________________________________
      9     ***************|__________________________________
     12     _**************|__________________________________
     13     _**************|__________________________________
     14     __*************|__________________________________
     15     __*************|__________________________________
     16     __*************|__________________________________
     40     ___________****|__________________________________
     30     _______********|__________________________________
    150     _______________|**********************************
    130     _______________|***************************_______
    120     _______________|***********************___________
    120     _______________|***********************___________
    125     _______________|*************************_________
```

Example 6

This example displays data at the observation level but with two reference points. The report shows an observation's value relative to values around the data set mean. In this case, the boundaries are plus and minus one standard deviation from the mean. Since plus or minus one deviation may fall outside the display area, they are plotted with the special symbols "[" and "]". Notice that the plot symbols and locations for the deviations are constant throughout the data set. This allows us to perform the calculations only once, when _N_ is 1, and RETAIN their values.

```
data _null_;
set one;
file 'ex06.txt' notitles;

retain bar_size 50 st_col 10 plus1 minus1 meanloc;
retain pluschr '>' minuschr '<';

if _n_ = 1 then do;
   Determine size of gap between Mean and Standard Deviation
   back     = &mean. - &std.;

   What is print location for the Mean?
   frac    = (&range. - (&mx. - &mean.)) / &range. ;
   meanloc = st_col + (frac * (bar_size-1));

   Translate this difference into print positions
   fracback = (&range. - (&mx. - back)) / &range.;
   minus1   = floor(st_col + (fracback * (bar_size - 1)));
   if minus1 < st_col then do;
      If one standard deviation below the mean falls outside the
      data range adjust print symbol and set print location to the
      start of the display area.
      minuschr = '[';
      minus1   = st_col;
      end;

   Similar logic to previous statements, only for one SD above the
   Mean.
   ahead    = &mean. + &std.;
   fracforw = (&range. - (&mx. - ahead)) / &range.;
   plus1    = floor(st_col + (fracforw * (bar_size -1)));
   if plus1 > st_col + bar_size then do;
      pluschr = ']';
      plus1   = st_col + bar_size;
      end;
   end;

bar = repeat('_', bar_size-1);

if size ^= . then do;
   fract = (&range. - (&mx. - size)) / &range.;

   loc = st_col + (fract * (bar_size -1));
   put @(st_col) bar
```

```
        @minus1    minuschr
        @plus1     pluschr
        @meanloc   '|'
        @loc       '*'
        @1         size 5.;
    end;
run;
```

Output 5: Display Observation Plus Group Measures (Mean, Standard Deviation)

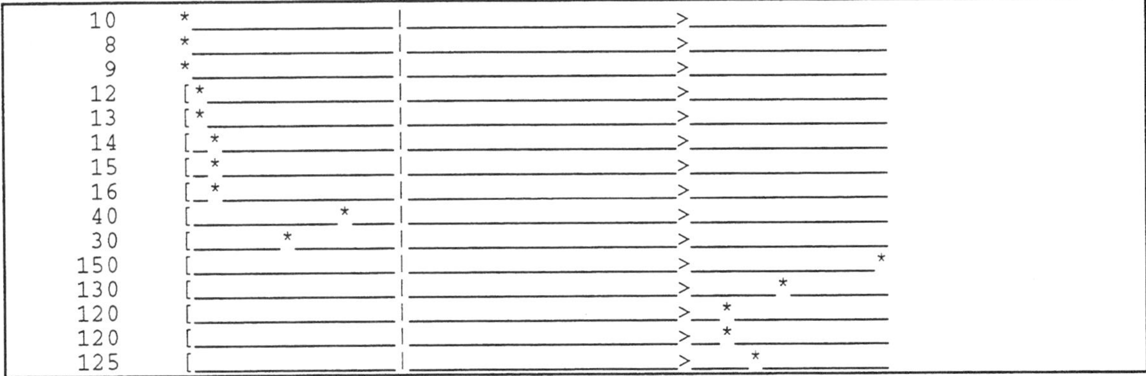

Example 7

This example displays a horizontal bar for each observation. Bar length is a function of the observation's value relative to the range of the data. Thus an observation with a value halfway through the range of the data will have a bar .5 times the number of print positions allocated for the bar (.5 times 50, or 25 print positions, in this case).

The display is not terribly different from a histogram produced by the CHART procedure. Recall, though, the advantage of hand-coding these displays: supporting text could be added to enhance the reader's understanding of the report. In addition to the value being plotted, the report could contain background information and other graphic components. The customized combining of text and graphic elements is not possible using PROCs.

```
data _null_;
set one;
file 'ex07.txt' notitles;

length obs_bar $50;
retain bar_size 50 st_col 10 obs_bar;

if size ^= . then do;
   fract   = (&range. - (&mx. - size)) / &range.;
   barsize = fract * (bar_size - 1);
   if barsize ^= . then do;
      obs_bar = repeat('*', barsize);
      end;

   if barsize ^= . then put @1 size @(st_col) obs_bar;
      else             put @1 size 5.;
   end;
run;
```

Output 6: Display Both Histogram and Data Values

```
10        *
8         *
9         *
12        **
13        **
14        ***
15        ***
16        ***
40        ************
30        ********
150       **************************************************
```

Output 6: Display Both Histogram and Data Values *(continued)*

```
130          *******************************************
120          ***************************************
120          ***************************************
125          *****************************************
```

Example 8

Unlike earlier examples, which displayed a graphic element for each observation in a data set, this example performs BY-group processing. A line is written only at the end of a BY group. Rather than write, say, 20 lines of data for a BY-group, we write only one line containing up to 20 plot symbols. In this example, the analysis variable is an event date. Thus the leftmost value in the display is the earliest date and the rightmost value the latest. Collisions, or multiple data points in the same print location, are displayed with an "M" rather than "*".

The display is built differently than previous examples. Rather than simply print the underlying row of dashes and one or more plot symbols, we build and RETAIN a character variable containing this information. At the beginning of each BY group, we create a bar of dashes. Then each observation changes the appropriate location in the string to a "*" or an "M" by using the SUBSTR "pseudovariable." The variable is actually written at the end of a BY group (LAST.var equals 1).

```
data _null_;
set dates;
by subject;
file 'ex08.txt' notitles;

length obs_bar $50;
retain bar_size 50 st_col 10 obs_bar;

Write a new bar at the start of each SUBJECT (BY variable)
if first.subject then obs_bar = repeat('-', bar_size-1);

if date ^= . then do;
   fract = ((&daterng. - (&datemax. - date)) / &daterng.);

   Unlike previous examples, loc is a location in a character string
   rather than an actual print position.
   loc = fract * (bar_size -1) + 1;
   if substr(obs_bar, loc, 1)^= '-' then substr(obs_bar,loc,1) = 'M';
      else                              substr(obs_bar,loc,1) = '*';
   end;

Write only when we are at the end of a subject and thus have
summary data. Only bars with at least one plotted observation will
be printed.
if last.subject & indexc(obs_bar, 'M', '*') > 0 then
   put @st_col obs_bar;
run;
```

Output 7: One Line Represents Multiple Observations

```
         *M-----------------*-----------------------------
         -----------*--------*------*-----------M--------*
```

Example 9

This example is similar to Example 8, but with a twist on interpretation. Here, each BY group begins in the leftmost (earliest date) position of the bar. Thus the distribution of plotted points along the bars represents the number of days from the first non missing date. In Example 8, the n'th print position represented a particular event. In this example, however, the n'th print position represents the same number of days from the earliest date. The data could, for example, represent clinical trials activities such as enrollment, adverse events, and scheduled visits. The report facilitates comparison of the patients: we can readily see if events were evenly spaced, grouped near the enrollment date, and so on.

Note that some preprocessing of the data needs to be done. Rather than use the individual BY groups' minimum, maximum, and range values, we need to use the maximum range of the analysis variable

DATE. This is done by selectively merging the summary data set at the beginning (_N_ = 1) of the report-writing DATA step.

```
proc means noprint data=dates;
class subject;
var date;
output out=summ(drop=_freq_) min=mindate range=daterng
                             max=maxdate;
run;

data _null_;
merge dates summ(where=(_type_=1));
by subject;
file 'ex09.txt' notitles;

length obs_bar $50;
retain dayprpos st_date;
retain bar_size 50 st_col 10 obs_bar;

At start of data set, get largest range.  This, along with the bar
size, determines how many days represented by each print position.
if _n_ = 1 then do;
   set summ(where=(_type_=0) rename=(daterng=typ0rnge));
   dayprpos = typ0rnge / bar_size;
   end;

Write a new bar at the beginning of each subject
if first.subject then do;
   obs_bar = repeat('-', bar_size-1);
   st_date = mindate;
   end;

Determine the gap between the current observation and the minimum
(earliest) date.  Print location LOC is this difference, expressed
in multiples of DAYPRPOS.
if date ^= . then do;
   loc = (date - st_date) / dayprpos ;
   if loc = 0 then loc = 1;
   if substr(obs_bar, loc, 1)^= '-' then substr(obs_bar,loc,1) = 'M';
      else                               substr(obs_bar,loc,1) = '*';
   end;

if last.subject & indexc(obs_bar, "M", "*") > 0 then
   put st_date date7.
       @st_col obs_bar;
run;
```

Output 8: Standardize Display Starting Date

```
01JAN94  M-------------------*----------------------------
15MAR94  *--------*------*-----------**-------*------------
```

Example 10

Rather than plot event dates, this example plots values of an analysis variable for each date. The analysis is conducted at the BY-group level and has both vertical and horizontal components. The horizontal axis represents dates, while the vertical is the quartile of the analysis variable at a given date. A height of four plot symbols indicates a value in the highest quartile, while a single symbol represents the lowest quartile. Four lines are required for display of the data. These are stored in four character variables, each with a length equal to the print positions in the horizontal axis (in this case, 50). The variables are modified via the SUBSTR function, much the same way as in Example 8.

As in Example 9, a preprocessing PROC is used here to create summary data. PROC UNIVARIATE is used to create percentiles, and this information is merged with the DATES data set in the report-writing DATA step.

```
proc univariate noprint data=dates;
by subject;
var value;
```

```
output out=summdate q1=_25 median=_50 q3=_75;
run;

data _null_;
merge dates summdate;
by subject;

file 'ex10.txt' notitles linesleft=ll;

length obs_bar1-obs_bar4 baseline $50 ;

retain bar_size 50 st_col 10 obs_bar1-obs_bar4 baseline;
array obs_bar(4);
format obs_bar1-obs_bar4 $char50.;

At start, write a line of dashes which will be used as the base line
for all displays.
if _n_ = 1 then baseline = repeat('-', bar_size-1);

Clear display variables at start of each subject (BY-group).
if first.subject then do;
   do i = 1 to 4;
      obs_bar(i) = ' ';
   end;
   end;

if date ^= . then do;
   Determine **where** the bar goes
   fract = (&daterng. - (&datemax. - date)) / &daterng.;
   loc   = fract * (bar_size -1) + 1;

   Now determine **how high** the bar should be
   if          (  . < value <= _25) then quartile = 1;
      else if (_25 < value <= _50) then quartile = 2;
      else if (_50 < value <= _75) then quartile = 3;
      else if value > _75          then quartile = 4;

   if quartile ^= . then do;
      Set values for up to 4 print positions
      do i = 1 to quartile;
         if substr(obs_bar(i), loc, 1) ^= ' ' then
                 substr(obs_bar(i),loc,1) = 'M';
            else substr(obs_bar(i),loc,1) = '*';
      end;

      Go back and reset to M (Multiple obs at print position) if
      necessary.
      if substr(obs_bar(1), loc, 1) = 'M' then do;
         do i = 2 to 4;
            if substr(obs_bar(i),loc,1) = "*" then
               substr(obs_bar(i),loc,1) = "M";
         end;
         end;
      end;  QUARTILE ^= . DO group
   end;     DATE ^= . DO Group

if last.subject & indexc(obs_bar(1), 'M', '*') > . then do;
   if ll <= 8 then put _page_;
   $CHAR format is important, since it preserves leading blanks and
   thus ensures proper column alignment.
   put / "Subject: " subject /
       @st_col obs_bar4 $char50. /
       @st_col obs_bar3 $char50. /
       @st_col obs_bar2 $char50. /
       @st_col obs_bar1 $char50. /
       @st_col baseline $char50.;
   end;
run;
```

Output 9: Two-Dimensional Display for Each Subject- Value of Analysis Variable by Date

```
Subject: 1
          M
         *M
         *M
         *M                    *
          ---------------------------------------------

Subject: 2
                    *
                    *         *                       *
                    *         *                M      *
                    *         *      *         M      *
          ---------------------------------------------
```

Example 11

This example begins to show more of the explanatory power of graphics by combining multiple graphic techniques. Each line of the report displays an observation in a data set. Quartiles for two variables, "pre" and "post" measures, are displayed. The date of the measurement is displayed, along with the actual measurements, their respective quartiles, and a bar showing the positioning of the two measurements in greater detail. "Pre" values use a plot symbol of "1"; "post" values use "2". Collisions are indicated by "*".

The complexity of the display is reflected in the bulky DATA step. The program, however, separates the graphic elements as much as possible and thus makes fairly straightforward reading. The horizontal bar's plot locations are calculated first, then the quartiles and their plot locations. No attempt is made to achieve computational efficiency. It is easier to calculate what we need in separate sections of the DATA step and incur some relatively minor performance penalties.

```
proc univariate noprint data=dates;
var value value2;
output out=summdate q1=_25 median=_50 q3=_75;
run;

proc sql noprint;
select max(value), max(value2), range(value), range(value2)
  into :max,       :max2,       :rng,         :rng2
  from dates;
quit;


data _null_;
file 'ex11.txt' header=pagetop print notitles;
length obs_bar $50 col_head $1;
retain bar_size 35 st_col 2 obs_bar range max;

array  val(2) value value2 ;
array plot(2) $ ;
array    q(2) ;

if _n_ = 1 then do;
   set summdate;
   obs_bar = repeat('-', bar_size-1);
   Bar scaling will be determined by the maximum range and value of
   the two analysis variables.
   range    = max(&rng., &rng2.);
   max      = max(&max., &max2.);
   end;

set dates;

First, determine print positions and symbols for analysis variables
VALUE and VALUE2. Symbols are for horizontal bar.
prop1 = ((range - (max - value )) / range);
prop2 = ((range - (max - value2)) / range);
loc1  = (prop1 * (bar_size-1));
loc2  = (prop2 * (bar_size-1));
loc1  = int(loc1);
```

```
loc2  = int(loc2);
if loc1 = loc2 then do;
   bplot1 = '*';
   bplot2 = '*';
   end;
   else do;
        bplot1 = '1';
        bplot2 = '2';
        end;

Determine quartiles
do i = 1 to 2;
   if          (   . < val(i) <= _25) then q(i)  = 1;
      else if (_25 < val(i) <= _50) then q(i)  = 2;
      else if (_50 < val(i) <= _75) then q(i)  = 3;
      else if val(i) > _75              then q(i)  = 4;
end;

Now determine symbols to plot for quartile display.
qplot1 = '1';
qplot2 = '2';
if q1 = q2 then do;
   qplot1 = '*';   qplot2 = '*';
   end;

Finally ... plot
put @st_col                 date date7.
    @(st_col+10)            value 2.
    @(st_col+12 +(3*q1)) qplot1
    @(st_col+12 +(3*q2)) qplot2
    @(st_col+28)            value2 2.
    @(st_col+33)            obs_bar
    @(st_col+33+loc1)       bplot1
    @(st_col+33+loc2)       bplot2
    ;
return;

pagetop: put @(st_col)      'Date'
             @(st_col+10) 'Pre '
             @(st_col+27) 'Post'
             @(st_col+14) ' '
             @
             ;
         do col_head = '1', '2', '3', '4';
            put (col_head)($3.) @;
         end;
         put ;
         return;
run;
```

Output 10: Graphic and Numeric Elements Combined to Display Pre/Post Data

```
Date       Pre  1  2  3  4  Post
01JAN94    12         *      15    ------------1--2-------------------
12JAN94     8   2  1          6    ----2--1---------------------------
13JAN94    20         *      10    ---------2-----------1-------------
15MAY94     8   2  1          5    ---2---1---------------------------
11NOV94    10      2  1       8    -------2-1-------------------------
15MAR94    30         2  1   15    ---------------2-------------------1
20MAY94    25         2  1   20    ----------------------2-----1-------
02JUL94     2   *             6    1---2------------------------------
18SEP94     4   1     2      10    --1------2-------------------------
20SEP94     6   1     2      14    ----1---------2--------------------
```

Example 12

This example combines two graphic styles in a single report. One summarizes the data; the other gives detailed information. The data are Adverse Events in a clinical trial. A self-rated pain index measures discomfort at the onset of the incident (time 0), two hours later, and four hours later (variables T0, T2, and T4). Discomfort scores range from 1 (none) to 5 (extreme).

The report's summary element is a timeline representing change from earliest to latest score. Thus the values range from plus 4 (5 changes to 1) to minus 4 (1 changes to 5). Positive scores are plotted as vertical bars of "+" characters, negative scores as a bar of "-" below a reference (value of 0) axis. The report's detail elements are boxes containing the date and description of the event. Below it are bars indicating the magnitude of the discomfort score at each time measured.

Considerable data "massaging" needs to be done here. For the summary portion of each person's report we need to know the first and last observation number for the person, as well as their minimum and maximum dates. This is performed in the DATA step at the top of the example.

At the start of each BY group, or patient, we pass through all observations for the group so we can plot the score differences. Then for each observation in the group, we write the boxes with the detailed information. The program makes extensive use of the FILE statement options which monitor column and line usage. The critical feature of the detail section is knowing when a new row of boxes or a new page needs to be written.

```
proc sort data=case1;
by id descending date;
run;

Create a data set with summary data: one observation per SUBJECT,
containing start/end observation numbers and min/max dates.
data ex12summ(drop=date);
set  case1(keep=id date);
by id;
retain _st _min _max;
if first.id then do;
   _st = _n_;
   _min = .;  _max = .;
   end;
_min = min(_min, date);
_max = max(_max, date);
if last.id then do;
   _fin = _n_;
   output;
   end;
format _min _max date7.;
run;

options nodate nocenter nonumber;

%let ps=66;
%let ls=78;

data _null_ ;
merge case1 ex12summ;
by id ;

file 'ex12.txt' header=pagetop n=ps notitles print ps=&ps. ls=&ls.
                col=colptr;
retain row col 0;
length varname $8;
array times(3) t0 t2 t4;
array bars(3) $5 ;

We need more rows at the start of a subject (ID) than other obs. Set
LINE2USE accordingly.
if first.id then do;
   line2use = 14;
   link newrow;
   end;
   else line2use = 7;

Before trying to write anything, see if we have to go to a new row or
a new page.
if &ls. < col + 22       then link newrow;
if &ps. < row + line2use then put _page_;

if first.id then do;
   non_plot = 0;
```

```
   nevent = _fin - _st + 1;
   put #(row)   "Patient: " id  "  Number of events: " nevent @;
   save_col = colptr;
   put #(row+6) &ls.*'-';

   Plot all events. Use vertical orientation.
   do i = _st to _fin while (eof ^= 1);
      set case1 end=eof point=i;
      What is the range of dates for this person?
      range = _max - _min;
      fract = (range - (_max - date)) / range;

      Create DIFF, the change between the earliest and latest
      measurements. Use the most widely spaced pair of non-missing
      values (e.g., if T0, T2, and T4 are all non-missing, use T0 and
      T4 rather than T2 and T4).
      valid = n(t0, t2, t4);
      if valid >= 2 then do;
         if t0 ^= . then st  = t0;
            else         st  = t2;
         if t4 ^= . then end = t4;
            else         end = t2;
         diff = st - end;
         end;
         else do;
              diff = .;
              non_plot + 1;
              end;

      if fract ^= . & diff ^= . then do;
         loc = fract * (&ls. - 1);
         Draw vertical bars indicating positive or negative change.
         if diff  =  4 then put #(row+2)  @loc '+';
         if diff >=  3 then put #(row+3)  @loc '+';
         if diff >=  2 then put #(row+4)  @loc '+';
         if diff >=  1 then put #(row+5)  @loc '+';
                            put #(row+6)  @loc '*';
         if diff <= -1 then put #(row+7)  @loc '-';
         if diff <= -2 then put #(row+8)  @loc '-';
         if diff <= -3 then put #(row+9)  @loc '-';
         if diff <= -4 then put #(row+10) @loc '-';
         end;
   end;

   Add some annotation to the chart - the min/max of the dates just
   plotted
   put #(row+11) @1 '^' @&ls. '^' /
       #(row+12) @1 _min date7. @(&ls.-6) _max date7.;

   if non_plot > 0 then
      put #(row) @(save_col+1) "Events which could not be displayed "
                               non_plot;
   Reposition analysis data set
   set case1 point=_st;

   Reset row, column pointers. When individual events are plotted
   they will begin in a new row. If a new page is required, page
   handling will be done in PAGETOP label.
   link newrow;
   end;   Finally .. end of FIRST. processing

Build the bars for each event (time 0, 2, and 4)
do i = 1 to 3;
   if 1 <= times(i) <= 5 then bars(i) = repeat('*', times(i)-1);
end;

If we cannot fit an event description in the alloted space, mark last
character.
if length(event) > 17 then substr(event, 17, 1) = '>';

Write text and data
put #(row+1) @(col+2) 'Date: ' date date7. ;
put #(row+2) @(col+2) event $17.;
```

```
do i = 4 to 6;
   call vname(times(i-3), varname);
   put #(row+i) @(col+2 ) varname
                @(col+6 ) bars(i-3)
                @(col+18) times(i-3) 1.;
end;

Draw boxes (8 rows by 21 columns)
put #row @col '+'   19*'-' '+';
do i = 1 to 6;
   put #(row+i) @col '|'   @(col+20) '|' ;
end;
put #(row+7) @col '+'   19*'-' '+'   #row;

col + 22;
return;

newrow:  col = 1;
         if first.id then row + 14;
           else           row +  9;
         return;
pagetop: put _page_  ;
         page + 1;
         put 'Adverse event history' @(&ls.-5) 'Pg ' page 3.;
         row = 3;  col = 1;
         return;
run;
```

Output 11: Patient Summary Display Combined with Observation-Level Detail

```
Adverse event history                                                Pg   1

Patient: 1   Number of events: 16

     +     +                                                    +     +
     +     +   +                                                +    ++    +
     +     +   +                                                +    ++    +
++   +  +  +  ++                                          + +   +  + ++ + +
**---*--*--*--**------------------------------------------*-*----*--*-**-*-*-




^                                                                          ^
01JAN94                                                              10APR95

+-------------------+ +-------------------+ +-------------------+
| Date: 10APR95     | | Date: 02APR95     | | Date: 17MAR95     |
|                   | |                   | |                   |
|                   | |                   | |                   |
| T0  *****       5 | | T0  ***         3 | | T0  *****       5 |
| T2  *****       5 | | T2  ***         3 | | T2  ****        4 |
| T4  **          2 | | T4  **          2 | | T4  *           1 |
+-------------------+ +-------------------+ +-------------------+

------------------------- Some lines omitted -------------------------

+-------------------+ +-------------------+ +-------------------+
| Date: 01MAR94     | | Date: 10FEB94     | | Date: 15JAN94     |
| headache          | | severe cluster h> | | nausea            |
|                   | |                   | |                   |
| T0  ***         3 | | T0  *****       5 | | T0  ****        4 |
| T2  ***         3 | | T2  ***         3 | | T2  ****        4 |
| T4  **          2 | | T4  *           1 | | T4  ***         3 |
+-------------------+ +-------------------+ +-------------------+
```

Output 11: Patient Summary Display Combined with Observation-Level Detail *(continued)*

```
Adverse event history                                                    Pg    2

+-------------------+
| Date: 01JAN94     |
| headache          |
|                   |
| T0   *****      5 |
| T2   ****       4 |
| T4              . |
+-------------------+




Patient: 2   Number of events: 6  Events which could not be displayed: 2


  +       +
+ +       +
*-*-------*----------------*----------------------------------------------------
                           -
                           -


^                                                                              ^
01JAN94                                                                  01APR94

+-------------------+ +-------------------+ +-------------------+
| Date: 01APR94     | | Date: 02FEB94     | | Date: 15JAN94     |
| unknown           | |                   | |                   |
|                   | |                   | |                   |
| T0              . | | T0   **         2 | | T0   *****      5 |
| T2              . | | T2   **         2 | | T2              . |
| T4              . | | T4   ****       4 | | T4   ***        3 |
+-------------------+ +-------------------+ +-------------------+

+-------------------+ +-------------------+ +-------------------+
| Date: 10JAN94     | | Date: 05JAN94     | | Date: 01JAN94     |
| headache          | | felt dizzy        | | dizziness         |
|                   | |                   | |                   |
| T0              . | | T0              . | | T0   *****      5 |
| T2              . | | T2   *****      5 | | T2   *****      5 |
| T4   *          1 | | T4   ***        3 | | T4   ****       4 |
+-------------------+ +-------------------+ +-------------------+
```

Example 13

This example demonstrates implementation of Example 3 in the macro language. The process is, essentially, a series of questions about the report and how it will be used. Will the user want to vary the minimum and maximum values displayed? Should values out of range be printed? What plot value should be used? How many print positions should be in the display area? What column should it start in? Do we always want to print the value next to the graphic element?

Once the questions are identified, the macro code comes relatively easily. In some cases it is simply direct substitution of a macro variable into an expression. For example, "loc = &startcol. + (&barsize. -1);" In other cases, parameters determine whether code should be included. An example of this is the %IF statement used to insert the printing of the analysis variable.

We see from the macro version of the program that the code which is actually executed (the non-macro language code) is actually a bit more compact than the original. _RANGE can be calculated directly, and we do not need to define and retain BAR_SIZE and ST_COL.

```
%macro ex13(barsize=50, startcol=10, min=0, max=120,
            pr_val=N,symbol=#,
            only_ok=N);
data _null_;
```

```
set one end=eof;
file 'ex13.txt' notitles;

bar = repeat('_', &barsize.-1);

if size ^= . then do;
   if size < &min. then do;
      loc = &startcol.;
      symbol = '<';
      outlier + 1;
      end;
      else if size > &max. then do;
           loc = &startcol. + (&barsize. - 1);
           symbol = '>';
           outlier + 1;
           end;
      else do;
           fract = ((&max.-&min.) - (&max. - size)) / (&max.-&min.);
           loc   = &startcol. + (fract * (&barsize. - 1)) ;
           symbol= "&symbol.";
           end;

   %if %upcase(&only_ok.) = Y %then %do;
       if symbol = "&symbol." then
       %end;
   put @(&startcol.) &barsize.*'-'   @loc symbol
       %if %upcase(&pr_val.) ^= N %then %do;
           @1 size 5.
           %end;
           ;
   end;
%if %upcase(&only_ok.) = Y %then %do;
    if eof & outlier > 0
       then put /  "# obs out of print range (&min. to &max.) = "
            outlier;
  %end;
run;
%mend;

options mprint;
%ex13(barsize=40, startcol=20, min=10, max=50, pr_val=n,
      only_ok=y);
```

Output 12: Generalization of Example 3 Using the Macro Language

```
                                #---------------------------------------
                                -#--------------------------------------
                                --#-------------------------------------
                                ---#------------------------------------
                                ----#-----------------------------------
                                -----#----------------------------------
                                ------------------------------#---------
                                --------------------#-------------------

  # obs out of print range (10 to 50) = 7
```

Conclusion

The appeal of colorful, high-resolution graphics cannot be denied. However, as we have seen in this chapter, a wide variety of information-rich, appealing displays can be achieved by using relatively few procedures and DATA step statements. These character -based graphic displays are often more appropriate for the analysis task at hand than SAS/GRAPH, can be quickly printed, and require knowledge of only a small portion of the base SAS language. Once you know what you want to communicate and how the ideas should be displayed it is largely a matter of preparing the data and then writing a DATA step.

The tools for this process are straightforward. Procedures such as SORT, SQL, and MEANS are used for pre processing the data. The actual report writing is carried out in a DATA step with FILE and PUT statements along with functions and other DATA step features. These are presented in Tables 1 through

5. The reports can be as simple or complex as needed, and always have the advantage of being able to freely mix graphic, textual, and numeric elements, a feature not readily available or apparent in other forms of SAS graphics.

Reference

Tufte, Edward (1983), *The Visual Display of Quantitative Information*, Cheshire, CT: Graphics Press.

CHAPTER 10

Using a Word-Wrap Macro on Long Text Variables

by John E. Hewlett

Abstract

Some database systems accessible by SAS software allow very large varying-length fields that can be used as word processing-like notepads. The problem is to have an easy way to print this free-form text in reports so that words are not split. These reports must also accommodate text columns devoted to the text fields, where the text columns vary in width from report to report. This chapter shows how to solve these problems using a macro called WORDRAP.

Specifications

The code in this chapter was developed and tested with Release 6.08 of the SAS System under the MVS and VM environments. Use of the code with other releases of the SAS System or other environments may require user modification. Modified code is not supported by the author.

About the Author

John Hewlett is an independent SAS Consultant/Contractor with three years of experience using SAS software. He has a BS degree in Engineering Science from Case Institute of Technology and an MBA degree from UCLA. His areas of expertise include report writing, SAS/AF software, and VSAM files.

Questions and Comments Should be Directed to:

John Hewlett
1340 Rolling Hills Drive
Fullerton, CA 92635
Telephone: 714-990-2693

Examples from this book are available online, see inside back cover for details.

Using a Word-Wrap Macro on Long Text Variables

J. E. Hewlett

Introduction

The SAS System allows variables up to only 200 characters long. This chapter shows you how to access and print variables of virtually unlimited size. You may have a single variable that is 8000 bytes long when you work with database systems that the SAS System can access, such as the TeraData DBC/1012. Such databases use long fields to hold free-form comments. In other words, the field acts like a word processing notepad where the user can record unstructured facts about a particular record.

Since such fields are used in a word processing manner, when it's time to print them, you need some rudimentary printing capabilities similar to those provided by word processing software. Two capabilities are crucial:

1. Word break
   When the field can't be printed on a single line, you want each line to end at a word break; in essence you want a ragged right margin for the field.
2. Varying field width
   In one report you might be able to devote a width of 110 characters to print this field. In a more crowded report you might only be able to allocate a width of 63 characters to print this field. If a particular record contained a 400 byte field, it would take at least 7 lines to probably print it in 4 lines. You want a way to easily specify (in each report) how much horizontal room is to be provided for the field and then let the software rearrange the text so that each line ends on a word boundary and no line is longer than the specified maximum.

This chapter shows you how to program these capabilities, primarily through a macro called WORDRAP. This macro was developed by Andy Gunn of Nashville Tennessee, with my participation in the design phase. The code for this macro is supplied in Appendix A and is very well documented. Therefore, the intricate details of how the macro works will not be repeated here. Instead, this chapter concentrates on understanding how to use the macro.

An example of using the macro in a practical situation is provided. The example also shows you how to read the original variable length field into an array, thus getting around the 200 character limitation of SAS. The WORDRAP macro expects to find its input in such an array.

Overview of logic

1. Use the SAS/AF SCL environment to allow the user to specify selection criteria for the report.
2. Use the SAS/AF SCL variables to create a database program to extract the required data into a normal (varying-length) file.
3. Run the database program from within SAS.
4. Use a SAS DATA step to process the external file into a SAS data set that contains arrays of the large text fields.
   a) Use the macro VARCHAR to turn the large varying-length text field into an array of 200 byte fields.
   b) Use the macro WORDRAP to turn the 200 byte array into a new array whose length is the length that you have room for on your printed report.
   As the text in the first array is parsed into the second array, WORDRAP ensures that no words are split; i.e. that each variable in the second array always starts with the first letter of a word.
5. Use a SAS DATA _NULL_ step to process the SAS data set and print the report.

Example Program with Explanation

Lines 1 through 15

Imagine that your actual data exist in a large TeraData database. The first thing you must do is write a TeraData program to extract the fields and records that you want and write them to a normal file.

```
01 /* ---------------------------------------------------------*/
02 /* Create the BTEQ program to get the data from the Teradata.*/
03 /* This is done in an interactive environment where the */
04 /* user's answers to SAS/AF SCL questions are used to create */
05 /* a customized BTEQ program which contains SQL code. */
06 /* ---------------------------------------------------------*/
07 /* The purpose of this example is not to teach you how to */
08 /* write TeraData code, so the proper code isn't shown here. */
09 /* ---------------------------------------------------------*/
```

Once the TeraData program has been created, we execute it from within SAS.

```
10
11 /* ---------------------------------------------------------*/
12 /* Execute the BTEQ program and create the TERA file */
13 /* ---------------------------------------------------------*/
14 x 'runbteq WREXAMPL';
15
```

Lines 16 through 30

Now you get to the heart of the matter. You have created a varying-length file whose records consist of a small fixed portion, followed by two potentially very large text fields. The first one might be as large as 5000 bytes, whereas the second one is limited to 2000 bytes.

```
16 /* ---------------------------------------------------------*/
17 /* Process the TERA file into a SAS data set */
18 /* ---------------------------------------------------------*/
```

Lines 19 through 27 read the fixed portion of each record using a FILENAME statement and a DATA step consisting of INFILE and INPUT statements.

```
19 filename TERA 'J4EHEWL.TERA.EXTRACT';
20 data RPT;
21 infile TERA;
22 input
23 VAR1 $char30.
24 VAR2 ib4.
25 VAR3 pd3.4
26 VAR4 $char10.
27 @;
```

Note the @ sign in line 27. This leaves the SAS pointer positioned at the beginning of the first varying-length text field.

Line 28 uses the macro VARCHAR to process the first text field into an array called LONG1. Note that the length parameter is set to 200. Although the macro allows you to use any length less than 201, you don't need to use any length other than 200. The third parameter in line 28 is 25. The first varying-length text field can be 5000 bytes long. 5000/200=25 Therefore, 25 array variables 200 characters long are required to hold the maximum possible field. For more information about the VARCHAR macro, see "Explanation of the VARCHAR Macro" and Appendix B later in this chapter.

```
28 %varchar(LONG1,200,25);
```

Line 29 processes the second text field into an array called LONG2. Since the second text field is limited to 2000 bytes, the third parameter is 10 (2000/200).

```
29 %varchar(LONG2,200,10);
30 run;
31 /* ---------------------------------------------------------*/
32 /* Write the Report */
33 /* ---------------------------------------------------------*/
```

Lines 34 through 44

You now have a SAS data set where each SAS record contains two arrays (plus the four fixed length fields). The following statements set up the DATA _NULL_ step used to write the report.

```
34 data _null_;
35 set RPT end=EOF;
36 file PRINT header=HEADING linesleft=LINES notitles
37 linesize=120;
```

Lines 38 through 40 use the WORDRAP macro to turn the 200 byte array called LONG1 into a 110 byte array called TEXT1. INLEN is set to 200 because the second parameter in line 28 is 200. INVARS is set to 25 because the third parameter in line 28 is 25. OUTLEN is set to the amount of room you want to allow for printing, in this case 110. This is the variable that changes in each use of WORDRAP; sometimes you have a wide area to print in, and sometimes it's fairly narrow.

Note that OUTVARS is larger than just text-field length divided by OUTLEN. In other words, 5000 / 110 = 46, but 50 is used here. You should always make OUTVARS about 10% bigger than the exact calculation. If you used 46, you would not be guaranteed that the reformatted text would fit in 46 array variables.

```
38 %wordrap(inbase=LONG1,outbase=TEXT1,inlen=200,outlen=110,
39 invars=25,outvars=50);
40 MAX1 = WORDRAOP;
```

Line 40 is critical and line 43 is used for consistency. You must save the value in WORDRAOP in line 40 before you use WORDRAP a second time (in line 41).

Lines 41 through 43 turn the array LONG2 into the array TEXT2. This time, INVARS is set to 10 because the third parameter of line 29 is 10.

```
41 %wordrap(inbase=LONG2,outbase=TEXT2,inlen=200,outlen=110,
42 invars=10,outvars=20);
43 MAX2 = WORDRAOP;
44 if LINES < 6 then link FOOTING;
```

For more information on the WORDRAP macro, see Appendix A.

Lines 45 through 49

You print the 4 fixed variables in the normal manner, using a PUT statement.

```
45 put @1 VAR1
46 @33 VAR2
47 @45 VAR3
48 @65 VAR4
49 /;
```

Lines 50 through 53

These statements print the first text field. As many rows as necessary are used to print your text; however, remember the width of the field is limited to 110.

```
50 if MAX1 > 0 then do I = 1 to MAX1;
51 put @11 TEXT1(I);
52 if LINES < 4 then link FOOTING;
53 end;
```

Line 54

If there is a first text field, this statement creates a blank line between it and the second text field. Remember, it's possible for the first text field to be empty and the second text field to contain some data.

```
54 if MAX1 > 0 then put;
```

Lines 55 through 58

These statements print the second text field. Again, only the correct number of rows are used to print the field.

```
55 if MAX2 > 0 then do I = 1 to MAX2;
56 put @11 TEXT2(I);
57 if LINES < 4 then link FOOTING;
58 end;
```

Lines 59 through 76

This code prints a title, column headings, and footnotes on each page.

```
59 if EOF then link FOOTING;
60 return;
61 HEADING:
62 put @31 'Title';
63 put @1 'Variable 1'
64 @33 'Variable 2'
65 @45 'Variable 3'
66 @65 'Variable 4'
67 /;
68 return;
69 FOOTING:
70 do while(LINES > 2);
71 put;
72 end;
73 put @21 'Footing Line 1';
74 put @21 'Footing Line 2';
75 return;
76 run;
```

Explanation of the VARCHAR Macro

Look at Appendix B. VARCHAR is a short macro and is fairly straight-forward. The only part that needs explaining is the ELSE clause in the IF statement. In this example you had a potential 5000 byte text field, followed by a potential 2000 byte text field. Suppose that for some reason, you only wanted to print out the first 1000 bytes of the first field. You would make the third parameter of VARCHAR a 5 instead of the normal 25.

But you we still have to process the pointer across the entire length of the actual field. This is the purpose of the ELSE clause, to get the pointer to the beginning of the next field in those cases where you are not outputting 100% of the current text field.

Also note the ib2. on the input TL statement. This assumes that your varying-length text field uses a 2 byte binary value in front of the data to define the length of the field. If you were ever in a situation that didn't use 2 bytes, you'd have to adjust the ib value accordingly. For example, you would use ib4. if your system's software uses a 4 byte field to define length.

Appendix A - WORDRAP Macro

```
%macro WORDRAP(INBASE=,OUTBASE=,INLEN=,OUTLEN=,INVARS=,OUTVARS=,
               INARRAY=,OUTARRAY=,CLEAROUT=NO);
/*--------------------------------------------------------------------
|      WORDRAP               1/91                                      |
|                                                                      |
|                                                                      |
| Macro WORDRAP copies text from one set of character variables       |
| to another set while trying to prevent word-splitting.  This        |
| macro assumes that a stream of text has been stored in the input    |
| set of character variables by breaking the text stream into         |
| fixed-length segments for storage in SAS variables, so that word    |
| splits have occurred.  During the copy to an output set of          |
| character variables, words are recombined and padded with blanks    |
| so that words are not split in the output character variables.      |
|                                                                      |
|                                                                      |
| NOTES:                                                               |
|                                                                      |
|   1. The input variable names have to be XXX1,XXX2,...,XXX10,etc.   |
|      where INBASE=XXX.  Names containing leading zeros in the        |
|      suffix, such as XXX01, will NOT work.                           |
|                                                                      |
|   2. INVAR and OUTVAR must be 2 or greater.                          |
|                                                                      |
|   3. INLEN and OUTLEN must be 3 or greater.                          |
|                                                                      |
|   4. A LENGTH statement is generated for the OUTBASE variables,      |
|      so it is NOT necessary to pre-define the output variables.      |
|                                                                      |
|   5. You may need more total bytes of space in the output            |
|      character variables than are in the input since some padding   |
|      with blanks may occur.                                          |
|                                                                      |
|                                                                      |
| Usage Example:                                                       |
|                                                                      |
|   The SAS data set X contains the 25 text variables called LONG1    |
|   through LONG25, each $200.  Copy to $100 strings, SHORT1          |
|   through SHORT52, for printing.                                    |
|                                                                      |
|      data _null_;                                                    |
|        set X:                                                        |
|        %WORDRAP(INBASE=LONG,OUTBASE=SHORT,INLEN=200,OUTLEN=100,     |
|                 INVARS=25,OUTVARS=52);                              |
|        LINESOUT=WORDRAOP;                                            |
|        do J = 1 to LINESOUT;                                         |
|          put @13 LONG(J);                                            |
|        end;                                                          |
|      run;                                                            |
|                                                                      |
| Requirements:                                                        |
|                                                                      |
```

1. Input must be in a set of SAS variables, all with the SAME length, and all in a variable naming sequence; e.g., DESCR1-DESCR25.

2. Output must also be a set of SAS variables, all with the SAME length, and all in a variable naming sequence; e.g., OUT1-OUT25.

3. A minimum of 2 variables are required for both input and output.

4. If your DATA step contains a "retain", then set CLEAROUT=YES to ensure that output variables are always initialized to blanks each time through the data loop.

Input:

INBASE= The base portion of the names of the set of variables in which text that is to be transferred can be found. For example, if DESC1-DESC25 is the text source, then INBASE=DESC.

OUTBASE= The base portion of the names of the set of variables in which word-wrapped versions of the input text are to be placed. For example, if OUT1-OUT50 is the text target, then OUTBASE=OUT.

INLEN= Length of Source Text variables, $1 to $200 200 is the usual value.

OUTLEN= Length of Target Text variables, $1 to $200. 100 (or less) is the usual value.

INVARS= Number of variables in set of source variables.

OUTVARS= Number of variables in set of target variables.

INARRAY= Name to use as the array name for the array of input variables. If not specified, &INBASE is used.

OUTARRAY= Name to use as the array name for the array of output variables. If not specified, &OUTBASE is used.

Output:

1. Text in INBASE variables is word-wrapped into OUTBASE variables.

2. As part of the process, array names are assigned to the set of input variables and the set of output variables (see INARRAY= and OUTARRAY= above). The array names can be used in processing later in the same DATA step. The arrays are explicit arrays.

```
|   3. Variable WORDRSLT tells what stopped the process.          |
|      'INVAR Empty' indicates all text was successfully transferred|
|      'OUTVAR Full' indicates there was NOT enough room in the    |
|                    OUTVAR variables to hold all the reformatted  |
|                    text.                                         |
|                                                                  |
|   4. Variable WORDRAOP tells how many OUTVARs had data transferred|
|      to them.  If WORDRAOP = 0, then the first input text vari-  |
|      able was blank and no text was transferred.                 |
|      Note:                                                       |
|           WORDRSLT and WORDRAOP are dropped from the output data |
|           set.  To save this info for later processing, store    |
|           them in another variable; e.g.,                        |
|               LINESOUT = WORDRAOP;                               |
|                                                                  |
|                                                                  |
| Code Notes:                                                      |
|                                                                  |
| To simplify code, the Macro %PSEUDO was written to simulate a    |
| SUBSTRING function that operates on a text string of any         |
| length that consists of the concatenated values of the set of    |
| input text strings.  The text value returned from %PSEUDO can be |
| a maximum of 200 bytes.  For efficiency, a completely blank      |
| string in the input set will flag the end of the input text.     |
|                                                                  |
 -----------------------------------------------------------------*/

%if &INBASE= or &OUTBASE= or &INLEN= or &OUTLEN= or &INVARS= or
    &OUTVARS= %then %do;
                    %put *-*- For Macro WORDRAP you must specify;
                    %put      all of the following:;
                    %put         INBASE  INLEN  INVARS;
                    %put        OUTBASE OUTLEN OUTVARS;
                    %goto EXIT;
                   %end;

/* To allow multiple calls to WORDRAP in a step, labels must differ
*/

%let WORDSKIP = WORDS&sysindex;
%let WORDEXIT = WORDX&sysindex;

%if  &INARRAY= %then %let  INARRAY = &INBASE;
%if &OUTARRAY= %then %let OUTARRAY = &OUTBASE;

/*-----------------------------------------------------------------
|     Description of variables                                     |
|     ------------------------                                     |
|  PSEUDOFC First character of a string                           |
|  PSEUDOLC Last  character of a string                           |
|  PSEUDO1  Pointer to 1st input text string involved in a Pseudo- |
|           substring                                              |
|  PSEUDOR1 Pointer to 1st involved character of 1st involved     |
|           string in Pseudo-substring                             |
```

```
|  PSEUDO2  Pointer to last input text string involved in a Pseudo-  |
|           substring                                                 |
|  PSEUDOR2 Pointer to last involved character of last involved       |
|           string in Pseudo-substring                                |
|  PSEUDOE  Pointer to last character in sum total string of text     |
|           for Pseudo-substring                                      |
|  PSEUDOJ  Pointer for stepping backwards, to avoid splitting        |
|           a word                                                    |
|  PSEUPTR  Pointer used during construction of output string         |
|  WORDMAXC Sum total of input text characters to transfer            |
|  WORDRAIP Pointer to  input text variable list                      |
|  WORDRAOP Pointer to output text variable list                      |
|  WORDRPPS Pointer to sum total string for start of string to        |
|           extract                                                   |
|  WORDRPPE Pointer to sum total string for end   of string to        |
|           extract                                                   |
|  WORDRSLT Text string describing macro result.                      |
 --------------------------------------------------------------------*/

/*--------------------------------------------------------------------
|  Embedded Macro: %PSEUDO   Pseudo-SUBSTRING Function                |
|                                                                     |
| Acts like SUBSTRING function on a long text string of               |
| concatenated values in &INBASE.  One version is for strings of      |
| length 1; the other is for all other lengths.                       |
 --------------------------------------------------------------------*/

%macro PSEUDO(PSEUDOS,PSEUDOL,OUTVAR);
  &OUTVAR = '';

/* Generate Pointer and Offset to first variable in INBASE.
*/

  PSEUDO1  = int((&PSEUDOS-1)/&INLEN)+1;
  PSEUDOR1 = mod(&PSEUDOS,&INLEN);
  if PSEUDOR1 = 0 then PSEUDOR1 = &INLEN;

/* The use of %quote prevents the automatic %eval from causing a
   macro error.
*/
  %if %quote(&PSEUDOL) = 1          /* simple code if length is 1 */
     %then %do;
             WORDRAIP = PSEUDO1;
             &OUTVAR  = substr(&INARRAY(WORDRAIP),PSEUDOR1,1);
            %end;

     %else %do;
             PSEUDOE  = &PSEUDOS + &PSEUDOL - 1;
             PSEUDO2  = int((PSEUDOE-1)/&INLEN)+1;
             PSEUDOR2 = mod(PSEUDOE,&INLEN);
             if PSEUDOR2 = 0 then PSEUDOR2 = &INLEN;

            do WORDRAIP = PSEUDO1 to PSEUDO2;
```

```
          if WORDRAIP = PSEUDO1 and WORDRAIP = PSEUDO2
            then do;
                      /* only one text variable involved */
                 &OUTVAR = substr(&INARRAY(WORDRAIP),PSEUDOR1,
                                  &PSEUDOL);
                 end;
            else if WORDRAIP = PSEUDO1 and WORDRAIP < PSEUDO2
                   then do;

                /* first of many vars - take to end of string */

                         &OUTVAR = substr(&INARRAY(WORDRAIP),
                                   PSEUDOR1);
                         PSEUPTR = &INLEN - PSEUDOR1 + 2;
                        end;
            else if WORDRAIP > PSEUDO1 and WORDRAIP < PSEUDO2
                   then do;

                      /* middle variable - take it all */

                  substr(&OUTVAR,PSEUPTR) = &INARRAY(WORDRAIP);
                         PSEUPTR + &INLEN;
                        end;

                    /* last variable - take from beginning */

                   else do;
                         substr(&OUTVAR,PSEUPTR) =
                             substr(&INARRAY(WORDRAIP),1,PSEUDOR2);
                        end;
        end;
       %end;
%mend PSEUDO;

/*-------------------------------------------------------------------
|  Start of SAS Code                                                 |
 -------------------------------------------------------------------*/

PSEUDOLC = ' ';       /* set length with assignment so no warning */
PSEUDOFC = ' ';       /* assoc. with mult. lengths if mult. use   */
drop WORDMAXC PSEUDOFC PSEUDOLC WORDRPPS WORDRPPE PSEUPTR
     WORDRAIP WORDRAOP PSEUDO1  PSEUDOR1 PSEUDO2  PSEUDOR2
     PSEUDOE  PSEUDOJ  WORDRSLT;
array  &INARRAY {*}            &INBASE.1 -  &INBASE&INVARS;
array &OUTARRAY {*} $&OUTLEN &OUTBASE.1 - &OUTBASE&OUTVARS;

/* Clear out output vars, in case of RETAIN.
*/
%if &CLEAROUT=YES %then %do;
   do WORDRAOP = 1 to dim(&OUTARRAY);
     &OUTARRAY(WORDRAOP) = ' ';
   end;
 %end;
```

```
/* For efficiency, set up stop point; i.e. WORDMAXC
*/
WORDRAOP = 0;

/* Find first blank text line.
*/
do WORDRAIP = 1 to &INVARS until(&INARRAY(WORDRAIP)=' ');
end;
if WORDRAIP = 1                     /* 1st input is blank */
  then goto &WORDEXIT;
  else do;
        WORDRAIP = WORDRAIP - 1;  /* Point at Last entry */
        WORDMAXC = length(&INARRAY(WORDRAIP)) + (WORDRAIP-1)*&INLEN;
       end;

/* Initialize Pointers.
*/
WORDRAIP = 1;
WORDRAOP = 1;
WORDRPPS = 1;

/* Loop - until no more input text OR output text is full.
   Continuously track where in 8000+ bytes you are.
   Use %PSEUDO to do SUBSTRINGS on 8000+ bytes.
*/
do until(0);

/* Calculate ending point in Pseudo-String.  You already know the
   starting point.
*/
  WORDRPPE = WORDRPPS + &OUTLEN - 1;
  if WORDRPPE > WORDMAXC then WORDRPPE = WORDMAXC;

  %PSEUDO(WORDRPPE,1,PSEUDOLC);              /* Get Last char  */
  if WORDRPPE < WORDMAXC
    then do;
          %PSEUDO(WORDRPPE+1,1,PSEUDOFC);  /* Get First char  */
         end;
    else PSEUDOFC = ' ';

/* If last char of current string AND first char of next string are
   both non-blank, then we're in the middle of a word!
*/
  if PSEUDOLC ¬= ' ' and PSEUDOFC ¬= ' ' then do;
    PSEUDOJ = 0;
    do until(0);
      PSEUDOJ +1;
      WORDRPPE + (-1);            /* Decrement pointer */
      %PSEUDO(WORDRPPE,1,PSEUDOFC);

/* Look backwards for a blank until a blank is found, OR we've gone
   back 20 characters, OR we've gone back 1/2 a string.
*/
```

```
        if PSEUDOFC = ' ' then goto &WORDSKIP;
        if PSEUDOJ  = 20  then goto &WORDSKIP;
        if PSEUDOJ  > &OUTLEN/2 then goto &WORDSKIP;
      end;
&WORDSKIP:

 /* Set to full length if no blank was found; i.e. the word will be
    split!
 */
     if PSEUDOFC ^= ' ' then WORDRPPE = WORDRPPS + &OUTLEN - 1;
    end;         /* End of if PSEUDOLC ^= ' ' etc. */

 /* Now load value into OUTVAR.
 */
   %PSEUDO(WORDRPPS,(WORDRPPE-WORDRPPS+1),&OUTARRAY(WORDRAOP));

 /* Set value of next start at first non-blank character.
    This ensures that the output text is always left justified.
 */
   WORDRPPS = WORDRPPE;
   PSEUDOFC = ' ';
   do while(PSEUDOFC = ' ');
     WORDRPPS +1;
     if WORDRPPS > WORDMAXC then do;
                                 WORDRSLT = 'INVARS Empty';
                                 goto &WORDEXIT;
                                end;
     %PSEUDO(WORDRPPS,1,PSEUDOFC);
   end;

 /* Increment OUTVAR Pointer.  Stop if full!
 */
   WORDRAOP +1;
   if WORDRAOP > &OUTVARS then do;
                               WORDRSLT = 'OUTVARS Full';
                               goto &WORDEXIT;
                              end;
 end;         /* End of Main Loop  */
&WORDEXIT:;
%EXIT:
%mend WORDRAP;
```

Appendix B - VARCHAR Macro

```
%macro VARCHAR(ARRAY,ARYLEN,ARYCNT);
   array &ARRAY(&ARYCNT) $ &ARYLEN &ARRAY.1-&ARRAY.&ARYCNT;
   input TL  ib2. @;        /* TL = Text Length */
    do J = 1 by 1 while(TL>0);
     CURLEN = min(200,TL);
      if J <= &ARYCNT then input &ARRAY(J) $varying200. CURLEN @;
                      else input +CURLEN @;
/*-----------------------------------
| The ELSE clause is needed because the array might fill up before  |
 | the pointer has been moved to the end of the input field.         |
  -----------------------------------*/
     TL = TL - CURLEN;
   end;
%mend;
```

CHAPTER 11

Five Nifty Reports Using PROC SQL Views in the SASHELP Library

by Bernadette Johnson

Abstract

New PROC SQL views in the SASHELP data library offer run-time information about current SAS processes. These views offer immediate access to information about SAS data set structures, SAS library and catalog definitions, SAS system option values, and external files associated with the current SAS session. Sample programs and output demonstrate the ease of using five PROC SQL views: VCATALG, VTABLE, VCOLUMN, VOPTION, and VEXTFL.

Specifications

The code in this chapter was developed and tested with Release 6.07 of the SAS System under the VMS environment. Use of the code with other releases of the SAS System or other environments may require user modification. Modified code is not supported by the author.

About the Author

Bernadette Johnson, Director of Clinical Computing at Pharmaceutical Product Development, Inc., has been a SAS software user for seven years. Her areas of expertise include application development using SAS/AF and SAS/FSP software and program development using base SAS software.

Questions and Comments Should be Directed to:

Bernadette Johnson
Pharmaceutical Product Development Inc.
1400 Perimeter Park Drive, Suite 100
Morrisville, NC 27560
Telephone: 919-380-2000

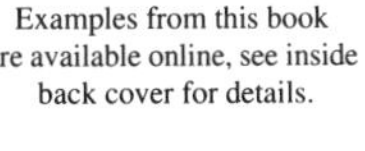

Examples from this book are available online, see inside back cover for details.

Five Nifty Reports Using PROC SQL Views in the SASHELP Library

Bernadette Johnson

Introduction

New, easy-to-use, run-time information is now available in PROC SQL views in the SASHELP data library. Until now, reporting information about current SAS processes has required the user to run a SAS utility procedure or to accept default output from a SAS procedure. PROC SQL views, automatically supplied in the SASHELP library, now contain descriptive information about the current SAS process. These views, used just like regular SAS data sets, provide the user with immediate access to information about SAS data set structures, SAS library and catalog definitions, SAS system option values, and external files associated with the current SAS session.

Fourteen PROC SQL views are available. These views require no SQL procedure programming, give the user access to run-time information, require no additional CPU time to generate the data, and make it easy for users to create custom reports. This chapter highlights five reports. See Figure 11 for a list of all the views.

If You Like PROC CATALOG, You Will Love SASHELP.VCATALG

The CATALOG procedure provides information about SAS data libraries, catalogs, and catalog entries. The default procedure output can be lengthy since a separate page is printed for each catalog in the current SAS session. The PROC SQL view, SASHELP.VCATALG, provides the same information as PROC CATALOG (Figure 1). The sample program maximizes the information printed on each page and produces the report in Figure 2.

Figure 1: A Summary of SASHELP.VCATALG

SAS VARIABLE NAME	TYPE/LENGTH	DESCRIPTION
LIBNAME	$ 8	Library Name
MEMNAME	$ 8	Member Name
MEMTYPE	$ 8	Member Type
OBJNAME	$ 8	Object Name
OBJTYPE	$ 8	Object Type
OBJDESC	$ 40	Object Description
MODIFIED	$ 8	Date Modified
ALIAS	$ 8	Object Alias

```
proc print data=sashelp.vcatalg label;
where libname="MASTER";
by libname memname ;
id libname memname ;
var objname objtype objdesc modified;
title "Example A: List of catalog entries in a SAS data library";
run;
```

Figure 2: SASHELP.VCATALG Output

Example A: List of catalog entries in a SAS data library

Library Name	Member Name	Object Name	Object Type	Object Description	Date Modified
MASTER	FORMULA	TIMELOG	FORMULA	FSVIEW formula for to view daily log	06/07/93
MASTER	PROFILE	AF	AFGO		10/14/93
		PRINTER	FORM	PRINTER.FORM	07/06/93
		PROJECT	FORMULA	FSVIEW formulas for TIMELOG.TIMELOG.	06/07/93
		TRACKING	FORMULA	FSVIEW formulas for TRACK.TRACKING.	03/30/93
		BUILD	KEYS	Function Key Definitions	06/01/93
		DM	KEYS	Function Key Definitions	11/19/92
		DMKEYS	KEYS	Function Key Definitions	09/30/93
		FSEDIT	KEYS	Function Key Definitions	09/30/93
		FSLETTER	KEYS	Function Key Definitions	01/28/93
		FSLIST	KEYS	Function Key Definitions	01/15/93
		REPORT	PROFILE	PROC REPORT user profile	01/15/93
		ASSIST	SOURCE		11/04/92
		DMSDEF	WSAVE	DMS window save information	07/13/93
		MSG	WSAVE	MSG window save information.	03/05/93
		OUTLIST	WSAVE	OUTLIST window save information.	11/18/92
MASTER	TIMELOG	JOBMAST	REPT	job mast	08/03/93

If You Like PROC CONTENTS, You Will Love SASHELP.VTABLE and SASHELP.VCOLUMN

The CONTENTS procedure provides a data file summary and details on each variable in the data files. The default procedure output combines the data file summary and the variable attribute listing. The PROC SQL view SASHELP.VTABLE, described in Figure 3, contains the data file summary, and SASHELP.VCOLUMN, described in Figure 5, contains the attributes of each variable. The program following Figure 3 creates a data file summary report (Figure 4). To create a variable attribute report (Figure 6), use the program following Figure 5.

Figure 3: A Summary of SASHELP.VTABLE

SAS VARIABLE	TYPE/LENGTH	DESCRIPTION
LIBNAME	$ 8	Library Name
MEMNAME	$ 8	Member Name
MEMTYPE	$ 8	Member Type
MEMLABEL	$ 40	Dataset Label
TYPEMEM	$ 8	Dataset Type
CRDATE	8	Date Created
MODATE	8	Date Modified
NOBS	8	Number of Observations
OBSLEN	8	Observation Length
NVAR	8	Number of Variables
PROTECT	$ 3	Type of Password Protection
COMPRESS	$ 8	Compression Routine
REUSE	$ 3	Reuse Space
BUFSIZE	8	Bufsize
DELOBS	8	Number of Deleted
INDXTYPE	$ 9	Type of Indexes

```
proc print data=sashelp.vtable label noobs ;
label nvar="# of Vars" nobs="# of Obs" indxtype="Index Type"
   compress="Com- press";
id libname;
by libname;
var memname  memlabel crdate modate nvar nobs compress bufsize;
title "Example B: Dataset Summary";
run;
```

Figure 4: SASHELP.VTABLE Output, a Data File Summary

```
                                          Example B: Dataset Summary
Library Member                                                                          # of # of   Com-
 Name    Name    Dataset Label                         Date Created      Date Modified   Vars  Obs  press Bufsize

MASTER  BUILD   Quarterly building supply sales      04NOV92:15:58:01 04NOV92:15:58:01   5    41    NO     8192
        CLASS   Student information                  04NOV92:15:58:03 04NOV92:15:58:03   5    19    NO    22528
        COLOR                                        12NOV92:14:42:50 12NOV92:14:42:52   1     1    NO     9728
        CRIME   Crime rates per 100,000 pop. by state 04NOV92:15:58:04 04NOV92:15:58:05  9    50    NO    21504
        FITNESS Exercise/fitness study data set      04NOV92:15:58:06 04NOV92:15:58:07   8    31    NO    14848
        HIGHWAY Motor vehicle accident data          04NOV92:15:58:07 04NOV92:15:58:08   5    24    NO    17920
        HOUSES  Residential housing for sale         04NOV92:15:58:08 04NOV92:15:58:09   6    15    NO    15872
        INGOTS  Foundry data                         04NOV92:15:58:10 04NOV92:15:58:10   4    19    NO    11776
        ORANGES Data on sale of oranges              04NOV92:15:58:12 04NOV92:15:58:12   6    36    NO    10240
        RETAIL  Memphis retail sales                 04NOV92:15:58:13 04NOV92:15:58:13   2    58    NO    10752
        SASPARM                                      04NOV92:15:57:48 07JAN93:14:36:38   5    72    NO    26624
        VENEER  Wood veneer wear data                04NOV92:15:58:14 04NOV92:15:58:14   2    20    NO     9728


SASHELP SASAPPL                                      11DEC92:17:06:52 11DEC92:17:07:38   8    41    YES   27648


SASUSER COLOR                                        29APR93:09:11:36 08SEP93:13:28:50   1     1    NO     8192
```

Figure 5: A Summary of SASHELP.VCOLUMN

SAS VARIABLE NAME	TYPE/LENGTH	DESCRIPTION
LIBNAME	$ 8	Library Name
MEMNAME	$ 8	Member Name
MEMTYPE	$ 8	Member Type
NAME	$ 8	Column Name
TYPE	$ 4	Column Type
LENGTH	8	Column Length
NPOS	8	Column Position
VARNUM	$ 40	Column Number in Table
LABEL	$ 16	Column Label
FORMAT	$ 16	Column Format
INFORMAT	$ 16	Column Informat
IDXUSAGE	$ 9	Column Index Type

```
proc print data=sashelp.vcolumn label split=' ' width=min;
where libname="MASTER";
by libname memname;
id libname memname;
var name type length npos varnum label format informat;
title "Example C: List of data sets and variables in a SAS data library";
run;
```

Figure 6: SASHELP.VCOLUMN Output, a Variable Attribute Report

Example C: List of data sets and variables in a SAS data library

Library Name	Member Name	Column Name	Column Type	Column Length	Column Position	Column Number in Table	Column Label	Column Format	Column Informat
MASTER	BUILD	INCOME	num	8	0	1	Disposable personal income		
		STARTS	num	8	8	2	U.S. housing starts		
		MORT	num	8	16	3	Mortgage rates		
		SALES	num	8	24	4	Sales of building supplies		
		DATE	num	8	32	5		YYQ4.	
MASTER	CLASS	NAME	char	8	0	1	First name		
		SEX	char	1	8	2	Gender		
		AGE	num	8	9	3	Age in years		
		HEIGHT	num	8	17	4	Height in inches		
		WEIGHT	num	8	25	5	Weight in pounds		
MASTER	CRIME	STATEN	char	15	0	1	State name		
		STATE	num	8	15	2	FIPS code		
		MURDER	num	8	23	3			
		RAPE	num	8	31	4			
		ROBBERY	num	8	39	5			
		ASSAULT	num	8	47	6			
		BURGLARY	num	8	55	7			
		LARCENY	num	8	63	8			
		AUTO	num	8	71	9			
MASTER	FITNESS	AGE	num	8	0	1	Age in years		
		WEIGHT	num	8	8	2	Weight in kg		
		RUNTIME	num	8	16	3	Min. to run 1.5 miles		
		RSTPULSE	num	8	24	4	Heart rate while resting		
		RUNPULSE	num	8	32	5	Heart rate while running		
		MAXPULSE	num	8	40	6	Maximum heart rate		
		OXYGEN	num	8	48	7	Oxygen consumption		
		GROUP	num	8	56	8	Experimental group		
MASTER	HOUSES	STYLE	char	8	0	1	Style of homes		
		SQFEET	num	8	8	2	Square footage		
		BEDROOMS	num	8	16	3	Number of bedrooms		
		BATHS	num	8	24	4	Number of bathrooms		
		STREET	char	16	32	5	Street address		
		PRICE	num	8	48	6	Asking price	DOLLAR12.	COMMA12.

If You Like PROC OPTIONS, You Will Love SASHELP.VOPTION

The default OPTIONS procedure output prints a list of the current SAS System options to the SAS log file. With the SASHELP.VOPTION view, shown in Figure 7, the option information can be accessed easily for reports. The following sample program produces the report in Figure 8.

Figure 7: A Summary of SASHELP.VOPTION

SAS VARIABLE NAME	TYPE/LENGTH	DESCRIPTION
OPTNAME	$ 16	Session Option Name
SETTING	$200	Session Option Setting
OPTDESC	$ 80	Option Description

```
proc report data=sashelp.voption nofs panels=2 headline;
column  optname setting ;
define  optname / display  width=12 flow;
define  setting / display  width=20 flow;
title "Example D: List of SAS System options";
run;
```

Figure 8: SASHELP.VOPTION Output

```
                    Example D: List of SAS System options

Session          Session Option
Option Name      Setting
------------------------------------
BATCH            BATCH
BUFNO            1
BUFSIZE          0
BYERR            BYERR
BYLINE           BYLINE
CAPS             NOCAPS
CARDIMAGE        NOCARDIMAGE
CATCACHE         0
CBUFNO           0
CENTER           CENTER
CHARCODE         NOCHARCODE
CLEANUP          CLEANUP
CMDMAC           NOCMDMAC
COMPRESS         NO
CPUID            CPUID
DATE             NODATE
DBCS             NODBCS
DBCSLANG
DBCSTYPE
DETAILS          NODETAILS
DEVICE
DKRICOND         ERROR
DKROCOND         WARN
DMR              NODMR
DMS              NODMS
DMSBATCH         NODMSBATCH
DSNFERR          DSNFERR
ECHOAUTO         NOECHOAUTO
ENGINE           V607
ERRORABEND       NOERRORABEND
ERRORS           20
FIRSTOBS         1
FMTERR           NOFMTERR
FMTSEARCH
FORMCHAR         |----|+|---+=|-
                 \<>*
FORMDLIM
FORMS            DEFAULT
GWINDOW          GWINDOW
IMPLMAC          NOIMPLMAC
INITSTMT
INVALIDDATA
LABEL            LABEL
LINESIZE         80
MACRO            MACRO
MAPS             MAPS
MAUTOSOURCE      MAUTOSOURCE
MERROR           MERROR
MISSING
MLOGIC           NOMLOGIC
MPRINT           NOMPRINT
MRECALL          NOMRECALL
MSGCASE          NOMSGCASE
MSGLEVEL         N

Session          Session Option
Option Name      Setting
------------------------------------
MSTORED          NOMSTORED
MSYMTABMAX       24576
MVARSIZE         80
NEWS             SAS$NEWS
NOTES            NOTES
NUMBER           NONUMBER
OBS              MAX
OVP              OVP
PAGENO           1
PAGESIZE         60
PARM
PARMCARDS        FT15F001
PRINTINIT        NOPRINTINIT
PROBSIG          0
PROC             PROC
REMOTE
REPLACE          REPLACE
REUSE            NO
RSASUSER         NORSASUSER
S                0
S2               0
SASAUTOS         SASAUTOS
SASFRSCR
SASHELP          SAS$HELP
SASMSG           SAS$MSG
SASMSTORE
SASSCRIPT
SASUSER          SAS$USER
SEQ              8
SERROR           SERROR
SETINIT          NOSETINIT
SITEINFO         SAS$SITEINFO
SKIP             0
SORTSEQ
SORTSIZE         -1
SOURCE           SOURCE
SOURCE2          NOSOURCE2
SPOOL            SPOOL
SYMBOLGEN        NOSYMBOLGEN
SYSPARM
TAPECLOSE        LEAVE
TERMINAL         NOTERMINAL
TRANTAB
USER
VNFERR           VNFERR
WORK             $1$DIA7:[SASTEMP.SAS
                 $WORK20E00A52]
WORKINIT         WORKINIT
WORKTERM         WORKTERM
YEARCUTOFF       1900
_LAST_           _NULL_
```

If You Like To Know Your Filenames, You Will Love SASHELP.VEXTFL

Currently, none of the SAS procedures prints the definitions of files used by the current SAS session to a SAS print file. The FILENAME statement prints the definition in the SAS log file. The SASHELP.VEXTFL view, described in Figure 9, provides all of the current SAS filerefs and the path names of the files. The following sample program generates the report in Figure 10.

Figure 9: A Summary of SASHELP.VEXTFL

SAS VARIABLE NAME	TYPE/LENGTH	DESCRIPTION
FILEREF	$ 8	Fileref
XPATH	$ 80	Path Name
XENGINE	$ 8	Engine Name

```
proc print data=sashelp.vextfl label;
id fileref;
var xpath xengine;
title "Example E: List of external files defined to current SAS session";
run;
```

Figure 10: SASHELP.VEXTFL Output

```
        Example E: List of external files defined to current SAS session
                                                                  Engine
           Fileref     Path Name                                   Name

           SAS+0000    $1$DIA2:[SAS607.TOOLS]SAS607.CFG
           SAS+0002    $1$DIA1:[JOHNSONBH.SASBOOK]EX8.SAS
           SAS+0003    $1$DIA1:[JOHNSONBH.SASBOOK]EX8.LIS
           SAS+0004    $1$DIA1:[JOHNSONBH.SASBOOK]EX8.LOG
           SAS+0005    SYS$OUTPUT:
           SAS+0006    SAS$MSG
           SAS+0007    SAS$MSG:MSGDIR.MSG
           SAS+0008    SAS$MSG:HOST.MSG
           SAS+0009    SAS$MSG:CORE.MSG
           JAN         $1$DIA1:[JOHNSONBH.SASBOOK]JANUARY.DAT
           FEB         $1$DIA1:[JOHNSONBH.SASBOOK]FEBRUARY.DAT
           MAR         $1$DIA1:[JOHNSONBH.SASBOOK]MARCH.DAT
           SAS+0010    SAS$MSG:BASE.MSG
           SAS+0011    SAS$MSG:SQL.MSG
```

Conclusion

The five reports highlighted here are just a sample of the reports that can be easily generated from the SASHELP SQL views. Fourteen PROC SQL views(Figure 11) are available in the SASHELP library. Each one can be used in a data step or SAS procedure just like a regular SAS data set.

Figure 11: Complete List of the SASHELP PROC SQL views

PROC SQL View Name	Description
SASHELP.VMEMBER	SAS data library names, member names and types, external path names for libraries
SASHELP.VTABLE	SAS data library names, data set size and structure information
SASHELP.VCOLUMN	SAS data library names, data set variable definitions
SASHELP.VCATALG	SAS data library names, SAS catalog names and entries
SASHELP.VEXTFL	SAS file references, external filenames, and engine specification
SASHELP.VVIEW	SAS data library names, SAS data view names and types, and engine specification
SASHELP.VINDEX	SAS data library names, SAS data file and variable names, and indexing information
SASHELP.VOPTION	List of SAS system options and the current setting
SASHELP.VSLIB	SAS data library names and corresponding external path names
SASHELP.VSTABLE	SAS data library names and SAS data file names
SASHELP.VSCATLG	SAS data library names and SAS catalog names
SASHELP.VSACCES	SAS data library names and SAS/ACCESS view names
SASHELP.VSVIEW	SAS data library names and SAS data view names
SASHELP.VSTABVW	SAS data library names, SAS data set and SAS data view names

For Further Reading

SAS Institute Inc. (1991), SAS Technical Report P-222: *Changes and Enhancements to Base SAS Software, Release 6.07*, Cary, NC: SAS Institute Inc.

CHAPTER 12

Computing Average Run Lengths for Various Control Charts Using SAS Software

by Dennis W. King

Abstract

SAS/QC software, a component of the SAS System, allows users to construct many types of control charts to monitor process characteristics. The average run length (ARL) of a control chart has been shown to be a quantitative tool for measuring the ability of the control chart to detect changes in a process parameter. In this chapter, the ARL for several types of control charts is computed using ARL functions available in SAS/QC software, the DATA step, and SAS/IML software. The computed ARLs are then summarized and compared using PROC TABULATE.

Specifications

The code in this chapter was developed and tested with Release 6.08 of the SAS System under the OS/2 environment. Use of the code with other releases of the SAS System or other environments may require user modification. Modified code is not supported by the author.

About the Author

Dennis King is President of STATKING Consulting Inc. and has been a SAS software user for 13 years. He has a BA degree in Mathematics from Eastern Illinois University, an MS degree in Statistics from the University of Wyoming, and a Ph.D. degree in Statistics from Texas A&M University. Dennis' areas of expertise include using SAS software for all types of statistical methods; base SAS, SAS/STAT, SAS/ETS, SAS/IML, SAS/QC, and SAS/GRAPH software; and macro language.

Questions and Comments Should be Directed to:

Dennis King
STATKING Consulting Inc.
5813 Coachmont Drive
Fairfield, OH 45014
Telephone: 513-858-2989

Computing Average Run Lengths for Various Control Charts Using SAS® Software

Dennis W. King

The Background of Control Charts

In the 1920's, Dr. Walter Shewhart introduced the control chart as a means to monitor and improve manufacturing processes. A manufacturing process consists of a sequence of steps performed in the assembly of a product or a component of the product. The *control chart* is a graphical method of tracking characteristics related to product quality over time.

In the decades up to and including the 1990's, the use of the control chart to monitor processes has spread to other industries beyond the manufacturing sector. For example, control charts are now used by service industries and medical and analytical laboratories to monitor and improve products and services. Their popularity is due to the fact that they (a) eliminate rework by focusing quality efforts on problems with the process, (b) provide a graphical feedback on patterns of defects and (c) provide information on process parameters.

The widespread use of control charts in the 90's was fueled by an explosion of research on the statistical theory of control charts in the 60's, 70's and 80's. A bibliography of control chart research by Vance (1983) indicates the multitude of types of control charts explored and invented by statistical researchers. As a group of charts emerged for monitoring the same process parameter, it became necessary for researchers to concentrate on performance measures for control charts. Pioneering papers by Page (1954,1955) and Brook and Evans (1972) have led to what has become the standard performance measure of control charts, *average run length* (ARL).

The quality control component of the SAS System, SAS/QC software, is a powerful tool for creating and displaying many types of control charts. SAS Technical Report P-188, *SAS/QC Software Examples, Version 6* gives many examples of code for creating a variety of charts. What has not been documented to this point is the ability to compute the ARL performance measure for the various charts using SAS software. It is the focus of this chapter to show how to use the DATA step and the matrix language (SAS/IML) to calculate ARL for many commonly used charts.

The Parts of a Control Chart

Although this chapter is not a summary of how to design and construct control charts using SAS software, it is helpful to become familiar with the parts of the control chart and how the chart is used to monitor a process. The control chart is a plot of a statistic used to summarize a quality characteristic versus a sample number or time. Overlaid on the plot are the centerline and upper and lower control limits (UCL,LCL) as shown in Figure 1. The centerline of the control charts marks the center of the distribution of the quality characteristic under study. It may be a targeted (known) value for the process or it may be estimated from data collected during a preliminary study of the process. The control limits define the boundary between data generated from a process operating under only chance causes of variability and data generated in the presence of assignable causes of variability.

Figure 1. Sample Control Chart

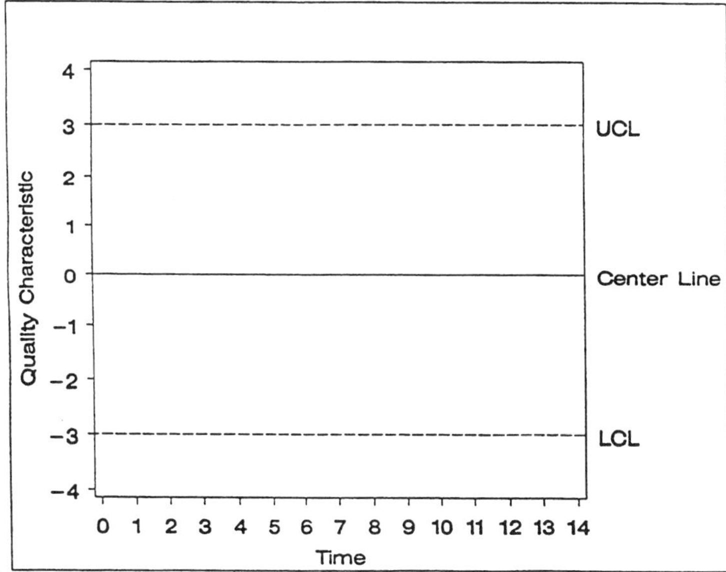

Each time the process is sampled, the quality characteristic calculated on the sample data varies. This is because not all items produced by the process are exactly alike in terms of the quality characteristic. It is hoped that a process operates most of the time under chance causes of variability only. Chance causes of variability are those inherent to the process. Small fluctuations in the response data over which those operating the process have no control. When the data from the process falls in the region between the control limits, only chance causes of variability are present and the process is said to be operating in an in-control state. When a shift in the process occurs due to the presence of assignable causes of variability, some points will fall outside of the control limits and the process is said to be out-of-control. Examples of assignable causes of variability are a change in operators, environmental changes or equipment problems. The process is then shut down, the assignable cause is identified and eliminated, and the process resumes operating in an in-control state.

The positioning of the control limits on the control chart is critical to the performance of the chart in detecting an out-of-control process. If the control limits are placed too close to the center line, the result will be that points will fall outside the control limits simply by chance giving a false indication of an out-of-control process. If the control limits are set too far away from the center line, the chart will fail to signal when an assignable cause of variability is present.

A general statistical model for all control charts, as given by Montgomery (1991), is as follows. Let X denote a sample statistic that measures some quality characteristic of interest. The mean or long term average of X is μ_X and the standard deviation of X is σ_X. The empirical rule then states that a large portion of the data observed from the process will lie between $\mu_X \pm 3\sigma_X$ no matter what control chart statistic is used. This led to the commonly used "Shewhart 3σ" control limits. The general definition for the control limits are then

$$UCL = \mu_x + k\sigma_x$$

$$Centerline = \mu_x$$

$$LCL = \mu_x - k\sigma_x$$

where k is commonly chosen to be 3. The mean, μ_X, and standard deviation, σ_X, of the control statistic are known as process parameters and are either known or can be estimated from the data collected on the process.

Figure 2. Distribution of Quality Characteristic Relative to Control Chart Limits

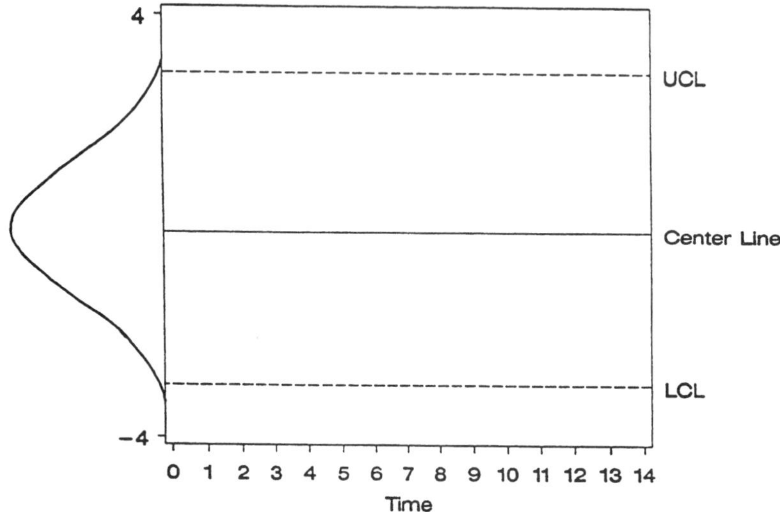

As an example, consider Figure 2. If the quality characteristic being measured follows a normal distribution, the control limits are chosen so that 99.7% of the observations would fall within these limits. Points falling outside the control limits may be due to random chance (though there is <1% chance of this) or they may be a signal that the process is out-of-control, i.e., some assignable cause is acting on the process.

Types of Control Charts

Control charts fall into two general categories, *variables control charts* and *attribute control charts*. Variables control charts are constructed for quality characteristics measured on a continuous scale. Attribute control charts are constructed for quality characteristics which are of a conforming/non conforming nature or counts of defects. Within these general categories, many types of charts are available to monitor a particular process parameter. In this chapter, the monitoring of the center of the process distribution for a continuous quality characteristic will be discussed. Several charts are available for this purpose, including the Shewhart $\overline{X}$ chart, the median control chart, the Run Sum control chart and the Shewhart $\overline{X}$ chart with supplemental run rules. The performance of all of these charts will be discussed in terms of ARL in the following sections.

Control Chart Average Run Length

The average run length (ARL) of a control chart is one way the performance of one control chart versus another can be measured. The following discussion of ARL will center on the monitoring of the process distribution mean for independent, normally distributed data with single observations at each time point but the concept of ARL applies equally as well to all other types of control charts.

As an example, consider the monitoring of the fill level in large containers of juice drink. Rather than measuring the contents of the bottle directly, the quality control technician marks a fill line 6 centimeters from the top of a sampled bottle and records the fill level relative to the line in millimeters. Suppose that the process average fill differential is $\mu_0=0$ (i.e., no underfill or overfill) and the fill differential is known to have a standard deviation of $\sigma=1$ centimeter from previous data. A single bottle is sampled from each hour's production. It has been determined by the quality assurance team and management that, on average, a one centimeter or greater underfill or overfill is critical in terms of customer satisfaction and profits.

In Figure 3, we see a sequence of data values from the filling process plotted on a 3σ Shewhart control chart. At time point 11, a point is plotted above the upper control limit. The Shewhart control chart is indicating that the process mean fill level differential has shifted upwards (an out-of-control signal) and that, on average, bottles are being overfilled with product. The cause of this out-of-control point needs to be investigated.

Figure 3. Example Data Sequence

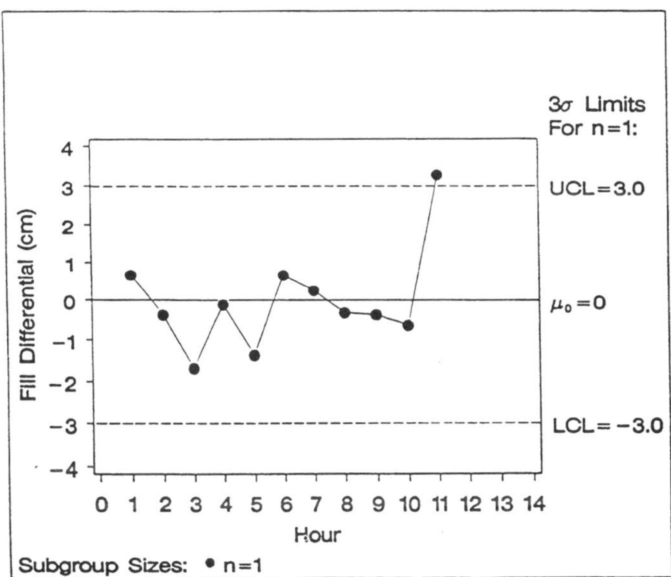

The run length, denoted *N*, for a sequence of data is the number of time points which elapse until an out-of-control signal is generated by the control chart. Each sequence of data recorded from the process will have a run length before an out-of-control signal is given. The run length for the pictured sequence of data is $N=11$.

The run length, *N*, is a random variable which can take on positive integer values. The expected value of *N*, denoted *E(N)*, is the average run length. It can be shown that the expected value of *N*, ARL, is the infinite sum

$$ARL = E(N) = \sum_{i=1}^{\infty} P(N \geq i).$$

The exact form of the terms in this sum is specific to each type of control chart. The first to be discussed is the ARL for the Shewhart chart.

ARL for the Shewhart Chart

For a Shewhart chart, the probability that the run length is longer than i is the probability of getting $i-1$ observations in a row inside the control limits. If the probability that an observation is between the control limits is denoted as p then

$$ARL = E(N) = \sum_{i=1}^{\infty} p^{i-1} = (1-p)^{-1}. \qquad (1)$$

If it is further assumed that the process characteristic that is being measured follows a normal distribution with mean μ and variance σ^2, then p can be calculated explicitly and, using p, the ARL can be computed for a specific chart.

For a Shewhart $\overline{X}$ chart with 3σ control limits, the probability of an observation being between the control limits is

$$p = P_{\mu}(\mu_0 - 3\sigma / \sqrt{n} < \overline{X} < \mu_0 + 3\sigma / \sqrt{n})$$

where μ_0 is the target mean level of the process. If the mean shifts upwards from μ_0 to μ_1 by some multiple δ of the standard deviation of the sample mean, $\sigma/\sqrt{n}$, then

$$\begin{aligned} p &= P((\mu_0 - \mu_1) - 3\sigma / \sqrt{n} < \overline{X} - \mu_1 < (\mu_0 - \mu_1) + 3\sigma / \sqrt{n}) \\ &= P((-3-\delta)\sigma / \sqrt{n} < \overline{X} - \mu_1 < (3-\delta)\sigma / \sqrt{n}) \qquad \text{since } \mu_1 = \mu_0 + \delta\sigma / \sqrt{n} \\ &= P(-3-\delta < Z < 3-\delta) \end{aligned}$$

i.e., p and, using (1), the ARL of the Shewhart control chart can be computed as a function of the multiplier of the standard deviation of the sample mean. All the ARLs shown in this chapter were computed for this standardized shift in the process mean, δ. Therefore, the shifts in the process mean shown in the tables in this chapter are the values of δ. For a specific application, these shifts can then be translated into the scale of the data units using the relation, $\Delta=\mu_1-\mu_0=\delta\sigma/\sqrt{n}$, where the process standard deviation is σ and the sample size at each time point is n. *Note the difference between Δ and δ.* The shift Δ is in the scale of the data units while the shift δ is in standardized units.

With independent, normally distributed process data, the quantity

$$p = P(-3+\delta < Z < 3+\delta)$$

can be computed for a variety of shifts, δ, in the process mean using the PROBNORM function available in base SAS software. The resultant value of p can then be used in (1) to compute ARL for the Shewhart chart.

The SAS macro SHEWARL, shown below, computes the Shewhart chart ARL for various shifts, δ, in the process mean, μ. The first column of Table 1 displays the results of these calculations. The arguments to the SHEWHART macro are the upper and lower shifts in the process mean for which ARLs will be calculated, DL and DU, and the increment value, D. The control limits are determined by the value of K.

```
%macro shewarl(dsn=,type=,dl=,du=,d=,k=);

data &dsn;
  length type $ 30;
  type="&type"; k=&k; lcl=-k; ucl=k;

  do delta = &dl to &du by &d;
    p=probnorm(ucl-delta) - probnorm(lcl-delta);
    arl = 1 / (1-p);
    output;
  end;
run;

%mend shewarl;
```

The macro call for the Shewhart 3σ chart is shown below.

```
%shewarl(dsn=arl1,type=Shewhart 3 sigma,dl=0,du=3,d=.2,k=3)
```

The resulting ARLs are shown in Table 1. This and all other comparison tables in this chapter were created using the TABARL macro shown below. The data sets containing the sequences of ARLs to be compared are given in the DSN argument. The table number is given in the TABNO argument.

```
%macro tabarl(dsn=,tabno=);

   data tabarl; set &dsn;

   proc tabulate data=tabarl format=10.2 order=data;
     class delta type;
     format delta 4.1;
     label type='Chart Type';
     var arl;
     table delta,type*arl*sum='   ';
   Title "Table &tabno.. ARL Comparison";
   run;

%mend tabarl;

%tabarl(dsn=arl1,tabno=1)
```

Table 1. ARLs for Shewhart 3σ Chart

	Chart Type
	Shewhart 3 sigma
	ARL
DELTA	
0.0	370.40
0.2	308.43
0.4	200.08
0.6	119.67
0.8	71.55
1.0	43.89
1.2	27.82
1.4	18.25
1.6	12.38
1.8	8.69
2.0	6.30
2.2	4.72
2.4	3.65
2.6	2.90
2.8	2.38
3.0	2.00

From Table 1, with δ=0, we get ARL=370.40. This is the in-control ARL. Since the tails of the Normal distribution overlap the control limits on the Shewhart chart, data values can be outside the control limits even when the process is operating in control. For this chart, a false out-of-control signal (or false alarm) will occur on the average once in every 370 time points. The out-of-control ARL at δ=1 ($\Delta=1\sigma/\sqrt{n}$) is 43.89. This means that the chart will signal on average after 44 time points have elapsed if a unit shift in the process mean occurs.

Modifications of the Shewhart 3σ Chart

While 3σ control limits have become the standard for statistical process control (SPC) applications, modifications of these limits are also commonly used. Two of these modifications will be discussed in this section. A sequence of ARLs can be computed for each of these modifications and these ARL sequences can be compared to the ARLs of the Shewhart 3σ chart.

In some SPC applications the control limits are narrowed slightly to $\mu \pm 2.5\sigma$. The ARL for this chart is calculated using (1) with

$$p = P(-2.5 + \delta < Z < 2.5 + \delta).$$

A call to the SHEWARL macro produces a sequence of ARLs for this chart. These ARLs are displayed in column two of Table 1.

```
%shewarl(dsn=arl2,type=Shewhart 2.5 sigma,dl=0,du=3,d=.2,k=2.5)
```

British standards use what is known as probability based control limits. The form of these limits is

$$\mu \pm Z_{\alpha/2}\sigma$$

where $Z_{\alpha/2}$ is the $\alpha/2$ percentage point of the normal distribution. With α=.002 the control limits are set such that 99.8% of the data are between the control limits when the process is operating in an in-control state.

The percentage points of the normal distribution can be calculated using the PROBIT function available in base SAS software. A call to the SHEWARL macro with k=PROBIT(.999) will calculate ARL for this chart using (1) with

$$p = P(-PROBIT(.999) + \delta < Z < PROBIT(.999) + \delta).$$

The macro call is

```
%shewarl(dsn=arl3,type=Prob. Limits .002,dl=0,du=3,d=.2,
          k=probit(.999))
```

The resulting ARLs for this chart along with that of the 2.5σ chart and the Shewhart $\overline{X}$ chart are shown side by side in Table 2. The macro call used to display the three ARL sequences in Table 2 is the following.

```
%tabarl(dsn=arl1 arl2 arl3,tabno=2)
```

Table 2. Comparison of ARLs for Various Shewhart Charts

	Chart Type		
	Shewhart 3 sigma	Shewhart 2.5 sigma	Prob. Limits .002
	ARL	ARL	ARL
DELTA			
0.0	370.40	80.52	500.00
0.2	308.43	70.47	412.32
0.4	200.08	50.68	262.37
0.6	119.67	33.69	153.96
0.8	71.55	22.20	90.46
1.0	43.89	14.92	54.59
1.2	27.82	10.32	34.05
1.4	18.25	7.37	21.98
1.6	12.38	5.43	14.69
1.8	8.69	4.13	10.15
2.0	6.30	3.24	7.26
2.2	4.72	2.62	5.36
2.4	3.65	2.17	4.08
2.6	2.90	1.85	3.21
2.8	2.38	1.62	2.59
3.0	2.00	1.45	2.15

From Table 2, it can be seen that narrowing the control limits has a dramatic effect on ARL. The in-control ARL is reduced to 80.52. This means that false alarms will be generated nearly five times faster than with the 3σ chart. Using this chart, the out-of-control ARL for a 1σ shift in the process center is a third of that of the 3σ chart. This tradeoff between a shortened in-control ARL versus a shortened ARL for a critical process shift must be weighed carefully before a type of chart is selected to monitor a process. The probability limits chart shows a higher in-control ARL and is slightly less responsive to shifts in the process center than the 3σ chart up to shifts of size 2.6σ.

ARL for the Median Control Chart

The Median control chart is an alternative to the Shewhart $\overline{X}$ chart for monitoring the center of the distribution of the quality characteristic under study. The development of this chart was spurred by two factors: (a) the simplicity of calculations used in setting up and maintaining the chart and (b) the decreased sensitivity of the median to sporadic large data values (sometimes called "flyers"). Since the median chart can easily be created using the SAS/QC procedure SHEWHART, factor (a) is no longer of interest. What is of interest is to compute the ARL for the median chart and compare it to the Shewhart charts from the previous section.

For a sample of size n at time point i, the median chart plots the sample median, $\tilde{X}$, of the data $(x_1, x_2, \ldots, x_n)$. When the data at time point i are ranked in order from smallest to largest (denoted $(x_{(1)}, x_{(2)}, \ldots, x_{(n)})$), the median is defined as

$$\begin{aligned} \tilde{X} &= x_{((n+1)/2)} && n \text{ odd} \\ &= (x_{(x/2)} + x_{(n/2+1)})/2 && n \text{ even.} \end{aligned}$$

Nelson (1982) and White and Schroeder (1987) give the control limits for this type of chart as

$$\mu_m \pm k\sigma_m$$

where μ_{m} is the targeted value and σ_{m} is the standard deviation of the median. It can be shown that $\sigma_{\mathrm{m}}=e(n)\cdot\sigma_{\mathrm{X}}$ where σ_{X} is the standard deviation of the data collected on the process and, for normally distributed process data, the factor *e(n)* is given by the STDMED function in SAS/QC software.

With k=3, n=5, σ_{X}=1 and normally distributed process data, the control limits are $\pm 3\cdot e(5) = \pm 3\cdot$ *STDMED*(5)=± 1.606. From a similar argument as was used for the Shewhart ARL, the ARL for the median chart is

$$ARL_m(\Delta) = (1-p)^{-1}$$

where, for a sample of size 5,

$$p = P(-1.606 + \Delta < \tilde{X} < 1.606 + \Delta).$$

Using the PROBMED function available in SAS/QC software, the MEDARL macro given below generates the ARLs for the median chart for selected shifts, δ, in the process center. The first six arguments for this macro are the same as those of the SHEWARL macro. The variable n gives the sample size at each time point. Note that this macro also generates ARLs for a Shewhart chart with control limits set at 2.977σ. This makes the in-control ARL for the Shewhart chart approximately equal to the in-control ARL for the median chart and allows a fair comparison of the two charts.

```
%macro medarl(dsn=,type=,dl=,du=,d=,k=,n=);

   data &dsn;
     length type $ 30;
     k=&k; n=&n;
```

```
      do delta = &dl to &du by &d;
         type="Shewhart 2.977 Sigma n=&n";
         p = probnorm(2.977-delta)-probnorm(-2.977-delta);
         arl=1/(1-p);
         output;
         type="&type";
         lcl=-k*stdmed(n); ucl=k*stdmed(n);
         shift=delta/sqrt(n);
         p = probmed(n,ucl-shift)-probmed(n,lcl-shift);
         arl=1/(1-p);
         output;
      end;
   run;

%mend medarl;
```

The median chart ARLs are created using the following macro call.

```
%medarl(dsn=arl4,type=Median 3 Sigma n=5,dl=0,du=3,d=.2,k=3,n=5)
```

Table 3 is then created by a call to the TABARL macro.

```
%tabarl(dsn=arl4,tabno=3)
```

Table 3. Comparison of Shewhart Chart and Median Chart ARLs

	Chart Type	
	Shewhart 2.977 Sigma n=5	Median 3 Sigma n=5
	ARL	ARL
DELTA		
0.0	343.54	343.76
0.2	286.76	304.11
0.4	186.93	222.88
0.6	112.35	149.53
0.8	67.48	98.03
1.0	41.57	64.66
1.2	26.46	43.38
1.4	17.42	29.72
1.6	11.87	20.82
1.8	8.36	14.92
2.0	6.09	10.94
2.2	4.57	8.20
2.4	3.55	6.29
2.6	2.83	4.93
2.8	2.33	3.95
3.0	1.96	3.23

From Table 3, it can be seen that the out-of-control ARLs for the median chart are larger than those of the Shewhart chart reflecting the decreased sensitivity of the median to large data values. When the control limits on the two charts are set such that the in-control ARLs are equal, the $\overline{X}$ chart provides better performance than the median chart for normally distributed data.

ARL for the Run Sum Control Chart

Roberts (1958) and Reynolds (1971) discuss another type of control chart used to monitor the center of the process distribution, the *run sum control chart*. The run sum control chart is operated by dividing the chart into regions that are one standard deviation wide on either side of the center line as shown in Figure 4. Each region is assigned a score. As each observation is plotted, it is assigned a score corresponding to the region of the chart in which the point falls. A running sum of the scores, S, is kept. For a two-sided chart, one that detects a shift from the target in both the negative and positive direction, S is reset to 0 at the end of each run of points on one side of the center line. The process center is shown to have shifted upwards when S exceeds h and downwards when S falls below $-h$.

Figure 4. Sample Run Sum Chart

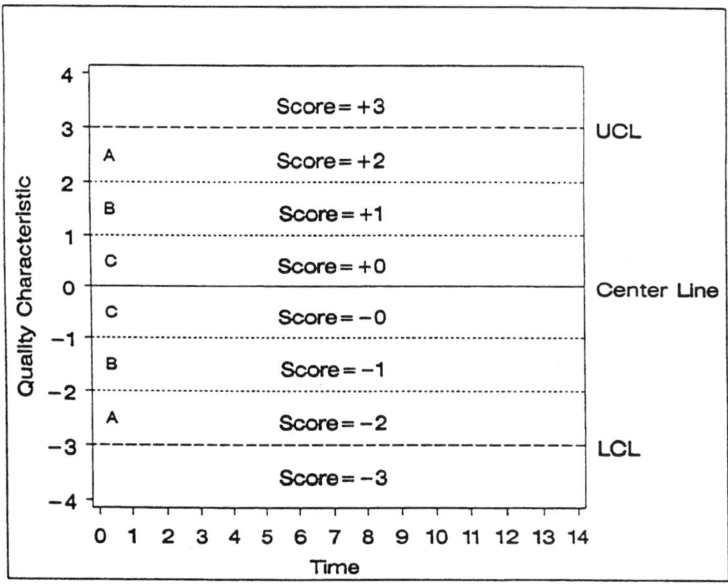

As shown in Figure 4, the chart is most easily operated when the scores 0,1,2,3,... are assigned to the zones above the center line and the corresponding negative scores are assigned to the zones below the center line. A formal notation for this chart is

$$RS_h[L_0(V_0), L_1(V_1), L_2(V_2), ...]$$

where L_i and V_i denote the limits and scores for each zone on the chart and h is the minimum run sum to signal an out-of-control process. An observation, X_j, is assigned a score of V_i if

$$\mu + L_i\sigma_x < X_j \le \mu + L_{i+1}\sigma_x .$$

The scores given in Figure 4 correspond to a symmetric two-sided version of

$$RS_h[0(0), 1(1), 2(2), ...].$$

Since this set of scores is most commonly used in practice, they will be used for the remainder of this chapter. The notation can then be shortened to RS_h.

Brook and Evans (1972) have shown that the ARL of many types of control charts can be computed by dividing the chart into regions or zones and considering the various possible data configurations recorded on the chart as the states of a Markov Chain. Let *s* denote the number of states necessary to describe the chart. For the run sum chart, the states correspond to the values of the running sum, *S*. For the one-sided RS_5 chart, the values that *S* can take on are 0, 1, 2, 3, 4 and ≥ 5. A total of six states (five in-control (0-4), one out-of-control(≥ 5)) would be necessary to describe the status of the chart. Let **P** be an *(s-1)x(s-1)* matrix whose elements are the probability of transitioning between any of the *s-1* in-control states which describe the control chart.

The matrix of in-control transition probabilities, **P**, can be used to compute ARL. The ij^{th} element of the matrix **P** is p_{ij}. So, for example, the element p_{12} is the probability of transitioning from state 1 to state 2 of the control chart. The ARL of a control chart is the first element of the vector

$$\text{ARL}=(\mathbf{I}\text{-}\mathbf{P})^{-1}\cdot\mathbf{J} \qquad (2)$$

where **I** is an *(s-1)x(s-1)* identity matrix and **J** is an *(s-1)* vector of ones.

For the run sum chart, the probability transition matrix consists of five in-control states. These states correspond to the values of *S* and are labeled as such in the matrix below. The element p_{00} is the probability that the running sum currently contains a value of 0 and stays at 0 after the next observation is scored. In terms of the data value plotted at time point *i*, X_i,

$$p_{00}(\Delta) = P(X_i \leq 1\sigma + \Delta).$$

In standardized units, this probability is

$$p_{00}(\delta) = P(Z \leq 1 + \delta).$$

For normally distributed data with δ=0, $p_{00}(0) = .8413$. Similarly, p_{13} is the probability that *S*=1 and will equal 3 after the next observation is scored. In terms of the data, the probability of obtaining a score of 2 on the next observation is

$$p_{13}(\Delta) = P(2\sigma + \Delta < X_i \leq 3\sigma + \Delta)$$

or in standardized units

$$p_{13}(\delta) = P(2 + \delta < Z \leq 3 + \delta).$$

With normally distributed data and δ=0, $p_{24}(0) = .34214$. In general, the probability transition matrix, **P**, is

$$
\begin{array}{c} \\ 0 \\ 1 \\ 2 \\ 3 \\ 4 \end{array}
\begin{array}{c}
\begin{array}{ccccc} 0 & 1 & 2 & 3 & 4 \end{array} \\
\begin{bmatrix}
p_{00} & p_{01} & p_{02} & p_{03} & p_{04} \\
p_{10} & p_{11} & & & \vdots \\
p_{20} & & \ddots & & \vdots \\
p_{30} & & & \ddots & \vdots \\
p_{40} & \cdots & \cdots & \cdots & p_{44}
\end{bmatrix}
\end{array}
$$

where the values along the border of the matrix give the possible values of S. Using (2), the ARL for the run sum chart can be calculated.

The probability transition matrix above is for a one-sided run sum chart. The ARL computed using this **P** matrix will thus be a one-sided ARL. Once the ARL has been computed for the one-sided case, the two-sided ARL can be computed using the approximate relation,

$$\frac{1}{ARL\,2(\delta)} \approx \frac{1}{ARL\,(\delta)} + \frac{1}{ARL\,(-\delta)} \tag{3}$$

derived by van Dobben de Bruyn(1968), where ARL2 is the two-sided ARL.

The SAS macro RSARL, shown below, can be used to compute ARLs for the run sum control chart. The first five arguments are the same as those of the SHEWARL macro presented earlier. The other variable, H, gives the minimum value of the run sum that will cause an out-of-control signal. All probabilities are calculated using standardized zone boundaries and standardized shifts, δ.

```
%macro rsarl(dsn=,type=,dl=,du=,d=,h=);

    proc iml;

      create &dsn var{shift arl};

      h=&h; row=0;
      do delta=&dl to &du by &d;
        arl2s=j(2,1,0);
        do side=1 to 2;
          if side=1 then sign=-1; else sign=1;
          shift=sign*delta;
          row=row+1; p=j(h,h,0);

          do i=1 to h;
            do j=1 to h;
              if j >= i then
                   p[i,j]=probnorm(j-i+1-shift) - probnorm(j-i-shift);
              if j=1 then p[i,j]=probnorm(0-shift);
              if j=1 & i=1 then p[i,j]=probnorm(1-shift);
            end;
          end;
          arlvec = inv(i(h)-p)*j(h,1,1); arl2s[side]=arlvec[1,1];
        end;
      arl = (arl2s[1]*arl2s[2])/(arl2s[1]+arl2s[2]);
      append;
      end;
      close &dsn;
      quit;

      data &dsn; set &dsn;
```

```
        length type $ 30;
        type="&type"; rename shift=delta;
    run;

%mend rsarl;
```

The sequence of ARLs for the RS_5 chart are generated from a call to the RSARL macro. Table 4, comparing the RS_5 and the Shewhart ARLs is created using the TABARL macro.

```
%rsarl(dsn=arl5,type=Run Sum h=5,dl=0,du=3,d=.2,h=5)

%tabarl(dsn=arl1 arl5,tabno=4)
```

Table 4. Comparison of Shewhart and Run Sum ARL

	Chart Type	
	Shewhart 3 sigma	Run Sum h=5
	ARL	ARL
DELTA		
0.0	370.40	343.73
0.2	308.43	190.72
0.4	200.08	74.69
0.6	119.67	33.93
0.8	71.55	18.47
1.0	43.89	11.67
1.2	27.82	8.24
1.4	18.25	6.31
1.6	12.38	5.11
1.8	8.69	4.32
2.0	6.30	3.76
2.2	4.72	3.34
2.4	3.65	3.02
2.6	2.90	2.77
2.8	2.38	2.56
3.0	2.00	2.39

From Table 4, it can be seen that the ARL of the RS_5 chart is slightly less than that of the Shewhart chart up to shifts of size 2.6σ. The shorter out-of-control ARLs are a result of (a) the fact that the RS_5 chart has a shorter in-control ARL than the Shewhart chart and (b) the sensitivity of the RS_5 chart to detect shifts in the process mean is better than the Shewhart chart. This increased sensitivity is due to the RS_5 chart's ability to consider sequences of data in reaching a decision on the process status. The Shewhart chart uses only the current time point to determine the status of the process.

ARL of Shewhart Chart with Supplemental Run Rules

A method of control charting that is similar to the run sum chart is to augment the Shewhart $\overline{X}$ with supplemental run rules. This type of chart also monitors the center of the process distribution. The sensitivity to shifts in the process center is increased by the addition of one or more supplemental run rules to the chart. These additional tests for runs are described by Nelson (1984) and can be added to the Shewhart chart using the TESTS= option in PROC SHEWHART. The purpose of this section is to show

how the ARL is calculated for this type of chart and to examine the effect of the added run rules by comparing the ARL of these charts to the ARL of the Shewhart chart.

Champ and Woodall (1987) and Chung and Pittman (1989) have shown that the ARL of this type of chart can also be calculated using the Markov chain approach. As was the case for the run sum chart, the in-control region is divided into zones that are one standard deviation wide on either side of the center line (see Figure 4). The states of the Markov chain represent the sequences of points that can occur in each region of interest.

For example, if we augment the Shewhart chart with a supplementary run rule of nine consecutive points on one side of the center line (which corresponds to specifying TESTS=1 2 in PROC SHEWHART), then an out-of-control process is signaled if one point falls outside the usual 3σ limits or if nine consecutive points fall in zones A, B or C on one side of center. Expressing the boundaries in standardized units, there are two one-sided regions to consider, R_1=(0,3) and R_2=($-\infty$,0) with probabilities of containment p_1 and p_2, respectively. The probability transition matrix, **P**, consists of nine in-control states. To remain in control, a point is observed in R_2 (state 1) or a run of eight or fewer consecutive points in R_1 is in progress (states 2-8). The transition matrix is **P** is

$$\begin{array}{ccccccccc} R_2 & R_1^1 & R_1^2 & R_1^3 & R_1^4 & R_1^5 & R_1^6 & R_1^7 & R_1^8 \end{array}$$
$$\begin{bmatrix} p_2 & p_1 & 0 & 0 & 0 & 0 & 0 & 0 & 0 \\ p_2 & 0 & p_1 & 0 & 0 & 0 & 0 & 0 & 0 \\ p_2 & 0 & 0 & p_1 & 0 & 0 & 0 & 0 & 0 \\ p_2 & 0 & 0 & 0 & p_1 & 0 & 0 & 0 & 0 \\ p_2 & 0 & 0 & 0 & 0 & p_1 & 0 & 0 & 0 \\ p_2 & 0 & 0 & 0 & 0 & 0 & p_1 & 0 & 0 \\ p_2 & 0 & 0 & 0 & 0 & 0 & 0 & p_1 & 0 \\ p_2 & 0 & 0 & 0 & 0 & 0 & 0 & 0 & p_1 \\ p_2 & 0 & 0 & 0 & 0 & 0 & 0 & 0 & 0 \end{bmatrix}$$

The superscript on the region denotes the number of consecutive points in that region. Since a single value below the center line breaks the run but does not cause an out-of-control signal, a single column for R_2 must appear in the **P** matrix. Many of the elements of the **P** matrix are 0 since, for example, a transition from one consecutive point in Zone A to one consecutive point in A is impossible.

If we assume that we are monitoring a process characteristic whose distribution is normal then

$$p_1 = P(0+\delta < Z < 3+\delta)$$

$$p_2 = P(Z < 0+\delta\ )$$

can be computed using the PROBNORM function in base SAS software. For a specified shift in the process center, δ, p_1 and p_2 can be computed and plugged into **P** so that the ARL can be calculated using (2). The two-sided ARL can be calculated using (3).

This example illustrates the form of the **P** matrix for *l out of l* supplemental run rules. King (1993) gives a summary of the computation of ARL for the Shewhart chart augmented with either an *l out of l* or an *l out of l+1* supplemental run rule. SAS macros are included that compute the ARLs. The remainder of this section will show how to compute ARL for Shewhart charts augmented with ***multiple run rules.***

Champ and Woodall (1990) have given a computer program useful for calculating ARL for Shewhart multiple run rule charts. This program has been written using SAS PROC IML by the SAS Institute staff. An abridged version of this program is shown in the appendix. For the purpose of this paper, the program has been made to operate as a macro and to generate a sequence of ARLs for the specified chart.

The operation of the code shown in the appendix is a two step process. The first step is to create data records describing the supplemental run rules to be applied to the chart. The type of the run for the region is given in the K and M variables. The lower and upper boundaries of the region are given in variables A and B. Note that when a region boundary is positive (negative) infinity a large positive (negative) number must be used as the argument to the macro. Values of 9 and -9 will produce satisfactory results. For example, to augment the Shewhart 3σ chart with a 2 out of 3 in zone A rule, four records are necessary. For the one consecutive point above the upper control limit, a record that assigns K=1, M=1, A=3 and B=9 is needed. The lower half of this rule requires K=1, M=1, A=-9 and B=-3. To designate the upper 2 out of 3 in zone A rule, a record that assigns K=2, M=3, A=2 and B=3 is needed. The lower half of this rule requires K=2, M=3, A=-3 and B=-2. The second step is to call the SHEWSUPP macro with the appropriate parameters. They are the same as those of the SHEWARL macro presented earlier. The macro calls that produced Table 5 below are shown at the end of the appendix.

In Table 5, the ARLs of several types of supplemental run rule charts are compared to the Shewhart 3 σ ARL. Column 2 of the chart shows the ARLs for a Shewhart chart augmented with a test for eight consecutive points on one side of center and a test for 2 out of 3 points in zone A. This chart gives an in-control ARL of 122.04. For a 1σ shift in the process mean, the ARL is 11.72. Note the improved responsiveness of the chart to a 1σ shift caused by the addition of the run rules. The ARLs for a chart augmented with a 4 out of 5 in zone B or C rule are comparable to those of the 2 out of 3 in zone C chart. As shown in column 4, when all three rules are applied to the Shewhart chart even shorter ARLs are obtained. The shorter out-of-control ARLs must be weighed against the in-control ARL of 91.74. This chart produces false alarms three time faster than the Shewhart chart.

Table 5. Comparison of Shewhart and Supplemental Run Rules Chart ARLs

	Chart Type			
	Shewhart 3 sigma	1,2/3,8/8 (1)	1,4/5,8/8 (2)	1,2/3,4/5-,8/8 (3)
	ARL	ARL	ARL	ARL
DELTA				
0.0	370.40	122.04	105.77	91.74
0.2	308.43	89.13	76.00	66.79
0.4	200.08	48.71	40.94	36.60
0.6	119.67	27.49	23.15	20.90
0.8	71.55	17.14	14.62	13.25
1.0	43.89	11.72	10.19	9.22
1.2	27.82	8.61	7.66	6.89
1.4	18.25	6.63	6.08	5.42
1.6	12.38	5.27	5.01	4.41
1.8	8.69	4.27	4.24	3.68
2.0	6.30	3.50	3.65	3.13
2.2	4.72	2.91	3.17	2.70
2.4	3.65	2.47	2.77	2.35
2.6	2.90	2.13	2.43	2.07
2.8	2.38	1.87	2.14	1.85
3.0	2.00	1.68	1.89	1.67

1/ This type of chart can be obtained in PROC SHEWHART
by coding TESTS=1 2 5   TEST2RUN=8
2/ This type of chart can be obtained in PROC SHEWHART
by coding TESTS=1 2 6   TEST2RUN=8
3/ This type of chart can be obtained in PROC SHEWHART
by coding TESTS=1 2 5 6 TEST2RUN=8

Summary

This chapter has presented a discussion of a quantitative measure of control chart performance known as average run length. A number of macros have been presented in this chapter that can be used to compute ARL for a variety of charts and then compare the calculated ARLs. While some comparisons of control chart ARLs have been discussed in this chapter, the user should now have the ability to make a comparison of ARLs for any subset of the chart types presented.

References

Brook, D. and Evans, D.A. (1972). "An Approach to the Probability Distribution of CUSUM Run Lengths", **Biometrika,** 59, 539-549.

Champ, C.W. and Woodall, W.H.(1987). "Exact Results for Shewhart Control Charts with Supplementary Run Rules", **Technometrics,** 29, no.4, 393-399.

Champ, C.W. and Woodall, W.H.(1990). "A Program to Evaluate the Run Length Distribution of a Shewhart Control Chart with Supplementary Run Rules", **Journal of Quality Technology,** 22, no.1, 68-73.

Chung, J. and Pittman, T.O.(1989). "A Simple Method for Computing the ARL of $\overline{X}$ -Charts with Zone Tests", **Communications in Statistics - Series B - Simulation and Computing,** 18(4), 1275-1293.

van Dobben de Bruyn, C.S.(1968). **Cumulative Sum Tests: Theory and Practice,** New York, NY: Hafner Publishing, 82p.

King, D.W. (1993). "Using SAS/QC Software to Select the "Best" Control Chart", **Observations, The Technical Journal for SAS Software Users,** vol.3, no. 1, 16-24.

Montgomery, D.C. (1991). **Introduction to Statistical Quality Control,** New York, NY: John Wiley & Sons, second edition.

Nelson, L. (1982). "Control Chart for Medians", **Journal of Quality Technology,** 14, no. 4, 226-227.

Nelson, L. (1984). "The Shewhart Control Chart - Tests for Special Causes", **Journal of Quality Technology,** 15, 237-239.

Page, E.S. (1954). "Continuous Inspection Schemes", **Biometrika,** 41, 100-114.

Page, E.S. (1955). "Control Charts with Warning Lines", **Biometrika,** 42, 243-257.

Reynolds, J.H. (1971). "The Run Sum Control Chart Procedure", **Journal of Quality Technology,** 3, no.1, 23-27.

Roberts, S.W.(1958). "Properties of Control Chart Zone Tests", **The Bell System Technical Journal,** 37, 83-114.

SAS Institute Inc.(1989). **SAS Technical Report P-188, SAS/QC Software Examples, Version 6,** Cary, NC: SAS Institute Inc., 374p.

White, E.M. and Schroeder, R. (1987). "A Simultaneous Control Chart", **Journal of Quality Technology,** 19, no. 1, 1-10.

Vance, L.C. (1983). "A Bibliography of Statistical Quality Control Chart Techniques, 1970-1980", **Journal of Quality Technology,** vol. 15, no. 2, 59-62.

Acknowledgments

The author would like to thank all the people at SAS Institute who helped make this article more readable and informative. Thanks to Jennifer Ginn and Liz Malcolm for all their excellent instructions on the formatting of the article and to the technical reviewers at SAS Institute. Special thanks go to Kathleen Giuseffi of the STATKING staff who typed the initial drafts of the chapter.

Appendix

```
/*  Input the Rules Defining the Chart   */

data rules;
  input k m a b;
  cards;
  1  1   3   9
  2  3   2   3
  4  5   1   3
  8  8   0   3
  8  8  -3   0
  4  5  -3  -1
  2  3  -3  -2
  1  1  -9  -3
  ;

proc print;
run;

%macro shewsupp(dsn=,type=,dl=,du=,d=);

 proc iml;

  use rules;  read all var {k m a b};
  create &dsn var{arl shf};

  do delta=&dl to &du by &d;

 /*********************************************************/
 /*  Input the Standarized Shift,                         */
 /*  the Upper Limit for the Calculation of ARL and Std,  */
 /*  and the Upper Limit for the CDF Graph                */
 /*********************************************************/

  shf    = delta;
  uppcal = 0.99999;
  uppgra = 0.99;

 /*   Find the Regions of the Chart   */

  r  = -9//a//b//9;
  r  = unique(r);
  nt = nrow(k);
  nr = ncol(r)-1;

 /***************************************************/
 /*   Find the Length of the State Vector           */
 /*   and the pointers to the End of the Subvector  */
 /*   Associated with Each Runs Rule                */
 /***************************************************/

  nv = sum(m)-nt;
  if(sum(m-k) = 0) then nv = nv+1;
  di = j(nt,1,0);
  di[1] = m[1]-1;
  do i = 2 to nt;
    if(m[i] > 1) then di[i] = di[i-1]+m[i]-1;
  end;

 /***************************************************/
 /*   Determine the Value of the Present            */
```

```
/*    Indicator Variable by Runs Rule and Region      */
/*    Combination                                     */
/****************************************************/

 a1 = j(nt,1,1);
 a1 = a1*r;
 x  = j(nt,nr,0);
 do j = 1 to nr;
   x[,j] = (a <= a1[,j])#(b >= a1[,j+1]);
 end;

/* Determine the State to State Transitions by Regions  */

 ps   = j(nv,1,0);
 s    = j(nt,1,0);
 a1   = j(1,nr,1);
 nx   = j(nv,1,0);
 qqns = 2**nv-1;
 ns   = 1;
 h    = 1;
 qq   = 0;
 q    = a1;
 do while ( h <= ns );
   qh = qq[h];
   do L = 1 to nv;
     ps[L] = qh-2*int(qh/2);
     qh = int(qh/2);
   end;
   do i = 1 to nt;
     s[i] = 0;
     if (m[i] > 1) then do
       L = di[i]-m[i]+2 to di[i];
       s[i] = s[i]+ps[L];
     end;
   end;
   do j = 1 to nr;
     sg = 0;
     do i = 1 to nt;
       if (sg = 0) then do;
         if (s[i]+x[i,j] >= k[i]) then sg = 1;
         else do;
           if (m[i] > 1) then nx[di[i]-m[i]+2] = x[i,j];
           if (m[i] > 2) then do
             L = di[i]-m[i]+3 to di[i];
             nx[L] = ps[L-1];
           end;
         end;
         if (x[i,j] = 0 & m[i] > 1) then do;
           tmp = s[i]-ps[di[i]]+1;
           L = di[i];
           ck = 0;
           do while ( ck = 0 & L >= di[i]-m[i]+2 );
             if (nx[L] = 1) then do;
               ck = 1;
               if (tmp < k[i]) then do;
                 nx[L] = 0;
                 tmp = tmp-1;
                 ck = 0;
               end;
             end;
             L = L-1;
             tmp = tmp+1;
           end;
         end;
       end;
```

```
      end;
      if (sg = 0) then do;
        qh = nx[1];
        do L = 2 to nv;
          qh = qh+nx[L]*(2**(L-1));
        end;
        ck = 0;
        do L = 1 to ns;
          if (ck = 0 & qh = qq[L]) then do;
            q[h,j] = qq[L];
            ck = 1;
          end;
        end;
        if (ck = 0) then do;
          ns = ns+1;
          qq = qq//qh;
          q[h,j] = qh;
        end;
      end;
      else
        q[h,j] = qqns;
    end;
    h = h+1;
    q = q//(qqns*a1);
  end;
  ns = ns+1;
  qq = qq//qqns;

  free / q qq ns nr r shf qqns uppcal uppgra delta k m a b;

/*******************************************/
/*   Sort the States in Ascending Order    */
/*     of Their Base Two Representations   */
/*******************************************/

  a1 = q;
  a1[rank(qq),] = q;
  q  = a1;
  a1 = qq;
  a1[rank(qq),] = qq;
  qq = a1;

/*   Remove any Duplicate States    */

  ck = 1;
  do while (ck = 1);
    ck = 0;
    i  = 1;
    do while (i <= ns-1);
      j = i+1;
      do while (j <= ns);
        if (q[i,] = q[j,]) then do;
            ck = 1;
            q  = q[remove(1:ns,j),];
            aaa= (q = (0*q+qq[j]));
            q  = (q#(1-aaa))+(qq[i]#aaa);
            qq = qq[remove(1:ns,j),];
            j  = j-1;
            ns = ns-1;
          end;
        j = j+1;
      end;
      i = i+1;
    end;
  end;
```

```
/*   Number the Next-State Transitions    */

 a1 = j(1,ns,1);
 a2 = (qq*a1)`;
 a3 = j(ns,nr,0);
 do j = 1 to nr;
   a3[,j] = ((q[,j]*a1) = a2)*((1:ns)`);
 end;
 a1 = (q < (0*q+qqns));
 q  = (ns#(1-a1))+(a3#a1);

 free qq qqns ck a2 a3;

/***********************************************************/
/*   Compute the Cumulative Distribution,                   */
/*   Function, the Average Run Length (ARL) and the         */
/*   Standard Deviation (STD) of the Run Length for a       */
/*   Given Standarized Shift (SHF) in the Mean.             */
/*                                                          */
/*   The Iterative Process for the Calculation of the       */
/*   CDF, ARL and STD stops when the CDF is > UPPCAL        */
/*                                                          */
/*   The Number of Recorded Points for the CDF Graph        */
/*   Stops When CDF is > UPPGRA                             */
/***********************************************************/

 pr = probnorm((r-shf)`);
 pr = (pr[2:nr+1,]//0)-pr;
 pr = pr[1:nr,];

 pt = j(ns,ns,0);
 do i = 1 to ns;
   do j = 1 to nr;
     pt[i,q[i,j]] = pt[i,q[i,j]]+pr[j];
   end;
 end;

 a1  = pt[1:ns-1,ns];
 pt  = pt[1:ns-1,1:ns-1];
 cdf = a1[1];
 acu = a1[1];
 n   = 1;
 do while ( acu <= uppcal );
   a1  = pt*a1;
   acu = acu+a1[1];
   if ( acu <= uppgra ) then n=n+1;
   cdf = cdf//a1[1];
 end;

 rl  = do(1,nrow(cdf),1);
 arl = rl*cdf;
 append;
 end;

 close &dsn;
quit;

data &dsn; set &dsn;
   length type $ 30;
   type="&type";
   rename shf=delta;
run;

%mend shewsupp;
```

```
%shewsupp(dsn=arl6,type=%str(1,2/3,8/8),dl=0,du=3,d=.2)

%shewsupp(dsn=arl7,type=%str(1,4/5,8/8),dl=0,du=3,d=.2)

%shewsupp(dsn=arl8,type=%str(1,2/3,4/5,8/8),dl=0,du=3,d=.2)

%tabarl(dsn=arl1 arl6 arl7 arl8,tabno=4)
```

Input Data Set for Shewsupp Macro
Values for 1,2/3,8/8 Run Rules

OBS	K	M	A	B
1	1	1	3	9
2	2	3	2	3
3	8	8	0	3
4	8	8	-3	0
5	2	3	-3	-2
6	1	1	-9	-3

Input Data Set for Shewsupp Macro
Values for 1,4/5,8/8 Run Rules

OBS	K	M	A	B
1	1	1	3	9
2	4	5	1	3
3	8	8	0	3
4	8	8	-3	0
5	4	5	-3	-1
6	1	1	-9	-3

Input Data Set for Shewsupp Macro
Values for 1,2/3,4/5,8/8 Run Rules

OBS	K	M	A	B
1	1	1	3	9
2	2	3	2	3
3	4	5	1	3
4	8	8	0	3
5	8	8	-3	0
6	4	5	-3	-1
7	2	3	-3	-2
8	1	1	-9	-3

CHAPTER 13

How to Automate Table Typesetting of SAS Output in Microsoft Word

by Rhena Seidman and Rick Aster

Abstract

Typesetting is often the best way to present tables, but table typesetting can be difficult to do manually. This chapter demonstrates an automated approach for producing typeset tables using a combination of SAS software and Microsoft Word word processing software.

Specifications

The code in this chapter was developed and tested with Releases 6.07 and 6.08 of the SAS System under various environments. Use of the code with other releases of the SAS System or other environments may require user modification. Modified code is not supported by the authors.

About the Author

Rhena Seidman is an Independent Consultant with 10 years of SAS software experience. She has a BA degree in Physics from Columbia University. Rick Aster is also an Independent Consultant with 10 years of SAS software experience. He has a BS degree in Economics and Mathematics from Lebanon Valley College. Between them, they have applied their knowledge of the SAS system in the fields of programming, statistics, data bases, insurance, computer performance evaluation, clinical research, marketing, banking, real estate, porting, translating, user interface design, documentation, and economics. They are authors of the book *Professional SAS Programming Secrets.*

Questions and Comments Should be Directed to:

Rhena Seidman
275 W. 96th Street, Suite 31F
New York, NY 10025
Telephone: 212-666-2773

Rick Aster
Oakwood Lane
Phoenixville, PA 19460
Telephone: 610-783-5371

Examples from this book are available online, see inside back cover for details.

How to Automate Table Typesetting of SAS® Output in Microsoft Word

Rhena Seidman and Rick Aster

Introduction

Typesetting, once a laborious and error-prone process, can now be the easiest and best way to present some kinds of SAS output. Popular word processing programs used with laser or ink-jet printers can produce typeset pages that combine standard text and graphics with SAS output. Using programmable word processing software such as Microsoft Word, it is possible to automate the process of assembling and typesetting the report. Automation saves time and effort, reduces error, and ensures a consistent format for the report.

Typesetting has important advantages. With the selection of the appropriate typeface and type size, typeset text is more readable and more compact than text that is not typeset, and it has a more attractive and professional appearance. Typesetting also allows graphical features such as rules and shading; text formatting such as bold and italic typefaces, subscript, and superscript characters, justification, and line spacing; and page layout features such as margins, page headers, and columns.

Figures 1a and 1b demonstrate some of the possible differences in appearance between typeset and non-typeset output of the same data.

Figure 1a. A non-typeset table produced by the PRINT procedure.

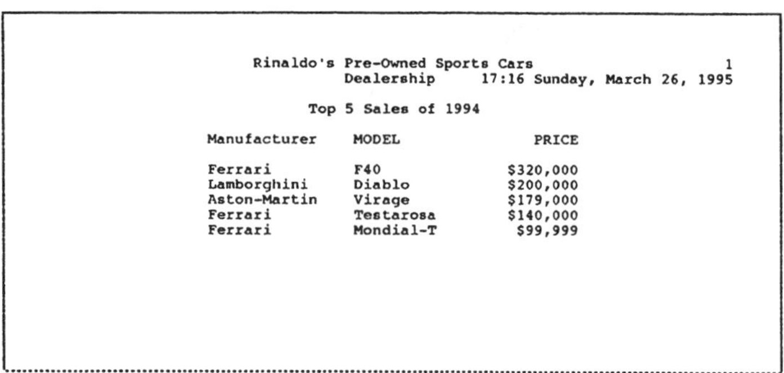

```
                  Rinaldo's Pre-Owned Sports Cars                    1
                            Dealership      17:16 Sunday, March 26, 1995

                      Top 5 Sales of 1994

         Manufacturer     MODEL                 PRICE

         Ferrari          F40                $320,000
         Lamborghini      Diablo             $200,000
         Aston-Martin     Virage             $179,000
         Ferrari          Testarosa          $140,000
         Ferrari          Mondial-T           $99,999
```

Figure 1b. The same data in typeset format.

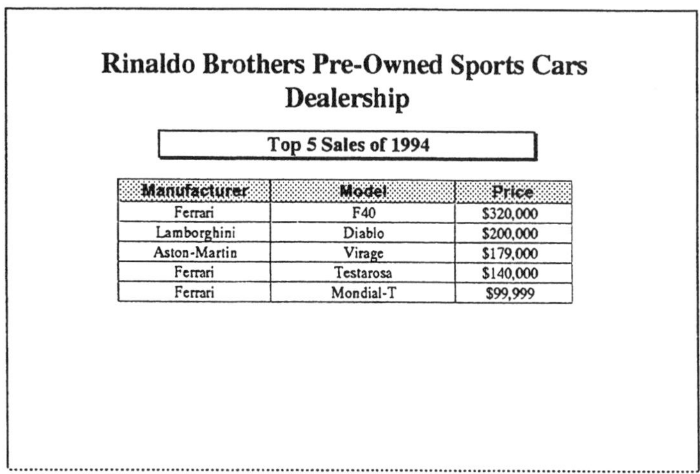

Rinaldo Brothers Pre-Owned Sports Cars Dealership

Top 5 Sales of 1994

Manufacturer	Model	Price
Ferrari	F40	$320,000
Lamborghini	Diablo	$200,000
Aston-Martin	Virage	$179,000
Ferrari	Testarosa	$140,000
Ferrari	Mondial-T	$99,999

Figure 1a is produced by this PROC step:

```
title1 "Rinaldo's Pre-Owned Sports Cars";
title2 "Dealership";
title4 "Top 5 Sales of 1994";
proc print data=top5 noobs label;
  label make='Manufacturer';
  format price dollar12.;
run;
```

Figure 1b is produced by a SAS program in combination with a BASIC program, as described in the next few pages.

In this chapter, we describe a process for automatically loading output from a SAS program into a word processing template to produce a report. The output can include tables and parameters. The word processing template is a Microsoft Word document. The process of importing the output is automated by a macro written in BASIC, which Microsoft Word uses as a macro programming language.

The process we describe demonstrates the general problem of automating the transfer of SAS output to a word processing or page layout program. A similar approach can be used to assemble and format SAS output in other programmable word processing and page layout software.

The specific examples shown are from Microsoft Word 6.0 for Microsoft Windows.

Overview of the Process

The automated report process requires the following components:

- A SAS program to generate the output for the report
- An interface file to take the output from the SAS program to the BASIC program
- A Microsoft Word document template that contains the formatting information for the report
- A BASIC program that combines the data with the template to produce the report.

SAS software and Microsoft Word software are required. However, they do not need to be running at the same time or on the same computer.

A Single Table

Our first example is the simple case of a report that consists of a single table.

Producing the Interface File

A SAS program can produce the output for automated typesetting in various different ways. The only requirement is that it produce the table data with the specific set of variables or columns. In our example, we take data from the SAS dataset TOP5.

We use the backslash character (\) as a delimiter between fields. The delimiter could be any character that does not appear in the data values.

This simple SAS program produces the interface file, using the fileref OUT:

```
data _null_;
  set top5;
  file out noprint;
  put make +(-1) '\' model +(-1) '\' price : dollar12.;
run;
```

The NOPRINT option defines the file as a text data file, rather than a print file.

The colon is used as formatting control in the PUT statement for list-style output, to omit leading and trailing blanks. The pointer control +(-1) acts as a backspace, to remove the one trailing blank that list output produces. It may not always be necessary to remove blanks, so sometimes you could use a standard formatted PUT statement.

The interface file looks like this:

```
Ferrari\F40\$320,000
Lamborghini\Diablo\$200,000
Aston-Martin\Virage\$179,000
Ferrari\Testarosa\$140,000
Ferrari\Mondial-T\$99,999
```

Moving the Interface File

If SAS and Microsoft Word software are running on different computers, you need to move the interface file from the computer where the SAS program produces it to the computer where it will be imported into Microsoft Word. In some cases, this will involve translating it from the EBCDIC character set to the ASCII character set. The character translation is done automatically by most communications software and should not present a problem.

The Microsoft Word Document Template

The document template for the report contains all of the formatting and standard text of the report. The table contains headings and formatting. It has only two rows where the data would be. The data rows are empty, but they contain the formatting information that will be used to format the data.

The template table does not have to have as many rows as the report table will have, because Microsoft Word automatically adds rows when the BASIC program copies the data values into the table.

Figure 2 shows the template for the report in Figure 1B.

Figure 2. The document template.

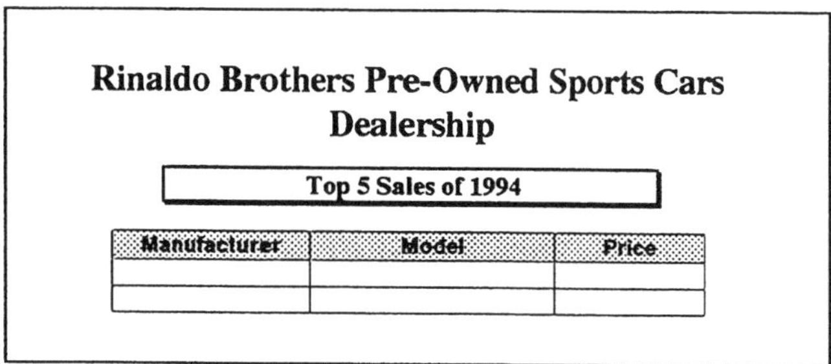

Even though the data cells are empty in this document template, they contain formatting information that is applied to the table cells in the final report. Formatting options include type face, style, and size, line spacing, and alignment. You could type dummy data into the template cells to see the formatting.

You can mark important points in or segments of a Microsoft Word document using a named marker called a bookmark. In the document template, a bookmark is needed at the beginning of the second empty data row in the table. That is the point where the table data will be inserted into the table. In our example the bookmark is named T0001.

When you create a table in a document template, include two empty rows after the column headings. Select the empty cells and apply formatting commands. Insert a bookmark at the beginning of the second empty row.

The BASIC Program

The BASIC program adds the data values to the template to produce the report. The BASIC program is stored in a separate document template.

The Microsoft dialect of BASIC includes many features that are similar to those of the SAS language. It uses two data types and control flow statements such as If-Then, While, GoTo, and Select.

To create a BASIC program and use it in the Microsoft Word environment as a macro, first create and save a new, empty document template. Then use the Macro dialog box to name the new macro and edit it. When you save the macro, it is stored as part of the template. Later, you can run the macro from the Macro dialog box.

The actions of the BASIC program are the same actions you could take as a Microsoft Word user. The program opens the interface file and modifies it. It opens the document template and saves it under a new name as the report file. It then copies data from the interface file to the report file. It makes a few adjustments in the appearance of the report. Finally, it saves the completed report and closes the files.

This is the BASIC program:

```
REM This macro fills in one table
Sub MAIN
	REM Turn off prompts
	FileConfirmConversions 0
	ToolsOptionsSave .SummaryPrompt = 0
	REM Open interface file
	FileOpen .Name = "EX1.TXT", .ConfirmConversions = 0
	REM Change \ to tabs
	EditReplace .Find = "\", .Replace = Chr$(9), .ReplaceAll
	REM Convert the interface data to table form and copy it to the clipboard
	EditSelectAll
	TextToTable
	StartOfRow
	TableSelectColumn
	EndOfRow 1
	EditCopy
	REM Duplicate the template
	FileOpen "EXAMPLE1.DOT"
	FileSaveAs .Name = "REPORT1.DOC"
	EditGoTo "T0001"
	EditPaste
	REM Format the new cells to match the format of the template columns
	REM Then delete the empty format row
	Dim ff As FormatFont
	Dim fp As FormatParagraph
	EditGoTo "T0001"
	LineUp
	TableSelectRow
	NumberOfColumns = SelInfo(18)
	CharLeft
```

```
For Column = 1 To NumberOfColumns
        GetCurValues ff
        GetCurValues fp
        LineDown
        EndOfColumn 1
        FormatParagraph fp
        FormatFont ff
        LineUp
        NextCell
        Next Column
    EditGoTo "T0001"
    LineUp
    TableDeleteRow
    REM Save changes and close report file
    FileClose 1
    REM Close interface file without saving the changes
    FileClose 2
End Sub
```

The main program is marked off by the Sub MAIN and End Sub statements. The BASIC program could include other routines, which can be functions or subroutines.

REM statements are remarks, or comment statements. Most statements in a BASIC program correspond to Microsoft Word commands and user actions.

Variable names of string variables end in a dollar sign ($). The same rule applies to functions. Dim statements declare the variables ff and fp as composite variables, called *records*. The two records have different types and can be used only in association with specific functions and subroutines that are associated with those record types.

The program produces a report in a separate file that is ready to be opened and customized or printed. If you use the interface file and document template shown previously, the report will look like the one in Figure 1b.

Notice how the report in the figure maintains the formatting of the document template. To change the appearance of the report, it is only necessary to change the template; the BASIC program does not need to be changed.

Multiple Tables

To produce a report that combines several tables, a more complicated approach is required. We demonstrate this using the SAS datasets COUNTRY, MAKE, and SALESMAN as the source of data for the tables. This SAS program produces Figure 3, showing the SAS datasets:

```
title 'Sales By Country of Origin';
proc print data=country label noobs;
  format sales avgprice dollar12.;
  label country='Country'
        qnt='Total Cars'
        avgprice='Average Price'
        sales='Total Sales';
  var country sales qnt avgprice;
run;
```

```
title 'Sales By Manufacturer';
proc print data=make label noobs;
  format sales avgprice dollar12.;
  label make='Manufacturer'
        qnt='Total Cars'
        avgprice='Average Price'
        sales='Total Sales';
  var make sales qnt avgprice;
run;
title 'Sales By Salesman';
proc print data=salesman label noobs;
  format sales avgprice dollar12.;
  label salesman='Salesman'
        qnt='Total Cars'
        avgprice='Average Price'
        sales='Total Sales';
  var salesman sales qnt avgprice;
run;
```

Figure 3. The SAS datasets used in the example.

Sales By Country of Origin 1
18:15 Sunday, March 26, 1995

Country	Total Sales	Total Cars	Average Price
England	$937,200	20	$46,860
Germany	$850,199	21	$40,486
Italy	$959,499	8	$119,937
Japan	$276,900	22	$12,586
USA	$298,400	27	$11,052

Sales By Manufacturer 2
18:15 Sunday, March 26, 1995

Manufacturer	Total Sales	Total Cars	Average Price
Aston-Martin	$310,700	2	$155,350
BMW	$134,000	5	$26,800
Chevrolet	$298,400	27	$11,052
Ferrari	$639,499	7	$91,357
Jaguar	$551,600	16	$34,475
Lamborghini	$320,000	1	$320,000
Lotus	$74,900	2	$37,450
Mazda	$95,500	8	$11,938
Mercedes	$244,199	6	$40,700
Mitsubushi	$67,400	6	$11,233
Nissan	$114,000	8	$14,250
Porsche	$472,000	10	$47,200

Sales By Salesman 3
18:15 Sunday, March 26, 1995

Salesman	Total Sales	Total Cars	Average Price
Andrew Evans	$214,200	8	$26,775
Blake Ward	$423,098	9	$47,011
Claude Jonson	$199,000	16	$12,438
Dora Samuels	$471,200	13	$36,246
Jane Ellington	$161,000	14	$11,500
John Sanders	$897,600	11	$81,600
Kelly Masters	$302,500	5	$60,500
Kristy Young	$121,800	11	$11,073
Oliver Griswold	$531,800	11	$48,345

Parameters

Two macro variables are used as parameters. The BASIC program uses the parameters as the file name for storing the report and in the report title. Additional parameters could be used to control any text in a report that might vary.

The Interface File

The parameters and tables are put into one text interface file. The first lines in the file contain the parameter values, one on each line. The beginning of each table is marked by a code and the table number, which corresponds to a specific table in the template. Each row of the table is contained on one line in the file.

This SAS program creates the interface file.

```
%let repname=RINALD.DOC;
%let store=Rinaldo Brothers;
data _null_;
  file out noprint;
  put "&repname"/
      "&store";
run;
data _null_;
  file out noprint mod;
  set country;
     if _n_=1 then put '##TABLE0001';
     put country +(-1) '\' sales : dollar12. +(-1) '\'
         qnt +(-1) '\' avgprice : dollar12.;
run;
data _null_;
  file out noprint mod;
  set make;
     if _n_=1 then put '##TABLE0002';
     put make +(-1) '\' sales : dollar12. +(-1) '\'
         qnt +(-1) '\' avgprice : dollar12.;
run;
data _null_;
  file out noprint mod;
  set salesman;
     if _n_=1 then put '##TABLE0003';
     put salesman +(-1) '\' sales : dollar12. +(-1) '\'
         qnt +(-1) '\' avgprice : dollar12.;
run;
```

The MOD option in the FILE statement prevents the second and subsequent DATA steps from erasing the output from the earlier steps.

Using the SAS datasets shown previously, the interface file looks like this:

```
RINALD.DOC
Rinaldo Brothers
##TABLE0001
England\$937,200\20\$46,860
Germany\$850,199\21\$40,486
Italy\$959,499\8\$119,937
Japan\$276,900\22\$12,586
USA\$298,400\27\$11,052
##TABLE0002
Aston-Martin\$310,700\2\$155,350
```

```
BMW\$134,000\5\$26,800
Chevrolet\$298,400\27\$11,052
Ferrari\$639,499\7\$91,357
Jaguar\$551,600\16\$34,475
Lamborghini\$320,000\1\$320,000
Lotus\$74,900\2\$37,450
Mazda\$95,500\8\$11,938
Mercedes\$244,199\6\$40,700
Mitsubushi\$67,400\6\$11,233
Nissan\$114,000\8\$14,250
Porsche\$472,000\10\$47,200
##TABLE0003
Andrew Evans\$214,200\8\$26,775
Blake Ward\$423,098\9\$47,011
Claude Jonson\$199,000\16\$12,438
Dora Samuels\$471,200\13\$36,246
Jane Ellington\$161,000\14\$11,500
John Sanders\$897,600\11\$81,600
Kelly Masters\$302,500\5\$60,500
Kristy Young\$121,800\11\$11,073
Oliver Griswold\$531,800\11\$48,345
```

The Document Template

The document template contains three tables, corresponding to the three SAS datasets. Each table has two bookmarks. As in the previous example, the first bookmark in each table is placed at the beginning of the second data row, and is named T0001, T0002, and T0003, respectively. An additional bookmark for each table contains the headings and column headers of the table; these bookmarks are labeled TH0001, TH0002, and TH0003.

The document template, shown in Figure 4, contains the code ##STORE where the report title will appear. The BASIC program finds this code and replaces it with the parameter value. Any distinctive code or phrase could be used as a place-holder for a parameter value.

Figure 4. The document template, with three tables.

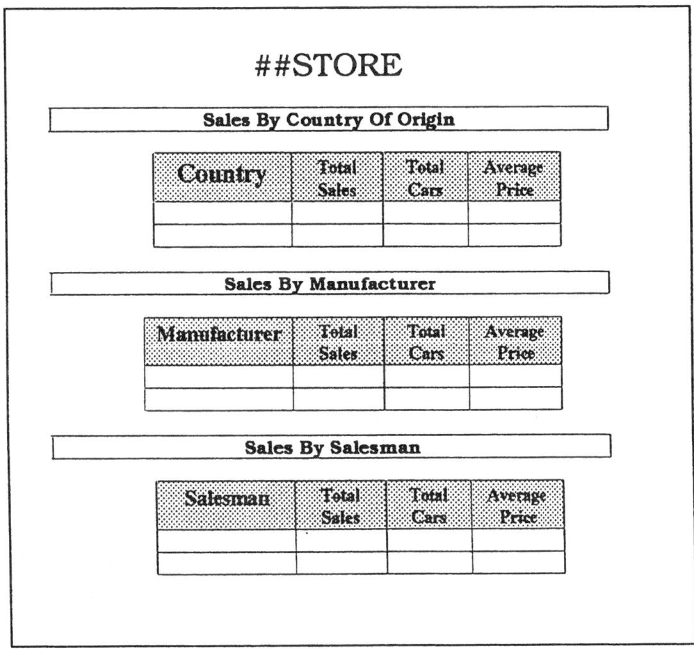

The BASIC Program

Because there are several tables, the BASIC program contains a loop for processing the tables.

```
REM This macro fills in many tables from one interface file
Sub MAIN
	REM Set number of tables
	NumberOfTables = 3
	REM Turn off prompts
	FileConfirmConversions 0
	ToolsOptionsSave .SummaryPrompt = 0
	REM Open the interface file containing the unformatted table data
	FileOpen "EX2.TXT"
	REM Change \ to tabs
	StartOfDocument
	EditReplace .Find = "\", .Replace = Chr$(9), .ReplaceAll
	StartOfDocument
	REM Set up variables to hold current formatting
	Dim ff As FormatFont
	Dim fp As FormatParagraph
	EndOfLine
	StartOfLine 1
	RepName$ = Selection$()
	LineDown 1
	EndOfLine
	StartOfLine 1
	Store$ = Selection$()
	LineDown 1
	StartOfLine
	REM open the template EXAMPLE2.DOT and save it as RepName$
	FileOpen "EXAMPLE2.DOT"
	FileSaveAs .Name = RepName$
	REM Fill in store name
	EditReplace .Find = "##STORE", .Replace = Store$, .ReplaceAll
	REM Return to Interface File
	Activate "EX2.TXT"
	REM Loop once for each table in the data until the end of the interface file:
	While CmpBookmarks("\Sel", "\EndOfDoc")
		REM Select table number from the current line and store it as TableNum$
		CharRight 7
		CharRight 4, 1
		TableNum$ = Selection$()
		REM Select all data for that table
		ParaDown
		EditBookmark .Name = "Begin", .Add
		EditFind .Find = "##TABLE", .Direction = 0
		If SelType() = 2 Then
			CharLeft 1
		Else
			EditGoTo "\EndOfDoc"
		End If
		EditBookmark .Name = "End", .Add
		EditGoTo "Begin"
		ExtendSelection
		EditGoTo "End"
```

```
        REM Convert the selected data to table form and copy it to the clipboard
        TextToTable
        SelType 1
        StartOfRow
        TableSelectColumn
        EndOfRow 1
        EditCopy
        SelType 1
        TableSelectTable
        CharRight
        REM Go to the template and insert the data at the appropriate bookmark
        Activate RepName$
        EditGoTo "T" + TableNum$
        EditPaste
        REM Format the new cells to match the format of the template columns
        REM Then delete the empty format row
        EditGoTo "T" + TableNum$
        LineUp
        TableSelectRow
        NumberOfColumns = SelInfo(18)
        CharLeft
        For Column = 1 To NumberOfColumns
            GetCurValues ff
            GetCurValues fp
            LineDown
            EndOfColumn 1
            FormatParagraph fp
            FormatFont ff
            LineUp
            NextCell
            Next Column
        EditGoTo "T" + TableNum$
        LineUp
        TableDeleteRow
        REM Return to unformatted data file to get the next table of data
        Activate "EX2.TXT"
        Wend
    REM Close EX2.TXT without saving changes
    FileClose 2
    REM Save changes and close the report file
    Activate RepName$
    FileClose 1
End Sub
```

The program could work without modification for any number of tables. To add a fourth table to the report, you would only need to add it to the SAS program and the document template.

In this case, the final report contains three tables, as shown in Figure 5.

Figure 5. The resulting typeset report, with three tables.

Rinaldo Brothers

Sales By Country Of Origin

Country	Total Sales	Total Cars	Average Price
England	$937,200	20	$46,860
Germany	$850,199	21	$40,486
Italy	$959,499	8	$119,937
Japan	$276,900	22	$12,586
USA	$298,400	27	$11,052

Sales By Manufacturer

Manufacturer	Total Sales	Total Cars	Average Price
Aston-Martin	$310,700	2	$155,350
BMW	$134,000	5	$26,800
Chevrolet	$298,400	27	$11,052
Ferrari	$639,499	7	$91,357
Jaguar	$551,600	16	$34,475
Lamborghini	$320,000	1	$320,000
Lotus	$74,900	2	$37,450
Mazda	$95,500	8	$11,938
Mercedes	$244,199	6	$40,700
Mitsubushi	$67,400	6	$11,233
Nissan	$114,000	8	$14,250
Porsche	$472,000	10	$47,200

Sales By Salesman

Salesman	Total Sales	Total Cars	Average Price
Andrew Evans	$214,200	8	$26,775
Blake Ward	$423,098	9	$47,011
Claude Jonson	$199,000	16	$12,438
Dora Samuels	$471,200	13	$36,246

Salesman	Total Sales	Total Cars	Average Price
Jane Ellington	$161,000	14	$11,500
John Sanders	$897,600	11	$81,600
Kelly Masters	$302,500	5	$60,500
Kristy Young	$121,800	11	$11,073
Oliver Griswold	$531,800	11	$48,345

Conditional Formatting

In some reports, you may want to call attention to some text that has a distinctive meaning by formatting it differently. In this section, we demonstrate a technique for doing this.

As our example, we produce a table in which bold characters and shading mark table rows that contain subtotals and totals. The same technique can be used for any typographic feature, such as italics, borders, and type size.

The example uses data taken from the SAS dataset TABLE. The following SAS program prints the SAS dataset, which is shown in Figure 6.

```
proc sort data=table;
  by make model;
run;
title 'First Quarter Sales By Manufacturer';
proc print data=table label noobs;
  by make;
  sum qnt sales;
  var make model qnt sales;
  format sales dollar12.;
  label make='Manufacturer'
        qnt ='Total Cars'
        sales='Total Dollars';
run;
```

Figure 6. The SAS dataset TABLE.

```
                 First Quarter Sales By Manufacturer                  1
                                          08:55 Monday, April 3, 1995

---------------------------- Manufacturer=BMW ----------------------------

                                           Total           Total
              Manufacturer      MODEL      Cars          Dollars

                  BMW           535i         1           $22,000
                  BMW           M5           2           $81,000
                                           -----     -----------
                  MAKE                       3          $103,000

-------------------------- Manufacturer=Ferrari --------------------------

                                           Total           Total
              Manufacturer      MODEL      Cars          Dollars

                Ferrari          348         1           $87,000
                Ferrari          F40         1          $320,000
                Ferrari       Mondial-T      1           $99,999
                Ferrari       Testarosa      1          $140,000
                                           -----     -----------
                 MAKE                        4          $646,999

-------------------------- Manufacturer=Porsche --------------------------

                                           Total           Total
              Manufacturer      MODEL      Cars          Dollars

                Porsche          911         1           $41,000
                Porsche          928         2          $130,000
                Porsche          944         3          $101,000
                                           -----     -----------
                   MAKE                      6          $272,000
                                           =====     ===========
                                            13        $1,021,999
```

The SAS Program

The SAS program calculates subtotals and totals from the SAS dataset TABLE and then writes the interface file. In the interface file, it writes the codes ##GRAY for table rows that should have a gray background and ##BOLD for table rows with bold type.

```
proc summary data=table nway;
   class make;
   var qnt sales;
   output out=sum sum=;
run;
proc summary data=sum nway;
   var qnt sales;
   output out=grandsum sum=;
run;
data _null_;
  set table sum end=last;
  by make;
  file out;
  if first.make then
```

```
      put make +(-1)
           '\' model +(-1) '\' qnt +(-1)
           '\' sales : dollar12.;
   else if not last.make then
      put '\' model +(-1) '\' qnt +(-1)
           '\' sales : dollar12.;
   else put '##GRAY##BOLDSubtotal\\'
            qnt +(-1) '\' sales : dollar12.;
   if last then do;
      set grandsum;
      put '\\\' /
          '##GRAY##BOLDGrand Total\\'
          qnt +(-1) '\' sales : dollar12.;
      end;
run;
```

The Interface File

The formatting codes appear at the beginning of rows in the interface file:

```
BMW\535i\1\$22,000
\M5\2\$81,000
##GRAY##BOLDSubtotal\\3\$103,000
Ferrari\348\1\$87,000
\F40\1\$320,000
\Mondial-T\1\$99,999
\Testarosa\1\$140,000
##GRAY##BOLDSubtotal\\4\$646,999
Porsche\911\1\$41,000
\928\2\$130,000
\944\3\$101,000
##GRAY##BOLDSubtotal\\6\$272,000
\\\
##GRAY##BOLDGrand Total\\13\$1,021,999
```

Many of the table cells are empty. The backslash for that cell still has to be present in the interface file to create a complete row of cells.

The Document Template

Figure 7 shows the document template. The table contains the heading row that you can see and two additional rows that do not have borders or shading.

Figure 7. The template.

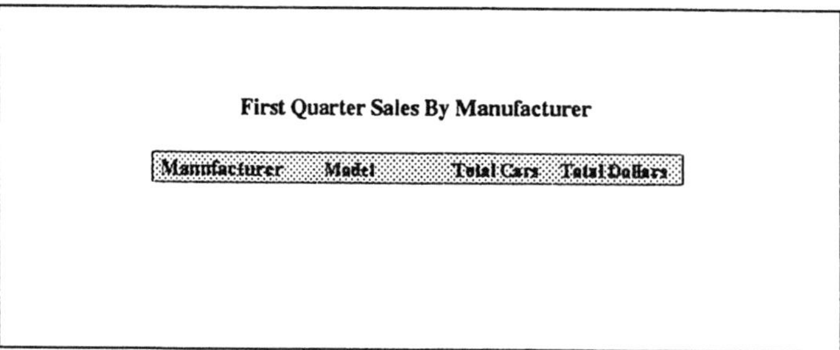

The BASIC Program

The BASIC program is similar to that of the first example, but with additional statements to find embedded codes and convert them to the corresponding formatting.

```
REM This macro fills in one table, but handles embedded typesetting codes
Sub MAIN
	REM Turn off prompts
	FileConfirmConversions 0
	ToolsOptionsSave .SummaryPrompt = 0
	REM Open raw data file
	FileOpen "EX3.TXT"
	REM Change \ to tabs in raw data
	StartOfDocument
	EditReplace .Find = "\", .Replace = Chr$(9), .ReplaceAll
	REM Convert the raw data to table form and copy it to the clipboard
	EditSelectAll
	TextToTable
	StartOfRow
	TableSelectColumn
	EndOfRow 1
	EditCopy
	REM open the template EXAMPLE3.DOT and save it as REPORT3.DOC
	FileOpen .Name = "EXAMPLE3.DOT"
	FileSaveAs .Name = "REPORT3.DOC"
	Dim ff As FormatFont
	Dim fp As FormatParagraph
	EditGoTo "T0001"
	EditPaste
	REM Format the new cells to match the format of the template columns
	REM Then delete the empty format row
	EditGoTo "T0001"
	LineUp
	TableSelectRow
	NumberOfColumns = SelInfo(18)
	CharLeft
	For Column = 1 To NumberOfColumns
		GetCurValues ff
		GetCurValues fp
		LineDown
		EndOfColumn 1
		FormatParagraph fp
		FormatFont ff
		LineUp
		NextCell
		Next Column
	EditGoTo "T0001"
	LineUp
	TableDeleteRow
	REM Format rows with embedded typesetting codes
	StartOfDocument
	EditFind .Find = "##GRAY", .Direction = 0
	While EditFindFound()
		EditClear
		TableSelectRow
		FormatBordersAndShading .Shading = 4, .ApplyTo = 2
```

```
            CharRight
            EditFind .Find = "##GRAY", .Direction = 0
            Wend
        StartOfDocument
        EditFind .Find = "##BOLD", .Direction = 0
        While EditFindFound()
            EditClear
            TableSelectRow
            FormatFont .Bold = 1
            CharRight
            EditFind .Find = "##BOLD", .Direction = 0
            Wend
        REM Close report file and save changes
        FileClose 1
        REM Close the raw data without saving the changes
        FileClose 2
End Sub
```

The EditFind, EditClear, FormatBordersAndShading, and FormatFont statements, found near the end of the BASIC program, are the main statements used to apply the formatting codes.

The report appears as shown in Figure 8.

Figure 8. The report, with gray shading and bold type used for some rows.

First Quarter Sales By Manufacturer

Manufacturer	Model	Total Cars	Total Dollars
BMW	535i	1	$22,000
	M5	2	$81,000
Subtotal		**3**	**$103,000**
Ferrari	348	1	$87,000
	F40	1	$320,000
	Mondial-T	1	$99,999
	Testarosa	1	$140,000
Subtotal		**4**	**$646,999**
Porsche	911	1	$41,000
	928	2	$130,000
	944	3	$101,000
Subtotal		**6**	**$272,000**
Grand Total		**13**	**$1,021,999**

The preceding example shows formatting that is applied to entire rows. However, formatting codes could just as easily be applied to individual cells, words, or characters.

Template Design

There is no need for a document template to be designed by the programmer who implements the report automation. Often, the template design is more appropriately handled by the specialists responsible for writing, editing, word processing, and document design. With two people working on a document template, special attention must be paid to the correct placement of bookmarks.

A report typically includes text, art, and tables. The text, sometimes the largest part of the report, may include a title, table of contents, several paragraphs or pages of introduction and explanation, credit lines, page headers and footers, headings, table titles, column headings for tables, footnotes, and other elements. Artwork can be used as in any document, such as a letterhead, logo, or clip art on the title page or in the page header. In addition, graphs can be used to provide a different perspective on the data values. Any of these elements can be added to the document template, and will then appear in the final report. When all the elements of a report are contained in a single word processing document, you can print the entire document together, eliminating the manual process of assembling the pages of the report.

The report design includes typeface, size, and style, line spacing, and alignment for each text element in the report, including the table column headers and each column in the table. It also includes the column width and row height in tables, the page margins, page numbering, page breaks, locations of header, footer, and footnote, and other document characteristics. Formatting for the body of the table is done in empty table rows, even though there is no text there to show the text formatting.

When there are multiple tables, the design includes the question of whether there are page breaks between tables. Each table could start on a separate page or, with short tables, two or more could be placed on the same page.

Wide tables often present special problems. You might use a narrow typeface, small type size, and minimal space between columns to make the table fit. Alternatively, you might design the page in landscape orientation, use larger paper for the report, or print the table across facing pages. Sometimes it is better to divide the table columns among two or more tables.

Table automation is easiest when the same formatting is used for an entire column of data. However, there are occasions when it is appropriate to use variations in formatting. These can be coded in the interface file, as in the last example, or they can be applied algorithmically by the BASIC program. Some situations where this is appropriate are described in the next section.

Besides table output, it is possible to create SAS/GRAPH output that can be imported into Microsoft Word, with each graphic contained in a separate file.

Additional Document Formatting and Processing

Microsoft Word and BASIC allow many possibilities for additional formatting and processing of a document after importing table data. The standard word processing features that you might use include these:

- Table of contents (with page numbers)
- Index
- Footnotes
- Headers
- The current date (usually in header or footer)
- Print merge (to produce copies of a report in a form letter format or with different titles or other variations).

In addition, you can use BASIC for just about any kind of standard processing, including these possibilities:

Omitting tables when there is no data. The BASIC program can delete tables that have no data in the interface file, or where all data values are zero or blank. The same could be done for individual table rows or columns.

Conditionally including text based on data values. In a financial report, for example, you might want to include one paragraph if a table shows a profit and a different paragraph if it shows a loss. A BASIC program can read a data value at any location in a table and modify the document based on that data value.

Making page breaks conditional. A BASIC routine could delete the page break between two small tables that can fit on one page.

Formatting missing values. Cells with missing values could be displayed as blank, or with an abbreviation such as N/A. The same could be done for cells with zero values. Special missing values might appear in the interface file as capital letters, but you could translate them to the conventional form for a footnote reference in a table: a lowercase superscript italic letter in a slightly smaller type size.

Formatting cells conditionally. Cells with special or unusual values can be highlighted with special formatting. For example, you could use bold type to call attention to cells with especially large values.

Sorting. You can use the sorting feature of Microsoft Word to display the same table sorted differerent ways.

Shading alternate rows. Using row shading or horizontal rules in a table sometimes makes wide rows easier to read. Another common approach is to insert additional vertical space after every five rows.

You can use a BASIC program to control the production of a list of reports that use the same template but different data. The BASIC program could pass a list of accounts, for example, to the SAS program for processing. The SAS program could produce one interface file, or a series of them. The BASIC program then produces each report as a separate document.

Conclusion

The combination of SAS software and automated typesetting can take most of the effort out of creating routine reports, even complex ones. A production system can produce enormous volumes of typeset reports with little human effort. You can look for potential applications anyplace where reports, especially those centered around tables, are created routinely or where regular reporting would be useful.

Where typeset reports are already being produced, the increased productivity from automation can allow more reports to be created faster and can allow more effort to be directed toward the quality and design of the reports. Where routine reports are not already typeset, automated typesetting can improve and standardize their appearance, reduce the effort of assembling them, and make them easier to read.

CHAPTER 14

Reporting and SAS Tool Selection

by Jack Shostak

Abstract

With so many SAS tools for reporting, it has become a challenge to choose the most efficient and effective reporting tool for any given task. After the essential design questions have been answered for a task, it is time to select the procedures and methods for reporting.

This chapter uses the answers to the design questions to critique several procedures and methods for their potential benefits and drawbacks. PROC REPORT and PROC TABULATE are discussed followed by a grouped discussion of PROC SQL, PROC PRINT, PROC FREQ, PROC UNIVARIATE, and PROC MEANS. Using a DATA_NULL_ step with PUT statements is discussed as an alternative to SAS procedures. Finally, a hybrid SAS procedure and DATA_NULL_ method is presented in order to capture both procedural efficiency and DATA_NULL_ flexibility.

Specifications

The code in this chapter was developed and tested with Release 6.08 of the SAS System under the OpenVMS environment. Use of the code with other releases of the SAS System or environments may require user modification. Modified code is not supported by the author.

About the Author

Jack Shostak is a Senior Programmer/Analyst with Pharmaceutical Research Associates. He has been a SAS software user for seven years and has a BS degree in Statistics from Virginia Polytechnic Institute and State University. Jack's areas of expertise include base SAS, SAS/STAT, SAS/GRAPH software and the macro facility.

Questions and Comments Should be Directed to:

Jack Shostak
Pharmaceutical Research Asssoc., Inc.
2400 Old Ivy Road
Charlottesville, VA 22903
Telephone: 804-977-2772
E-Mail: Jack@PRA-WW.com

Examples from this book are available online, see inside back cover for details.

Reporting and SAS® Tool Selection

Jack Shostak

Introduction

This chapter is intended for beginner to intermediate SAS software users who have a general knowledge of SAS reporting methodology and procedures. The goal of this chapter is to help SAS programmers select the best programming tools for their reporting needs. It is assumed the programmer is capable of basic data manipulation with SAS and is looking for a cohesive and efficient way of listing and summarizing data for an end user. This chapter does not attempt to discuss graphical data presentation.

Every task you encounter can benefit from proper tool selection. If you pick the right tool, then a task can be easily solved. Just as easily, poor tool selection can lead to disaster. If you have ever stripped a nut or a bolt using the wrong size wrench, then you know all about poor tool selection. Finally, you may have successfully completed a task only to find yourself wondering if the tool used was the best tool for the job. Sometimes this question is not so easily answered.

To know whether the right tool was selected, you usually have to evaluate the tool's performance at the end of the job. Was the job finished on time in a fashion acceptable to both the worker and the end user? There are many variables involved in answering this question that this chapter will address. However, let us not lose sight of the tools themselves.

Over the years, SAS Institute and others have added tools to the report-generation toolbox. Today, SAS programmers have a broad range of reporting tools to choose from. The variety of procedures makes reporting tool selection much more challenging. In some cases, many tools will serve to solve the same task.

The content of this chapter is dated in the sense that it is based on the SAS products currently available, but its spirit will always apply. The spirit I would like to instill in this chapter is that you should gain the most from what tools you currently have. Don't reinvent the wheel. As my father once said, "Let the tool do the work." We do not know what SAS tools will be presented to us in the future to solve our report-generation problems. However, by knowing the most about the abilities of your tools and your task at hand you can make the best decision about which tools to employ today.

Determining End User Needs and Project Parameters

To understand what tools you need to complete a task, you must first truly understand your task. Reporting duties in SAS can range from a simple quick-and-dirty data listing to a multiple project conglomeration of aesthetically pleasing listings and summaries. At this point you must have definite specifications of end user needs. Keep in mind, however, that you must be aware of your programming project environment. For instance, a shovel might indeed be a poor tool choice to excavate a fishpond when you have a deadline of one day. So to select the proper SAS reporting tool for a job, you must determine project parameters while fully understanding end user needs. Here are five guidelines for determining end user needs and project parameters.

Know thy end user

By end user, I mean the person that will ultimately own the report that you generate. The end user is the person that the report is programmed for in the first place. If you are the end user yourself, then this step is quite simple. You will report whatever and however you wish. Sometimes, defining the end user is by no means easy. Perhaps the end user is so far removed from the reporting process that he or she cannot be consulted on what is wanted. If this is your situation, stop now and remedy it because it will be difficult to produce a product that the unknown end user will like. Once you have found the end user of your report, consider what type of user he or she is.

To simplify, there are three basic types of end user:

I. The first type of end user knows exactly what they want in a report. They can give you detailed up-front specifications on what they need generated. These end users exist, albeit rare.

II. The second type of end user is the most common type. They seemingly know what they want at first, but after exploration of the data, they change their minds. It is human nature to change your thinking, especially if you are involved in exploratory analysis.

III. The third type of end user is admittedly fickle in what they want in the report. These end users aren't especially common, but when someone tells you this before programming, you need to account for it in your tool selection.

Sure, it is easy to categorize end users here on paper, but in reality it is a bit different. The only way to really know what an end user is like is from historical analysis. Perhaps you have worked for this person before, or you can get references. A good guess is that the end user is of the second type, but if you cannot afford mistakes in tool choice, a conservative and safe bet is the third type of end user. It is better to be prepared for changing output specifications early in the programming design phase rather than be forced into some rigid construction later.

Know thyself

Know your workload capacity before engaging a reporting task. This usually only applies to large, multiple project reporting applications, but it is usually a good thing to keep in mind. In general, use only the tools you know how to use or have time to learn how to use well. There isn't a feeling much worse than trying to teach yourself an advanced application of a new and unfamiliar SAS procedure under heavy time pressure. The bottom line is that you should be comfortable with what you choose to use, otherwise disaster can result.

Know your time constraints

One of the most important factors in tool selection for a reporting task is knowing how fast it has to be completed. I generally break reporting tasks down into two main categories regarding time: those projects that need to be done extremely quickly and those that don't. Requests such as "I need this ASAP" or "I need this by yesterday" are not uncommon, and you need a plan of attack for those when they occur. Reporting tasks that allow a little more breathing room and flexibility in presentation also allow for a bit more leeway in tool selection.

Know your aesthetic requirements

To complete a reporting job to the end user's satisfaction, you need to be attuned to the aesthetic requirements. Aesthetic requirements define how 'pretty' the SAS output needs to be for the report. Remember, beauty is in the eyes of the end user. I generally classify aesthetic requirements into three categories. The prettiest output is required when the end user allows for no compromise in presentation. The output must look a specific way requiring full-page control of the presentation. A more moderate approach allows some compromise over issues of aesthetics when efficiency is at risk. Finally, there is the 'quick-and-dirty' task where information exchange is of highest importance and aesthetic quality is of little or no concern. Most reporting tasks will be in the moderate to high range of aesthetic demand.

Know the scope of your reporting

A very important factor in tool selection that is often overlooked is scope of programming. You would want to seriously consider tool selection if the same tool had to serve well over a series of projects across many databases. Think of the simple volume of code that will need to be written for large reporting applications. Tools that lend themselves to fewer lines of code will excel in project maintenance on large projects. Another consideration is code portability. Determine if the same code needs to work across a series of projects. Also, data type is of great importance. How varied are the data types that your tool will need to operate on, and will those variables reported on change data types over time? Whether it be a large multi-tasking project or a simple listing should have an impact on your tool selection.

To adequately select a SAS tool for reporting requires that you know everything about the job that you can. When a project parameter cannot be determined, make a conservative guess. It is better to complete a task ahead of expectation then to lag behind and allow quality and timeliness to suffer. Now that you have all the end user needs and project parameters defined, you can start to look at what SAS has to offer for reporting tables and listings.

SAS Tools

In this section I present a brief look at each reporting procedure's capabilities. First, the REPORT procedure will be examined. PROC REPORT is SAS Institute's newest and strongest reporting procedure yet. A PROC TABULATE presentation is next, followed by a brief discussion of the SQL and PRINT procedures and a mention of the FREQ, UNIVARIATE, and MEANS procedures. Finally, the DATA _NULL_ with PUT statements and a hybrid DATA _NULL_ approach will be presented.

A fictional subject demography data set is used for all programming examples in this chapter. Here is the source code and data that create the sample set:

```
data demog;

input age 1-3 gender $ 5 height 7-11 weight 13-17 marital $ 19 income 21-26
      region $ 28-29 title $ 31-75;

datalines;
 28 M  72.5 165.3 S  30000 SE Electrician
 45 F  65.4 118.6 M  45695 SW Assistant Editor and Senior Correspondent
 18 M  68.0 135.0 S  18000 MW Food Technician
 61 M  69.5 150.0 M  95000 NE Chief Executive Officer
 22 F  62.0 105.2 S  20500 NW Retail Salesperson
 35 F  75.0 160.0 S  45250 MW European Investments Consultant
 17 M  62.5 170.2 S   9000 SE Night Clerk/Student
 52 F  60.0 139.2 M  37000 NE Assistant for Accounting and Payroll
 26 M  70.5 165.0 S  25250 SE Carpenter
 32 M  61.0 140.0 S  16025 NE Entrepreneur
;
```

PROC REPORT

PROC REPORT is SAS Institute's newest tool in the report generator's toolbox. You can easily learn how to use this procedure in either interactive or batch mode. I recommend *SAS Guide to the REPORT Procedure, Usage and Reference, Version 6, First Edition*, SAS Technical Report P-258, *Using the REPORT Procedure in a Nonwindowing Environment, Release 6.07*, and the section on PROC REPORT in SAS Technical Report P-222, *Changes and Enhancements to Base SAS Software, Release 6.07*. *SAS Guide to the REPORT Procedure* focuses heavily on the interactive application of PROC REPORT, but with a little effort the PROC REPORT syntax can be mastered by studying the source code examples throughout the book. SAS Technical Report P-258 would be a valuable asset to those running SAS primarily in batch mode. PROC REPORT is SAS Institute's most advanced and elaborate reporting procedure yet for tables, summaries, and listings. This section will show PROC REPORT's ability to create listings and summary tables and the advantages and drawbacks of the procedure.

Data Listings

As of this writing, PROC REPORT's capacity for data listings is nearly unsurpassed. PROC REPORT is capable of rather complicated and aesthetically pleasing raw data listings without much effort.

Example 1:

```
options ls=80 nodate nonumber;

proc format;
 value $gender 'F' = 'Female'
               'M' = 'Male';
 value $marital 'S' = 'Single'
                'M' = 'Married';
 value $region 'SW' = 'Southwest'
               'NE' = 'Northeast'
               'SE' = 'Southeast'
               'NW' = 'Northwest'
               'MW' = 'Midwest';
run;
```

```
proc report
 data = demog
 headline
 headskip
 spacing = 2;

 column ("--" region ("_Physical_" age gender height weight) marital income
            title);

 define region/order 'Geographic Region' order=data width=10 format=$region.;

 define age/display 'Age'  format=3. center;
 define gender/display 'Gender' format = $gender. width=6 left;
 define height/display 'Height (in)' format=5.1 width=6 center;
 define weight/display 'Weight (lbs)' format=5.1 width=6 center;
 define marital/display 'Marital Status' format=$marital.;
 define income/display 'Annual Income' format=dollar8.;
 define title/display 'Occupation' width=18 flow;

title1 "Listing of Demographics";
run;
```

Output 1: PROC REPORT Data Listing

```
                         Listing of Demographics

 --------------------------------------------------------------------------
                  ________Physical__________
 Geographic                   Height  Weight  Marital    Annual
 Region       Age  Gender     (in)    (lbs)   Status     Income  Occupation
 --------------------------------------------------------------------------

 Southeast     28  Male       72.5    165.3   Single    $30,000  Electrician
               17  Male       62.5    170.2   Single     $9,000  Night Clerk
                                                                 Student
               26  Male       70.5    165.0   Single    $25,250  Carpenter
 Southwest     45  Female     65.4    118.6   Married   $45,695  Assistant Editor
                                                                 and Senior
                                                                 Correspondent
 Midwest       18  Male       68.0    135.0   Single    $18,000  Food Technician
               35  Female     75.0    160.0   Single    $45,250  European
                                                                 Investments
                                                                 Consultant
 Northeast     61  Male       69.5    150.0   Married   $95,000  Chief Executive
                                                                 Officer
               52  Female     60.0    139.2   Married   $37,000  Assistant for
                                                                 Accounting and
                                                                 Payroll
               32  Male       61.0    140.0   Single    $16,025  Entrepreneur
 Northwest     22  Female     62.0    105.2   Single    $20,500  Retail Salesperson
```

The essential structure of PROC REPORT lies in the COLUMN and DEFINE statements. COLUMN statements simply state what columns will be presented on the page in order from left to right. DEFINE statements fully describe each column. These two statements are then augmented by others for line drawing, summarization, and customized DATA step statements.

Example 1 presents a relatively simple listing and shows a few of the features of PROC REPORT. PROC REPORT allows for varied column justification. Center, left, and right justification can be done to the column header and the data in the column itself. The COLUMN and DEFINE statements allow for variable underlining and variable group underlining. Another feature is the presentation of data for groups. By specifying ORDER in the DEFINE statement, you can make PROC REPORT print just the first observation in a group of like observations. Do not confuse the ORDER usage qualifier with the ORDER= option. The ORDER= option specifies exactly what type of sorting to perform on the data, and the ORDER usage qualifier simply defines the variable as an order variable.

Another addition to PROC REPORT is the FLOW option in the DEFINE statement. The FLOW option allows the observation to wrap over to the next line of the report automatically within the defined width of that column. The FLOW option is used in the presentation of the TITLE variable in Example 1. Word splitting in column titles and within the column itself can be controlled by using the SPLIT= option. Another feature worth noting is that PROC REPORT makes use of the FORMCHAR string if you wish to change simple dashes to solid lines or other aesthetically pleasing printer dependent box-drawing characters.

Data Summaries

PROC REPORT is quite capable of generating data summaries as well as listings.

Example 2:

```
options ls=80 nodate nonumber;

proc format;
 value $gender 'F' = 'Female'
               'M' = 'Male';
 value $marital 'S' = 'Single'
                'M' = 'Married';
 value $region 'SW' = 'Southwest'
               'NE' = 'Northeast'
               'SE' = 'Southeast'
               'NW' = 'Northwest'
               'MW' = 'Midwest';
run;

proc report
 data = demog
 headskip;

 column gender marital region,(age=agen age=agemean);
   define gender /group 'Gender' format=$gender.;
   define marital /group 'Marital Status' format=$marital.;
   define region /across center 'Age across the Region' '--' format=$region.;
   define agen/analysis 'n ---' n f=3.;
   define agemean/analysis 'mean -----' mean f=5.1;

 break after gender /skip;

title 'Summary of Age';
run;
```

Output 2: PROC REPORT Data Summary

```
                              Summary of Age

                                 Age across the Region
                       -----------------------------------------------------
                        Midwest    Northeast   Northwest   Southeast   Southwest
              Marital   n   mean   n   mean   n   mean   n   mean   n   mean
    Gender    Status   ---  -----  ---  -----  ---  -----  ---  -----  ---  -----

    Female    Married   0    0.0   1   52.0   0    0.0   0    0.0   1   45.0
              Single    1   35.0   0    0.0   1   22.0   0    0.0   0    0.0

    Male      Married   0    0.0   1   61.0   0    0.0   0    0.0   0    0.0
              Single    1   18.0   1   32.0   0    0.0   3   23.7   0    0.0
```

In Example 2, we see a relatively simple summary of age across region by gender and marital status. This example uses the ACROSS variable in the definition of REGION. ACROSS variables create one column for each formatted value of the variable. This is a very useful generic feature that also allows for nested ACROSS variables. Some of the other features of PROC REPORT not shown in the previous example are useful in producing summaries.

PROC REPORT allows a type of DATA step interface with the COMPUTE, BREAK, and RBREAK statements. BREAK statements allow you to perform certain DATA step computations directly before or after a group of observations, while RBREAK allows computation at the beginning or end of the report. The COMPUTE statement provides variable computation using many regular SAS DATA step statements along with the LINE statement, which mimics PUT statements. It is with these LINE statements that you can customize your report to present special summary lines.

Though it is powerful, PROC REPORT does have some limitations. The procedure cannot produce median values, but can produce most other variable statistics. Even when using the FORMCHAR= option to alter the line drawing characters or LINE statements, PROC REPORT suffers from a bit of a limited look created by a lack of full page control. Within the borders defined by the top of the column to the bottom of the data, you have good output presentation control, but outside that range PROC REPORT is somewhat limited by what you can do with TITLE and FOOTNOTE statements. Finally, PROC REPORT cannot easily summarize both continuous and categorical variables from a horizontal perspective as it is driven essentially by the COLUMN statement.

At the time of this writing, there are several items to watch closely when using PROC REPORT:

- When using the FLOW or SPLIT= option, remember that the character '/' is the default split character. To avoid unwanted splits on the character '/', specify SPLIT=" " as a PROC REPORT option.
- When using break lines with NOPRINT columns and underlining, you may find a slight mismatch in underline lengths.
- If you run PROC REPORT in batch mode, you may want to pay special attention to the creation of your PROFILE catalog. PROC REPORT will save REPORT options in your PROFILE catalog and those options will be in effect on the next run whether you like it or not. A fairly good work-around is to delete your PROFILE catalog and specify RSASUSER at SAS invocation to prevent writing to the PROFILE catalog.

In conclusion, PROC Report is a very powerful tool. For basic data listings it is invaluable. PROC Report can handle most data summaries quite easily as well. With a little compromise here and there, this tool can be the workhorse of any reporting effort. Also, by creative use of the macro facility, you can make PROC REPORT perform most generic tasks in any environment with little or no aesthetic compromise.

PROC TABULATE

PROC TABULATE is a SAS procedure designed for cross-tabular data summaries. To the SAS programmer who is new to the world of PROC TABULATE, I recommend the book *SAS Guide to TABULATE Processing*. This book is a well-written and comprehensive manual on PROC TABULATE.

Example 3:

```
options ls=80 nodate nonumber missing = '0';

proc format;
 value $gender 'F' = 'Female'
               'M' = 'Male';
 value $marital 'S' = 'Single'
                'M' = 'Married';
 value $region 'SW' = 'Southwest'
               'NE' = 'Northeast'
               'SE' = 'Southeast'
               'NW' = 'Northwest'
               'MW' = 'Midwest';
run;
```

```
proc tabulate
 data = demog;

 class region marital gender;
 var age height weight;
 tables (region ='Geographic Region')*(marital='Marital Status')
        (all='Total')*(marital='')
        (all='Overall Total'),
     age='Age'*(n='n'*f=3. mean='Mean'*f=5.1)
     height='Height'*(n='n'*f=3. mean='Mean'*f=5.1)
     weight='Weight'*(n='n'*f=3. mean='Mean'*f=5.1)
     gender='Gender'*(n='n'*f=3. pctn<region*marital all*marital
                     all>='%'*f=4.1)
     /rts=30;

 format region $region. marital $marital. gender $gender.;
 title 'Tabulation of Demographics';
run;
```

OUTPUT 3: PROC TABULATE Data Summary

Tabulation of Demographics

		Age		Height		Weight		Gender			
								Female		Male	
		n	Mean	n	Mean	n	Mean	n	%	n	%
Geographic Region	Marital Status										
Midwest	Single	2	26.5	2	71.5	2	147.5	1	25.0	1	16.7
Northeast	Married	2	56.5	2	64.8	2	144.6	1	25.0	1	16.7
	Single	1	32.0	1	61.0	1	140.0	0	0	1	16.7
Northwest	Single	1	22.0	1	62.0	1	105.2	1	25.0	0	0
Southeast	Single	3	23.7	3	68.5	3	166.8	0	0	3	50.0
Southwest	Married	1	45.0	1	65.4	1	118.6	1	25.0	0	0
Total	Married	3	52.7	3	65.0	3	135.9	2	50.0	1	16.7
	Single	7	25.4	7	67.4	7	148.7	2	50.0	5	83.3
Overall Total		10	33.6	10	66.6	10	144.9	4	100	6	100

The fundamental structure of PROC TABULATE is within the TABLES statement. Any tabulation can contain page, row, and column dimensions. A two-dimensional table consists of row and column dimensions, while a one-dimensional table is simply a table of columns. CLASS statements define categorical divisions while VAR statements define continuous variables to be analyzed.

In this third example, we see what a useful tool PROC TABULATE can be for data summaries. With a few lines of code, we can create a rather elaborate matrix of summary information. Categorical information is summarized next to numeric with underlying totals easily read. Data can also be formatted with the FORMAT statement and the "*f=" format modifier.

There are some limitations to PROC TABULATE. One of the most common complaints is that it looks "boxy". Even when using the FORMCHAR option to modify line drawings in PROC TABULATE, the result is a rather rigid display of data. Formatting row and column titles can appear awkward as well since the procedure doesn't implement word splitting very well, and the width of your column title is determined by the data format used. As with PROC REPORT, medians are not optional statistics. Also, getting percentages correct can be rather difficult with complex tables. Those who have computed complicated percentages with PROC TABULATE know how difficult getting the denominator definition correct can be at times.

PROC TABULATE is the easiest procedure to use when you wish to quickly summarize some data. Also, with just a few minor alterations to the TABLES statement, you can dramatically change the appearance and function of the summary. This coding feature makes PROC TABULATE flexible and quite handy at generating various summary presentations on the fly. PROC TABULATE is also easy to simply pick up and start using, but like PROC REPORT it can take a little while to master.

Other Procedures

PROC SQL:

PROC SQL is SAS Institute's interface with Structured Query Language (SQL). By implementing this procedure, you can begin writing code in SQL within the SAS program. SQL is covered quite nicely in the *SAS Guide to the SQL Procedure: Usage and Reference, Version 6, First Edition.* SQL is a wonderful tool for database manipulation, and it even presents some summary capabilities. PROC SQL can be used as a data listing tool as well, but there is a lack of aesthetic control over the output. You are limited to FORMAT and LABEL statements for column control and display.

Example 4:

```
proc format;
 value $gender 'F' = 'Female'
               'M' = 'Male';
 value $marital 'S' = 'Single'
                'M' = 'Married';
 value $region 'SW' = 'Southwest'
               'NE' = 'Northeast'
               'SE' = 'Southeast'
               'NW' = 'Northwest'
               'MW' = 'Midwest';
run;

title 'Summary of Age';

proc sql;
 select region format = $region. label='Region',
        marital format = $marital. label = 'Marital Status',
        n(age) as nage format = 3. label = 'Age N',
        mean(age) as meanage format = 5.1 label = 'Age Mean',
        std(age) as stdage format = 5.1 label = 'Std Age'

  from demog

   group by region, marital
   order by region, marital;
```

Output 4: PROC SQL Summary

```
                    Summary of Age

                   Marital  Age    Age    Std
Region             Status     N   Mean    Age
---------------------------------------------
Midwest     Single     2   26.5   12.0
Northeast   Married    2   56.5    6.4
Northeast   Single     1   32.0     .
Northwest   Single     1   22.0     .
Southeast   Single     3   23.7    5.9
Southwest   Married    1   45.0     .
```

PROC PRINT:

With the arrival of PROC REPORT, PROC PRINT has been mildly overrun in its abilities. However, PROC PRINT can still be useful for quick-and-dirty data presentations. In fact, it can be quicker to code a PROC PRINT since each variable doesn't need as much definition as may be needed in PROC REPORT's DEFINE statements. Here is an example of PROC PRINT imitating as best it can what was done with PROC REPORT in Example 1. Notice that PROC PRINT does not have the FLOW option, so it will wrap observations to make it fit on the 80-character page.

Example 5:

```
proc format;
 value $gender 'F' = 'Female'
               'M' = 'Male';
 value $marital 'S' = 'Single'
                'M' = 'Married';
 value $region 'SW' = 'Southwest'
               'NE' = 'Northeast'
               'SE' = 'Southeast'
               'NW' = 'Northwest'
               'MW' = 'Midwest';
run;

proc print
 data = demog
 noobs
 label
 split="*";

 var region age gender height weight marital income title;

 label  region = 'Geographic*Region*-----------'
        age = 'Age*---'
        gender = 'Gender*------'
        height = 'Height*(in)*------'
        weight = 'Weight*(lbs)*------'
        marital = 'Marital*Status*-------'
        income = 'Annual*Income*--------'
        title = 'Occupation*-----------------------------';
format region $region. gender $gender. height weight 5.1 marital $marital.
       income dollar8. title $45.;
title1 "Listing of Demographics";
title2 "------------------------------------"
       "-----------------------------------";
run;
```

Output 5: PROC PRINT Listing

```
                         Listing of Demographics
      ----------------------------------------------------------------------

      Geographic                        Height    Weight    Marital     Annual
        Region       Age    Gender       (in)      (lbs)    Status      Income
      -----------    ---    ------      ------    ------    -------    --------

       Southeast      28    Male         72.5     165.3     Single      $30,000
       Southwest      45    Female       65.4     118.6     Married     $45,695
       Midwest        18    Male         68.0     135.0     Single      $18,000
       Northeast      61    Male         69.5     150.0     Married     $95,000
       Northwest      22    Female       62.0     105.2     Single      $20,500
       Midwest        35    Female       75.0     160.0     Single      $45,250
       Southeast      17    Male         62.5     170.2     Single       $9,000
       Northeast      52    Female       60.0     139.2     Married     $37,000
       Southeast      26    Male         70.5     165.0     Single      $25,250
       Northeast      32    Male         61.0     140.0     Single      $16,025


      Occupation
      -----------------------------

      Electrician
      Assistant Editor and Senior Correspondent
      Food Technician
      Chief Executive Officer
      Retail Salesperson
      European Investments Consultant
      Night Clerk/Student
      Assistant for Accounting and Payroll
      Carpenter
      Entrepreneur
```

PROC FREQ:

PROC FREQ is an excellent tool for quick-and-dirty crosstabulation tables and frequency counts on categorical data. An essential reporting feature of PROC FREQ is the OUT= option in the TABLES statement. Once created, the data set contains statistics that can be manipulated by the DATA _NULL_ method of reporting. (See Example 6 later in this chapter.)

PROC UNIVARIATE:

PROC UNIVARIATE is a useful tool for a comprehensive, numeric quick-and-dirty look at continuous variables. PROC UNIVARIATE also has an output data set capability in the OUTPUT statement which allows the creation of a data set containing quite a diverse set of descriptive statistics. The cherished median value can be obtained from PROC UNIVARIATE along with many other univariate statistics for reporting purposes.

PROC MEANS:

PROC MEANS is good for producing many univariate statistics on continuous variables. PROC MEANS allows for some aesthetic control of summary output which makes it a fairly attractive quick-and-dirty summary tool. Once again, this procedure also has an output data set feature with the OUTPUT statement that writes the statistics to a data set. These statistics could then be manipulated using the DATA _NULL_ method described in the next section.

DATA _NULL_

The DATA _NULL_ step is simply a DATA step that doesn't write out a SAS data set. One of the most common uses for a DATA _NULL_ is report file generation, where a FILE statement is used with one or more PUT statements to create a report file. Over the years, this form of reporting in SAS has been and continues to be the most flexible and limitless form of summary and listing generation. A DATA _NULL_ report has complete page control, which means that DATA _NULL_ can put anything desired on the page at any time in any place. This complete page control can be accomplished by "PUT @" and "PUT #" statements for column and row designations, respectively. Of course, this high level of control over the output comes at a cost.

DATA _NULL_ steps require more raw SAS coding than any other reporting method. For a listing in this format, very little if any data manipulation may be required. Summaries, however, sometimes require that a DATA _NULL_ be preceded by one of many SAS analysis procedures followed by further data restructuring. Some common front-end procedures for the DATA _NULL_ are PROC FREQ, PROC UNIVARIATE, and PROC MEANS. Each of these procedures is fine for producing quick-and-dirty tables, but are rarely used in final reports as stand alone output. Here is an example of how to replicate the results in Example 2 with a DATA _NULL_ step.

Example 6:

```
options ls=80 nodate nonumber;

proc format;
 value $gender 'F' = 'Female'
               'M' = 'Male';
 value $marital 'S' = 'Single'
                'M' = 'Married';
 value $region 'SW' = 'Southwest'
               'NE' = 'Northeast'
               'SE' = 'Southeast'
               'NW' = 'Northwest'
               'MW' = 'Midwest';
run;

proc sort
 data=demog;
  by gender marital region;

proc means
 data=demog;
  by gender marital region;

  var age;
  output out=demsum n=n mean=mean;
run;

data _null_;
 set demsum;
  by gender marital;

  file print header=H;

  array ns {5} _temporary_;
  array means {5} _temporary_;

  if first.marital then
   do i = 1 to 5;
    ns{i} = 0;
    means{i} = 0;
   end;

  index = (region = 'MW')*1 + (region = 'NE')*2 + (region = 'NW')*3 +
          (region = 'SE')*4 + (region = 'SW')*5;

  ns{index} = n;
  means{index} = mean;

  if first.gender then
```

```
     put @4 gender $gender. @;

   if first.marital then
     put @12 marital $marital. @;

   if last.marital then
     put @21 ns{1} 3. @26 means{1} 5.1
         @33 ns{2} 3. @38 means{2} 5.1
         @45 ns{3} 3. @50 means{3} 5.1
         @57 ns{4} 3. @62 means{4} 5.1
         @69 ns{5} 3. @74 means{5} 5.1;

   if last.gender then
      put;

return;

H: put /
   @39 'Age across the Region' /
   @21 '-----------------------------------------------------------' /
   @22 'Midwest     Northeast    Northwest    Southeast    Southwest' /
   @12 'Marital     n    mean    n    mean    n    mean    n    mean    n    mean' /
   @4  'Gender  Status    ---  -----  ---  -----  ---  -----  ---  -----  ---'
       '-----'/;
return;
title 'Summary of Age';
run;
```

Output 6: DATA _NULL_ Step Summary

```
                                  Summary of Age

                                     Age across the Region
                     -------------------------------------------------------------
                      Midwest     Northeast    Northwest    Southeast    Southwest
           Marital    n   mean    n   mean    n   mean    n   mean    n   mean
   Gender  Status    ---  -----  ---  -----  ---  -----  ---  -----  ---  -----

   Female  Married    0    0.0    1   52.0    0    0.0    0    0.0    1   45.0
           Single     1   35.0    0    0.0    1   22.0    0    0.0    0    0.0

   Male    Married    0    0.0    1   61.0    0    0.0    0    0.0    0    0.0
           Single     1   18.0    1   32.0    0    0.0    3   23.7    0    0.0
```

As shown in Example 6, it takes a bit more programming using a DATA _NULL_ approach to arrive at the same results obtained through using PROC REPORT. The above program assumes that only the data for gender and marital status need to be present to create a row. Additional code would need to be added to report the case where a gender by marital status crossing was completely absent in the data.

The beauty of the DATA _NULL_ approach is that it is completely adaptable. This summary could be presented in absolutely any fashion imaginable given the programmer has the time to create the output format. DATA _NULL_ steps also allow for specialized table or listing headers and footers that are data driven. If a special footnote needs to appear based on the presence of a certain data value in an observation, a DATA _NULL_ can handle that case. If elaborate title construction is required or is data dependent, a DATA _NULL_ can do this also.

Hybrid DATA _NULL_ Approach

This section discusses a hybrid DATA _NULL_ approach to SAS report generation. Essentially, this method involves simply extracting text output from a SAS procedure into a DATA _NULL_ and then modifying it. The possibilities are rather limitless for what can be done with the hybrid approach.

However, this method is best suited for reporting output that isn't very lengthy. The following example shows how footnotes and customized standard output footers can be appended to any SAS output with the %FOOTER macro.

Example 7:

```
options ls=80 nodate nonumber ps=20;

proc format;
 value $gender 'F' = 'Female'
               'M' = 'Male';
 value $marital 'S' = 'Single'
                'M' = 'Married';
 value $region 'SW' = 'Southwest'
               'NE' = 'Northeast'
               'SE' = 'Southeast'
               'NW' = 'Northwest'
               'MW' = 'Midwest';
run;


%macro footer(L) / parmbuff;

  footnote "PAGEHERE ";  **** paging footnote for PROC;
  run;

  proc printto;

  %let repfile=%scan(&syspbuff,2,|);
  %let wide=%scan(&syspbuff,3,|);

  data lines;
   infile "&repfile"
          lrecl=&wide  missover recfm=v noprint pad linesize=&wide end=eof;

   input all $char&wide..;

   drop width startat;
   retain width 0 startat;

   index + 1;

   **** determine width and beginning column of output;
   if length(trim(left(all))) > width and
      (index(all,'---') > 0 or index(all,'___') > 0) then
    do;
     startat = indexc(all,'_-');
     width = length(trim(left(all))) - 1;
    end;

   placem = indexc(all,'01234567890123456789O-=_+',
                  'qwertyuiopasdfghjklzxcvbnm',
                  'QWERTYUIOPASDFGHJKLZXCVBNM',
                  '{[}]:;|\><,.?/',
                  '"');

   /**** DRAW UNDERLINES ****/
```

```
   if index(all,"PAGEHERE") or eof then
    do;
     all = repeat("-",width);
     placem = startat;
     output;
     if eof then                          /**** LAST PAGE ****/
      do;
       all = repeat("-",width);
       placem = startat;
       output;
      end;
     else                                 /**** BOTTOM OF ANY BUT LAST PAGE ****/
      do;
       all = '(Continued)';
       placem = startat + width - 10;
       output;
      end;

     /**** PLACE FOOTNOTES ****/
     %let stop=%length(&syspbuff);
     %do i=4 %to &stop;
      %let foot =%scan(&syspbuff,&i,|);
      %if "&foot" ne ")" %then
       %do;
        all = "&foot";
        placem = startat;
        output;
       %end;
      %else %let i=&stop;
     %end;
    end;
   else output;
  run;

  proc sort
   data=lines;
    by index;

  /**** OUTPUT FILE ****/
  data _null_;
   set lines;

    file "&repfile" lrecl= &wide recfm=f pad linesize= &wide new;
    put @placem all;
  run;

%mend footer;


proc printto
  print='repnul.lis' new;

proc report
 data = demog
 headline
 headskip
```

```
spacing = 2;

column ("--" region ("_Physical_" age gender height weight) marital income
    title);

define region/order 'Geographic Region' order=data width=10 format=$region.;

define age/display 'Age'  format=3. center;
define gender/display 'Gender' format = $gender. width=6 left;
define height/display 'Height (in)' format=5.1 width=6 center;
define weight/display 'Weight (lbs)' format=5.1 width=6 center;
define marital/display 'Marital Status' format=$marital.;
define income/display 'Annual Income' format=dollar8.;
define title/display 'Occupation' width=18 flow;

title1 "Listing of Demographics *";
%footer(|repnul.lis|80|* Data collected for 1993.|);
run;
```

Output 7: Hybrid DATA _NULL_ Summary

```
                       Listing of Demographics *

 --------------------------------------------------------------------------------
              _________Physical__________
 Geographic               Height  Weight  Marital     Annual
 Region      Age  Gender   (in)   (lbs)   Status      Income  Occupation
 --------------------------------------------------------------------------------

 Southeast    28  Male     72.5   165.3   Single     $30,000  Electrician
              17  Male     62.5   170.2   Single      $9,000  Night Clerk
                                                              Student
              26  Male     70.5   165.0   Single     $25,250  Carpenter
 Southwest    45  Female   65.4   118.6   Married    $45,695  Assistant Editor
                                                              and Senior
                                                              Correspondent
 Midwest      18  Male     68.0   135.0   Single     $18,000  Food Technician

 --------------------------------------------------------------------------------
                                                                    (Continued)
 * Data collected for 1993.
```

```
                       Listing of Demographics *

 --------------------------------------------------------------------------------
              _________Physical__________
 Geographic               Height  Weight  Marital     Annual
 Region      Age  Gender   (in)   (lbs)   Status      Income  Occupation
 --------------------------------------------------------------------------------

 Midwest      35  Female   75.0   160.0   Single     $45,250  European
                                                              Investments
                                                              Consultant
 Northeast    61  Male     69.5   150.0   Married    $95,000  Chief Executive
                                                              Officer
              52  Female   60.0   139.2   Married    $37,000  Assistant for
                                                              Accounting and
                                                              Payroll
              32  Male     61.0   140.0   Single     $16,025  Entrepreneur
 Northwest    22  Female   62.0   105.2   Single     $20,500  Retail Salesperson

 --------------------------------------------------------------------------------
 --------------------------------------------------------------------------------
 * Data collected for 1993.
```

%FOOTER documentation:

```
%FOOTER will create underlines at the bottom of any SAS output along
 with any required footnotes left justified to the left most part of
 the SAS output.  The final page is indicated by a double underline
 and the other pages indicate a continuing output stream by the presence
 of the '(continued)' string at the bottom of the page.

Requires:   1) CC=CR
            2) Use of PROC PRINTTO in the calling program
            3) %FOOTER is called *before the RUN* statement following the PROC
Parameters:
            %FOOTER(|p1|p2|p3|.....|pn|)
    where
            p1      = the full path name of where the procedure
                      output is going.
            p2      = linesize of the output.
            p3-pn   = any footnotes desired.
            '|'     = delimiter for all parameters.
```

Output 7 is a modification of Output 1. This program simply underlines the PROC REPORT output with page-dependent underlining and left-justified footnotes. This may seem simple, but it cannot be accomplished with PROC REPORT and FOOTNOTE statements alone. Admittedly, this type of processing is memory intensive as it turns an output file into a large data set itself. However, this method grants a lot of flexibility to canned SAS procedures when there is no other way of getting that essential extra touch. The %FOOTER macro presented can easily be modified into a header macro routine to place special information at the top of any output. Perhaps a single character isn't enough information to truly represent missing values and the only other solution is to format every numeric field. The %FOOTER macro could be modified to search out and replace the single character with a more meaningful string.

Once again, this hybrid approach to reporting is computer resource expensive, but it can otherwise lend a lot of flexibility to SAS procedures that have reached their limits otherwise. This hybrid DATA _NULL_ method could conceivably be used to post-process SAS output from any SAS procedure.

Comparison of Approaches

Once the reporting task objectives are clear and the SAS reporting tools are available, you must decide which tool to use. Each reporting approach will lend itself to different results based on end user needs and project parameters. So, let us compare each tool with respect to the end user, time constraints, output aesthetics, and programming scope.

Of the reporting tools mentioned in this chapter, some are affected more severely by the changing demands of the end user. PROC TABULATE and PROC REPORT can be rather accommodating under changing specifications, so they are good to use unless you are certain they cannot meet output requirements. Both procedures can allow for major restructuring of the output with just a few statement modifications and at much less cost than a DATA _NULL_ step approach. If the changes to the PROC REPORT or PROC TABULATE output are cosmetic and just outside the limits of the procedures, then a hybrid DATA _NULL_ step approach can be used. The DATA _NULL_ step approach is the most flexible if the end user changes the output requirements dramatically. The code may not have to be scrapped, even if some fairly extensive and expensive modifications need to be made. Of course, if the procedural output is of the quick-and-dirty variety, and is not likely to be changed by the end user later, the SQL, FREQ, UNIVARIATE, MEANS, and PRINT procedures will suffice. If one of these quick-and-dirty reports needs to be quickly modified, most of them have output data set options that can be ported to a DATA _NULL_.

Time is always a critical factor, and it plays a large part in determining which reporting approach to take. By far, the DATA _NULL_ and hybrid DATA _NULL_ approaches take the most time to write, maintain, and modify. If a very aggressive deadline is set for the project, these approaches may be prohibitive. This is where the beauty of PROC REPORT and PROC TABULATE shines. Both procedures can quickly lead to summary and listing output of moderately complex design without a lot of coding. Also, PROC REPORT and PROC TABULATE are very easy to maintain since error trapping is greatly simplified. If there isn't the time for coding PROC REPORT or PROC TABULATE, the basic output from them can usually be generated by one of the other quick-and-dirty procedures: SQL, FREQ, UNIVARIATE, MEANS, or PRINT.

Output aesthetics as defined by the end user play a primary role in tool selection. Again, the DATA _NULL_ approach is limitless in what can be done. If the end user has extremely detailed demands, the

DATA _NULL_ may be the only logical choice. If the output specifications are a bit less extravagant, a hybrid DATA _NULL_ or preferably PROC REPORT or PROC TABULATE can be used. These methods have some limitations in presentation, but will meet most every listing or summary specification. Finally, if the aesthetics of the output is of minimal importance and what really matters are simply the raw results, one of the quick-and-dirty procedures mentioned earlier will suffice.

Finally, project scope may effect which tool you choose to use for reporting. A broad project scope may involve carrying the same programs across several databases or analyzing varied data types within a project. Look back at the distinctive appearance of PROC TABULATE. Let us suppose that you chose PROC TABULATE to be the workhorse procedure for a set of summary tables across several projects. Half of the way through the tables, you discover that you simply cannot create the table you need with PROC TABULATE. This can be depressing, because you either need to create a time consuming DATA _NULL_ to imitate a PROC TABULATE, or you go back and select a whole new approach leaving you to rewrite many programs. The key here is to pick a reporting tool or set of tools that will allow enough flexibility to complete the project without a rewrite. At a cost, you will rarely ever find yourself in a jam with the DATA _NULL_ or hybrid DATA _NULL_. On rare occasion, PROC REPORT and PROC TABULATE alone can lead to some problems in presenting a consistent and aesthetically pleasing broad scope reporting package.

Here is a brief summary of each reporting tool in strengths and weaknesses:

PROC REPORT:
Capable of attractive and complex listings and summaries.
Can compute a number of statistics.
Quick to produce.
Easy to maintain.
Moderately adaptable to change including DATA step interface.

PROC TABULATE:
Capable of attractive, yet distinctive complex summary tables.
Can compute a number of statistics, including complex percentages.
Quick to produce for simple tables.
Easy to maintain.
Very adaptable within PROC TABULATE language limits.

PROC SQL:
Capable of advanced data manipulation, summary and listings.
Quick to produce.
Easy to maintain if proficient in structured query language.
Adaptable, but limited in aesthetic control of output.

Other Quick-and-Dirty Procedures:
Includes PROC PRINT, MEANS, UNIVARIATE, FREQ.
Very quickly produced.
Easiest to maintain.
Extremely limited in aesthetic control as stand alone procedures.
MEANS, UNIVARIATE, FREQ can produce data sets of statistics.

DATA _NULL_:
Capable of any type of listing or summary.
Production time based on complexity. May be slow and expensive to produce.
More difficult to maintain due to large volume of code.
Most adaptable, at a cost.

Hybrid DATA _NULL_:
Capable of almost any type of listing or summary.
Initial coding implementation and computer resource demand.
Average maintenance time since majority of code is procedural.
Quite adaptable for projects large in scope.

Conclusion

Times have changed for SAS programmers and reporting. There was a time when standard quick-and-dirty output or the DATA _NULL_ was all there was in the way of reporting tools. Now, SAS has given us new high-power reporting tools for descriptive statistics and data listings with the REPORT, TABULATE, and SQL procedures. With the introduction of the new tools along with the old, SAS programmers have more options when deciding which tool would suit their needs best. The correct tool selection is based on two points. You must know what you have to report, and you must know what tools you have to report with. Only by fully understanding these two factors can you make the best decision at the time. Remember, make the tool do the work.

References

SAS Institute Inc. (1990), *SAS Guide to the Report Procedure: Usage and Reference, Version 6, First Edition*, Cary, NC: SAS Institute Inc.

SAS Institute Inc. (1990), *SAS Guide to TABULATE Processing, Second Edition*, Cary, NC: SAS Institute Inc.

SAS Institute Inc. (1989), *SAS Guide to the SQL Procedure: Usage and Reference, Version 6, First Edition*, Cary, NC: SAS Institute Inc.

SAS Institute Inc. (1991), SAS Technical Report P-222: *Changes and Enhancements to Base SAS Software, Release 6.07*, Cary, NC: SAS Institute Inc.

SAS Institute Inc. (1993), SAS Technical Report P-258: *Using the REPORT Procedure in a Nonwindowing Environment, Release 6.07*, Cary, NC: SAS Institute Inc.

CHAPTER 15

Producing Multiple Reports from Typical Survey Data

by Pamela G. Spurrier

Abstract

A survey is a frequently used method of obtaining information. Typical questions elicit four kinds of response: yes/no, a rating, a category selection, or a quantitative value. This chapter presents and discusses a series of SAS programs that edit the collected data, format the data for ease of analysis, and produce reports for each of the four types of questions. The programs were written for survey data that were collected using simple random sampling. The use of macros and features of macro processing allow the programs to be adapted to surveys with a varying number of questions, and to surveys that use a different point scale for rating questions.

Specifications

The code in this chapter was developed and tested with Release 6.04 of the SAS System under the DOS environment. Use of the code with other releases of the SAS System or other environments may require user modification. Modified code is not supported by the author.

About the Author

Pamela Spurrier is an Independent Statistician/Consultant with 20 years of experience using SAS software. She has a BS degree in Mathematics from Nazareth College and an MA degree in Statistics from the University of Missouri -·Columbia. Her areas of expertise include base SAS and SAS/STAT software, report writing, and the macro facility.

Questions and Comments Should be Directed to:

Pamela Spurrier
1709 Quail Valley West
Columbia, SC 29212-1540
Telephone: 803-781-2340

Examples from this book are available online, see inside back cover for details.

Producing Multiple Reports from Typical Survey Data

Pamela G. Spurrier

Introduction

A survey is a frequently-used method of obtaining information. Typical questions elicit one of four kinds of response: yes/no, a rating, a category selection, or a quantitative value. This chapter will present and discuss a series of SAS programs that edit the collected data, format the data for ease of analysis, and produce reports for each of the four types of questions. The programs were written for survey data that were collected using simple random sampling to select the respondents. These programs are for intermediate to advanced SAS users who have a basic understanding of the `MACRO` facility.

A Sample Report Writing Task: The Employee Opinion Survey

The Employee Opinion Survey (Figure 1) was developed for a study conducted in 1991. It will serve as the example for this chapter. The Employee Opinion Survey demonstrates all four types of typical questions:

Questions to which the respondent indicates "yes" or "no." Section 1 of the Employee Opinion Survey contains such questions. The information of interest is usually the percentage that indicated "yes." In this chapter, questions of this type are referred to as Section 1 questions.

Questions that ask the respondent to rate an item. The rating is often on a scale of 3 or more. Section 2 of the Employee Opinion Survey contains two such questions asked about four groups of employees. Several estimates may be of interest for these types of questions. Often the average or median rating is of primary interest. Others are interested in the percentage of respondents that rated the item at each value of the scale. In this chapter, questions of this type are referred to as Section 2 questions.

Questions that ask the respondent to check the appropriate category. The first four questions of Section 3 of the Employee Opinion Survey are this type of question. The percentage of respondents indicating each category is to be estimated. In this chapter, questions of this type are referred to as Section 3 categorical questions.

Questions that ask for a quantitative value. The last two questions of Section 3 of the Employee Opinion Survey, which ask for years of service, are this type of question. The average or mean value for each quantitative value must be estimated. In this chapter, questions of this type are referred to as Section 3 quantitative questions.

Creating Reports from Survey Data

Nine SAS programs have been written to accomplish the tasks of data editing, data re-coding, data analysis, and report generation. The program `EDIT.SAS` generates a list of errors in the raw data file; `S1P1.SAS`, `S2P1.SAS`, `S2P2.SAS`, `S2P3.SAS`, and `S3P1.SAS` generate the final reports.

The use of macros and features of macro processing allow the programs to be adapted to surveys with varying number of questions and to those that use a different point scale for rating questions. Informats are used to accommodate varying keying schemes by re-coding the data for analysis purposes. Formats are used to edit the raw data file and to customize the final reports.

`FORMAT.SAS` - Creates formats that customize the final reports and informats that re-code data for analysis purposes.

Figure 1: 1991 Employee Opinion Survey

Section 1: We are interested in **your overall assessment** of the services listed below. Please **circle** your response. If you are not familiar with an administrative service or *if you provide the service*, please circle "**N/A**" (Not Applicable).

1. Do you receive sufficient information from the finance area to plan your budget? YES NO N/A
2. Are available benefits as well as changes in benefits explained in sufficient detail? YES NO N/A
3. Are the necessary instructional materials ordered properly and received in sufficient number prior to the beginning of each term? YES NO N/A
4. Do you feel that the publications produced for and about this institution create a positive image for the school? YES NO N/A

Section 2: Please rate the **overall performance** of the following groups of employees *on the service that they provide*.

If you have not had any contact with a group or **if you are a member of the group**, check "N/A".

For the groups with which you have had contact, **check the appropriate response** for each of the two questions.

	WHEN YOU CALL UPON THEM FOR ASSISTANCE, ARE THESE EMPLOYEES HELPFUL?					DO THESE EMPLOYEES RESPOND TO YOUR NEEDS AND/OR REQUESTS IN A TIMELY MANNER?				
	NEVER	SOMETIMES	MOST TIMES	ALWAYS	N/A	NEVER	SOMETIMES	MOST TIMES	ALWAYS	N/A
1. Food Service										
2. Cashiers										
3. Security										
4. Personnel										

Section 3: Please **provide** the appropriate information about you.

Employee Type: Faculty _____ Staff _____

Status: Full-time _____ Part-time _____

Functional Area of Assignment: Academic Programs/Services _____ Student Services _____

Maintenance _____ Administration _____

On what campus are you located? ______________________

How long have you been employed at this campus? _______ years

How long have you been employed at Area Technical College? _______ years

FIRST.SAS - Sets parameters to customize programs for a specific survey. The values set in this program are used by all the programs except **FORMAT.SAS** to customize the programs to a specific survey.

EDIT.SAS - Edits the data and produces a list of surveys that need correction.

DATA.SAS - Creates the SAS data set that is used to produce the estimates and the reports. Informats are used to re-code the raw data. Data from questions such as those in Section 1 of the Employee Opinion Survey must be re-coded to "1" for "yes" responses, "0" for "no" responses, and "." (missing) for both "N/A" and non-response. Data from questions such as those in Section 2 of the Employee Opinion Survey must be re-coded to the rating scale of interest; the scale must be discrete, sequential values. Data from questions such as those in Section 3 of the Employee Opinion Survey must be re-coded so that non-response is coded as missing (".").

S1P1.SAS - Produces the estimates for questions in Section 1. The percentage of respondents indicating "yes" is estimated as is the 95% confidence interval for the estimate.

S2P1.SAS - Produces estimates of the average rating for questions in Section 2. The 95% confidence interval for the average rating is also estimated.

S2P2.SAS - Produces estimates of the median rating for Section 2 questions. The 25th. and 75th. percentiles are printed instead of a 95% confidence interval.

S2P3.SAS - Produces estimates of the percentage of respondents that rate the item at each value of the scale. For example, if a scale of 0 to 3 is used for the Section 2 questions, the program would produce estimates of the percentage of respondents that rated the item 0, that rated the item 1, that rated the item 2, and that rated the item 3. The 95% confidence intervals for these estimates are also calculated.

S3P1.SAS - Produces estimates for the two types of questions in Section 3. For the categorical questions, the percentage of respondents indicating each category is estimated. Here, the number of response categories varies by question. For quantitative questions such as years of service, the average or mean value is estimated. The 95% confidence intervals for the estimates are produced.

The variable names used in the SAS programs were chosen to facilitate the use of DO loops, arrays, abbreviated variable lists, and features of MACRO processing. The variable names for Sections 1 and 3 took the form **SxQy** where **x** indicated the section of the Employee Opinion Survey from which the question came (**x**=1 or 3) and y indicated the question number within the section with questions numbered sequentially from 1 (y=1, 2, ...). Each question in Section 2 has two parts: a helpfulness part and a timeliness part. To identify parts, the variable names for this section took the form **SxQyPz** where **z** indicated the part (**z**=1 or 2). **SxQ** is referred to as the prefix. The programs and macros that produce final reports have been written so that the prefix can be changed to meet survey needs. The sequential numbering of questions and of parts of questions must be retained.

Coding and Re-Coding Data for a Survey

The process of producing valid final reports for a survey begins at the design step. As the questions are planned, the keying scheme should be considered. The keying scheme used for the Employee Opinion Survey was designed to minimize keying errors. Possible responses were given sequential odd number values beginning with 1. For example, the questions in Section 1 were keyed as 1 for a "yes" response, 3 for a "no" response, 5 for an "N/A" response, and 7 for non-response. The use of sequential odd numbers prevents some keying errors that can occur if sequential numbers are used. The appearance of an even number in the data automatically signals an error to the individuals performing data entry. Informats re-code the data for analysis in the program **DATA.SAS**. For questions in Section 1, the informat yv given in the program **FORMAT.SAS** is used to re-code the data to "1" for a "yes" response, "0" for a "no" response, and "." for an "N/A" response or for non-response. The informat rv was used to re-code the questions in Section 2. The second digit of the format s3ev suggests how each of the categorical questions in Section 3 was keyed.

Making Changes for a Specific Survey

The code of FORMAT.SAS creates a format library that is used by the other programs. The PICTURE and VALUE statements will be discussed with the programs that use them. This program must be customized to the specific survey in order to re-code data to the required formats based on the keying schemes used and to format the output of the final reports to reflect the actual questions asked on the survey. The PROC CATALOG statements at the end of the program produce documentation of the formats, informats, and pictures stored on the library.

```
****** FORMAT.SAS - FORMATS FOR EMPLOYEE OPINION SURVEY ***;
options pagesize=55 linesize=80 nodate nonumber;
libname library 'c:\mysas\satech';
proc format library=library fmtlib;

*** informat for Section 1 questions;
   invalue yv '1'=1 '3'=0 '5'=. '7'=.;
*** informat for Section 2 questions;
   invalue rv '1'=0 '3'=1 '5'=2 '7'=3 '9'=.;

*** pictures used in final reports;
   picture confl low-high='0009.99%' (prefix='(');
   picture confu low-high='0009.99% )';
   picture estv low-high='0009.99%';
   picture conf2l low-high='0009.9' (prefix='(');
   picture conf2u low-high='0009.9 )';
   picture est2v low-high='0009.9';

*** output formats for identifiers of questions in Sections 1 and 2;
   value $enamev 's1q1'='Sufficient financial info - planning?'
                 's1q2'='Benefits explained sufficiently?'
                 's1q3'='Materials ordered & received?'
                 's1q4'='Publications create positive image?'
                 's2q1'='Food Service'
                 's2q2'='Cashiers'
                 's2q3'='Security'
                 's2q4'='Personnel'
                 's2q1p0'='Food Service: Overall'
                 's2q1p1'='             : Helpful'
                 's2q1p2'='             : Timely Response'
                 's2q2p0'='Cashiers     : Overall'
                 's2q2p1'='             : Helpful'
                 's2q2p2'='             : Timely Response'
                 's2q3p0'='Security     : Overall'
                 's2q3p1'='             : Helpful'
                 's2q3p2'='             : Timely Response'
                 's2q4p0'='Personnel    : Overall'
                 's2q4p1'='             : Helpful'
                 's2q4p2'='             : Timely Response'
                 's3q1'='Employee Type'
                 's3q2'='Status'
                 's3q3'='Assignment Area'
                 's3q4'='Campus'
                 's3q5'='Yrs at Campus'
```

```
                    's3q6'='Yrs in System'
;

*** output format for rating scale in Section 2;
   value s2ratev 1='Never' 2='Sometimes' 3='Most Times' 4='Always';
*** output format for parts of questions in Section 2;
   value s2catv 1='Helpful' 2='Timely Response';
*** output format for responses to question in Section 3;
   value s3ev 11='Faculty'  13='Staff'  15='Not Reported'
              21='Full-time'  23='Part-time'  25='Not Reported'
              31='Academic Programs/Services'
              33='Student Services'
              35='Maintenance'
              37='Administration'
              39='Not Reported'
              41='Main'
              43='South Center'
              45='Other'
              47='Not Reported'
;
proc catalog c=library.formats et=format;
   contents;
   run;
   quit;
```

Setting Parameters to Adapt Programs to a Specific Survey

After the survey is designed, the keying structure is determined, and the variable names are assigned, the parameters that will adapt the SAS programs to a specific survey are known. `FIRST.SAS` contains these parameters. They must be known when any of the other SAS programs are run. On an interactive system, the program `FIRST.SAS` is run before any other programs. On batch systems, the statements in `FIRST.SAS` should be appended to the beginning of the other programs. The code for `FIRST.SAS` describes the values needed and gives the appropriate values for the Employee Opinion Survey.

```
******************* FIRST.SAS ********************************

  This program sets the parameters for all survey programs.

  Check each program for additional changes required before
     execution.

******************************************************************;

options pagesize=55 linesize=80 nodate nonumber;

*** identify locations of libraries and raw data file
    and give names to SAS data sets created in programs;

libname library 'c:\mysas\satech'; *** location of SAS format
library;
libname out 'c:\mysas\satech';  *** location of SAS data sets;
%let rawdsn=c:\mysas\satech\scsurvey.dat; *** name and location of
     the raw data file;

%let dsn1=employ; *** name used for SAS data set created
```

```
     in DATA.SAS;
%let dsnout=emp; *** prefix used for SAS data sets that store
     estimates - use maximum of 4 characters;

*** set parameters based on number of questions;

%let sec1=4;    *** number of questions in section 1;
%let sec2=4;    *** number of questions in section 2;
%let s2part=2; *** # of parts to each question in section 2;
%let sec3=6;    *** number of questions in section 3;
%let sec3t1=4; *** number of categorical questions in section 3;
%let sec3t2=2; *** number of quantitative questions in section 3;

*** set parameters that hold population and sample size;

%let npop=273; %* population size;
%let nsamp=94; %* sample size;

*** create two title statements for the final reports;
title1 '1991 Employee Opinion Survey';
title2 'Area Technical College';
```

Editing the Employee Opinion Survey

After you have collected and keyed the survey data, the next step is to edit the data. Several features of SAS software make this task relatively easy. `EDIT.SAS` accomplishes this task using `PROC FORMAT` and the `PUT` function. Output 1 shows a portion of theeport generated by `EDIT.SAS`.

Output 1: Sample Report Generated by EDIT.SAS

```
                         1991 Employee Opinion Survey
                            Area Technical College

ID1=1 S1Q2=9
      S3Q5=5.5 S3Q6=5
   TOTAL ERRORS FOUND= 2

ID1=2 S2Q2P2=6
      S2Q4P2=8
   TOTAL ERRORS FOUND= 2

ID1=3 S1Q3=2
   TOTAL ERRORS FOUND= 1

DATA CARD MISSING: ID1=4 ID2=4 ID3=5
```

`PROC FORMAT` is used to create one format for each possible keying scheme used for variables with discrete responses. Only three were needed for the Employee Opinion Survey: `r5v`, `r7v`, and `r9v`. Notice that all permissible values for a keying scheme are assigned to the value 'x'. The arrays `CHK1` and `CHK2` hold the values of the variables corresponding to Sections 1 and 2 of the survey. Within the data step, the data are read and edited; error messages are generated as needed.

As indicated by the input statement, each observation consists of three lines of data. Each data line contains the observation identification number called `id1` on the first data card, `id2` on the second data card, and `id3` on the third data card. After setting the error counter for the observation, `count`, to 0, the first edit checks that the data have been read properly. If all three identification numbers match, no error has occurred. Otherwise, some data have been lost. The program increments the variable `count`, generates an error message, and calls `LOSTCARD`. `LOSTCARD` instructs SAS not to output the observation. SAS will attempt to build an observation beginning with the second line of data using the input specifications. This process continues until a valid observation, one for which all three identification numbers match, is obtained. Then the edit program continues.

The variables for Section 1 are edited using the format `r7v`. Within a `DO` loop that runs from 1 to the upper bound of the array `chk1`, found using `HBOUND(chk1)`, each variable is written with the format `r7v` by the `PUT` function. If the variable is not written as an "x," an error exits. The error `count` for the observation is increased by 1, and an error message is written to the print file. In similar fashion, the variables for Section 2 are edited using the format `r9v`.

The variables in Section 3 do not all use the same keying scheme. They are not edited within a `DO` loop, but the approach is the same. Separate SAS statements write each variable using the `PUT` function and the appropriate format and determine whether an error exists.

Any logical edits are added at the end of the program. Here, the only logical edit is a comparison of `s3q5`, the number of years employed at the campus, and `s3q6`, the number of years employed by the technical college.

```
******************** EDIT.SAS ********************************

The location and name of the raw data file is given in FIRST.SAS.

Customize PROC FORMAT to reflect the keying scheme used.

This program may require significant changes to reflect a specific
survey.

*****************************************************************;

%let prefix=s2q; *** prefix for Section 2 questions;

%macro section2(start,stop,question);
   %do i=&start %to &stop;
         &prefix&i.p1-&prefix&i.p&question
      %end;
%mend section2;

proc format;
   value  r5v 1,3,5='x';
   value r7v 1,3,5,7='x';
   value r9v 1,3,5,7,9='x';
run;

data temp;
   array chk1 {*} s1q1-s1q&sec1;
   array chk2 {*} %section2(1,&sec2,&s2part);
   retain ecount 0;
   infile "&rawdsn" end=eof;  *** name and location of data file;
   file print;
   input @1 id1 3. @5 (s1q1-s1q&sec1) (1. +1) /
      @1 id2 3. @5 ( %section2(1,&sec2,&s2part)) (1. 1. +1) /
      @1 id3 3. @5 s3q1-s3q&sec3 ;
```

```
*** initialize error counter and edit for lost data;
   count=0;
   if id1^=id2 or id2^=id3 then do;
      count=count+1;
      put / 'DATA CARD MISSING: ' id1= id2= id3=;
      lostcard;
      end;

*** edit Section 1 data;
   do i=1 to hbound(chk1);
      if put(chk1{i},r7v.)^='x' then do;
         count=count+1;
         if count=1 then put / id1= chk1{i}=;
         else put '       ' chk1{i}=;
         end;
      end;

*** edit Section 2 data;
   do i=1 to hbound(chk2);
      if put(chk2{i},r9v.)^='x' then do;
         count=count+1;
         if count=1 then put / id1= chk2{i}=;
         else put '       ' chk2{i}=;
         end;
      end;

*** edit Section 3 data;
   if put(s3q1,r5v.)^='x' then do;
         count=count+1;
         if count=1 then put / id1= s3q1=;
         else put '       ' s3q1=;
         end;
   if put(s3q2,r5v.)^='x' then do;
         count=count+1;
         if count=1 then put / id1= s3q2=;
         else put '       ' s3q2=;
         end;
   if put(s3q3,r9v.)^='x' then do;
         count=count+1;
         if count=1 then put / id1= s3q3=;
         else put '       ' s3q3=;
         end;
**** edits for s3q4, s3q5 and s3q6 must be changed to reflect coding
used
     at each institution.;
   if put(s3q4,r7v.)^='x' then do;
         count=count+1;
         if count=1 then put / id1= s3q4=;
         else put '       ' s3q4=;
         end;

*** logical edits;
   if s3q5>s3q6 then do;
         count=count+1;
         if count=1 then put / id1= s3q5= s3q6=;
         else put '       ' s3q5= s3q6=;
```

```
         end;

     ecount=ecount+count;
     if count>0 then put / '    TOTAL ERRORS FOUND= ' count / ;
     if eof and ecount=0 then put / 'NO ERRORS FOUND IN DATA SET' / ;
  run;
```

Creating a SAS Data Set Containing the Corrected Survey Data

After the raw data file has been corrected, it is read using `DATA.SAS`, and the SAS data set `&dsn1.ssd` is created. `&dsn1.ssd` is located on the library defined in `FIRST.SAS`.

The program resembles `EDIT.SAS`. On the `INPUT` statement, however, informats used to read the data are those that re-code the data for analysis purposes. The variables in Section 1 are read with the `yv` informat, and those in Section 2 are read with the `rv` informat. The variables in Section 3 are read as keyed. Recall that each question in Section 2 contained two parts. The macro `SEC2` generates code that creates a variable for each of these questions. This variable, named `&prefix&i` where `&i` identifies the specific question, contains the average rating based on the values for the parts. The average is computed for those observations with non-missing values for all the parts. If a respondent failed to rate each part, the average is missing for the observation. These variables will be used in the programs that produce final reports for this section of the survey.

```
********************* DATA.SAS ***********************************

     This program reads the raw data file and creates the SAS data
file &DSN1.SSD on the library defined in FIRST.SAS.

 Provide the correct prefix for Section 2 variables in the %LET
statement.

     The SAS data set &DSN1.SSD is used in all the programs
that produce reports for the employee survey.
*******************************************************************;

%let prefix=s2q; *** prefix used for Section 2 variables;

%macro section2(start,stop,question);
   %do i=&start %to &stop;
         &prefix&i.p1-&prefix&i.p&question
      %end;
%mend section2;

%macro sec2;
   %do i=1 %to &sec2;
      if nmiss(of &prefix&i.p1-&prefix&i.p&s2part)=0 then
         &prefix&i=mean(of &prefix&i.p1-&prefix&i.p&s2part);
      %end;
   %mend sec2;

data out.&dsn1;
   array chk1 {*} s1q1-s1q&sec1;
   array chk2 {*} %section2(1,&sec2,&s2part);
   retain ecount 0;
   infile "&rawdsn" end=eof;  *** name and location of data file;
   input @1 id1 3. @5 (s1q1-s1q&sec1) (yv. +1) /
      @1 id2 3. @5 ( %section2(1,&sec2,&s2part)) (rv. rv. +1) /
```

```
      @1 id3 3. @5 s3q1-s3q&sec3;
   %sec2
run;
```

Analyzing Section 1 Questions

Section 1 contains questions to which the respondent indicated "yes" or "no." Not all respondents answered every question in this section. The final report provides the number of respondents answering the question, the percentage of respondents answering the question that indicated "yes," and the 95% confidence interval for the percentage.

Output 2: Percentage of Respondents Indicating Yes

1991 Employee Opinion Survey
Area Technical College
Section 1: Overall Assessment of Services
Percentage of Respondents Indicating Yes

Service	Number Responding	% With Yes Response	95% Confidence Interval Lower Endpoint	Upper Endpoint
Sufficient financial info - planning?	44	77.27%	(66.92%	87.62%)
Benefits explained sufficiently?	46	73.91%	(63.31%	84.51%)
Materials ordered & received?	87	80.46%	(73.54%	87.38%)
Publications create positive image?	80	78.75%	(71.30%	86.20%)

Notice several features of this report. The percentage responding "yes" is printed with a "%" sign as are the lower and upper endpoints. The confidence interval is given within parentheses. The former is accomplished using the picture `estv`; the latter is accomplished using the pictures `confl` and `confu`. Finally, notice that the services listed under the column `Service` are descriptive. This is accomplished using the format enamev, found in `FORMAT.SAS`. The values to the left of the equal sign in the `VALUE` statement creating enamev will be discussed below.

Output 2 was produced using the program `S1P1.SAS`.

```
*********************** S1P1.SAS *********************************
   This program produces estimates of the percentage of respondents
   that answered yes to each question in Section 1 of the Employee
   Survey.  The program also produces estimates of the
   95% confidenceinterval.
*******************************************************************;

%let prefix=s1q; %* variable name prefix Section 1;

proc means data=out.&dsn1   noprint;
   var &prefix.1-&prefix&sec1;
   output out=temp n=n1-n&sec1 mean=est1-est&sec1
      stderr=se1- se&sec1;
run;
```

```
data last (keep=name n est lower upper);
   length name $ 6.;
   array tn {*} n1-n&sec1;
   array test {*} est1-est&sec1;
   array tse {*} se1-se&sec1;
   set temp;
   wt=sqrt((&npop-&nsamp)/&npop);
   do i=1 to &sec1;
      name="&prefix" || left(i);
      n=tn{i};
      est=test{i};
      dif=2*wt*tse{i};
      lower=max(round((est-dif)*100,.01),0);
      upper=min(round((est+dif)*100,.01),100);
      est=round(est*100,.01);
      output;
      end;
run;

proc print data=last split='*' d uniform;
   var n est lower upper;id name;
   format est estv. lower confl. upper confu. name $enamev.;
   label n='Number*Responding'
         est='% With*Yes*Response'
         lower='95%*Confidence*Lower*Endpoint'
         upper=' *Interval*Upper*Endpoint'
         name='Service';
title3 'Section 1: Overall Assessment of Services';
title4 'Percentage of Respondents Indicating Yes';
run;

data out.&dsnout.s1p1 (label='estimates for section 1');
   set last;
run;
```

S1P1.SAS uses PROC MEANS to produce the estimates. The data for Section 1 have been re-coded to "1" for a "yes" response, "0" for a "no" response, and "." (missing) for an "N/A" response or for non-response. The value of MEAN produced by PROC MEANS for such variables is the proportion of observations coded "1." Here, this corresponds to the proportion of respondents indicating "yes." Notice that PROC MEANS is customized to the survey using &prefix and &sec1. The value of &prefix is assigned in this program; the value of &sec1 is set in the program FIRST.SAS. PROC MEANS creates an output data set, called temp, that contains the values of N, MEAN, and STDERR for each question in Section 1. There is only one observation in this output data set.

The data set last sets the output data set temp and creates one observation for each question. Notice the correspondence between the question number and the suffix of the variables that hold its values of N, MEAN, and STDERR. This correspondence is used within the DO loop to assign the correct values to the variables n, est, dif, lower, and upper and to assign a value to the variable name, used to identify the percentage. This is the variable that is printed under the column Service in the final report using the format enamev. name is assigned a value by concatenating the current value of i to &prefix. Hence, the value of "s1q1" is assigned to name for the first question. The format enamev associates the value "Sufficient financial info - planning?" with the value "s1q1."

PROC PRINT is used to produce the report. The options SPLIT, D, and UNIFORM are used. A FORMAT statement and a LABEL statement further define the output. Additional TITLE statements are also defined. Recall that `TITLE1` and `TITLE2` are in the program `FIRST.SAS`. The final statements of the program create a SAS data set that contains the estimates. If the report portion of the program must be run again, it can be run using only the `PROC PRINT` statements by changing `data=last` to `data=out.&dsnout.s1p1`.

Analyzing Section 2 Questions

Section 2 contained the questions that asked respondents to rate an item. Here there were two ratings for each group of employees. The first was a rating of helpfulness, the second a rating of timeliness. The data for this section have been re-coded to a scale from 0 to 3, with 0 for "never" and 3 for "always." Responses of N/A and non-response have been re-coded to missing (".").

Three final reports could be produced for this section. If the average rating is of interest, the report produced by `S2P1.SAS` would be used. If the median rating is of interest, the report produced by `S2P2.SAS` would be used. If the percentage of respondents giving the group each possible rating is of interest, the report produced by `S2P3.SAS` would be used. The first two reports, and the programs that produce them, are quite similar.

Producing Average Ratings of Service Groups

Output 3: Average Ratings by Service Groups

```
                              1991 Employee Opinion Survey
                                Area Technical College
                      Section 2: Average Ratings of Service Groups
                Ratings: 0-Never, 1-Occasionally, 2-Most of the Time, 3-Always
             Overall Rating=Average of Ratings for All Characteristics : Range 0-3

------------------------------ Page Number=1 ------------------------------
                                                                95%
                                                           Confidence  Interval
                                      Number     Average      Lower      Upper
   Group: Characteristic            Responding   Rating     Endpoint   Endpoint

Food Service: Overall                   68         1.9        (1.8       2.1 )

            : Helpful                   74         2.0        (1.8       2.1 )

            : Timely Response           68         1.9        (1.7       2.0 )

Cashiers    : Overall                   57         2.5        (2.3       2.6 )

            : Helpful                   65         2.5        (2.3       2.6 )

            : Timely Response           57         2.4        (2.3       2.6 )

Security    : Overall                   75         2.2        (2.1       2.4 )

            : Helpful                   83         2.3        (2.1       2.4 )

            : Timely Response           75         2.2        (2.1       2.3 )

Personnel   : Overall                   76         1.9        (1.8       2.1 )

            : Helpful                   85         2.0        (1.9       2.1 )

            : Timely Response           77         1.9        (1.8       2.1 )
```

Output 3 is produced by S2P1.SAS. For each service group, the average rating for helpfulness and the average rating for timeliness are given. An overall rating based on the average rating of those who rated the employee group on both characteristics is also given.

The overall rating is based on the &prefix&i variables that were created by the macro SEC2 in DATA.SAS. The individual ratings are based on the values of the variables &prefix&i.p1 and &prefix&i.p2. Here, &i identifies the specific question. The information printed under the column Group: Characteristic in the report is produced using the format enamev. The pictures est2v, conf2l, and conf2u are used to print the values of the mean and the lower and upper endpoints of the 95% confidence interval.

This program is similar to S1P1.SAS. The values of the lowest possible rating for a part and of the highest possible rating for a part must be assigned in %LET statements. **PROC MEANS** is used to compute the values of N, MEAN, and STDERR for the overall rating and the rating for each part for each question. The macro LISTIT generates the code for the VAR statement to accomplish this. The remainder of the program follows the pattern of S1P1.SAS. The data step last creates three observations per question corresponding to the overall rating, the helpfulness rating, and the timeliness rating. Values are assigned to the variable name for each of these by concatenating the value &prefix with the value of i (identifies a question), the character "p" and the value of k (identifies a part of a question). The value of "&prefix&i.p0" is given to the variable name for the overall ratings. Finally, the report is printed using PROC PRINT, and a SAS data set is created that contains the estimates.

The code that produced Output 3 is given below.

```
************************ S2P1.SAS *********************************
   This program produces estimates of the average rating given by
   respondents to each part of each question in Section 2 of
   the Employee Opinion Survey.  The average overall rating
   is also produced, as are the estimates of the
   95% confidence intervals.

   Verify that the values in the %LET statements for LOWR and HIGHR
   are correct for your survey.
*******************************************************************;

%let upper=%eval(&sec2*%eval(&s2part+1));  %* quest*(parts+1);
%let lowr=0;  %* value of lowest rating for part;
%let highr=3;  %* value of highest rating for part;
%let prefix=s2q; %* variable name prefix for Section 2;
%let pagechk=%eval(40/%eval((&s2part+1)*2));

%macro listit;
   %do i=1 %to &sec2;
      &prefix&i &prefix&i.p1-&prefix&i.p&s2part
      %end;
   %mend listit;

proc means data=out.&dsn1   noprint;
   var %listit  ;
   output out=temp n=n1-n&upper mean=est1-est&upper
      stderr=se1- se&upper;
run;

data last (keep=page name n est lower upper);
   length name $ 8.;
```

```
    retain page 1 wt;
    array test {*} est1-est&upper;
    array tse {*} se1-se&upper;
    array tn {*} n1-n&upper;
    set temp;
    wt=sqrt((&npop-&nsamp)/&npop);
    do i=1 to &sec2;
       j=((&s2part+1)*(i-1)+1);
       do k=0 to &s2part;
          m=j+k;
          name="&prefix" || left(i) || "p" || left(k);
          n=tn{m};
          est=test{m};
          dif=2*wt*tse{m};
          lower=max(round((est-dif),.1),&lowr);
          upper=min(round((est+dif),.1),&highr);
          est=round(est,.1);
          output;
          end;
       if mod(i,&pagechk)=0 then page=page+1;
       end;
run;

proc print data=last split='*' d uniform;
    var n est lower upper;id name;
    format est est2v. lower conf2l. upper conf2u. name $enamev.;
    label n='Number*Responding'
          est='Average*Rating'
          lower='95%*Confidence*Lower*Endpoint'
          upper=' *Interval*Upper*Endpoint'
          name='Group: Characteristic'
          page='Page Number'
;
    by page notsorted;
    pageby page;
title3 'Section 2: Average Ratings of Service Groups';
title4 'Ratings: 0-Never, 1-Occasionally, 2-Most of the Time, 3-
Always';
title5 'Overall Rating=Average of Ratings for All Characteristics :
Range 0-3';
run;

data out.&dsnout.s2p1 (label='estimates of average ratings:sec 2');
    set last;
run;
```

Producing Median Ratings of Service Groups

The report produced by `S2P2.SAS` contains median ratings and the 25th. and 75th. percentiles. Otherwise, it looks like the report produced by `S2P1.SAS`.

The program `S2P2.SAS` uses `PROC UNIVARIATE` to produce the estimates of the `median` and the 25th. and 75th. percentiles. The only other differences between `S2P1.SAS` and `S2P2.SAS` are those required to change from reporting the 95% confidence interval to reporting the 25th. and 75th. percentile.

Output 4: Median Ratings of Service Groups

```
                          1991 Employee Opinion Survey
                            Area Technical College
                    Section 2: Median Ratings of Service Groups
            Ratings: 0-Never, 1-Occasionally, 2-Most of the Time, 3-Always
         Overall Rating=Average of Ratings for All Characteristics : Range 0-3

------------------------------ Page Number=1 --------------------------------

                                  Number      Median     25th        75th
     Group: Characteristic      Responding    Rating   Percentile  Percentile

 Food Service: Overall              68         2.0      (1.5        2.3 )

             : Helpful              74         2.0      (1.0        3.0 )

             : Timely Response      68         2.0      (1.0        2.0 )

 Cashiers    : Overall              57         2.5      (2.0        3.0 )

             : Helpful              65         3.0      (2.0        3.0 )

             : Timely Response      57         2.0      (2.0        3.0 )

 Security    : Overall              75         2.0      (2.0        3.0 )

             : Helpful              83         2.0      (2.0        3.0 )

             : Timely Response      75         2.0      (2.0        3.0 )

 Personnel   : Overall              76         2.0      (1.5        2.5 )

             : Helpful              85         2.0      (2.0        3.0 )

             : Timely Response      77         2.0      (1.0        2.0 )
```

The code that produced Output 4 is given below.

```
********************* S2P2.SAS ***********************************
   This program produces estimates of the median rating given by
   respondents to each part of each question in Section 2 of
   the Employee Opinion Survey.  The median overall rating
   is also produced as are the 25th. and 75th. percentiles.

   Verify that the values in the %LET statements for LOWR and HIGHR
   are correct for your survey.
******************************************************************;

%let upper=%eval(&sec2*%eval(&s2part+1));
%let highr=3; %* highest rating for a part;
%let lowr=0; %* lowest rating for a part;
%let prefix=s2q; %* variable name prefix for Section 2;
%let pagechk=%eval(40/%eval((&s2part+1)*2));

%macro listit;
   %do i=1 %to &sec2;
```

```
      &prefix&i &prefix&i.p1-&prefix&i.p&s2part
      %end;
   %mend listit;

proc univariate data=out.&dsn1 noprint;
   var %listit  ;
   output out=temp n=n1-n&upper median=est1-est&upper
      q1=q1v1- q1v&upper q3=q3v1-q3v&upper;
run;

data last (keep=page name n est lower upper);
   length name $ 8.;
   retain page 1;
   array tn {*} n1-n&upper;
   array test {*} est1-est&upper;
   array tq1 {*} q1v1-q1v&upper;
   array tq3 {*} q3v1-q3v&upper;
   set temp;
   do i=1 to &sec2;
      j=((&s2part+1)*(i-1)+1);
      do k=0 to &s2part;
         m=j+k;
         name="&prefix" || left(i) || "p" || left(k);
         n=tn{m};
         est=round(test{m},.1);
         lower=max(round(tq1{m},.1),&lowr);
         upper=min(round(tq3{m},.1),&highr);
         output;
         end;
      if mod(i,&pagechk)=0 then page=page+1;
      end;
run;

proc print data=last split='*' d uniform;
   var n est lower upper;id name;
   format est est2v. lower conf2l. upper conf2u. name $enamev.;
   label n='Number*Responding'
         est='Median*Rating'
         lower='25th*Percentile'
         upper='75th*Percentile'
         name='Group: Characteristic'
         page='Page Number'
;
   by page notsorted;
   pageby page;
title3 'Section 2: Median Ratings of Service Groups';
title4 'Ratings: 0-Never, 1-Occasionally, 2-Most of the Time, 3-
Always';
title5 'Overall Rating=Average of Ratings for All Characteristics :
Range 0-3';
run;

data out.&dsnout.s2p2 (label='median estimates for section 2');
   set last;
run;
```

Producing the Percent of Ratings in Each Category

The final report produced for Section 2 provides the number and percentage of respondents rating a service group 0, 1, 2, or 3 on each characteristic. The first page of the report is shown in Output 5. Results for two groups of employees appear on a page.

Output 5: Percent of Ratings in Each Category Provided by Service Groups

```
                    1991 Employee Opinion Survey
                       Area Technical College
             Section 2: Percent of Ratings in Each Category
                     Provided By Service Groups

---------------------- PAGE=1 Employee Group=Food Service ----------------------
                                                         95%
                                                   Confidence    Interval
                                 Number     % With     Lower        Upper
PART              Response     Responding  Response   Endpoint     Endpoint

Helpful           Never             1        1.35%    (0.00%        3.54% )

Helpful           Sometimes        18       24.32%    (16.19%      32.46% )

Helpful           Most Times       36       48.65%    (39.17%      58.12% )

Helpful           Always           19       25.68%    (17.40%      33.96% )

Timely Response   Never             1        1.47%    (0.00%        3.85% )

Timely Response   Sometimes        21       30.88%    (21.74%      40.02% )

Timely Response   Most Times       31       45.59%    (35.73%      55.44% )

Timely Response   Always           15       22.06%    (13.86%      30.26% )

------------------------ PAGE=1 Employee Group=Cashiers ------------------------
                                                         95%
                                                   Confidence    Interval
                                 Number     % With     Lower        Upper
PART              Response     Responding  Response   Endpoint     Endpoint

Helpful           Never             1        1.54%    (0.00%        4.03% )

Helpful           Sometimes         4        6.15%    (1.29%       11.02% )

Helpful           Most Times       23       35.38%    (25.70%      45.06% )

Helpful           Always           37       56.92%    (46.90%      66.95% )

Timely Response   Never             0        0.00%    (0.00%        0.00% )

Timely Response   Sometimes         2        3.51%    (0.00%        7.49% )

Timely Response   Most Times       28       49.12%    (38.30%      59.94% )

Timely Response   Always           27       47.37%    (36.56%      58.17% )
```

The estimates given in this report are produced within the data step of the program `S2P3.SAS`. Prior to running the program, the values of `category` and `prefix` must be assigned in the `%LET` statements. Within the data step, the number of respondents indicating a specific response for a question is counted for all questions and stored in the array `COUNTS`. The total number of respondents answering each question is counted and stored in the array `NT`. When the end of the data set is reached, a `DO` loop assigns values to the variables `name`, `part`, `response`, `n`, `est`, `lower`, and `upper`. `part` identifies the part of the question. `response` identifies the specific response. Here 1 corresponds to a response of "never" and 4 to a response of "always." One observation is output for each rating category for each part of each question. The number of observations output to the data set one is the same as the value of `&top2` computed in a `%LET` statement at the beginning of the program. The estimates are now printed using `PROC PRINT`. Two additional formats are used: `s2ratev` is used to print the value of the variable `response`; `s2catv` is used to print the value of the variable `part`. A SAS data set is created that stores the estimates created in the data step.

```
*********************** S2P3.SAS ********************************
   This program produces estimates for Section 2
   of the Employee Opinion Survey.

   For each question, the percentage of employees responding
   to each category and the 95% confidence intervals are estimated.

   Verify that the values in the %LET statement for CATEGORY and
   PREFIX arecorrect for your survey.
*****************************************************************;

%let category=4;  %* number of response categories;
%let top1=%eval(&sec2 * &s2part);
%let top2=%eval(&sec2 * &s2part * &category);
%let prefix=s2q; %* variable name prefix;
%let pagechk=%eval(40/%eval((&s2part * &category * 2)+3));

%macro sec2;
    %do i=1 %to &sec2;
       &prefix&i.p1-&prefix&i.p&s2part
       %end;
   %mend sec2;

data one;
   set out.&dsn1 (keep=%sec2) end=eof;
   array temp {&sec2,&s2part} %sec2;
   array nt {&sec2,&s2part} n1-n&top1;
   array counts {&sec2,&s2part,&category} ct1-ct&top2;
   retain page 1 n1-n&top1 ct1-ct&top2 0 wt;
   length name $ 4;
   if _n_=1 then do;
      wt=sqrt((&npop-&nsamp)/&npop);
      end;
   do i=1 to &sec2;
      do i2=1 to &s2part;
         if temp{i,i2}^=. then do;
             j=temp{i,i2}+1;
             counts{i,i2,j}=counts{i,i2,j} + 1;
             nt{i,i2}=nt{i,i2} + 1;
             end;
         end;
      end;
   if eof then do i=1 to &sec2;
      name="&prefix" || left(i) ;
```

```
      do i2=1 to &s2part;
         part=i2;
         do j=1 to &category;
            response=j;
            n=counts{i,i2,j};
            est=counts{i,i2,j}/nt{i,i2} *100;
            dif=2*wt*sqrt(est*(100-est)/(nt{i,i2}-1));
            lower=max(round((est-dif),.01),0);
            upper=min(round((est+dif),.01),100);
            est=round(est,.01);
            output;
            end;
         end;
      if mod(i,&pagechk)=0 then page=page+1;
      end;
run;

proc print data=one split='*' d uniform;
   var response n est lower upper;id part;
   by page notsorted name notsorted;
   pageby page;
   format est estv. lower confl. upper confu. name $enamev.
          response s2ratev. part s2catv.;
   label n='Number*Responding'
          est='*% With*Response'
          lower='95%*Confidence*Lower*Endpoint'
          upper=' *Interval*Upper*Endpoint'
          name='Employee Group'
          response='Response';
title3 'Section 2: Percent of Ratings in Each Category';
title4 'Provided By Service Groups';
run;

data out.&dsnout.s2p3 (label='estimates by category for section 2');
   set one;
run;
```

Analyzing Section 3 Questions

The final program produces the report for Section 3. Two types of questions were asked in Section 3: questions with categorical responses and questions with quantitative responses. The report is produced in two parts corresponding to the types of questions.

Reporting Demographics Based on Categorical Questions

Output 6 shows the first part of the report. It provides the number and percentage of respondents indicating each category of response for a question. In addition, the 95% confidence interval for the percentage is given.

The program `S3P1.SAS` requires that the categorical questions have variable names `&prefix&i` with `&i` ranging from `t1start` to `t1stop` and that the quantitative questions have sequential variable names `&prefix&i` with `&i` ranging from `t2start` to `t2stop`. The parameters `t1start`, `t1stop`, `t2start`, and `t2stop` must be given values in the `%LET` statements at the beginning of the program.

Output 6: Demographics from Categorical Questions

1991 Employee Opinion Survey
Area Technical College
Section 3: Demographics

---------------------------- Question=Employee Type ----------------------------

Response	Number Responding	% With Response	95% Confidence Lower Endpoint	Interval Upper Endpoint
Faculty	49	52.13%	(43.74%	60.52%)
Staff	40	42.55%	(34.25%	50.86%)
Not Reported	5	5.32%	(1.55%	9.09%)

------------------------------- Question=Status -------------------------------

Response	Number Responding	% With Response	95% Confidence Lower Endpoint	Interval Upper Endpoint
Full-time	64	68.09%	(60.26%	75.91%)
Part-time	21	22.34%	(15.35%	29.34%)
Not Reported	9	9.57%	(4.63%	14.52%)

--------------------------- Question=Assignment Area ---------------------------

Response	Number Responding	% With Response	95% Confidence Lower Endpoint	Interval Upper Endpoint
Academic Programs/Services	48	51.06%	(42.67%	59.46%)
Student Services	14	14.89%	(8.91%	20.87%)
Administration	14	14.89%	(8.91%	20.87%)
Not Reported	18	19.15%	(12.54%	25.76%)

------------------------------- Question=Campus -------------------------------

Response	Number Responding	% With Response	95% Confidence Lower Endpoint	Interval Upper Endpoint
Main	75	79.79%	(73.04%	86.53%)
South Center	1	1.06%	(0.00%	2.79%)
Other	4	4.26%	(0.87%	7.64%)
Not Reported	14	14.89%	(8.91%	20.87%)

The macro `FLIP` is used to produce the required estimates for each of the categorical questions. For each categorical question, `FLIP` does the following. First, `PROC FREQ` is used to output the number of respondents indicating each category of response for the specific question to the output data set `temp`. Second, the data step `countit` sums the counts for each cell of the frequency table to obtain the total number of respondents for the question. Third, the data step `temp2` uses the output data file `temp` and creates the variables name, `response`, n, `est`, `lower`, and `upper` that hold the values to be printed. At the end of the data step, `temp` contains one observation for each response category present in the data. Fourth, the data set `last` "collects" these values. When these four steps have been completed for each categorical question, `PROC PRINT` produces the final report.

To hold the estimates in a single data set and to print that data set, the variable `response` is created to identify the estimates. The value of `response` is based on the value of the variable `&prefix&i` and the current value of the `DO` loop, `&i`:

```
response=(&i*10) + &prefix&i;
```

For the Employee Opinion Survey, the values of `response` are two digit values: the first digit indicates the question number, `&i`, and the second digit indicates the code used for the response category. For example, question `S3Q1` had 3 response categories coded "1" for faculty, "3" for staff, and "5" for non-response. The values of `response` assigned by the program are "11" for faculty, "13" for staff, and "15 for non-response. With this coding scheme, the data can be stored and printed together using only one format value, `s3ev`, to print the value of `response`. Depending on a survey's keying scheme, the values assigned to `response` may need to be changed.

Reporting Demographics Based on Quantitative Questions

The second part of the report, shown in Output 7, is for the quantitative questions in Section 3. For each quantitative question, the report provides the number of respondents to the question, the average response, and the 95% confidence interval for the average response.

Output 7: Demographics from Quantitative Questions

```
                        1991 Employee Opinion Survey
                           Area Technical College
                          Section 3: Demographics

                                                    95%
                                                Confidence     Interval
                         Number                   Lower         Upper
      Question         Responding    Average     Endpoint      Endpoint


    Yrs at Campus          94          5.6        (4.7          6.5 )

    Yrs in System          94          7.4        (6.5          8.3 )
```

The portion of the program `S3P1.SAS` that generates this report is similar to the program `S2P2.SAS`. The reports generated by these two programs differ only in the titles and in the first column of information. Two SAS data sets are created at the end of this program. The first stores the estimates for the categorical variables, and the second stores the estimates for the quantitative variables.

```
************************ S3P1.SAS **********************************
   This program produces estimates for Section 3 of the
   Employee Opinion Survey.

   For categorical questions, the percentage of employees responding
   to each category and the 95% confidence intervals are estimated.

   For quantitative questions, the mean value and the
```

```
   95% confidence interval are estimated.

   Verify that the values in the %LET statements for T1START,
   T1STOP, T2START and T2STOP are correct for your survey.
****************************************************************;

%let prefix=s3q; %* variable name prefix for Section 3;
%let t1start=1; %* question number of first categorical value;
%let t1stop=4; %* question number of last categorical value;
%let t2start=5; %* question number of first quantitative value;
%let t2stop=6; %* question number of last quantitative value;

*** Part 1 to produce estimates for Section 3 categorical variables
*** starts here.;

%macro flip;
   %do i=&t1start %to &t1stop;
      proc freq data=out.&dsn1;
          tables &prefix&i / out=temp noprint;
      run;

      data countit (keep=ntotal);
         set temp end=eof;
         retain ntotal 0;
         ntotal=ntotal + count;
         if eof then do;
            put "for &prefix&i, " ntotal;
            output;
            end;
      run;

      data temp2 (keep=name response n est lower upper);
         length name $ 5.;
         set temp;
         if _n_=1 then do;
            set wts;
            set countit;
            end;
         name="&prefix" || "&i";
         response=(&i*10) + &prefix&i;
         n=count;
         est=percent;
         dif=2*wt*sqrt(percent*(100-percent)/(ntotal-1));
         lower=max(round((est-dif),.01),0);
         upper=min(round((est+dif),.01),100);
         est=round(est,.01);
         output;
      run;

      %if &i=1 %then %do;
         data last;set temp2;
         %end;
      %else %then %do;
         data last;set last temp2;
         %end;
         run;
```

```
      %end;
   %mend flip;

 data wts;
    wt=sqrt((&npop-&nsamp)/&npop);
    put wt=;
 run;

%flip

proc print data=last split='*' d uniform;
   var n est lower upper;id response;
   by name notsorted;
   format est estv. lower confl. upper confu. name $enamev.
          response s3ev.;
   label n='Number*Responding'
          est='*% With*Response'
          lower='95%*Confidence*Lower*Endpoint'
          upper=' *Interval*Upper*Endpoint'
          name='Question'
          response='Response'
;
title3 'Section 3: Demographics';
run;

*** Part 2 to produce estimates for Section 3 quantitative
*** variables starts here.;

proc means data=out.&dsn1   noprint;
   var &prefix&t2start-&prefix&t2stop;
   output out=temp n=n&t2start-n&t2stop mean=est&t2start-est&t2stop
      stderr=se&t2start-se&t2stop;
run;

data last2 (keep=name n est lower upper);
   length name $ 5.;
   array tn {&t2start:&t2stop} n&t2start-n&t2stop;
   array test {&t2start:&t2stop} est&t2start-est&t2stop;
   array tse {&t2start:&t2stop} se&t2start-se&t2stop;
   set temp;
   wt=sqrt((&npop-&nsamp)/&npop);
   do i=&t2start to &t2stop;
      name="&prefix" || left(i);
      n=tn{i};
      est=test{i};
      dif=2*wt*tse{i};
      lower=round((est-dif),.1);
      upper=round((est+dif),.1);
      est=round(est,.1);
      output;
      end;
run;

proc print data=last2 split='*' d uniform;
   var n est lower upper;id name;
   format est est2v. lower conf2l. upper conf2u. name $enamev.;
```

```
   label n='Number*Responding'
         est='Average'
         lower='95%*Confidence*Lower*Endpoint'
         upper=' *Interval*Upper*Endpoint'
         name='Question'
;
title3 'Section 3: Demographics';
run;

data out.&dsnout.s3p1 (label='estimates for section 3-categorical');
   set last; run;

data out.&dsnout.s3p2 (label='estimates for section 3-
quantitative');
   set last2; run;
```

Making Estimates Based on Respondent Numbers

A common problem in surveys is item non-response. Not all the respondents answer all of the questions. Estimates are usually desired for the sub-population of respondents that answered a particular question. Therefore, the statistical formulas on which the SAS programs are based produce estimates based on the number of respondents answering a particular question. The formulas follow.

Formulas to Estimate the Mean and Variance for a Sub-population from a Simple Random Sample

Let

N = the population size
n = the sample size
m = the size of the sub-population in the sample, $m \leq n$.

i indicate the individual in the sub-population of interest, $i=1,\ldots,m$
Σ indicate summation over i

y indicate the value of a characteristic of interest
y_m indicate the estimate of the mean of the characteristic
V indicate the estimate of the variance

$$y_m = \Sigma y_i / m$$

$$V(y_m) = (N\text{-}n)/N * \Sigma (y_i - y_m)^2 / [m * (m\text{-}1)]$$

Note 1: y_m is the value of `MEAN` produced by `PROC MEANS`. The square root of $\Sigma (y_i - y_m)^2 / [m * (m\text{-}1)]$ is the value of `STDERR` produced by `PROC MEANS`.

Note 2: A proportion (p) is the mean of a variable that takes on only the values of 0 and 1. The formula for y_m is also the formula for estimating a proportion.

Note 3: The formula for the estimate of the variance of a proportion can be derived from the formula for $V(y_m)$. It can also be written as follows:

$$V(p) = (N-n)/N * [p*(1-p) / (m-1)]$$

Here, the square root of [p*(1-p) / (m-1)] is the value of `STDERR` produced by `PROC MEANS`.

Conclusion

The nine SAS programs presented in this chapter provide a flexible system of programs for analyzing the results of many common surveys. Although `FORMAT.SAS`, `FIRST.SAS`, `EDIT.SAS`, and `DATA.SAS` require customization to reflect a specific survey, following the guidelines for keying schemes and variable name assignment will minimize this work. The final report programs are customized by the computer using the parameters in the `%LET` statements in `FIRST.SAS` and in the report programs themselves.

CHAPTER 16

Online Report Generation Using SAS Display Manager

by Michael L. Sternberg

Abstract

The Display Manager component of base SAS software, when used in conjunction with SAS macros, can be a very powerful tool for developing online reporting systems. To illustrate these capabilities, this chapter presents the steps used in building a marketing report system. More specifically, the overall design, key SAS programs, and use of SAS macros is discussed. The chapter concludes with the presentation of a generic framework which can be used when building any online reporting application.

Specifications

The code in this chapter was developed and tested with Release 6.08 of the SAS System under the Windows environment. Use of the code with other releases of the SAS System or environments may require user modification. Modified code is not supported by the author.

About the Author

Michael Sternberg is a Systems Technology Planner with AAA Michigan. He has BSA and MBA degrees in Information Systems from the University of Michigan. As an independent SAS consultant, Michael provides SAS programming, training, and application development for a variety of clients. A SAS software user for nine years, his areas of expertise include base SAS, SAS/AF, and SAS/FSP software and SAS macros.

Questions and Comments Should be Directed to:

Michael Sternberg
2736 Pembroke
Birmingham, MI 48009
Telephone: 313-436-7335

Online Report Generation Using SAS® Display Manager

Michael L. Sternberg

Introduction

SAS Institute provides two excellent (but additional cost) products (SAS/AF and SAS/FSP software) which can be used to support the development of online reporting systems. However, it is also possible to create extremely sophisticated online reporting applications using the Display Manager component of base SAS. This chapter will discuss the creation of such applications by presenting the steps used in building a custom market research application. This in turn will provide a general framework which can be used for any online reporting system to be created with SAS Display Manager.

In designing a Display Manager-based reporting system there are two important components to consider, the main menu and the reports. To allow for an in-depth analysis of the design process, this chapter will concentrate on the main menu and a single, Customer Frequency report. However, once the basic concepts are understood, you could add any number of additional reports using the same overall approach.

Architecture

In today's changing business environment, it is important to build applications which can be easily modified in support of changing business requirements. For this reason, any online reporting system should use a modular design. To illustrate the concept, consider the marketing application mentioned above. Basically, this application is composed of two types of high-level modules:

Main Menu	-	This module is used to call and execute each report.
Report	-	The report modules prompt the user for input and build the final reports.

Each report module is composed of two sub-modules:

Screen	-	This module prompts the user for input and records user selections.
Process	-	The process module uses the information entered in the screen module to produce a final report.

Figure 1 - Reporting System Architecture

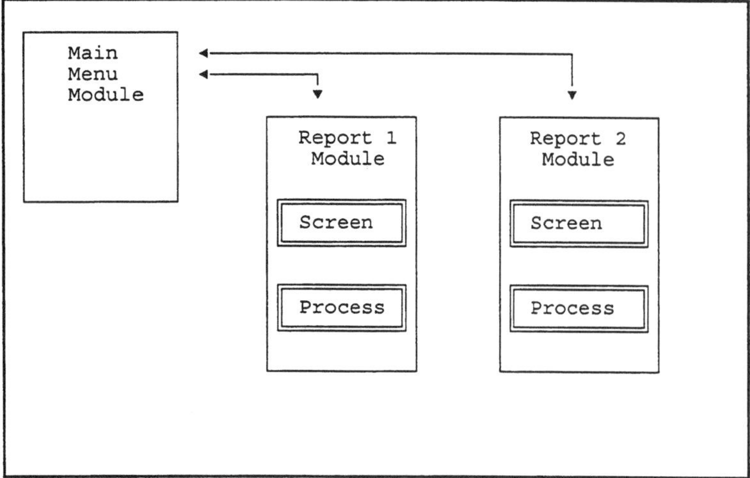

Figure 1 presents a graphical view of the reporting system architecture. The arrows indicate that control passes from the main menu to a report and then from the report back to the main menu. Notice how the design lends itself to extension; to add a new report, one would simply create a new report module and provide the links to and from the main menu.

In terms of programs, the main menu module is made up of one SAS program, while each report module is made up of two SAS programs: one for screens and another for processing. Execution begins with the main menu program, which displays a list of possible choices for the marketing application. The choices are provided on the top of the user's screen via an action bar. To select a particular option, the user moves the cursor to the appropriate entry and presses enter.

When the user selects a particular report option, the main menu program causes the screen program for that particular report to be executed. This program asks the user various questions and stores user responses in macro variables. Once all questions have been answered, the screen program calls a processing program which reads in the macro variables and uses this information to generate the final output. After reporting is complete, the processing program calls the main menu program and places the user back at the original starting point.

Customer Frequency Report

As stated earlier, the specific report to be discussed is the Customer Frequency report. This report provides a demographic analysis for a specific group of customers. The demographic aspect consists of a series of variables such as age, income, sex, number of children, number of adults in household, etc. Users can select from a great variety of these variables. Each variable selected will be used to generate a table for inclusion in the final report. Figure 2 illustrates the format of a single table. Please note that a complete report would include many of these tables.

Figure 2 - Sample Customer Frequency Table

INSURANCE CUSTOMERS

CHARACTERISTIC	# OF CUSTOMERS	PERCENT
CUSTOMER AGE:		
00 - 18	4,000	5
19 - 24	8,000	10
25 - 30	14,400	18
...	...	...
...	...	...
...	...	...

All the tables in a report are generated for a particular customer group. In this case, the customer group is households with an insurance product. The first column in the table divides a variable of interest, age, into discrete ranges. The second column presents the number of insurance customers within that particular age range. The final column indicates the percentage of total customers that fit into a particular age category.

Main Menu

The initial program for the marketing application displays a main menu from which numerous marketing related options can be selected. The main menu screen has the following format:

Screen 1 - Main Menu Screen

```
FREQ  SEGMENT  PROFILE  LIFT  END  BYE

          WELCOME TO THE

              X CORP

         MARKETING SYSTEM

  SELECT ONE OF THE ABOVE AND PRESS ENTER
```

The marketing application was developed for an IBM mainframe environment, so all the system screens are character based. Even so, the system can take full advantage of the SAS PMENU feature. This feature provides the capability to place action bars at the top of screens. For example, the main menu screen uses an action bar to control access to each of the functions available in the marketing application. To access a particular function, the user moves the cursor to one of the action bar selections and presses enter.

The action bar selections perform the following functions:

FREQ	- Accesses the Frequency report screens
SEGMENT	- Accesses the Segment report screens
PROFILE	- Accesses the Profile report screens
LIFT	- Accesses the Lift report screens
END	- Exits to SAS Display Manager
BYE	- Completely exits SAS

The main menu is created by a simple stand-alone SAS program. The program consists of a single DATA step which contains a WINDOW statement, a DISPLAY statement, and a DO loop. The DATA step code (assuming an IBM Mainframe environment) used to create the main menu is presented in Example 1:

Example 1 - SAS code to create the main menu

```
DM  'PMENU';
LIBNAME MLIB 'XXX.SASLIB';
FILENAME MCODE 'XXX.CODELIB';

DATA _NULL_;

WINDOW MAIN MENU=MLIB.MASTER.OPTS
    #1  @14 '                                          ' A=HIGHLIGHT
    #2  @14 '                                          ' A=HIGHLIGHT
```

```
     #3  @14 '        WELCOME  TO  THE          ' A=HIGHLIGHT
     #4  @14 '                                  ' A=HIGHLIGHT
     #5  @14 '            X CORP                ' A=HIGHLIGHT
     #6  @14 '                                  ' A=HIGHLIGHT
     #7  @14 '      MARKETING APPLICATION       ' A=HIGHLIGHT
     #8  @14 '                                  ' A=HIGHLIGHT
     #15 @14 'SELECT ONE OF THE ABOVE AND PRESS ENTER'
              A=HIGHLIGHT;

  DO WHILE(UPCASE(_CMD_) NE 'MIKE');
  DISPLAY MAIN;
  END;

  STOP;
  RUN;
```

The important statements used in the menu program are discussed below:

DM 'PMENU'
This statement turns on the PMENU feature of SAS Display Manager so that action bars can be used in the main menu window and throughout all other screens in the marketing application.

LIBNAME MLIB 'xxx.SASLIB'
This statement provides the name of the SAS library containing the action bar entry used on the main menu. An explanation of this library will be presented in "Action Bar Creation", which follows.

FILENAME MCODE 'xxx.CODELIB'
Many of the action bar selections cause other SAS programs to be executed. This statement identifies the storage location for the files that contain these SAS programs.

DATA _NULL_
Because the only purpose of this DATA step is to display a main menu window, the step does not need to create a SAS data set. For this reason, a DATA _NULL_ statement is used. The _NULL_ saves computational resources when a DATA step does not need to create a SAS data set.

WINDOW MAIN MENU=MLIB.MASTER.OPTS
The WINDOW statement defines a full-screen window containing the main menu for the marketing application. Notice that the WINDOW statement contains a MENU= option. This option links the window to a SAS library entry containing the action bar shown in Screen 1. The action bar is not defined with the WINDOW statement. Instead, it is created in a separate program which calls PROC PMENU. The three-level qualifier used with the MENU= option identifies the action bar to be displayed with the window. The qualifier consists of a libref (MLIB), a catalog (MASTER) and a PMENU entry name (OPTS).

DO WHILE(UPCASE(_CMD_) NE 'MIKE')
This DO loop is used to assure the main menu screen will display until the user selects an option from the action bar. The WHILE condition has been purposely designed so that it can never be satisfied. The action bar selection, however, overrides the WHILE condition and causes processing to continue.

DISPLAY MAIN
This statement is used to display the main menu window. It is placed in a DO loop so that the main menu will continue to display until the user selects an option from the action bar. When using this technique it is important to provide at least one option to cancel processing if users do not want to continue. For example, on Screen 1, the END or BYE action bar options can always be selected to

exit from the main menu window.

STOP

This statement is used to end the DATA step. STOP is normally required when a DATA step does not process any observations because SAS cannot detect an end-of-file condition and complete the DATA step. The use of action bar options to handle this processing negates the need for the STOP statement, but it is still good practice to include it. This will avoid confusing problems if at some future point the action bar feature is not being utilized.

Action Bar Creation

All the action bars for the marketing application were created using one SAS program which calls PROC PMENU. This section will display and discuss the specific statements that were used. PROC PMENU also has many other options and parameters. For a detailed description of these, please refer to the PMENU chapter in the *SAS Procedures Guide, Version 6, Third Edition.*

Example 2 - SAS code for the action bar program

```
/* CREATE MENU ENTRIES FOR MARKETING SYSTEM*/

LIBNAME MLIB 'XXX.SASLIB';        /*ACTION BAR SAS LIBRARY */
FILENAME MCODE 'XXX.CODELIB';     /*SOURCE CODE LOCATION */

PROC PMENU CAT=MLIB.MASTER;

/* DEFINE MAIN ACTION BAR FOR MAIN MENU SCREEN */

MENU OPTS;
   ITEM 'FREQ'     SELECTION=OPT1;
   ITEM 'SEGMENT'  SELECTION=OPT2;
   ITEM 'PROFILE'  SELECTION=OPT3;
   ITEM 'LIFT'     SELECTION=OPT4;
   ITEM 'END';
   ITEM 'BYE';

   /* CALL PGM TO DISPLAY FREQUENCY REPORT SCREENS */
   SELECTION OPT1 'END;INCLUDE MCODE(FRQSCRN);SUBMIT';

   /* CALL PGM TO DISPLAY SEGMENT REPORT SCREENS */
   SELECTION OPT2 'END;INCLUDE MCODE(SEGSCRN);SUBMIT';

   /* CALL PGM TO DISPLAY PROFILE REPORT SCREENS  */
   SELECTION OPT3 'END;INCLUDE MCODE(PROSCRN);SUBMIT';

   /* CALL PGM TO DISPLAY THE LIFT REPORT SCREEN    */
   SELECTION OPT4 'END;INCLUDE MCODE(LIFTSCRN);SUBMIT';
RUN;

/* SET UP AN ACTION BAR FOR LAST FREQUENCY SCREEN */

MENU FL;
   ITEM 'MAIN'     SELECTION=FL1;
   ITEM 'CONTINUE' SELECTION=FL2;
```

```
    /* RETURN TO MAIN MENU */
    SELECTION FL1 'END;INCLUDE MCODE(MAINSCRN);SUBMIT';

    /* CALL FREQUENCY PROCESSING PROGRAM */
    SELECTION FL2 'END;INCLUDE MCODE(FREQPROC);SUBMIT';
RUN;

/* SET UP ANOTHER ACTION BAR FOR OTHER FREQUENCY SCREENS */

MENU FF;
    ITEM 'MAIN'   SELECTION=FF1;

    /* RETURN TO MAIN MENU */
    SELECTION FF1 'END;INCLUDE MCODE(MAINSCRN);SUBMIT';

RUN;
QUIT;
```

The important statements used in the action bar program are discussed below:

LIBNAME MLIB 'xxx.SASLIB'

This statement defines the output SAS data library which will contain the action bars produced when the PROC PMENU program is executed. Within the PMENU program, the libref (MLIB) is used when referring to the action bar library.

FILENAME MCODE 'xxx.CODELIB'

Many of the action bar selections cause other SAS programs to be executed. This statement identifies the storage location which contains these programs. The fileref (MCODE) will be used throughout the marketing application to access various SAS programs.

PROC PMENU CAT=MLIB.MASTER

This SAS procedure is used to create action bars. The action bars are stored as a catalog entry using the name identified in the CAT= option of the PROC PMENU statement (MASTER). Also, notice how the libref (MLIB) in the CAT= option points to the library defined in the previous LIBREF statement.

MENU ...

This statement marks the beginning of an action bar definition and provides a name for that action bar. To illustrate, the name on the first MENU statement is OPTS. This name is also the third-level qualifier used in the MENU= option on the WINDOW statement (see the WINDOW statement in Example 1).

ITEM ...

The ITEM statement defines what is displayed on the action bar. There is an ITEM statement for each possible entry on the action bar. In the case of the main menu, these items are: FREQ, SEGMENT, PROFILE, LIFT, END, and BYE. The SELECTION= option on the ITEM statements is used to link these particular items with some action that is defined on the SELECTION statements which follow. The ITEM statements without SELECTION= options contain actual Display Manager commands which SAS will execute if this item is chosen. For example, if the user selects BYE, the SAS BYE command is executed and the SAS session is ended.

SELECTION ...

This statement is used in conjunction with the ITEM statement to define a command or series of commands that are submitted when the user selects a particular action bar item. The SELECTION= option on the ITEM statement is the link between the SELECTION and ITEM statements. To illustrate, the ITEM statement for the FREQ action bar option has SELECTION=OPT1. There is also a SELECTION statement that begins with SELECTION OPT1. This statement causes SAS to end the current main menu window, include the code for the Frequency report screen program and submit this code for execution. SELECTION statements can also be used for other tasks such as defining pull-down menus. Please see the *SAS Procedures Guide* for all the possible options.

RUN

A single execution of PROC PMENU can define many different action bars. However, all the statements for a particular action bar must be in the same run group. For this reason, each action bar definition ends with a RUN statement.

QUIT

The QUIT statement is used to end the execution of PROC PMENU. It should be the last statement in the action bar definition program.

Looking closely at Example 2 it is possible to see three groups of MENU - RUN statements. This means that three action bars are being defined. The first action bar, OPTS, provides the user with command and report options on the main menu. The second action bar, FL, is used on the last window of the Frequency screen program and provides the user with two choices, MAIN and CONTINUE. MAIN returns the user to the main menu, and CONTINUE starts execution of the Frequency report processing program. The final action bar, FF, simply provides the MAIN option for all other Frequency report screens.

The action bar program must be run one time, prior to any executions of the marketing application. This will create a catalog of action bars stored in a SAS data library. To access the action bars in a SAS program, a WINDOW statement with a MENU= option is utilized. For example, the MENU= option for main menu window is: MENU=MLIB.MASTER.OPTS. MLIB is the fileref for the SAS data library, MASTER is the PMENU catalog and OPTS is the particular action bar entry.

Screen Program

When a user selects FREQ from the main menu action bar, SAS includes the program FRQSCRN from the location with libref MCODE and begins executing it. This program sequentially displays a series of windows which ask the user questions about how to create the final Frequency report. The actual screen program is quite large and it would not be possible to show every screen. However, some of the more important screens are shown below:

```
MAIN

  PLEASE ENTER AN OVERALL TITLE
  FOR THIS FREQUENCY RUN:
```

Screen 2 - Title Entry Window. On this window the user enters a title which will be displayed on the final report.

```
MAIN

  DEFINE THE CUSTOMER GROUP
  (CHOOSE 1 OR 2)

     1. REGION

     2. SAS CODE              1
```

Screen 3 - Customer Definition Window. This window provides two options for how the Frequency report customer group will be identified.

MAIN

SELECT REGION
(CHOOSE 1, 2, 3 OR 4)

1. NORTH
2. SOUTH
3. EAST
4. WEST _

Screen 4 - Region Selection Window. If the user selects REGION in screen 3 then screen 4 is displayed. Here, the user must select a report region.

MAIN

ENTER CONDITION PORTION OF:

IF <CONDITION> ;

PRESS ENTER WHEN COMPLETE

Screen 5 - Code Entry Window. When the user selects SAS code in screen 3, screen 5 is displayed. Here, the user enters actual SAS code.

MAIN

PLEASE SELECT A CATEGORY OF VARIABLES:

1. HOUSEHOLD
2. AUTOMOTIVE
3. SPECIAL _

Screen 6 - Variable Selection Window. This window allows the user to select a category of variables for the final report.

MAIN CONTINUE

PREPARATION FOR THE FREQUENCY RUN IS NOW COMPLETE

OUTPUT WILL BE PLACED IN
UID.FREQOUT

PLEASE SELECT ONE OF THE ABOVE AND PRESS ENTER

Screen 7 - Summary Window. This window provides a name for the report file and asks the user to select MAIN or CONTINUE.

The screen program consists of a single DATA step which defines and displays the windows presented above. When a user enters selections, the program validates what has been input and stores the appropriate information as macro variables. Some representative code from the screen program is shown in Example 3:

Example 3 - Frequency Report Screen Program

```
/****  DISPLAY SCREENS FOR THE FREQUENCY REPORT *****/
DATA _NULL_;

WINDOW TLE MENU=MLIB.MASTER.FF
    #4 @4 'PLEASE ENTER AN OVERALL TITLE FOR THIS FREQUENCY
              RUN:'
    #6 @4  TOP $70. REQUIRED=YES;

DISPLAY TLE;

WINDOW DEFN MENU=MLIB.MASTER.FF
    #4  @4  'DEFINE THE CUSTOMER GROUP'
    #6  @4  '(CHOOSE 1 OR 2)'
    #11 @4  '1. REGION'
    #13 @4  '2. SAS CODE'
    #13 @41 DEF     $1.;

DEF='1';
DISPLAY DEFN;

DO WHILE(DEF NE '1' AND DEF NE '2');
  _MSG_ ='??? WARNING YOU MUST ENTER A 1 OR 2';
  DISPLAY DEFN BELL;
END;

WINDOW REGION MENU=MLIB.MASTER.FF
    #4  @4  'SELECT REGION'
    #6  @4  '(CHOOSE 1, 2, 3 OR 4)'
    #11 @4  '1. NORTH'
    #13 @4  '2. SOUTH'
    #15 @4  '3. EAST'
    #17 @4  '4. WEST'
    #17 @41 REG     $1.;

WINDOW CODE MENU=MLIB.MASTER.FF
    #6  @4  'ENTER CONDITION PORTION OF:'
    #8  @4  'IF <CONDITION>;'
    #10 @4  SCODE1 $70. REQUIRED=YES AUTO=YES
    #11 @4  SCODE2 $70. AUTO=YES
    #15 @4  'PRESS ENTER WHEN COMPLETE';

IF DEF='1' THEN
    DO;
      DISPLAY REGION;
      DO WHILE(REG NE '1' AND REG NE '2' AND REG NE '3' AND
              REG NE '4');
          _MSG_ ='??? WARNING YOU MUST ENTER A 1, 2, 3 OR 4';
```

```
          DISPLAY REGION BELL;
        END;
      END;
ELSE IF DEF='2' THEN DISPLAY CODE;

WINDOW VARSEL MENU=MLIB.MASTER.FF
    #5  @10 'PLEASE SELECT A CATEGORY OF VARIABLES'
    #6  @10 '(CHOOSE 1, 2 OR 3)'
    #9  @10 '1. HOUSEHOLD'
    #10 @10 '2. AUTOMOTIVE'
    #11 @10 '3. SPECIAL'
    #11 @55 VARS $1.;

DISPLAY VARSEL;

DO WHILE(VARS NE '1' AND VARS NE '2' AND VARS NE '3');
     _MSG_ ='??? WARNING YOU MUST ENTER A 1, 2 OR 3';
    DISPLAY VARSEL BELL;
END;

CALL SYMPUT('TOP',TOP);
CALL SYMPUT('DEF',DEF);

/* STORE SAS CODE OR REGION CODE FOR PROCESSING PROGRAM */
IF DEF='2' THEN
    CALL SYMPUT('CUSCODE',SCODE1 || SCODE2);
ELSE IF DEF='1' THEN
     CALL SYMPUT('CUSCODE',REG);

/* STORE VARIABLES TO BE PROCESSED */
IF VARS = '1' THEN
     CALL SYMPUT('OVERMAC', 'BUS HOME RES ADX KIDS');
ELSE IF VARS='2' THEN
     CALL SYMPUT('OVERMAC', 'GMCAR FORDCAR TOYCAR HONCAR
          CHRYCAR');
ELSE IF VARS='3' THEN
     CALL SYMPUT('OVERMAC', 'SP1 SP2 SP3 SP4 SP5');

JOB="&SYSJOBID";
FORMAT UID $4.;
UID=SUBSTR(JOB,1,4);
FNAME=UID||'.FREQOUT';

WINDOW FIN MENU=MLIB.MASTER.FL
    #3 @5 'PREPARATION FOR FREQUENCY RUN IS NOW COMPLETE'
    #5 @5 'OUTPUT WILL BE PLACED IN'
    #5 @48 FNAME $13.
    #9 @5 'PLEASE SELECT ONE OF THE ABOVE AND PRESS ENTER';

DO WHILE(UPCASE(_CMD_) NE 'MIKE');
   DISPLAY FIN;
END;
STOP;
RUN;
```

The important statements used in the screen program are discussed below:

DATA _NULL_

The screen program is composed of a single DATA step. Because the only purpose of this DATA step is to display various screens, the DATA step does not need to create a SAS data set. For this reason, a DATA _NULL_ statement is used. The _NULL_ saves computational resources when an output data set is not required.

WINDOW TLE MENU=MLIB.MASTER.FF

This statement defines the Title Entry (TLE) window. The WINDOW statement has a MENU= option which links to the FF action bar. This action bar will display the option MAIN at the top of the user's screen. If the user selects this option, the Frequency run will be canceled, and the user will be returned to the main menu program. The FF action bar was defined previously in the action bar program presented in Example 2.

The next few lines in the WINDOW statement define the specific contents of the window. For example, the statement after WINDOW defines the constant text, "PLEASE ENTER ...", which will be displayed on line 4 starting in column 4. The next line defines the variable TOP (starting at line 6, column 4), which will be used to hold the title that the user types in. The REQUIRED= option on the TOP variable means that something must be entered or SAS will return an error message and force the user to enter a title.

DISPLAY TLE

This statement causes the TLE window to be displayed for the user. The user would then enter a title and press enter.

WINDOW DEFN MENU=MLIB.MASTER.FF

This statement defines the Customer Definition window (DEFN). The variable DEF is included in the definition. This variable will hold the user's selection. Once again the window has a MENU= option to link to a previously defined action bar. Notice that this window references the same action bar (FF) as the previous window. This is perfectly legal in SAS and simply means that the action bar for this window will be the same as that of the previous window. If a user selects the action bar option (MAIN) they will be returned to the main menu, just as in the previous Title Entry window.

DEF='1'

This statement provides an initial value for the variable DEF. Notice how the variable is assigned a value prior to the DISPLAY statement for the DEFN window. This is done so that the DEFN window will be displayed with a default value for DEF (see Screen 3 earlier). The user can then press enter to accept the default value or input a new value to override it.

DISPLAY DEFN

This statement causes the Customer Definition window (DEFN) to be displayed for the user.

DO WHILE(DEF NE '1' AND DEF NE '2')

The DO loop is used to validate the user's entry for the DEF variable. If an entry is invalid (DEF is not equal to 1 or 2), then the _MSG_ variable is set to an appropriate error message and the DEFN window is redisplayed. _MSG_ is a special SAS defined variable which is automatically displayed when a window is displayed. The BELL option makes a sound so the user will realize an invalid entry has been made. Once the user enters the proper selection, the DO loop is exited.

WINDOW REGION MENU=MLIB.MASTER.FF
WINDOW CODE MENU=MLIB.MASTER.FF

These statements define screens for accepting a region or SAS code from the user. Only one of the windows will be displayed depending on the user's choice in the previous DEFN window. Once again, both windows utilize the FF action bar.

IF DEF='1' THEN DO
DISPLAY REGION
...
...
END
ELSE IF DEF='2' THEN DISPLAY CODE

This statement will display either the REGION or the CODE window based on the value assigned to the variable DEF. DEF was defined in the DEFN window by a user entry or acceptance of the default value, '1'. For the REGION window, additional SAS statements are included to validate the user's entry of a particular region. For the CODE window no special validations are performed.

WINDOW VARSEL MENU=MLIB.MASTER.FF
DISPLAY VARSEL
DO WHILE (VARS NE '1' AND VARS NE '2' AND VARS NE '3') ...

In this block of SAS code, the WINDOW statement defines the VARSEL window, which again uses the FF action bar. This window asks the user for the group of variables that should be included in the Frequency report. The user can select only one group of variables per run. The other statements are used to display the window and validate user input.

CALL SYMPUT('TOP',TOP)
CALL SYMPUT('DEF',DEF)

These CALL SYMPUT routines are used to create macro variables which contain the values of the DATA step variables TOP and DEF. The use of macro variables allows the marketing application to pass values between the screen and processing programs. This concept is of vital importance to Display Manager-based reporting systems and will be discussed in detail in the sections that follow. Note: for those that are curious, it is perfectly legal in SAS to have macro variables with the same names as SAS variables.

IF DEF='2' THEN CALL SYMPUT('CUSCODE', SCODE1 || SCODE2)
ELSE IF DEF ='1' THEN CALL SYMPUT('CUSCODE', REG)

This IF statement causes either region codes or SAS code to be stored in the macro variable CUSCODE, depending on the user's previous selection in the Customer Definition window (see Screen 3 earlier). Thus, if the user selected region in Screen 3, CUSCODE will be assigned the region code entered by the user; if SAS code was selected, CUSCODE will be assigned the SAS code entered by the user.

IF VARS = '1' THEN ...

This next section of code consists of a series of nested IF statements and SYMPUT calls. The code is used to store all the variable names that correspond to a particular category in a single macro variable called OVERMAC. Thus, if the user selected household as the variable category then the names of all household variables will be placed in OVERMAC.

JOB="&SYSJOBID"
FORMAT UID $4.
UID=SUBSTR(JOB,1,4)
FNAME=UID || '.FREQOUT'

This series of statements extracts a user-id from an IBM mainframe system, appends it to the name FREQOUT and stores the result in a variable called FNAME. The value stored in FNAME will be used as the file name into which the final Frequency report will be written. Note: the exact format of the user-id will be specific to each site. In this case, a four character id is assumed.

WINDOW FIN MENU=MLIB.MASTER.FL
DO WHILE (UPCASE(_CMD_) NE 'MIKE')

These statements are used to define and display the Summary window (FIN). This window informs the user that the final report will be placed in data set uid.FREQOUT, where uid is a user-id. Recall that the name of the data set was created using the four statements discussed in the previous block of

SAS code. The DO loop is used to display the FIN window and to force the user to make a selection from the action bar. Any other option, such as pressing enter, will not satisfy the WHILE condition and will cause the window to be redisplayed. Notice that this window uses the FL action bar. A review of the previous action bar program will reveal that the choices on this action bar are MAIN and CONTINUE. As before, MAIN returns the user to the main menu. CONTINUE, however, is a new entry which causes the code for the processing program to begin executing.

Processing Program

The processing program reads in the macro variables created in the screen program and uses this information to build the Frequency report and place it in an output file. Once processing is complete, the user is returned to the main menu screen where he or she can execute another report or exit the marketing application. A sample of code from this program is presented in Example 4.

The processing program makes extensive use of SAS macros. The code for these macros would normally be found at the beginning of the processing program. However, to simplify the discussion, all macro code has been removed and will be discussed in a separate section.

Example 4 - Frequency Report Processing Program

```
*******************************************************************;
**   Author's Note: All macro routines would
**   normally be defined in this area.
*******************************************************************;

  DATA PREP;
  SET IN.CUSTFILE;

  KEEP &OVERMAC;

  ***********************************;
  * CALL MACRO TO SELECT CUSTOMERS*;
  ***********************************;
  %DEFCUST;

  PROC FREQ;
  *******************************;
  * CALL MACRO TO GEN FREQS*;
  *******************************;
  %FREQTAB

  PROC DATASETS;
  DELETE PREP;

  DATA DONE;
  SET &OVERMAC;
  LENGTH VARNAM $8.;
  IF _N_ < 0 THEN;    /* DUMMY IF SO MACRO CAN CODE ELSE IFS */

  ************************************;
  * CALL MACRO TO GEN VARVAL, VARNAM*;
  ************************************;
  %DATCOMB
```

```
DATA _NULL_;
SET DONE;
BY VARNAM NOTSORTED;

FILE FOUT NOTITLE HEADER=H;

IF _N_ < 0 THEN;   /* DUMMY IF SO MACRO CAN CODE ELSE IFS */

%POUT(HEAD1=NUMBER OF ADULTS
   PRESENT:,FORM=$PRES.,VAR=APRES)

%POUT(HEAD1=OCCUPATION OF,HEAD2=PRINCIPAL:,FORM=$OCCUP.,
   VAR=OCCUP)

%POUT(HEAD1=AGE OF PRINCIPAL:,FORM=$AGEX.,VAR=AGE)

%POUT(HEAD1=HOME VALUE:,FORM=$HOME.,VAR=HOME)


*************************************************************;
**  Author's Note: Nonessential code has been deleted
**  from this DATA step to conserve space.
*************************************************************;

RETURN;

H:  PUT _PAGE_ @5 "&TOP" //;
    PUT @47 '# OF';
    PUT @5 'CHARACTERISTIC' @47 'HOUSEHOLDS'
       @69 'PERCENT' OVERPRINT @5
         '_________________________________'
       @47 '_____________'
       @69 '_________' /;

RETURN;
RUN;

*****************************************************;
*  REDISPLAY MAIN MENU*;
*;
*  NOTE: FILEREF MCODE WAS ORIGINALLY ALLOCATED IN THE*;
*  SCREEN PROGRAM AND IS STILL ACTIVE FOR USE IN THE*;
*  PROCESSING PROGRAM*;
****************************************************;

%INCLUDE MCODE(MAINSCRN);
```

At first glance the processing program may seem to be quite small. However, much of the processing program code is generated by SAS macros and as such is not readily visible. The macro code will be discussed in a later section, but for now a review of each processing step will be presented.

DATA PREP
SET IN.CUSTFILE

These statements mark the beginning of the initial DATA step in the processing program. This step reads in a marketing data set which is referenced by the name IN.CUSTFILE. Note: the definition for libref IN was done previously and is not shown in the code samples presented.

The DATA step also uses a KEEP statement so that the output data set (PREP) will only contain the specific variables necessary for generating the Frequency report. Within the KEEP statement is a reference to the macro variable OVERMAC. At execution time, OVERMAC will be converted to a list of all the variables to be reported on. Recall, that a list of these variables was placed in the macro variable OVERMAC by the screen program.

The DATA step also contains a reference to DEFCUST. This is a macro routine, used to generate SAS code which will execute during this step. More specifically, the DEFCUST macro routine is used to determine if the current observation being processed is part of the customer group of interest. A detailed explanation of this routine and all other macro routines can be found in the "Application Macros" section, found later in this chapter.

PROC FREQ

The next step in the program is a PROC FREQ. No code is shown within this step because it is all generated by the macro routine FREQTAB. The purpose of this step is to create a separate frequency data set for each variable of interest. The name of each output data set is the same as the variable name. To illustrate the basic format, consider the variable AGE and assume for AGE=1, 100 observations, for AGE=2, 200 observations, and for AGE=3, 700 observations. Given this data, the resulting frequency data set would be:

AGE	COUNT	PERCENT
1	100	10.0
2	200	20.0
3	700	70.0

The AGE variable was in the original data set while the COUNT and PERCENT variables were generated by the PROC FREQ.

PROC DATASETS
DELETE PREP

The PREP data set was used as the input to the PROC FREQ step. Once the PROC FREQ step concludes, the PREP data set is no longer necessary. Thus, PROC DATASETS is used to delete this data set and free up valuable workspace for other tasks.

DATA DONE
SET &OVERMAC

This DATA step combines the data sets output from the PROC FREQ and calls the macro routine DATCOMB. This routine creates two new variables: VARNAM and VARVAL. VARNAM contains the names of each report variable, while VARVAL contains the values for each report variable. Also, notice the SET statement which uses the macro variable OVERMAC. Recall, that OVERMAC contains the names of all variables of interest and that the previous PROC FREQ created data sets using those variable names. To illustrate the output generated, assume two data sets were created by the PROC FREQ step: AGE with values 1 and 2 and INCOME with values 1, 2 and 3. Both data sets also include COUNT and PERCENT variables as defined earlier. When this DATA step concludes, the DONE data set will have the format:

VARNAM	VARVAL	COUNT	PERCENT	AGE	INCOME
AGE	1	20	20.0	1	
AGE	2	80	80.0	2	
INCOME	1	10	10.0		1
INCOME	2	40	40.0		2
INCOME	3	50	50.0		3

Note 1: Values for COUNT and PERCENT are assumed.

Note 2: VARNAM must be set to a length of 8 in the program because it contains the names of SAS variables, which can be up to 8 characters in length.

DATA _NULL_
SET DONE

This is the final reporting phase of the program. In this step an output table is produced for each variable selected by the user in the screen program. The input is the data set from the previous step. The BY statement is used to allow for the use of FIRST.*variable* processing (see FIRST.*variable* in *SAS Language: Reference, Version 6, First Edition* for more information). The macro routine POUT is used to generate the SAS code for printing table detail lines. The macro is executed multiple times - once for each possible output table. Note: the definition of fileref FOUT, used on the FILE statement, was done previously and is not shown in the code samples presented.

%INCLUDE MCODE(MAINSCRN)

This step returns control to the main menu for the marketing application. MCODE is a fileref which identifies the SAS code to include. Recall that this fileref was defined in the initial main menu program (see Example 1). Since the reporting program was executed via an INCLUDE from the main menu program, the fileref MCODE is valid in the processing program as well.

Application Macros

As stated earlier, the marketing application makes extensive use of SAS macros. The macros are used to pass information between the screen and processing programs and to generate SAS code. To understand the macros used, it is important to have a basic understanding of macro concepts and terminology. Readers unfamiliar with SAS macros may want to refer to the following SAS manuals:

SAS Macro Facility Tips and Techniques, Version 6, First Edition
SAS Guide to Macro Processing, Version 6, Second Edition

The screen program in the marketing application primarily uses macro variables to store user input and pass it on to the processing program. The important macro variables in the screen program are:

DEF - This macro variable contains the user's selection for how to define the customer group (1 = region code, 2 = user-entered SAS code).

TOP - This macro variable contains the title which will be placed on the final report.

CUSCODE - This macro variable contains either the region or the SAS code which will be used to define the customer group of interest in the processing program. The screen program places the appropriate value in this macro variable based on the user's selection in the Customer Definition window.

OVERMAC - This macro variable contains the names of all variables for which final output tables are to be produced. Exactly which variable names are in this macro variable will depend on user selections in the variable selection window of the screen program.

The processing program uses the macro variables created in the screen program as well as numerous macro routines to write its own code. In fact, each time the marketing application executes, the processing program will rewrite itself, tailoring its code to meet each user's report requests. To understand how this is implemented, please review the processing program macro routines which follow.

DEFCUST Macro

The DEFCUST macro is used to build a subsetting IF statement which selects only those customers that meet the criteria specified by the user in the screen program. The macro code for this routine is shown below:

Example 5 - DEFCUST Macro Code

```
%MACRO DEFCUST;

    %IF "&DEF"="1" %THEN %DO;
         IF REGION = "&CUSCODE";
    %END;

    %ELSE %IF "&DEF"="2" %THEN %DO;
         IF &CUSCODE;
    %END;

%MEND DEFCUST;
```

Recall that in the screen program the user was given the option of defining a customer group by selecting a region or by providing SAS code. The screen program then used this information to create the macro variable DEF. Thus, when &DEF evaluates to a '1', the user has selected to use region codes for defining the customer group; when &DEF evaluates to '2', the user has selected to define the customer group by specifying SAS code.

The screen program also stored the specific region or SAS code provided to define the customer group. This information was stored in a second macro variable called CUSCODE. Thus, based on the value of DEF, CUSCODE has two potential values. First, it could represent a region code. Secondly, it could represent actual SAS code.

In the DEFCUST macro, the value of DEF is used in a %IF macro statement to determine which subsetting IF statement to build, one using a region code or one using SAS code. The actual information required to build the IF statement was stored in the macro variable CUSCODE by the screen program. Thus, DEFCUST will build different IF statements depending on user selections in the screen program. To illustrate the process, suppose the user selected to use SAS code in the screen program and the code entered was: INCOME='7'. In this situation DEF would evaluate to a "1" and &CUSCODE would evaluate to INCOME='7'. This in turn would cause the DEFCUST macro to generate:

```
IF INCOME='7';
```

Next, suppose the user selected to use a region code and that the region chosen was North, a value of "1" in the Region Selection window. In this case DEFCUST would generate:

```
IF REGION='1';
```

In either case the call to the DEFCUST macro would place a subsetting IF into the initial DATA step of the processing program. The added code would then be interpreted and executed as part of the DATA step.

As a final point, it is important to understand why CUSCODE is enclosed in double quotes for region code processing but not for user-defined SAS code processing. The answer is that the double quotes cause the region code to be enclosed in quotes during DATA step processing. Since all the variables on the original input file are defined as character, the use of double quotes means that SAS will not have to convert a numeric value to character data. This makes the program more efficient.

In the case of user-defined SAS code, the CUSCODE macro variable contains SAS code which will be placed in an IF statement. In this case, there is no need to be concerned with character to numeric conversions and there is no need for double quotes.

FREQTAB Macro

The FREQTAB macro builds a series of TABLES statements which are used in conjunction with a FREQ procedure. The code for this macro is as follows:

Example 6 - FREQTAB Macro Code

```
%MACRO FREQTAB;

  %DO J=1 %TO 20;                                /* LOOP FOR VARS*/
    %IF %SCAN(&OVERMAC,&J) =  %THEN %GOTO DONE;

        TABLES  %SCAN(&OVERMAC,&J) /
             SPARSE NOPRINT MISSING OUT= %SCAN(&OVERMAC,&J);
  %END;

%DONE: %MEND FREQTAB;
```

The above routine contains a macro %DO loop that will generate one TABLES statement for each variable of interest. Recall that the names of these variables were placed in the OVERMAC macro variable by the screen program. The %SCAN macro function extracts one variable name at a time from the OVERMAC macro variable, based on the value of J. If J = 1 then the first variable name is extracted. If J = 2 then the second variable name is extracted and so on. When J becomes larger than the total number of variable names in OVERMAC, the %SCAN function in the %IF statement returns a null string. This causes control to pass to the %MEND statement, which effectively ends the %DO loop and the FREQTAB macro as well.

To illustrate how this macro operates, assume OVERMAC contains "ADULT ROUTE". In this case the generated code would be:

```
TABLES ADULT / SPARSE NOPRINT MISSING OUT=ADULT;
TABLES ROUTE / SPARSE NOPRINT MISSING OUT=ROUTE;
```

These statements would then be inserted and executed as part of the PROC FREQ step of the processing program. Notice how a separate TABLES statement is created for each variable name in &OVERMAC. This is because SAS only allows one output file to be created on a single TABLES statement.

DATCOMB Macro

The DATCOMB macro creates two variables, VARNAM and VARVAL. VARNAM contains the name of each variable for which an output table is to be generated, while VARVAL contains the values associated with each output table variable. The code for the DATCOMB macro is as follows:

Example 7 - DATCOMB Macro Code

```
%MACRO DATCOMB;

  %DO J=1 %TO 20;                              /* LOOP FOR VARS*/
     %IF %SCAN(&OVERMAC,&J) =  %THEN %GOTO FINI;

     ELSE IF %SCAN(&OVERMAC,&J) NE ' ' THEN
        DO;
          VARVAL= %SCAN(&OVERMAC,&J);
          CALL VNAME(%SCAN(&OVERMAC,&J),VARNAM);
        END;

  %END;

%FINI: %MEND DATCOMB;
```

As can be seen in the code above, the DATCOMB macro consists of a single %DO loop which increments the macro variable J from 1 to 20. The value of J is used in a %SCAN function to extract a variable name from OVERMAC. Thus, on the initial iteration of the loop, the first variable name in OVERMAC is extracted and on the second, the second variable name. This continues until all variable names have been processed. At this point the %SCAN function returns a null string which is detected by the %IF macro statement. This in turn causes both the %DO loop and the DATCOMB macro to end.

For each variable name that is extracted, a block of SAS code is built. This code will be used to create the VARVAL and VARNAM data set variables. As stated earlier, VARVAL will be used to hold the values associated with each user-selected variable, while VARNAM will contain the names of these variables. The VNAME call routine is used to extract the name of a variable and place it in the VARNAM variable. To illustrate the overall process, assume that a user has just finished executing the screen program and that from this run the OVERMAC variable was defined as "ADULT ROUTE". In this case the DATCOMB macro would generate the following:

```
ELSE IF ADULT NE ' ' THEN
     DO;
        VARVAL=ADULT;
        CALL VNAME(ADULT,VARNAM);
     END;

ELSE IF ROUTE NE ' ' THEN
     DO;
        VARVAL=ROUTE;
        CALL VNAME(ROUTE,VARNAM);
     END;
```

The above code indicates that the DATCOMB macro only produces ELSE IF statements. This is possible because a dummy IF, which can never be true, is coded in the DATA step which calls the DATCOMB macro. By eliminating the need to code IF and ELSE IF cases, macro coding can be simplified.

Another point to keep in mind is that the macro only generates code that corresponds to the table variables selected by the user in the screen program. Thus, for each run, different code may be generated, depending on the screen variables selected.

POUT Macro

The POUT macro is used to build the detail lines for the final Frequency report. The code for this macro is as follows:

Example 8 - POUT Macro Code

```
%MACRO POUT (HEAD1=,
         HEAD2=,
         FORM=,
         VAR=);

  %IF %INDEX(&OVERMAC,&VAR) %THEN
    %DO;

       ELSE IF TRIM(VARNAM)="&VAR" THEN
         DO;
            IF FIRST.VARNAM THEN
               DO;
                    PUT / @5  "&HEAD1";

                 %IF %LENGTH(&HEAD2) > 0 %THEN %DO;
                    PUT   @5  "&HEAD2";
                 %END;

                    PUT / @5  VARVAL   &FORM
                         @42 COUNT    COMMA12.
                         @69 PERCENT 6.2;
               END;

            ELSE
               DO;
                   PUT  @5   VARVAL   &FORM
                       @42  COUNT    COMMA12.
                       @69  PERCENT 6.2;
               END;
         END;
    %END;

%MEND POUT;
```

This macro differs somewhat from the previous examples in that it makes use of macro variable parameters. These are keyword parameters which have a default value of null. However, when the macro is executed with the appropriate call, the macro parameters are given values which can be used within the macro. For the macro, the following parameters are used:

HEAD1 - Provides a title line for a report table.

HEAD2 - Provides an additional title line for a report table.

FORM - Provides a format for variable printing. These can be SAS or user-defined formats.

VAR - Provides the name of the variable for which detail line code is to be generated.

The POUT macro is executed one time for each variable in the original input SAS data set. However, since the user can only select a subset of the available variables, there is the potential to build code which will not ever be needed. To avoid this situation, the first line in the macro does a test to see if the variable name passed to the POUT macro, via the VAR parameter, is in the OVERMAC macro variable. Remember that OVERMAC contains the names of all variables that the user has selected for a particular run. The code to perform this test is:

```
%IF %INDEX(&OVERMAC,&VAR) %THEN
```

Notice that this simple test allows the POUT macro to generate only code that is absolutely necessary for a particular run. Thus, the actual SAS code generated by POUT can change with each run, based on user selections in the screen program.

To illustrate macro execution, assume the POUT macro is called with the following parameter values:

```
%POUT(HEAD1=NUMBER OF ADULTS PRESENT,FORM=$PRES.,
      VAR=ADULTS);
```

If in the screen program the user had not selected ADULTS as a variable to be reported on, then ADULTS would not be found in the OVERMAC macro variable, and the statement below would stop the macro from generating any code.

```
%IF %INDEX(&OVERMAC,&VAR) %THEN
```

However, if ADULTS was a variable selected by the user in the screen program, the POUT macro will resolve to the SAS code which follows. Note: macro parameter replacements are shown in bold.

```
ELSE IF TRIM(VARNAM)="ADULTS" THEN
      DO;
         IF FIRST.VARNAM THEN
            DO;
               PUT / @5  "NUMBER OF ADULTS PRESENT";
               PUT / @5  VARVAL $PRES.
                     @50 COUNT COMMA12.
                     @79 PERCENT 6.2;
            END;

         ELSE
            DO;
                PUT  @5   VARVAL $PRES.
                     @50  COUNT COMMA12.
                     @79  PERCENT 6.2;
            END;
      END;
```

When reviewing this code, take note of the information that was passed to the POUT macro using macro variable parameters and how the parameter values were inserted into the SAS code within the macro. Notice how a one line call to the POUT macro generated a large block of code and that for each call made to POUT this code is modified slightly.

Also, notice that the macro is generating blocks of ELSE IF code. Since SAS requires an IF before an ELSE, this implies there must be an IF coded. Using the same technique mentioned earlier, a dummy IF has been coded in the step which calls the POUT macro. In this way the macro only needs to generate ELSE IF statements.

Framework

At the beginning of this chapter it was stated that a review of the marketing application would provide a framework for building online, Display Manager-based reporting systems. A summary of this framework is as follows:

Main Menu

The first step in building an online Display Manager application is to provide an overall point of control that can be used to drive all the other programs in the application. This is handled by a main menu program which utilizes an action bar to control overall system flow. With this approach, the user simply moves the cursor to the appropriate action bar option and presses enter. Use of a separate menu program is vital because it provides a starting point for access to any of the subsystems (e.g. reports) that make up the application. Also, the main menu program is the place where all subsystems return upon completion of their particular tasks.

Action Bars

Each screen in the marketing application has an action bar to provide overall control options. To improve ease-of-use characteristics, action bar choices should be consistent throughout the application. Also, make sure the action bars provide an option for the user to cancel processing at any point. Using this technique will assure that users unfamiliar with the application do not accidentally make runs which waste substantial computer resources.

PMENU Program

The action bars in the marketing application were created with a separate program which executes PROC PMENU. Recall that a single execution of this PROC creates many different action bars, each of which can be used in one or more windows. The PMENU program should be developed along with the application screens. As each new screen is added to the application, new entries can be added to the PMENU program. Thus, the PMENU program will be created gradually as the application screens are defined.

Although this application only used action bars, PROC PMENU is very flexible and can be used to create many different effects for the windows in an application. Some of these include: pull-down menus, dialog boxes and radio buttons. For details on how to use these and other PMENU features consult the *SAS Procedures Guide* and review the information for PROC PMENU.

Screen Program

The marketing application utilizes a separate program which displays screens to the user, collects their responses to various questions and stores this information in macro variables. It would also be possible to build a combined screen and processing program. However, there are some very good reasons for building a separate screen program. First, a separate screen program makes it easy to stop the application before any substantial processing is done. In the Frequency Report system this was of high importance because the input data set was very large and the user community was not familiar with SAS. Also, use of a separate screen program makes it easier to prototype screen changes without impacting the processing aspects of the application. Next, separating screen and processing logic makes it easier to distribute work since one person can work on screens while another works on processing logic. Lastly, independent screen and processing programs facilitate modular design and provide components which can be re-used in other applications.

Processing Program

One more component of the marketing application is the processing program. It is heavily macro oriented and uses information, in the form of macro variables, from the screen program to build a final report. The program basically consists of a series of macro routines which generate different code depending on the options selected by the user in the screen program. The use of macros means that the processing program can be flexible enough to support a wide range of options while still providing efficient processing. Overall, the use of a macro-oriented processing program is an extremely powerful approach that allows the marketing application to write its own code based on user input.

Libraries

The marketing application makes use of two key libraries. The first is a SAS code library which contains the source code for all of the programs that make up the marketing application. The second is a SAS data library which is used to hold the action bars output by the PROC PMENU run. By using libraries in this manner, the marketing application is able to utilize %INCLUDE statements to execute the appropriate SAS programs when needed.

Conclusion

This chapter has shown that it is possible to build an extremely sophisticated online reporting application using only features available with base SAS. The major SAS features utilized were the WINDOW statement, PROC PMENU, macro variables, macro routines and SAS Display Manager. The overall approach was to create a main menu program and a series of screen and processing programs. Taken as a group these programs represent a generic framework which can be utilized for any online Display Manager application.

References

For further information on SAS programming and SAS macros, refer to the following SAS Institute publications:

SAS Guide to Macro Processing,Version 6, Second Edition

SAS Language: Reference, Version 6, First Edition

SAS Procedures Guide, Version 6, Third Edition

SAS Macro Facility Tips and Techniques, Version 6, First Edition

CHAPTER 17

Exceptions Reports for Zero Observations

by Robert Virgile

Abstract

Many reports print the exception rather than the rule. But what happens when there are no exceptions to print? The user gets no report and therefore suspects that the program failed. What happens next? The user calls you. A better solution is to provide a report on zero observations, keeping the user informed. This chapter examines the issues involved and programming techniques needed to generate a report on zero observations.

Specifications

The programming techniques in this chapter are applicable to all recent releases and operating systems with one exception. Release 6.06 does not support the CALL EXECUTE statement.

About the Author

Robert Virgile is President of Robert Virgile Associates, Inc. A SAS software user for 14 years, he has an SB degree in Economics from MIT. Robert's areas of expertise include base SAS, macro language, SAS/FSP, SAS/GRAPH, and SAS/AF software.

Questions and Comments Should be Directed to:

Robert Virgile
3 Rock Street
Woburn, MA 01801
Telephone: 617-938-0307

Exceptions Reports for Zero Observations

Robert Virgile

Introduction

Reporting programs occasionally attempt to print zero observations. For example, these titles share a common theme:

> Finished Products with Defects
> Credit Card Purchases under $5
> Listing of Bad Data Values

Each report prints a subset of all data, listing the exception rather than the rule. The programs generating these reports may chug along nicely for a while, generating daily reports on the exceptions. But what happens when nothing goes wrong, and there are no exceptions? The user gets no printout. The user cannot tell whether the program failed, or whether nothing was printed because there were no exceptions. What happens next? The user calls you. How can we avoid this unpleasant turn of events? Print a report on zero observations.

This chapter examines programming techniques that inform the user when no exceptions were found. It also explains a related technique for DATA step reporting: how to detect end-of-file when subsetting the incoming data. Most sample programs solve one problem but introduce another. Therefore this chapter describes a series of issues and related programming techniques.

Checking for Bad Data: A Sample Program

Let's take a simple example which tests the values of two variables:

1. GENDER should be MALE or FEMALE.

2. PHONE should be seven characters long, should contain digits only, and cannot begin with a 0 or a 1.

This program checks for bad data and prints the bad values:

```
DATA BADDATA1 (KEEP=ID PHONE)
     BADDATA2 (KEEP=ID GENDER);
SET UNCLEAN;
IF (COMPRESS(PHONE) NE PHONE)
OR (COMPRESS(PHONE,'0123456789') NE ' ')
OR (LENGTH(PHONE) NE 7))
OR NOT ('2' <= SUBSTR(PHONE,1,1) <= '9')
THEN OUTPUT BADDATA1;
IF GENDER NOT IN ('MALE', 'FEMALE')
THEN OUTPUT BADDATA2;
```

```
PROC PRINT DATA=BADDATA1;
VAR ID PHONE;
TITLE 'BAD DATA FOR PHONE';

PROC PRINT DATA=BADDATA2;
VAR ID GENDER;
TITLE 'BAD DATA FOR GENDER';
```

Two quick notes about the program:

1. Missing values are being output as bad data. The program could be modified to ignore missing values.

2. The very first condition being checked detects embedded blanks. None of the other conditions accomplish that.

If a PROC PRINT receives a data set with zero observations, nothing prints. A message appears in the log:

```
NOTE:  No observations to print.
```

However, the user doesn't see this. The user notices that the program must be faulty because some of the output is missing.

Adding a Report on Zero Observations

The right programming modifications will inform the user about zero exceptions. To emphasize the programming techniques, sample programs contain these simplifying features:

1. Reports will print only a couple of variables.

2. Programs will check just two variables (PHONE and GENDER) for accuracy.

3. Programs will check the PHONE variable for its length only.

The first DATA step can print messages about those variables having no bad data. For example:

```
DATA BADDATA1 (KEEP=ID PHONE)
     BADDATA2 (KEEP=ID GENDER);
SET UNCLEAN END=LAST;
IF LENGTH(PHONE) NE 7 THEN DO;
   N1 + 1;
   OUTPUT BADDATA1;
END;
IF GENDER NOT IN ('MALE', 'FEMALE') THEN DO;
   N2 + 1;
   OUTPUT BADDATA2;
END;
```

```
IF LAST THEN DO;
   FILE PRINT NOTITLES;
   IF N1=0 THEN PUT // 'NO BAD DATA FOR PHONE';
   IF N2=0 THEN PUT // 'NO BAD DATA FOR GENDER';
END;

PROC PRINT DATA=BADDATA1;
VAR ID PHONE;
TITLE 'BAD DATA FOR PHONE';

PROC PRINT DATA=BADDATA2;
VAR ID GENDER;
TITLE 'BAD DATA FOR GENDER';
```

The syntax N1+1 both assigns N1 an initial value of zero and retains N1 from one observation to the next. Now the first section of the report mentions the variables being checked that had no bad data. A subsequent PROC PRINT may or may not generate output, but at least every variable is accounted for. This solution works, but may run into a few difficulties:

1. With many variables to check, it may be impractical to create a separate output dataset for each.

2. Besides the low aesthetic value of running PROC PRINT on an empty dataset, it takes some of a programmer's time to verify that the note about no observations to print can be ignored.

3. The order of the reports may change depending on which variable(s) contain no bad data.

Creating a Single Output Dataset

The first drawback is the number of output datasets. A viable alternative approach would combine all errors into a single dataset:

```
DATA BADDATA (KEEP=ID VARIABLE VALUE REASON);
SET UNCLEAN;
LENGTH VARIABLE $ 8 VALUE REASON $ 20;
IF LENGTH(PHONE) NE 7 THEN DO;
   VARIABLE='PHONE';
   VALUE=PHONE;
   REASON='NOT 7 CHARACTERS LONG';
   OUTPUT;
END;
IF GENDER NOT IN ('MALE', 'FEMALE') THEN DO;
   VARIABLE='GENDER';
   VALUE=GENDER;
   REASON='ILLEGAL VALUE';
   OUTPUT;
END;
```

Each observation indicates:

1. Which variable contains bad data,

2. What the bad value is, and

3. Why that value is bad.

If a single observation contains more than one bad data value, the output dataset will contain more than one observation for the same ID.

Note that VALUE is a character variable. If the program also checks numeric variables, they can be converted to character expressions using the PUT function:

```
VALUE = PUT(NUMVAR, fmtname.);
```

where fmtname might be a simple numeric format such as 3.0 or 5.1. Before printing, BADDATA could be sorted by ID or VARIABLE, whichever is easier for the user.

Saving Programmer Time Examining the Log

The second drawback is that running PROC PRINT on an empty data set generates a note on the log. Aside from the aesthetics involved, a programmer normally would examine notes to be certain that the program ran correctly. So the second drawback is really that the programmer spends a little extra time examining the output. A macro language tool, CALL EXECUTE, provides a way around this problem. This example checks just one variable:

```
DATA BADDATA1 (KEEP=ID PHONE);
SET UNCLEAN END=LAST;
IF LENGTH(PHONE) NE 7 THEN DO;
   OUTPUT BADDATA1;
   N1 + 1;
END;
IF LAST THEN DO;
   IF N1 THEN DO;
      CALL EXECUTE('PROC PRINT DATA=BADDATA1;');
      CALL EXECUTE('TITLE "BAD DATA FOR PHONE";');
   END;
   ELSE DO;
      FILE PRINT;
      PUT // 'NO BAD DATA FOR PHONE';
   END;
END;
RUN;
```

CALL EXECUTE stacks programming statements to be run once the DATA step ends. It requires that the macro processor be turned on, as well as a RUN statement ending the DATA step. In the example, CALL EXECUTE uses constant text as its argument. In more advanced applications, CALL EXECUTE could take the name of a DATA step variable, a macro variable, or a call to a macro, any of which could resolve into additional programming statements to be run once the DATA step ends.

Controlling the Order of Reports

The final drawback is that the order of the reports changes. Some users won't mind. Some will appreciate seeing an initial section summarizing the "no problem" areas. Some will insist on the reports appearing in the "proper" order. A couple of programming techniques would allow the program to control the order of the reports. The first technique uses no macro language, and begins with the original DATA step:

```
DATA BADDATA1 (KEEP=ID PHONE)
     BADDATA2 (KEEP=ID GENDER);
SET UNCLEAN;
IF LENGTH(PHONE) NE 7 THEN OUTPUT BADDATA1;
IF GENDER NOT IN ('MALE', 'FEMALE') THEN
   OUTPUT BADDATA2;
```

The program could proceed by taking each output data set (in the "proper" order) and printing an appropriate report. For example, this code would take care of BADDATA1:

```
DATA _NULL_;
IF LAST THEN DO;
   FILE PRINT;
   PUT // 'NO BAD DATA FOR PHONE';
END;
STOP;
SET BADDATA1 END=LAST;

PROC PRINT DATA=BADDATA1;
VAR ID PHONE;
TITLE 'BAD DATA FOR PHONE';
```

In this program, either the DATA step or PROC PRINT generates a report. The other step produces no output. Consider two possibilities:

1. BADDATA1 contains at least one observation. The DATA step produces no output. The END= condition is false since there are observations in BADDATA1 which have not yet been read. The STOP statement ends the DATA step without ever executing the SET statement. PROC PRINT then prints the observations.

2. BADDATA1 contains zero observations. The END= variable (LAST) receives a value of 1 as the DATA step is compiled, before executing any of the programming statements. This is the usual meaning of an END= variable: 0 means there are more observations to be read, while 1 means that the last observation has already been read. Therefore, when a data set contains 0 observations, the END= variable is initially set to 1, not 0. As a result, the DATA step finds that LAST is true and generates a report. As before, STOP then ends the DATA step. PROC PRINT finds no observations to be printed.

The most powerful and flexible approach uses macro language to generate PROC PRINTs if needed yet also controls the order of the reports. The program begins with a DATA step which outputs bad data as before but also creates macro variables counting the number of bad records in each data set.

```
DATA BADDATA1 (KEEP=ID PHONE);
     BADDATA2 (KEEP=ID GENDER);
SET UNCLEAN END=LAST;
IF LENGTH(PHONE) NE 7 THEN DO;
   N1 + 1;
   OUTPUT BADDATA1;
END;
IF GENDER NOT IN ('MALE', 'FEMALE') THEN DO;
   N2 + 1;
   OUTPUT BADDATA2;
END;
IF LAST THEN DO;
   CALL SYMPUT('N1', PUT(N1,4.));
   CALL SYMPUT('N2', PUT(N2,4.));
END;
```

Now macro language can examine individually the values of &N1 and &N2. Since macro language can conditionally generate SAS code, the program could use a value of 0 to generate a DATA step report or a value greater than 0 to generate a PROC PRINT. The PUT function in CALL SYMPUT controls the conversion of N1 and N2 from numeric to character. Without it, the SAS software would make the conversion (a necessary step since all macro variables are character strings) and generate a note on the Log about numeric to character conversion. The program above might continue:

```
%MACRO BADDATA;

   %IF &N1=0 %THEN %DO;
        DATA _NULL_;
        FILE PRINT;
        PUT // 'NO BAD DATA FOR PHONE';
   %END;
   %ELSE %DO;
        PROC PRINT DATA=BADDATA1;
        TITLE 'BAD DATA FOR PHONE';
   %END;

%MEND BADDATA;

%BADDATA
```

The macro could be extended to cover more than the PHONE variable. Given the flexibility of macro language, this program could generate the reports in any order:

1. All data sets with 0 observations could be described first.

2. Alternatively, a separate report could be printed for each data set, with the reports always appearing in the same order whether or not there are 0 observations.

Detecting End-of-File When Subsetting Data

Many programs in this chapter checked for end-of-file to generate a report. If a program also subsets the observations, the combination of subsetting and detecting end-of-file can produce an unusual result: no report but no error message. For example:

```
DATA BADDATA1;
SET UNCLEAN END=LAST;
IF STATE='NY';
IF LENGTH(PHONE) NE 7 THEN DO;
   OUTPUT BADDATA1;
   N1 + 1;
END;
IF LAST THEN DO;
   IF N1 THEN DO;
      FILE PRINT;
      PUT // 'NO BAD DATA FOR PHONE';
   END;
END;
```

The subsetting IF reads in each observation, deleting those that fail to meet the subsetting condition. If the last observation contains STATE='ME', it gets deleted. The remaining programming statements, including those that would have generated the report, do not get executed once the observation is deleted. If possible, replace IF with WHERE. WHERE subsets differently than IF: it looks ahead through the data set and only reads in the observations which satisfy the WHERE condition. As a result, WHERE sets the END= variable to 1 when the last desired observation is read in, whether or not this is the last record in the incoming data set. There could be some drawbacks, however:

1. WHERE works with SAS data sets not with raw data.

2. WHERE can be more expensive than IF. Although the relative costs vary depending on the operating system and release of the software, two key factors exist when comparing IF and WHERE: the larger the number of variables and the larger the percentage of deleted observations, the more efficient WHERE becomes.

Most programs can still use IF just by changing the order of the statements:

```
DATA BADDATA1;
IF LAST THEN DO;
   IF N1 THEN DO;
      FILE PRINT;
      PUT // 'NO BAD DATA FOR PHONE';
   END;
END;
SET UNCLEAN END=LAST;
IF STATE='NY';
IF LENGTH(PHONE) NE 7 THEN DO;
   N1 + 1;
   OUTPUT BADDATA1;
END;
```

This unusual looking form of the DATA step works with either IF or WHERE. The DATA step executes as a continuous loop: leave the DATA statement, execute the programming statements, and then return to the DATA statement (possibly outputting an observation at that point). The DATA step does not end just because UNCLEAN runs out of observations. The loop continues an extra time, not ending until the SET statement fails because there is no more data left to read. As a result, the program checks LAST, even after reading in the final observation from UNCLEAN. If the reporting section is lengthy, this form may be cumbersome. It may be more readable if the reporting section appears at the end of the DATA step. This can be accomplished if you are willing to use a GOTO statement:

```
DATA BADDATA1;
IF LAST THEN GOTO REPORT;
SET UNCLEAN END=LAST;
IF STATE='NY';
IF LENGTH(PHONE) NE 7 THEN DO;
   N1 + 1;
   OUTPUT BADDATA1;
END;
RETURN;
REPORT:
IF N1=0 THEN DO;
   FILE PRINT;
   PUT // 'NO BAD DATA FOR PHONE';
END;
STOP;
```

The STOP statement is safe but not necessary in the latest releases of the software. Current releases will automatically end the DATA step when the end of the programming statements is reached but no data was read. The message is:

```
DATA step ended due to looping.
```

meaning that the software executed the programming statements within the DATA step yet failed to read from any source of data.

Conclusion

This chapter examined programming techniques to report on zero observations. In one regard, it illustrates a broader issue in the data processing arena: unusual or unexpected occurrences in the incoming data. Programmers cannot assume that the data fit a certain mold. Throughout a program (not just in the final reporting step) programmers should consider possibilities and less likely events. Data often depart from the norm.

CHAPTER 18

Harnessing SAS Macro Power and Flexibility: Applications in Reporting and Graphics

by Robin E. Way, Jr.

Abstract

SAS users can design powerful, integrated statistics and graphics presentations to take appropriate advantage of the variety of information residing in their data. These integrated presentations are more effective at persuading or convincing audiences than a series of one-shot pictures. This chapter introduces intermediate SAS users to a variety of programming techniques that help maximize the scope of information conveyed in SAS statistical reports and graphics. These reports can be used individually or together, and they integrate DATA step techniques, statistical and graphics procedures, and macro coding to increase user productivity and presentation effectiveness.

Specifications

The code in this chapter was developed and tested with Release 6.08 of the SAS System under the Windows environment. Use of the code with other releases of the SAS System or other operating environments may require user modification. Modified code is not supported by the author.

About the Author

Robin Way is an Associate with Barakat and Chamberlin, Inc., which was founded in 1982 to provide economic and management consulting services to electric, gas, and water utilities and to clients doing business in energy and other regulated industries. Mr. Way specializes in econometric and qualitative choice analysis, forecasting, and the design and implementation of expert systems for the energy industry. A SAS software user for eight years, he has a BA degree in Psychology from the University of California at Berkeley. He is currently a candidate for an MS degree in Applied Psychology from Portland State University. His areas of expertise include base SAS, SAS/STAT, SAS/ETS, SAS/GRAPH, and SAS/AF software, macros, and applications development.

Questions and Comments Should be Directed to:

Robin Way
Barakat & Chamberlin
620 SW 5th Ave., Suite 810
Portland, OR 97204
Telephone: 503-224-3666

Examples from this book are available online, see inside back cover for details.

Harnessing SAS® Macro Power and Flexibility: Applications in Reporting and Graphics

Robin E. Way, Jr.

Introduction

Effective communication with statistics and graphics requires considering the audience and their familiarity with the context of the analysis. If the findings fail to capture the attention of decision-makers, important factors of the analysis might be misinterpreted or simply ignored. To avoid this fate, the analyst should invest time and effort in reviewing and improving the content, clarity, and effectiveness of their presentation. The user can address all three issues through a variety of techniques. Several that have proven useful to the author are presented in this chapter.

The benefit of thoughtfully-crafted statistical reports and graphics presentations far outweighs the time spent learning and developing the necessary SAS skills. Specifically, this chapter emphasizes several DATA step and macro programming techniques to help summarize data. These techniques are integrated with statistics and graphics procedures to distill and highlight the key insights of the data analysis presentation. With some practice and creativity, you can develop more sophisticated macros that apply these programming techniques in an almost object-oriented approach, leading to improved productivity and persuasiveness.

The chapter's three main sections describe some building blocks of this process, particularly macro-based processing techniques. The first section focuses on data processing control via macro statements and data-dependent macro variables. The next section describes how to stretch SAS statistics and reporting procedures to present the maximum scope of information from your data. The third section puts all the building blocks together. It describes macro coding with respect to presentation and graphics procedures. Finally, the summary recaps the lessons learned in this chapter and directs the user to further references.

Macro-Based Data Processing

The capabilities of the DATA step can be dramatically enhanced by including macro-based techniques in your programming repertoire. These techniques will pass data-dependent values to other parts of the application and also control processing of the DATA and PROC steps based on data-dependent values. Data can be passed throughout the application by using the SYMPUT routine, macro parameters, or the %LET statement. Data processing can be modified via iterative %DO--%END loops and conditional %IF statements. Both techniques are described in this section.

SYMPUT Routine

The SYMPUT routine is perhaps the most flexible method of passing values throughout a SAS application. SYMPUT assigns a value produced in the DATA step to a macro variable. Since SYMPUT is a SAS routine, it is invoked by using the CALL statement in a DATA step in the following manner:

```
call symput (name, value);
```

where *name* indicates the macro variable created by the routine, which can be one of the following:

- a character string enclosed in quotes,
- a DATA step character variable whose values are valid SAS names, or
- a character expression.

The character string creates a single macro variable with name *name*. The DATA step character variable creates a macro variable with a name equal to the value of the DATA step variable. The character expression creates macro variables based on the result of a character expression. For example, the statement:

```
call symput (mv||left(_n_), value)
```

creates one macro variable for each observation in the dataset, where the name of the macro variable has the text prefix "mv" and a numeric suffix equal to the internal SAS variable _N_. This variable is essentially equal to the number of the observation in the DATA step.

The *value* in the SYMPUT routine can be one of the following:

- a string (enclosed in quotes),
- the name of a DATA step variable, or
- a DATA step expression (such as put(*variable, format.*)).

The resolution of *value* is always a character expression. If the value passed by a DATA step variable or expression is numeric, it will be converted to a character string when the SYMPUT routine is resolved.

There is an important restriction on using the SYMPUT routine: it cannot pass a value through a macro variable in the DATA step in which it was created. Specifically, macro variables referenced with an ampersand are resolved at compilation. Thus, macro variables created with CALL SYMPUT cannot be referenced until after a step boundary is crossed. However, their value can be retrieved with CALL SYMGET in the same DATA step in which they are created..

Macro Parameters

Macro parameters can be used to initialize macro variables with specific values at the outset of a section of macro code. This method is less flexible than the SYMPUT routine, because macro parameter values cannot be dynamically assigned by variables in a SAS dataset. However, new parameter values can be assigned in each new macro call. Furthermore, macros can be nested inside one another, which provides one way of passing macro variable values dynamically. For example, the following example identifies one way of passing values between sections of macro code that behave like subroutines:

```
%global m n;
%macro loop1;
  %do j = 1 %to &m;
    (statements)
    %end;
%mend loop1;
%macro loop2;
  %do k = 1 %to &n;
    (statements)
    %end;
%mend loop2;
%macro main (m, n);
%loop1
%loop2
%mend main;
%main (5, 7)
%main (2, 4)
```

This series of macro statements creates three macros: Loop1,Loop2, and Main. Loop1 and Loop2 are called within the body of Main. The %DO loops inside Loop1 and Loop2 are iterated according to the values passed from the Main macro, which is called twice. The first time Main is called, Loop1 iterates from 1 to 5, and Loop2 iterates from 1 to 7. The next time Main is called, Loop1 iterates from 1 to 2, and Loop2 iterates from 1 to 4. The %GLOBAL statement ensures that the macro variables &M and &N are resolvable across macro environments--that is, they can be resolved "outside" the realm of the Main macro in which they are initialized.

%LET Statement

The %LET statement assigns a string to a single macro variable. Unlike the SYMPUT routine, the value of the macro variable created in the %LET statement is available immediately. However, %LET is less flexible than SYMPUT because it cannot create macro variables and assign values dynamically. A single %LET statement is equivalent to a SYMPUT routine creating a single variable with the value of a character string. Therefore, the two statements are equivalent (except, of course, for the restriction on the resolution of the SYMPUT call within the DATA step):

```
%let x = test;
call symput ('x', 'test');
```

%DO and %END Statements

Sections of code can be processed iteratively through the use of %DO--%END loops. Similar to DO--END, the macro version of iterative processing executes sets of statements based on an index-based set of parameters. One limitation of the %DO macro statement concerns the flexibility of index lists. While the DO statement can perform iterative looping based on discrete indexes, the %DO statement is limited to the simpler start/stop/by increment loop form. This is summarized in the following table:

Table 1: Comparison of DO and %DO Increment Flexibility

Version of DO loop	(%)do j = 0 to 10 by 2;	(%)do j = (2 4 5 7 9 13);
%DO	yes	no
DO	yes	yes

This flexibility issue has important implications for designing your application and for the method of arranging your data analysis. For example, say you have five datasets, each of which includes household characteristics for a unique city. If the analysis plan calls for treating each city's households as a distinct group, it would be wise to artificially assign each city a number (or identification code) from 1 to 5. In this way, you could write the same analysis program once, and run the five sets of data through the program individually.

Iterative processing is a relatively simple process if running separate analyses via BY-group processing is all you need to do. But what if you want to prepare a graphic presentation of each city-specific analysis, complete with customized titles, footnotes, and legends? The title "Mean Income for Households in City 5" isn't nearly as descriptive as "Mean Income for Households in Philadelphia". The former strategy (via BY-group processing) requires more time and development of repetitive code than writing the code once and using a %DO--%END loop.

%IF--%THEN--%ELSE Statements

Sections of code can also be conditionally processed via the %IF--%THEN--%ELSE macro statements. Again, macro-based conditional processing is very similar to the typical DATA step version of IF--THEN--ELSE statements. The condition specified in an %IF--%THEN macro statement can be based on macro variables, and combined with other macro statements, such as

```
%do x = 1 %to 5;
  (statements)
  %if (&x=2) %then %do;
    (statements)
    %end;
  %else %let j=5;
  (statements)
```

```
%end;
```

This macro-based technique is more flexible than the DATA step-based strategy, because it can run alternative sections of code contingent on the values contained in a macro variable. Note that the condition of an %IF--%THEN macro statement can also include DATA step variables, as long as the condition is tested within the DATA step itself.

Macro-Based Statistics and Reporting

The SAS System includes a wide variety of reporting and statistical procedures, as well as a suite of functions and CALL routines. These procedures, functions, and routines enable you to quickly and efficiently produce analyses which would have taken many times as long to run ten to fifteen years ago.

However, if one had to rely on only one procedure for summarizing and breaking down data into smaller chunks and presenting the salient details, I would pick PROC SUMMARY. This procedure offers broad analysis power and flexibility. Some of the tools included in PROC SUMMARY are described in Table 2:

Table 2: Selected Components of PROC SUMMARY

Task/Tool	PROC SUMMARY
Analysis Variable	VAR
Subsetting Variables	WHERE
Classification Variables	CLASS, BY
Weighted by Parameter	WEIGHT
Weighted by Observation	FREQ

The analysis variable tool identifies the continuous or discrete "target" of the analysis, such as dollars spent or widgets sold. The subsetting variables include only those observations that match a specified set of criteria, such as sales in January. The classification variables identify classes and sub-classes of the analysis, such as sales by department and by sales region. Finally, the analysis can weight the classified results either by the number of cases (or measures) contributing to the class or by a variable that measures some other meaningful weight of the class.

Features of the SUMMARY Procedure

I frequently use PROC SUMMARY when I need to distill the important trends and parameters from raw data. This procedure is fast and can calculate summary statistics for a multitude of classifications. This procedure is essentially the same product as PROC MEANS, which is also quite popular among SAS users. Instead of printed output, PROC SUMMARY creates an output dataset by default. PROC SUMMARY can calculate many of the same parameters as PROC FREQ, such as number of observations in a cross-tabulation, via the _FREQ_ variable included in the output dataset.

CLASS Statement

The output dataset from PROC SUMMARY contains one observation for every possible classification and sub-classification of the data. The classification scheme is specified via the CLASS statement. For example, assume we have a dataset for an analysis variable SALES, for which we want to summarize using two classification variables. The first class variable (DEPT) has three levels (such as lumber, paper, and pulp), and the second (REGION) has four levels (such as North, South, East, and West). PROC SUMMARY will create a total of 20 subclasses of the analysis variable summary statistics.

Why 20 classes instead of 12 (3 DEPT classes * 4 REGION classes = 12 classes)? PROC SUMMARY by default creates not only the two-way classification of DEPT * REGION but also one-way and zero-way classifications. So there are 12 two-way classes (DEPT * REGION), 7 one-way classes (three DEPT classes and four REGION classes), and one zero-way class (for all observations). If you desire only the maximum classification scheme (two-way, in this case), specify the NWAY option in the PROC SUMMARY statement.

BY Statement

The BY statement can also be used in PROC SUMMARY to create a classification scheme, but it requires that the data be sorted in order of the variables named in the BY statement. This increases the time required for the task, particularly for a large dataset.

Weighting Using the FREQ Statement

Weighting allows you to calculate weighted statistics, such as weighted means. The SUMMARY procedure assumes that every input observation represents one case or measurement. A variable (and only one variable) named in the FREQ statement allows you to specify that each input observation represents more than one case or measurement. This might be useful in a factorial design experiment. Note that the FREQ statement accepts only integer values. Any variable values which have decimal portions will be truncated, and any observations with a value of missing or less than one will be dropped from the output dataset.

Weighting Using the WEIGHT Statement

The WEIGHT statement allows you to specify a variable (and again only a single variable) containing values representing weights. That is, the value of the weight variable for each observation is the weight by which the same observation's analysis variable will be multiplied. This is different than the FREQ statement because the weight variable can include decimal values (i.e., non-integers). Both the FREQ and WEIGHT variables can be used in the same procedure.

WHERE Statement

The WHERE statement is legal in any procedure or DATA step, but is a welcome sight particularly in PROC SUMMARY. I find the WHERE statement very useful because it allows you to develop a new analysis of existing data without having to use the DATA step. This reduces run time because WHERE subsets the data as it is being read into the program data vector, rather than after all the data has been processed. The most important restriction on the WHERE statement is that it cannot use functions, cannot be executed conditionally (i.e., in an IF--THEN statement) and does not recognize DATA step BY-group processing (since the BY-group can't exist until all the data has been read into the program data vector). In addition to using traditional operators (including most arithmetic, comparison, and logical operators), the WHERE statement has its own special set of operators, such as IN, BETWEEN--AND, CONTAINS, IS MISSING, LIKE, and even "SOUNDS LIKE".

OUTPUT Statement

The OUTPUT statement creates the output dataset. The OUT= option names the dataset that is to receive the summarized data. All the statistics available in the MEANS procedure are also available in SUMMARY. Two of the most common statistics are expressed with the MEAN= and SUM= options. Various naming conventions create variables that contain the values of these statistics for each class. The one I use the most is also the most explicit. For each variable in the VAR statement, I create a new variable in the MEAN= or SUM= option of the OUTPUT statement. This can be entered as follows:

```
proc summary data=in.raw;
  var sales1-sales3;
  class dept region;
  output out=stats mean=avg1-avg3 sum=total1-total3;
```

```
run;
```

This procedure summarizes three analysis variables and the previously named classification variables. The OUTPUT statistics naming convention MEAN=AVG1-AVG3 creates one output statistics variable for each analysis variable, which contains the mean of SALES1, SALES2, and SALES3 for each class of DEPT and REGION. The same is true for the output statistics variables TOTAL1, TOTAL2, and TOTAL3, which contain the sum of the analysis variables for each class.

Putting It All Together: Macro-Based Techniques in Reporting and Graphics Procedures

Once the data has been treated, summarized, and distilled by the SUMMARY procedure (or perhaps by PROC MEANS or PROC FREQ), reporting procedures (such as PROC PRINT and PROC REPORT) and graphics procedures (such as PROC GPLOT and PROC GCHART) can present the results.

Macro variables are a useful tool in title and footnote statements in coordination with reporting and graphics procedures. One way of getting data-dependent values into macro variables is through PROC SUMMARY's output dataset combined with a "null" DATA step (i.e., DATA _NULL_). Null DATA steps create no actual dataset, although datasets can be read into a null DATA step and processed like any other dataset. However, they save on space, particularly if a duplicate copy of the data isn't needed. Null DATA steps are an excellent place to run the SYMPUT routine. For example, take our dataset from the section describing the SUMMARY procedure. Given 12 classes of statistics (using the NWAY option) on one analysis variable (SALES), 12 observations will be created by the OUTPUT statement. If we used the SYMPUT routine to create 12 macro variables, each of which contained the mean of SALES in each class, we would use the following statements:

```
proc summary data=in.raw nway;
  var sales;
  class dept region;
  output out=stats mean=xbar;
run;
data _null_;
  set stats;
  call symput ('smean'||left(_n_), put(xbar, comma10.2));
run;
```

This code creates 12 macro variables (named *&smean1* through *&smean12*), each of which contains the value of mean sales for each class in the output dataset from PROC SUMMARY.

This approach can be used for titles, for footnotes, and for specifying labels, such as axes and legends in plots and bar charts and for slices in pie charts. When you want to use a macro variable this way, remember that macro resolution follows a number of specific rules. First, when resolving a macro reference that is part of a title, footnote, or graphics label, you must use double quotes, not single quotes (the more common option). For example, consider the two following statements:

```
title 'Distribution of Sales for the &dept Department';
```

and

```
title "Distribution of Sales for the &dept Department";
```

The only difference between these two statements is the quote markers. When the SAS compiler sees the first title statement, it will read &DEPT as a character string. The compiler reads the second statement's

&DEPT as a macro reference, and it will resolve &DEPT into its current value. If &DEPT has not been created, SAS will write a warning to the log and treat the macro reference as a character string.

Second, when a macro reference is part of a character string, you will need to delimit the end of the macro reference. An example for macro variables *&day* and *&month* is as follows:

```
footnote "This report was generated on the &dayth day of &month.";
```

The intent is to print a footnote stating on which day of which month the report was created. The statement will generate a warning message instead, however, because the compiler will try to resolve a reference for macro variable *&dayth* instead of *&day*. This is due to the lack of a delimiter at the end of macro reference for *&day*. The correct syntax reads:

```
footnote "This report was generated on the &day.th day of &month.";
```

Note that no warning message would be generated for the reference to *&month*. This is because SAS interprets any non-alphabetic character, including a space, as a character not legal in a macro reference. Therefore, SAS recognizes that the reference for *&month* ends at the character to the left of the final period.

Naturally, a vast number of applications for this type of macro strategy abound. I probably use these strategies at least five to six times in programs that present data and analysis results. The next section of this chapter presents a variety of these strategies in a real program setting.

Does It Really Work?

This section presents a real-world application of many of the techniques described in the above sections. The SAS program, which was developed from a forecasting project, is shown section-by-section in the following pages and in its entirety in Figure 1. This SAS program develops a forecast of sales for each of six states and two types of sales as a function of number of customers, customer density (customers per square mile), and time. The program:

- reads in data from a permanent SAS dataset,
- transforms the dependent and independent variables into their logarithmic values,
- creates some macro variables through the SYMPUT routine for use in TITLE statements,
- runs ordinary least-squares regression (REG), correcting for autoregressive parameters conditional on specific data characteristics (AUTOREG), and
- prepares a graphics plot of the results, complete with customized symbols, axes, titles, and a legend.

Figure 2 shows sample SAS regression output, and Figure 3 shows the graphics output.

Through the description of this program, I will demonstrate some tools which I use frequently when I develop an analysis program in SAS. These tools are based on the building blocks already described. Since I believe the key to learning is to observe how these tools interact in a real setting, I will describe the intent of each section of the code, identify what tools are being used, and highlight some program development strategies. We will consider the program in separate sections.

The LIBNAME and MACRO Statements

```
libname forecast 'd:\sasuser\forecast';
%macro iter (i, state, sale, titl, inf1, inf2);
```

The LIBNAME statement defines the physical location of the permanent SAS datasets used in this analysis. The %MACRO statement defines a block of macro code called %ITER and creates six macro parameters (&I, &STAT, &SALE, &TITL, &INF1, and &INF2). The values of these parameters will change based on the state and type of sales forecasted. For example, there are six states and two sales types, and hence twelve macro calls (one for each combination of state and sales type). For each macro call the macro parameters define the items shown in this table:

Table 3: Application of Macro Variables

Macro parameter	Usage of macro variable
&I	Numeric identifier for state
&STATE	Text identifier for state
&SALE	Abbreviated text identifier for sales type
&TITL	Formal text identifier for sales type
&INF1	Year of inflection point 1 (for piecewise regression)
&INF2	Year of inflection point 2 (for piecewise regression)

The DATA _NULL_ Step

```
data _null_;
  set forecast.sales;
    where statenum = &i;
  time = year - 1974;
  ltime = log(time);
  lc = log(cust);
  if (&inf1=0) then do;
    %let lt1=0;  %let lr1=0;
    end;
  else if (year=&inf1) then do;
    call symput ('lt1', put(ltime, 8.2));
    call symput ('lr1', put(lc, 8.2));
    end;
  if (&inf2=0) then do;
    %let lt2=0;  %let lr2=0;
    end;
  else if (year=&inf2) then do;
    call symput ('lt2', put(ltime, 8.2));
    call symput ('lr2', put(lc, 8.2));
    end;
run;
```

The first DATA step has a name of _NULL_ which creates a DATA step environment without actually creating an output dataset. This tool is useful for creating macro variables through the SYMPUT routine, which is indeed the primary application of this DATA step. Null DATA steps are also useful for reading and writing flat files and other types of files that the user wants to save in a non-SAS file format. This DATA step reads in all the observations in the SAS dataset called FORECAST.SALES where the value of the variable *statenum* is equal to the current value of the macro variable &I. The next three lines of code perform a few manipulations of analysis variables by creating a time variable, a logarithmic time variable, and a logarithmic customer variable.

The final section of the null DATA step uses a combination of IF--THEN--ELSE statements and DO loops to create macro variables. The macro variables in turn are created by a combination of %LET statements and SYMPUT routines. These macro variables are specifying some predetermined inflection points in the dependent variable of the subsequent regression analysis. These inflection points represent systematic shifts in the slope of the dependent variable (sales) as a result of a discrete event in time--such as advertising strategies, price changes, etc. Each macro call defines up to two possible inflection points in the independent regression variables, which are fed back into macro parameters for purposes of descriptive documentation in title statements and so on. These customized title statements will be used later in the program for the printed output from regression and graphics procedures. For more detail on piecewise linear regression concepts, please consult *Econometric Models and Economic Forecasts* by R. Pindyck and D. Rubenfeld.

The logic of this part of the DATA step is as follows:

- if the first inflection point is zero (i.e., does not exist for this state and sales type), then assign the value of zero to the macro variables for the first inflection point;
- if the first inflection point is non-zero, assign the log value of the year in which the inflection point occurs and the log value of number of customers in that year to two macro variables (via the SYMPUT routine);
- follow the same tests for the second inflection point variables.

The DATA SALES&I Step

```
data sales&i;
  set forecast.sales;
    where statenum = &i;
  lc = log(cust);
  if year ge &infl then binl=1;
    else binl=0;
  if year ge &inf2 then bin2=1;
    else bin2=0;
  time = year - 1974;
  ltime = log(time);
  ltim&infl = (ltime - &ltl) * binl;
  ltim&inf2 = (ltime - &lt2) * bin2;
  lc&infl = (lc - &lrl) * binl;
  lc&inf2 = (lc - &lr2) * bin2;
  lt&sale.&i = log(t&sale);
run;
```

The second DATA step creates an output dataset SALES&I, which resolves into a state-specific dataset name (such as SALES1 for Oregon sales, SALES2 for Washington sales, etc.). This DATA step reads in the observations matching the desired state identifier and creates a logarithmic variable (for number of customers). The next four lines of code define two binary variables that indicate the status of the inflection point for the state and sales type. If the year of the current observation is greater or equal to the first inflection point (defined in the macro variable &INF1), then the variable BIN1 is set to 1. Otherwise, it is set to zero. The same logic applies for variable BIN2.

The next line defines the logarithmic variable for time. The following four lines of code define four variables, the names of which depend on the inflection point macro variables. For example, if the first inflection point occurs in 1978, then LTIM&INF1 resolves into LTIM1978. The variable's value is defined as the log of the current time value, minus the log of the first inflection point's time value, quantity multiplied by BIN1. Here the use of BIN1 effectively turns LTIM&INF1 on or off, depending on whether BIN1 is equal to one or zero, respectively. The same logic is used for the second inflection point and subsequently for the log value of the number of customers. The last line creates the log value of the cumulative amount of sales for state &i. This allows us to specify a log-log functional form for the autoregressive forecasting model.

The REG Procedure

```
proc reg data=sales&i;
  model t&sale.&i = density cust lc time ltime /
```

```
    selection=adjrsq adjrsq b stb vif;
  title "Cumulative sales OLS forecast: test for &state, &titl";
run;
```

This part of the program runs a stepwise series of ordinary-least squares regression modes for each state-specific dataset, then sorts the results by the value of the adjusted r-squared statistic. This model serves only as a test of some basic relationships which are expected between the dependent variable and key independent variables. We also print the value of the adjusted r-squared statistic, the regular and standardized regression coefficients, and the variance inflation factor (a measure of potential multicollinearity).

The AUTOREG Procedure

```
%if (&infl=0 and &inf2=0) %then %do;
  proc autoreg data=sales&i;
    model lt&sale.&i = ltime lc / backstep nlag=3;
    where statenum = &i;
    output out=reg&sale.&i p=lp&sale.&i lclm=ll&sale.&i uclm=lu&sale.&i;
    title 'Cumulative Sales (Log-Log Piecewise AutoRegressive) Forecast
Model';
    title2 "Western Division: &state, &titl";
    title3 "Log-Log model: No Slope Changes";
  run;
  %end;

%else %if (&infl>0 and &inf2=0) %then %do;
  proc autoreg data=sales&i;
    model lt&sale.&i = ltime ltim&infl lc lc&infl / backstep nlag=3;
    where statenum = &i;
    output out=reg&sale.&i p=lp&sale.&i lclm=ll&sale.&i uclm=lu&sale.&i;
    title 'Cumulative Sales (Log-Log Piecewise AutoRegressive) Forecast
Model';
    title2 "Western Division: &state, &titl";
    title3 "Log-Log model: Slope Changes in: &infl";
  run;
  %end;

%else %if (&infl>0 and &inf2>0) %then %do;
  proc autoreg data=sales&i;
    model lt&sale.&i = ltime ltim&infl ltim&inf2 lc lc&infl lc&inf2 /
backstep nlag=3;
    where statenum = &i;
    output out=reg&sale.&i p=lp&sale.&i lclm=ll&sale.&i uclm=lu&sale.&i;
    title 'Cumulative Sales (Log-Log Piecewise AutoRegressive) Forecast
Model';
    title2 "Western Division: &state, &titl";
    title3 "Log-Log model: Slope Changes in: &infl &inf2";
  run;
  %end;
```

Here we run the autoregressive forecasting model for cumulative sales for each state and sales type. Each model uses the backstep option to select the appropriate order of the autoregressive parameter. You will note the series of %IF--%THEN--%ELSE macro statements, which select the appropriate model for the number of inflection points in the current analysis dataset. That is, if all inflection points are equal to zero, the model is simply a function of log of customers and log of time (a simple linear time trend). However, if there is one inflection point, the model adds two piecewise parameters (i.e., LTIM&INF1 and LC&INF1). The model adds the second pair of piecewise parameters when two inflection points are present. The title statements identify the state and the type of sales forecasted by the current model, as well as the year in which the first and second inflection points occur.

Each model also creates an output dataset which contains three new variables: the predicted value and the upper and lower 95% confidence intervals about the predicted value. PROC REG and PROC AUTOREG will automatically calculate the value of the predicted value in the historical period, as well as into the future if you provide the values of the independent regression parameters in the forecast horizon. It is very persuasive to present both the forecasted value of the dependent variable and the "backcast," (i.e., to compare the predicted dependent variable with the actual value of the dependent variable).

Each variable has a name customized to the sales type variable &SALE and the state identifier variable &I, in the following manner:

```
output out=reg&sale.&i p=lp&sale.&i lclm=ll&sale.&i uclm=lu&sale.&i;
```

When defining the name of the output variables, the values of two macro variables are used jointly to uniquely identify the variable for each state and sales type. The macro variable references are delineated by a "dot " or period. This is not a necessary step, since SAS understands that an ampersand is not generally an allowable character in a macro variable name and therefore would delineate at that point anyway. For example, the macro variable reference LP&SALE.&I is equivalent to LP&SALE&I (but not to LP&&SALE&I, which is a different creature altogether and outside the scope of this discussion). However, I find the dot helps me to delineate visually the distinction between the first and second macro variable references, particularly during debugging.

If you are an experienced macro user, you may recognize that the three sections of PROC AUTOREG could be collapsed into a single section of code by more elegant programming. If I were to follow this strategy, I could reduce the program size and eliminate the need for redundant title statements. However, I would also need to create new macro variables to specify the model statement and the third title statement. I decided to maintain my code as shown here because it is easier to explain this code to a non-programmer, which is often part of my work. It sometimes comes down to optimizing your time rather than maximizing program elegance.

The SORT Procedure

```
proc sort data=reg&sale.&i;  by year;  run;
data pr&sale.&i;
  set reg&sale.&i;
  array in {4} lt&sale.&i lp&sale.&i ll&sale.&i lu&sale.&i;
  array out {4} t&sale.&i p&sale.&i l&sale.&i u&sale.&i;
  do i=1 to 4;
    out(i) = exp(in(i));
    end;
run;
```

The next section of code sorts each output dataset in turn by the YEAR variable, then converts the historical value, the predicted value, and the confidence limit values from their logarithmic form back to their base 10 form. I do this through a set of arrays and the EXP() function. This is done in preparation for plotting the results, since the log of predicted sales isn't nearly as interesting or relevant to a decision-maker as the value of actual sales.

Preparing the Symbols, Axes, and Legends

```
goptions reset=all;
symbol1 l=1 w=2 i=join h=1.5 v=dot c=black;
symbol2 l=1 w=2 i=join h=1.5 v=square c=black;
symbol3 l=2 w=1 i=join h=1 v=none c=black;
symbol4 l=2 w=1 i=join h=1 v=none c=black;
axis1 label=(h=1 j=l 'Cumulative' j=l 'Sales');
legend1 frame label=(h=1.5 "&state") across=2
  value=(h=1 t=1 'Actual' t=2 'Predicted' t=3 'Lower Forecast Range'
    t=4 'Upper Forecast Range');
```

From here on, the code prepares and creates some graphics plots of the forecast results. First, I reset all the graphics options to their prescribed defaults, in case I had modified them earlier in the current session. Then I prepare the symbols, axes, and legends. The first symbol option specifies a black dot joined by a solid line for the historical sales variable. The second symbol option specifies a hollow square, also joined by a solid line for the predicted value. The third and fourth symbols, which are the same, are used for the confidence intervals. These statements create a dashed line with no specific symbols (i.e., dots). The AXIS statement creates a left-aligned label at the top of the y-axis telling the user that the plotted variable represents cumulative sales. Finally, the LEGEND statement creates a legend at the bottom center of the page (the default position) surrounded by a frame. The label for the legend is the value of the text state identifier macro variable &STATE. The legend provides for two legend entries per line, via the ACROSS= option. The VALUE= option defines the printed names for the plotted variables.

The GOPTIONS Statement

```
goptions device=ps600 rotate=portrait ftitle=hwpsl007 ftext=hwpsl005
fby=hwpsl005 noprompt;
```

This statement defines the graphics options in effect for the subsequent GPLOT procedure. Here I have defined a 600 dpi Postscript driver. This is a modification of the PS driver that is supplied with SAS/GRAPH software. I created this driver in PROC GDEVICE. Unfortunately, a more detailed discussion of the graphic driver modification process is outside the scope of this chapter. Furthermore, I have asked for the plots to be rotated to a portrait mode, and I have specified hardware-specific fonts (Postscript Times Roman) for my main title (bold), subsequent titles and text (regular), and by-line text (regular). These are specified by the FTITLE, FTEXT, and FBY options, respectively. Finally, the NOPROMPT option keeps SAS from prompting me to check the printer for readiness, since I use a network printer that is always ready.

The GPLOT Procedure

```
proc gplot data=pr&sale.&i;
  plot (t&sale.&i p&sale.&i l&sale.&i u&sale.&i) * year /
    overlay legend=legend1 vaxis=axis1 href=1992 lhref=20;
  title1 h=2 ;
  title2 h=2 "Actual vs. Predicted &titl";
  title3 h=1.5 "Western Division: &state";
run;
quit;
```

The GPLOT procedure plots an overlay of the actual sales, the predicted sales, and the confidence limits against the year. It specifies the desired legend and vertical axis options, as well as a vertical reference line. This reference line meets the horizontal axis where the historical and forecast horizons meet (where YEAR=1992) and creates a dashed line (LHREF=20). The title statements present a general description of the plot's contents (with respect to sales type), and the state for which the plot is generated.

The PRINTTO Procedure

```
%mend iter;
proc printto new print='d:\-a';  run;
%iter (1, Oregon, new, New Sales, 1982, 0)
%iter (2, Washington, new, New Sales, 1982, 0)
%iter (3, Idaho, new, New Sales, 1985, 0)
%iter (4, Montana, new, New Sales, 1982, 0)
%iter (5, California, new, New Sales, 1982, 0)
%iter (6, Wyoming, new, New Sales, 1982, 1986)
%iter (1, Oregon, rpt, Repeat Sales, 1982, 0)
%iter (2, Washington, rpt, Repeat Sales, 1979, 0)
%iter (3, Idaho, rpt, Repeat Sales, 1980, 1982)
%iter (4, Montana, rpt, Repeat Sales, 0, 0)
%iter (5, California, rpt, Repeat Sales, 0, 0)
%iter (6, Wyoming, rpt, Repeat Sales, 1982, 0)
proc printto;  run;
```

Following the closure of the %ITER macro (the %MEND statement), PROC PRINTTO directs all printed output (from PROC REG and AUTOREG) to a physical file called D:\-A. Macro calls for each state and sales type follow, including the appropriate values for the macro parameters. The final PROC PRINTTO statement with no options releases SAS' control of the physical file created in the previous PRINTTO, allowing Windows to print the file to the printer, move it into a word processor, etc.

Summary

This chapter has presented, somewhat briefly, a tool kit of macro-based techniques for preparing customized output. These macro techniques can be particularly powerful when applied to SAS graphics. The SAS code example identified some tools to simplify the preparation and debugging of code. I would like to emphasize the strategies for data processing and value-passing to remove the data dependency from your programming efforts. By disconnecting SAS programs from the data, your SAS programs will start to approach the object-oriented strategies now in vogue.

Specifically, data can be captured and passed throughout the application through the SYMPUT routine, the %LET statement, and macro parameters. Macro statements, such as %DO--%END and %IF--%THEN--%ELSE, control the flow of data processing based on key conditions stored in macro variables. Statistics and reporting procedures often contain more options than commonly used, and some options can be harnessed to streamline the distilling of trends and summaries from raw data. When preparing printed output, users should also be aware of the appropriate methods for macro variable resolution. Finally, a variety of these tools can be put to work to customize your graphics output. This chapter has identified how to place data-specific details in titles, footnotes, axes, and legends. While the main example focused on line plots, all these options are valid in the area of bar charts, pie charts, map plots, and so on.

There are a multitude of graphics and other reporting options outside the scope of this chapter. The SYMBOL statement provides options for high-low stock plots, as well as data-dependent regression and spline interpolation. The PATTERN statement can define user-specified fills for areas in your graphics output. For example, the Annotate Facility and the Graphics Editor provide an even greater level of user control over graphics presentations. Please refer to the following resources for more information on SAS-based graphics presentations:

- SAS Graphics Software: Usage, Version 6, First Edition
- SAS Graphics Software: Reference (Volumes 1 and 2), Version 6, First Edition
- SAS Graphics Software: Graphics Editor, Version 6, First Edition
- SAS Technical Report P-215, SAS/GRAPH Software: Changes and Enhancements, Release 6.07

There are also more detailed macro options and macro-based strategies which are described in the SAS Guide to Macro Processing, Version 6, Second Edition. This manual covers the macro environment, macro referencing and resolution, macro windows and DATA step interfaces, and other useful ways of passing data and controlling the flow of processing.

The best source of macro-based strategies is your imagination. I have generally found that if I could conceive of an idea for controlling data processing or customizing output based on some critical variables, the SAS System provided the tools to get the job done. As you gain more experience in macro-based strategies, I hope you will come to appreciate the many SAS tools available and learn new ways of using them interactively. Furthermore, I hope the practical and relatively simple tools identified in this chapter will catalyze greater use of macro-based strategies.

References

Pindyck, R., and D. Rubenfeld, (1981), *Econometric Models and Economic Forecasts,* New York: McGraw-Hill

SAS Institute Inc. (1991), *SAS Graphics Software: Usage, Version 6, First Edition*, Cary, NC: SAS Institute Inc.

SAS Institute Inc. (1991), *SAS Graphics Software: Reference (Volumes 1 and 2), Version 6, First Edition*, Cary, NC: SAS Institute Inc.

SAS Institute Inc. (1991), *SAS Graphics Software: Graphics Editor, Version 6, First Edition*, Cary, NC: SAS Institute Inc.

SAS Institute Inc. (1991), *SAS Technical Report P-215, SAS/GRAPH Software: Changes and Enhancements, Release 6.07*, Cary, NC: SAS Institute Inc.

SAS Institute Inc. (1990), *SAS Guide to Macro Processing, Version 6, Second Edition*, Cary, NC: SAS Institute Inc.

Figure 1: Forecasting and Graphics SAS Code

```
libname forecast 'd:\sasuser\forecast';

%macro iter (i, state, sale, titl, inf1, inf2);

/*** This null data step creates some state-specific macro variables used
subsequently in the analysis and in title statements.  The data step creates
four macro variables (&lt1, &lr1, &lt2, &lr2) using either the %LET statement
or the SYMPUT routine, depending on an &IF--&THEN condition.  The values of
the %LET-created variables are conditional on the existence of pre-defined
inflection points in the dependent variable over time.  These inflection
points are contained in the macro parameters &inf1 and &inf2. ***/

  data _null_;
    set forecast.sales;
      where statenum = &i;
    time = year - 1974;
    ltime = log(time);
    lc = log(cust);
    if (&inf1=0) then do;
      %let lt1=0;  %let lr1=0;
      end;
    else if (year=&inf1) then do;
      call symput ('lt1', put(ltime, 8.2));
      call symput ('lr1', put(lc, 8.2));
      end;
    if (&inf2=0) then do;
      %let lt2=0;  %let lr2=0;
      end;
    else if (year=&inf2) then do;
      call symput ('lt2', put(ltime, 8.2));
      call symput ('lr2', put(lc, 8.2));
      end;
  run;

/*** The next data step creates the analysis variables for the OLS regression
and the autoregressive correction analyses for each state. It transforms all
the dependent and independent variables into their logarithmic values.  It
also constructs the piecewise variables ltim&inf1, ltimeinf2, lc&inf1, and
lc&inf2, which take advantage of the macro variables defined in the null data
step above. ***/

  data sales&i;
    set forecast.sales;
      where statenum = &i;
    lc = log(cust);
    if year ge &inf1 then bin1=1;
      else bin1=0;
    if year ge &inf2 then bin2=1;
      else bin2=0;
```

Figure 1 (continued): Forecasting and Graphics SAS Code

```
      time = year - 1974;
      ltime = log(time);
      ltim&inf1 = (ltime - &lt1) * bin1;
      ltim&inf2 = (ltime - &lt2) * bin2;
      lc&inf1 = (lc - &lr1) * bin1;
      lc&inf2 = (lc - &lr2) * bin2;
      lt&sale.&i = log(t&sale);
    run;

  /*** This procedure runs the OLS regression. ***/

  proc reg data=sales&i;
    model t&sale.&i = density lden cust lc time ltime /
      selection=adjrsq adjrsq b stb vif;
    title "Cumulative sales OLS forecast: test for &state, &titl";
  run;

  /*** The next set of procedures runs the regression analyses with
  autoregressive correction (AUTOREG).  The choice between the three available
  models depends on whether the data for each state and type of sales (new
  versus repeat sales) involves zero, one, or two historical inflection points.
   The output datasets from each model create three additional variables: the
  predicted value, the upper 95% confidence limit, and the lower 95% confidence
  limit. ***/

  %if (&inf1=0 and &inf2=0) %then %do;
    proc autoreg data=sales&i;
      model lt&sale.&i = ltime lc / backstep nlag=3;
      where statenum = &i;
      output out=reg&sale.&i p=lp&sale.&i lclm=ll&sale.&i uclm=lu&sale.&i;
      title 'Cumulative Sales (Log-Log Piecewise AutoRegressive) Forecast
  Model';
      title2 "Western Division: &state, &titl";
      title3 "Log-Log model: No Slope Changes";
    run;
    %end;

  %else %if (&inf1>0 and &inf2=0) %then %do;
    proc autoreg data=sales&i;
      model lt&sale.&i = ltime ltim&inf1 lc lc&inf1 / backstep nlag=3;
      where statenum = &i;
      output out=reg&sale.&i p=lp&sale.&i lclm=ll&sale.&i uclm=lu&sale.&i;
      title 'Cumulative Sales (Log-Log Piecewise AutoRegressive) Forecast
  Model';
      title2 "Western Division: &state, &titl";
      title3 "Log-Log model: Slope Changes in: &inf1";
    run;
    %end;
  %else %if (&inf1>0 and &inf2>0) %then %do;
    proc autoreg data=sales&i;
```

Figure 1 (continued): Forecasting and Graphics SAS Code

```
    model lt&sale.&i = ltime ltim&inf1 ltim&inf2 lc lc&inf1 lc&inf2 /
backstep nlag=3;
    where statenum = &i;
    output out=reg&sale.&i p=lp&sale.&i lclm=ll&sale.&i uclm=lu&sale.&i;
    title 'Cumulative Sales (Log-Log Piecewise AutoRegressive) Forecast
Model';
    title2 "Western Division: &state, &titl";
    title3 "Log-Log model: Slope Changes in: &inf1 &inf2";
  run;
  %end;

/*** This sorts the output datasets by year to ensure proper ploting: ***/

proc sort data=reg&sale.&i;  by year;  run;

/*** This data step uses the EXP() function to convert the logarithmic (i.e.,
base e) regression parameters back into their regular (i.e., base 10) values.
***/

data pr&sale.&i;
  set reg&sale.&i;
  array in {4} lt&sale.&i lp&sale.&i ll&sale.&i lu&sale.&i;
  array out {4} t&sale.&i p&sale.&i l&sale.&i u&sale.&i;
  do i=1 to 4;
    out(i) = exp(in(i));
    end;
run;

/*** This resets any graphics options different from the defaults. ***/

goptions reset=all;

/*** This series of graphics statements set up the plotting symbols and
interpolation options (symbol statements), the axis labels, and legend
options. ***/

symbol1 l=1 w=2 i=join h=1.5 v=dot c=black;
symbol2 l=1 w=2 i=join h=1.5 v=square c=black;
symbol3 l=2 w=1 i=join h=1 v=none c=black;
symbol4 l=2 w=1 i=join h=1 v=none c=black;
axis1 label=(h=1 j=l 'Cumulative' j=l 'Sales');
legend1 frame label=(h=1.5 "&state") across=2
  value=(h=1 t=1 'Actual' t=2 'Predicted' t=3 'Lower Forecast Range'
    t=4 'Upper Forecast Range');

/*** This states my preferred graphics options, including the graphics device
driver, the page orientation, the font selections for titles and text, and
turning off the prompt that asks the user to check the printer (since I work
on a network and this message is unnecessary for my workstation). ***/
```

Figure 1 (continued): Forecasting and Graphics SAS Code

```
goptions device=ps600 rotate=portrait ftitle=hwpsl007 ftext=hwpsl005
fby=hwpsl005 noprompt;

/*** This GPLOT procedure plots the historical and predicted sales, as well
as confidence limits around the predicted value.  The procedure also draws a
vertical dashed reference line at the point on the plot where the historical
period ends and the forecast horizon begins.  The title statements define the
state and sales type (new versus repeat), as well as creating a legend for
the lines plotted. ***/

proc gplot data=pr&sale.&i;
  plot (t&sale.&i p&sale.&i l&sale.&i u&sale.&i) * year /
    overlay legend=legend1 vaxis=axis1 href=1992 lhref=20;
  title1 h=2 ;
  title2 h=2 "Actual vs. Predicted &titl";
  title3 h=1.5 "Western Division: &state";
run;
quit;

%mend iter;

/*** The PROC PRINTTO statements define a physical file as the location in
which to save the printed output from PROC REG and PROC AUTOREG is to be
saved.  The macro calls specify the macro parameters for each iteration of
the macro-driven program. ***/

proc printto new print='d:\-a';  run;

%iter (1, Oregon, new, New Sales, 1982, 0)
%iter (2, Washington, new, New Sales, 1982, 0)
%iter (3, Idaho, new, New Sales, 1985, 0)
%iter (4, Montana, new, New Sales, 1982, 0)
%iter (5, California, new, New Sales, 1982, 0)
%iter (6, Wyoming, new, New Sales, 1982, 1986)

%iter (1, Oregon, rpt, Repeat Sales, 1982, 0)
%iter (2, Washington, rpt, Repeat Sales, 1979, 0)
%iter (3, Idaho, rpt, Repeat Sales, 1980, 1982)
%iter (4, Montana, rpt, Repeat Sales, 0, 0)
%iter (5, California, rpt, Repeat Sales, 0, 0)
%iter (6, Wyoming, rpt, Repeat Sales, 1982, 0)

proc printto;  run;
```

Figure 2: Sample SAS PROC AUTOREG Output

```
Cumulative Pole-Mile (Log-Log Piecewise AutoRegressive) Forecast
Western Division: Oregon, New Sales
Log-Log model: Slope Changes in: 1982

Autoreg Procedure

Dependent Variable = LTNDO1


Ordinary Least Squares Estimates

SSE           0.016359    DFE              13
MSE           0.001258    Root MSE   0.035474
SBC           -60.5266    AIC        -64.9785
Reg Rsq         0.9975    Total Rsq    0.9975
Durbin-Watson   0.5129


Variable      DF        B Value    Std Error   t Ratio Approx Prob

Intercept      1     4.38600751       12.725     0.345      0.7359
LTIME          1     0.94813877        0.095     9.988      0.0001
LTIM1982       1    -0.80049838        0.156    -5.142      0.0002
LRC            1     0.10394138        1.016     0.102      0.9201
LRC1982        1     1.22662920        1.437     0.854      0.4088


Estimates of Autocorrelations

  Lag  Covariance  Correlation -1 9 8 7 6 5 4 3 2 1 0 1 2 3 4 5 6 7 8 9 1

    0    0.000909     1.000000 |                    |********************|
    1    0.000633     0.696388 |                    |**************      |
    2    0.000143     0.157668 |                    |***                 |
    3    -0.00029    -0.320043 |              ******|                    |


Backward Elimination of Autoregressive Terms

Lag   Estimate     t-Ratio    Prob
  3   0.185910      0.5983  0.5629


Preliminary MSE = 0.000279
```

Figure 2 (continued): Sample SAS PROC AUTOREG Output

Estimates of the Autoregressive Parameters

Lag	Coefficient	Std Error	t Ratio
1	-1.13891499	0.23280725	-4.892094
2	0.63545939	0.23280725	2.729552

Yule-Walker Estimates

SSE	0.002968	DFE	11
MSE	0.00027	Root MSE	0.016426
SBC	-83.7725	AIC	-90.0051
Reg Rsq	0.9983	Total Rsq	0.9995
Durbin-Watson	1.9618		

Variable	DF	B Value	Std Error	t Ratio	Approx Prob
Intercept	1	2.55851439	8.7366	0.293	0.7751
LTIME	1	0.93695410	0.0540	17.337	0.0001
LTIM1982	1	-0.82700366	0.1368	-6.047	0.0001
LRC	1	0.24942185	0.6962	0.358	0.7269
LRC1982	1	1.47981117	1.2251	1.208	0.2524

Figure 3: Sample SAS PROC GPLOT Output

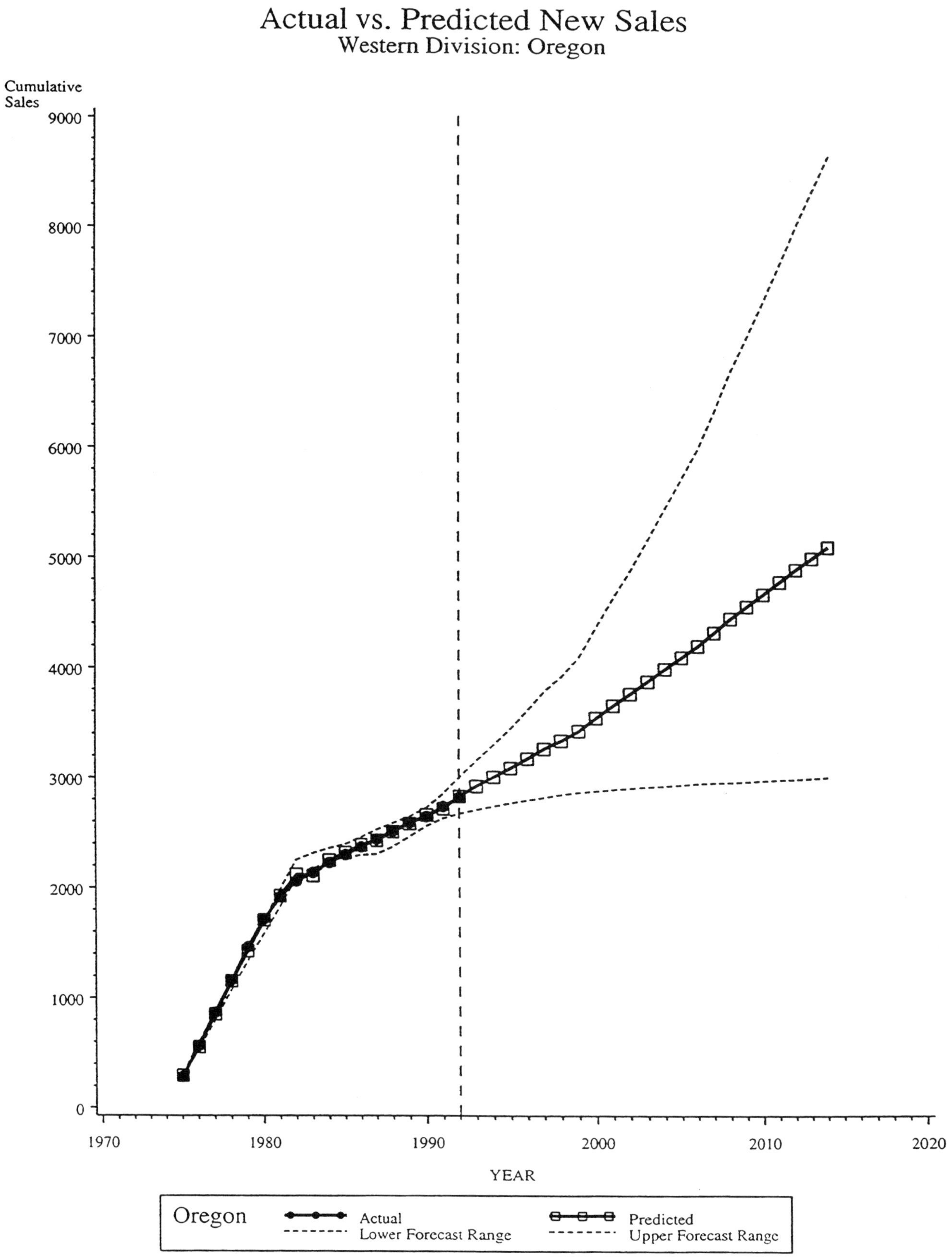

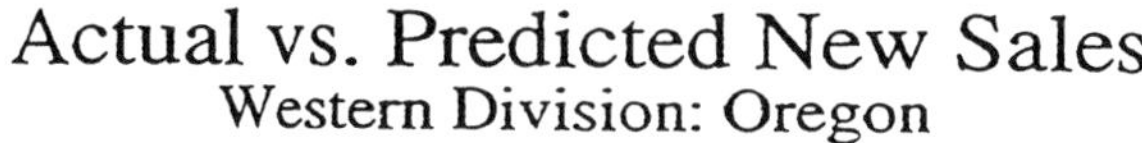

Actual vs. Predicted New Sales
Western Division: Oregon
Cumulative Sales
9000
8000
7000
6000
5000
4000
3000
2000
1000
0
1970
1980
1990
2000
2010
2020
YEAR
Oregon
Actual
Lower Forecast Range
Predicted
Upper Forecast Range

INDEX

D

E

F

G

N

O

S

T

U

V

W

Special Characters